W9-BBS-348

Memoirs of Dr. Charles Burney, 1726–1769

Burney as a young man, by Peter Toms, 1754.
Courtesy of the Osborn Collection.

Memoirs of

Dr. Charles Burney
1726–1769

Edited from

autograph fragments by

SLAVA KLIMA,

GARRY BOWERS, AND

KERRY S. GRANT

University of Nebraska Press

Lincoln and London

Copyright © 1988, University of Nebraska Press
All rights reserved
Manufactured in the United States of America

The paper in this book meets the minimum requirements of
American National Standard for Information Sciences –
Permanence of Paper for Printed Library Materials,
ANSI Z39.48-1984.

Library of Congress Cataloging-in-Publication Data
Burney, Charles, 1726–1814.
Memoirs of Dr. Charles Burney, 1726-1769.
Includes indexes and bibliographical references.
1. Burney, Charles, 1726–1814.   2. Musicologists –
England – Biography.   I. Klima, Slava.   II. Bowers,
Garry.   III. Grant, Kerry S. (Kerry Scott)   IV. Title.
ML423.B9A3   1988   780'.92'4 [B]   87-6060
ISBN 0-8032-1197-x (alk. paper)

ML
423
.B9
A3
1988

CONTENTS

Acknowledgments

We would first like to express our thanks to the Keeper of Manuscripts of the British Library, London; to Lola Szladits, Curator of the Berg Collection, New York Public Library; and to Stephen Parks, Curator of the Osborn Collection at Yale University, for giving us permission to publish the text of the present volume from manuscripts deposited in their respective collections.

Our thanks next go to Joyce Hemlow and Lars Troide of McGill University, who, over the many years we have been involved together in preparing Burney manuscripts for publication, have generously helped us elucidate difficult passages and obscure references.

Betty Rizzo of City College of New York, who is preparing a biography of Frances Greville, was most helpful with her comments on the Greville family, as was John A. Parkinson of the British Library with his comments on material relating to Thomas Arne. Martin Battestin helped us with a note on the young Fielding, and Commander A. Fountaine, R.N.R., very kindly allowed us to see at Narford Hall the copy of Swift's *Tale of a Tub* once owned by his ancestor Sir Andrew Fountaine, who showed it to Burney in 1751–52.

The archivists and librarians at the Norfolk and London Public Record Offices, the Stanley Library at King's Lynn, the Bath Public Library, and the Bodleian Library, Oxford, were very helpful in making manuscripts and rare books available to us.

We would also like to express our gratitude to the owners of Burney letters quoted in the notes to this edition—in particular to Michael Burney-Cumming, to John Comyn, to the Keeper of Manuscripts at the Bodleian Library, Oxford, as well as to the curators of the Coke, the Hyde, and the Pierpont Morgan Library collections, and to the Yale Center for British Art and British Studies—for permission to use them.

McGill students Barbara and Eugene Bereza helped with the transcription of the text, and Ruth Martin and Beverly Greeley did a great deal of typing and retyping. Special thanks to Elsie Wagner, who prepared the index.

We are grateful to the Social Sciences and Humanities Research Council of Canada, which has for years generously supported work on the Burney family papers. A special grant from McGill University's Humanities Research Grants Committee enabled us to complete work on the index. The university itself has long provided us with a place in which to work and made it possible for Kerry Grant to join us as our consultant for specifically musicological problems.

Short Titles

These abbreviated forms are used to cite the following texts and collections. Standard encyclopedias, biographical dictionaries, peerages, baronetages, knightages, school and university lists, lists of clergy, and town and city directories of all kinds have also been consulted but are not cited unless for a particular reason. The place of publication for all works cited is London unless otherwise specifically indicated.

AR	*The Annual Register, or a View of the History, Politics, and Literature . . . , 1758–.*
Armytage	*Register of Baptisms and Marriages at St. George's Chapel, Mayfair,* ed. G. S. Armytage, 1889.
Barker/Stenning	G. F. Barker and Alan H. Stenning, *The Record of Old Westminsters,* 1908.
Barrett	The Barrett Collection of Burney Papers, British Library, London.
Barrington	Daines Barrington, *Miscellanies,* 1781.
Beaven	Alfred B. Beaven, *The Aldermen of the City of London,* 1908.
Beinecke	The Beinecke Rare Book and Manuscript Library, Yale University Library, New Haven, Conn.
Bennett	J. H. E. Bennett, *The Rolls of the Freemen of the City of Chester,* pt. 2, 1700–1805, Chester, England, 1908.

Berg	The Henry W. and Albert A. Berg Collection, New York Public Library, New York.
BL	The British Library, London.
Black	Cecilia Black, *The Linleys of Bath,* 2d ed., 1926.
Boalch	Donald H. Boalch, *Makers of the Harpsichord and Clavichord, 1440–1840,* Oxford, 2d ed., 1974.
Bodleian	Bodleian Library, Oxford University, Oxford.
Bradfer-Lawrence	H. L. Bradfer-Lawrence, "The Merchants of Lynn," in *A Supplement to Blomefield's Norfolk,* ed. Christopher Hussey, pp. 143–203, 1929.
Bridge 1913	Joseph C. Bridge, *The Organists of Chester Cathedral,* Chester, England, 1913.
Bridge 1928	Joseph C. Bridge, "Town Waits and Their Times," *Proceedings of the Musical Association* 54 (21 Feb. 1928): 63–92.
BUCEM	*The British Union Catalogue of Early Music, Printed before the Year 1801 . . . ,* ed. Edith B. Schnapper, 1957.
Burne	R. V. H. Burne, *Chester Cathedral,* 1958.
Burney-Cumming	Collection of Burney letters owned by Michael Burney-Cumming, 5 King's Arms Lane, Polebrook, Oundle, near Peterborough, England.
Burns	Robert Burns, *Burns: Poems and Songs,* ed. James Kinsley, 1971.
Buss	Robert Woodward Buss, *Charles Fleetwood,* 1915.
Campbell	Colin Campbell, *Vitruvius Britannicus,* vol. 1, 1715.
Cat. Corr.	*A Catalogue of the Burney Family Correspondence, 1749–1878,* comp. Joyce Hemlow with Jeanne M. M. Burgess and Althea Douglas, 1971.
Cat. Misc. Lib.	*A Catalogue of the Miscellaneous Library of the late Charles Burney, Doctor of Music, and Fellow of the Royal Society . . . ,* 1814.

Cat. Mus.	*A Catalogue of the Valuable and Very Fine Collection of Music, Printed and MS., of the late Charles Burney, Mus.D., F.R.S. . . . , 1814.*
Chapman	*The Letters of Samuel Johnson,* ed. R. W. Chapman, 1952.
Charke	Charlotte Charke, *A Narrative of the Life of Mrs. Charlotte Charke* (1755), ed. L. R. N. Ashley, 1969.
Clifford	James L. Clifford, *Dictionary Johnson,* 1979.
Coke	The Gerald Coke Collection, Jenkyn Place, Bentley, Hants., England.
Commem.	Charles Burney, *An Account of the Musical Performances in Westminster Abbey and the Pantheon in Commemoration of Handel,* 1785.
Comyn	The John Comyn Collection of Burney Papers, Cross House, Vowchurch, Turnastone, Herts., England.
Crawford	Thomas Crawford, *Love, Labour and Liberty: The Eighteenth-Century Scottish Lyric,* 1971.
Davies 1780	Thomas Davies, *Memoirs of the Life of Garrick,* 1780.
Davies 1784	Thomas Davies, *Dramatic Miscellanies,* 1784.
Dawe	Donovan Dawe, *Organists of the City of London, 1666–1850,* 1983.
Deutsch 1948	O. E. Deutsch, "Poetry Preserved in Music: Bibliographical Notes on Smollett and Oswald, Handel, and Haydn," *MLN* 63 (1948): 73–88.
Deutsch 1955	O. E. Deutsch, *Handel,* 1955.
Dibdin	Charles Dibdin, *Professional Life of Mr. Dibdin,* 1803.
Eastman	Arthur M. Eastman, "The Texts from Which Johnson Printed His Shakespeare," *JEGP* 49 (April 1950): 182–91.
ED	*The Early Diary of Frances Burney, 1768–1778,* ed. Annie Raine Ellis, 1913.

Edwards	F. G. E. Edwards, *Musical Times* 45 (1904): 438.
EM	Autobiographical sketch by Charles Burney, *European Magazine* 3 (March 1785): 363.
Evans	G. Blakemore Evans, "The Text of Johnson's *Shakespeare* (1765)," *PQ* 28 (July 1949): 425–28.
Farrall	L. M. Farrall, *Parish Register of the Holy and Undivided Trinity of the City of Chester, 1522–1837,* ed. Laurence Meakin, 1914.
Fiske	Roger Fiske, *English Theatre Music in the Eighteenth Century,* Oxford, 1973.
Fitzpatrick	Horace Fitzpatrick, *The Horn and Horn-Playing and the Austro-Bohemian Tradition, 1680–1830,* 1971.
Fletcher 1911	*The Register of St. Mary's, Shrewsbury,* ed. W. G. D. Fletcher, 1911.
Fletcher 1918	*The Register of St. Chad's,* ed. W. G. D. Fletcher, 1918.
Folger	The Folger Shakespeare Library, Washington, D.C.
Gadd	David Gadd, *Georgian Summer: Bath in the Eighteenth Century,* 1971.
Garrick *Corr.*	*The Private Correspondence of David Garrick, with the Most Celebrated Persons of His Time* . . . [ed. James Boaden], 1831–32.
Garrick *Letters*	*The Letters of David Garrick,* ed. David M. Little and George M. Kahrl, 1963.
Genest	John Genest, *Some Account of the English Stage, from the Restoration in 1660 to 1830,* Bath, England, 1832.
GM	*Gentleman's Magazine,* 1731–1880.
Grant	Kerry Scott Grant, *Dr. Burney as Critic and Historian of Music,* Ann Arbor, Mich., 1983.
Green	Frederick Charles Green, *Minuet,* 1935.
Guthkelch/Nicholl Smith	Jonathan Swift, *A Tale of a Tub,* ed. A. C. Guthkelch and D. Nicholl Smith, 2d ed., 1958.

Hawkins	Sir John Hawkins, *A General History of the Science and Practice of Music*, 1776; rpt. 1963.
HFB	Joyce Hemlow, *The History of Fanny Burney*, Oxford, 1958.
Highfill	Philip H. Highfill, Jr., Kalman A. Burnim, and Edward A. Langhans, *A Biographical Dictionary of Actors, Actresses, Musicians, Dancers, Managers, & Other Stage Personnel in London, 1660–1800*, Carbondale, Ill., 1973– .
Hill	Constance Hill, *The House in St. Martin's Street*, 1907.
Hill/Powell	*Boswell's Life of Johnson . . .* , ed. George Birkbeck Hill, rev. L. F. Powell, 6 vols., Oxford, 1934–64.
Hillen	Henry J. Hillen, *History of the Borough of King's Lynn*, 1907.
Hist. Mus.	Charles Burney, Mus. D., F.R.S., *A General History of Music . . .* , 1776–89.
Holzman	James M. Holzman, *The Nabobs in England: A Study of the Returned Anglo-Indian*, 1926.
Horn	David Bayne Horn, *Diplomatic Representatives*, 1932.
Hudson/Luckhurst	Derek Hudson and Kenneth W. Luckhurst, *The Royal Society of Arts, 1754–1954*, 1954.
Hussey	Christopher Hussey, "Wilbury House, Wiltshire," *Country Life* 126 (1959): 1014–18, 1148–51.
Hyde	The Hyde Collection, Four Oaks Farm, Somerville, N.J.
JL	*The Journal and Letters of Fanny Burney (Madame D'Arblay)*, ed. Joyce Hemlow, Oxford, 1972–84.
Johnsonian Misc.	George Birkbeck Hill, *Johnsonian Miscellanies*, 1897.
Kassler	J. C. Kassler, "Burney's Sketch of a *Plan for a Public Music-School*," *Musical Quarterly* 58 (1972): 210–34.
Ketton-Cremer 1948	R. W. Ketton-Cremer, *A Norfolk Gallery*, 1948.
Ketton-Cremer 1957	R. W. Ketton-Cremer, *Norfolk Assembly*, 1957.

Kidson	F. Kidson, "James Oswald, Dr. Burney, and 'the Whole Temple of Apollo,'" *Musical Antiquary* 2 (1910–11): 39.
Knapp 1931	Lewis Mansfield Knapp, "Smollett's Verses and Their Musical Settings in the Eighteenth Century," *MLN* 46 (1931): 224–32.
Knapp 1944	Lewis Mansfield Knapp, "Dr. John Armstrong, Littérateur, and Associate of Smollett, Thomson, Wilkes, and Other Celebrities," *PMLA* 59 (1944):1019–58.
Leslie/Taylor	Charles Robert Leslie and Tom Taylor, *Life and Times of Sir Joshua Reynolds,* 1865.
Lewis	Mr. Wilmarth S. Lewis, Farmington, Conn.
Lewis *Walpole*	W. S. Lewis, *Horace Walpole's Fugitive Verses,* 1931.
Lloyds	Lloyds Bank Ltd., Cox's and King's Branch, 6 Pall Mall, London.
Lodge	John Lodge, *Peerage of Ireland,* 1789.
London Stage	*The London Stage, 1660–1800: A Calendar of Plays, Entertainments & Afterpieces Together with Casts, Box-Receipts and Contemporary Comment, Compiled from the Playbills, Newspapers, and Theatrical Diaries of the Period,* Carbondale, Ill.: pt. 3, ed. Arthur H. Scouten, 1961; pt. 4, ed. George Winchester Stone, Jr., 1962; pt. 5, ed. Charles Beecher Hogan, 1968; index, comp. Ben Ross Schneider, Jr., 1979.
Lonsdale 1960	Roger Lonsdale, "Dr. Burney, John Weaver and the *Spectator,*" *Bulletin of the New York Public Library* 65 (1960): 286–88.
Lonsdale 1965	Roger Lonsdale, *Dr. Charles Burney,* Oxford, 1965.
Lonsdale 1979	Roger Lonsdale, "Dr. Burney's 'Dictionary of Music,'" *Musicology* 5 (1979): 167–68.
Mackenzie	Alexander Mackenzie, *History of the Mackenzies,* Inverness, Scotland, 1894.

MacMillan	*Drury Lane Calendar, 1747–1776,* ed. Dougald MacMillan, 1938.
Maddison	A. R. Maddison, *Lincolnshire Pedigrees,* 1902.
Manwaring	G. E. Manwaring, *My Friend the Admiral: The Life, Letters, and Journals of Rear-Admiral James Burney, F.R.S.,* 1931.
Maxted	Ian Maxted, *The London Book Trades, 1775–1800,* 1977.
Mem.	Fanny Burney (Madame d'Arblay), *Memoirs of Doctor Burney, Arranged from His Own Manuscripts, from Family Papers, and from Personal Recollections,* 1832.
Mem. of Metastasio	Pietro Metastasio, *Memoirs of the Life and Writings of the Abate Metastasio,* ed. Charles Burney, 1796; rpt. 1971.
Mercer	Charles Burney, *A General History of Music,* ed. Frank Mercer, 1935; rpt. 1957.
Millican	Percy Millican, "Joseph Burney, the Dancing Master," *Norfolk Archaeology* 29 (1947): 238–50.
Mortimer	*Mortimer's Universal Director . . . ,* 1763.
Mus. Nbk	Musical Notebooks, Osborn Collection.
MS Cat.	"Catalogue of the Books, Tracts & Treatises of all the Original Authors Ancient & Modern, in Greek, Latin, German, French, Italian, Spanish, and English of the late Charles Burney," British Library, Add. MSS 18191.
Namier/Brooke	Lewis Namier and John Brooke, *The House of Commons, 1754–1790,* 1964.
Nash	Mary Nash, *The Provoked Wife: The Life and Times of Susannah Cibber,* 1977.
New Grove	*The New Grove Dictionary of Music and Musicians,* ed. Stanley Sadie, 1980.
Newman	William S. Newman, *The Sonata in the Classic Era,* Chapel Hill, N.C., 1963.

Newton	R. Newton, "The English Cult of Domenico Scarlatti," *Music and Letters* 20 (1939): 138–56.
Nichols	John Nichols, *Illustrations*, 1817–58.
Odell	G. C. D. Odell, *Shakespeare from Betterton to Irving*, 1920.
Oman	Carola Oman, *David Garrick*, 1958.
Osborn	The James Marshall and Marie-Louise Osborn Collection, Yale University Library, New Haven, Conn.
Owen	Hugh Owen, *Some Account of the Ancient and Present State of Shrewsbury*, 1810.
Owen/Blakeway	Hugh Owen and J. B. Blakeway, *History of Shrewsbury*, 1825.
Parker	Constance Anne Parker, *Mr. Stubbs the Horse Painter*, 1971.
Parkinson	John A. Parkinson, "An Unknown Violin Solo by Arne," *Musical Times* 117 (1976): 902.
Parson	Clement Parson, *David Garrick and His Circle*, 1906.
Paul	*The Scots Peerage*, ed. Sir James Balfour Paul, 1904–14.
Paulson	Ronald Paulson, *Hogarth: His Life, Art and Times*, 2 vols., 1971.
Percy	Thomas Percy, *Reliques of Ancient English Poetry* (1765), ed. Henry B. Wheatley, 1876–77; rpt. 1966.
Pilkington	Laetitia Pilkington, *Memoirs of Mrs. Pilkington* (1749), ed. Iris Barry, 1929.
PML	Pierpont Morgan Library, New York.
Poet. Nbk	Manuscript collection of Burney's verses, Osborn Collection.
Pohl	Carl Ferdinand Pohl, *Mozart and Haydn in London*, 1867.

Poole	Charles Burney, *Music, Men, and Manners in France and Italy, 1770,* ed. H. Edmund Poole, 1969; rpt. 1974.
Powicke/Fryde	F. M. Powicke and E. B. Fryde, *Handbook of British Chronology,* 2d ed., 1961.
Price	F. G. Hilton Price, *A Handbook of London Bankers,* 1876; rev. ed. 1890–91.
Pyle	Edmund Pyle, *Memoirs of a Royal Chaplain, 1729–1763,* ed. Albert Hartshorne, 1905.
Rees	Articles by Charles Burney in *The Cyclopaedia; or, Universal Dictionary of Arts, Sciences, and Literature,* ed. Abraham Rees, 1802–19.
Register of Condover	*The Register of Condover, 1570–1812,* 1906.
Richards	William Richards, *The History of Lynn,* 1812.
RISM	*Répertoire International des Sources Musicales, Series A/I/ 1 Einzeldrucke vor 1800,* Kassel, Basel, Tours, London, 1971– .
Roscoe, P. C.	P. C. Roscoe, "Arne and 'The Guardian Outwitted,'" *Music and Letters* 24 (1943): 237–45.
Roscoe, S.	Sydney Roscoe, *John Newbery and his Successors, 1740–1814,* 1973.
Ross	Janet Ross, *Italian Sketches,* 1887.
Roth	Cecil Roth, *The Great Synagogue, London, 1690–1940,* 1950.
Scholes 1942	Percy A. Scholes, "The Election of a London Organist Two Centuries Ago," *Musical Times* 83 (1942): 73–75, 157, 186.
Scholes 1948	Percy A. Scholes, *The Great Dr. Burney,* 1948.
Scholes 1954	Percy A. Scholes, *God Save the Queen! The History and Romance of the World's First National Anthem,* 1954.
Scott	A. Scott, "Arne's Alfred," *Music and Letters* 55 (1974): 385–97.

Seward	William Seward, *Anecdotes of Distinguished Persons,* 1798.
Sherbo	Arthur Sherbo, *Christopher Smart,* 1967.
Sherson	Erroll Sherson, *The Lively Lady Townshend and Her Friends,* 1926.
Sichel	Walter Sichel, *Bolingbroke and His Times,* 1901–2.
Spence	Joseph Spence, *Observations, Anecdotes and Characters of Books and Men,* ed. James M. Osborn, Oxford, 1966.
Swift	Jonathan Swift, *Journal to Stella,* ed. Harold Williams, 1948.
Thrale *Autobiography*	Hester Thrale, *Autobiography, Letters, and Literary Remains of Mrs. Piozzi (Thrale),* 2d ed., 1861.
Thraliana	*Thraliana: The Diary of Mrs. Hester Lynch Thrale (Later Mrs. Piozzi), 1776–1809,* ed. Katherine C. Balderston, 2d ed., Oxford, 1942.
Tipping	H. Avray Tipping, "Wilbury House, Wiltshire," *Country Life* 71 (1932): 96–102.
Tours	*Dr. Burney's Musical Tours in Europe,* ed. Percy A. Scholes, 1959.
Victor	Benjamin Victor, *A History of the Theatres in London and Dublin from 1730 to the present Time,* 1761–71.
Voltaire	François-Marie Arouet de Voltaire, *Oeuvres complètes,* ed. Adrien-Jean-Quentin Beuchot, 1829–80.
Walpole *Anecdotes*	Horace Walpole, *Anecdotes of Painting in England,* 1862.
Walpole *Memoirs*	Horace Walpole, *Memoirs of the Reign of King George III,* ed. Sir Denis Le Marchant, 1845.
Welsh	Charles Welsh, *A Bookseller of the Last Century,* 1885.
Wilkinson	Tate Wilkinson, *Memoirs,* 1790.
Worcester Mem.	Typescript of 1899 family chronicle by Col. Henry Edward Burney, "Memoranda of the Burney Family, 1603–1845," Osborn Collection.

Young	Arthur Young, *Autobiography,* ed. M. Betham-Edwards, 1898.
Yale Center	Yale Center for British Art and British Studies, Yale University, New Haven, Conn.
YW	*The Yale Edition of Horace Walpole's Correspondence,* ed. W. S. Lewis et al., New Haven, Conn., 1937–83.

Editors' Introduction

Burney's Career

Charles Burney was born at Shrewsbury on 7 April 1726 (Old Style), the twentieth child of a mercurial dancing-master, James MacBurney. When in 1729 his father was engaged as an actor in the newly opened Goodman's Fields Theatre in London, Charles and his elder brother Richard were sent to the nearby village of Condover, where they spent their childhood under the care of one Elleanor Ball and her husband. There Burney's taste for music first manifested itself in a fondness for bell-ringing. At about fifteen, while attending the Free School at Chester, he learned to play the organ from Edmund Baker, organist of Chester Cathedral, and for a time served as pupil-assistant to his half-brother James, organist of St. Mary's and St. Chad's in Shrewsbury.

In 1744 the theatrical composer Thomas Arne passed through Chester on his return from Ireland and took Burney with him to London as an apprentice. The discovery of the metropolis with its musical life at Drury Lane, Covent Garden, and Vauxhall Gardens was an important event in Burney's life. While he copied out music for Arne, played as a supernumerary in performances of Handel's oratorios, and earned a few shillings as a fiddler in the Drury Lane orchestra, he discovered at first hand the lively backstage life of Grub Street and met such formidable figures as George Frederick Handel and David Garrick.

Burney's enthusiasm for "modern" Italian music soon recommended him to Fulke Greville, a gentleman of means, greatly addicted to gambling, who one day heard the young musician perform a Scarlatti sonata at Jacob Kirckman's music shop. In 1748 he bought Burney out of his apprenticeship to Arne for £300 and set him up as music man at Wilbury, his elegant country seat in Wiltshire. Here Burney first met Samuel Crisp, one of Greville's boon companions from the beau monde. Here "he had his education," for the "company that visited Mᴿ Greville was of the first class for birth, breeding, and conversation,"[1] and proved invaluable to him later when, as music teacher, he moved at ease in the upper reaches of London society.

In 1749 Greville offered to take the young musician with him to Italy. Although Burney must have been very much tempted by this opportunity to visit the land of his favorite composers, he declined the offer in order to marry Esther Sleepe, who had already presented him with a daughter. Left to fend for himself, he gave music lessons, won an appointment as organist of St. Dionis Backchurch, organized the Society of the Temple of Apollo with James Oswald, and wrote music for Garrick's Drury Lane entertainments—*Robin Hood, Queen Mab,* and a new version of *Alfred.*

In 1751 Burney's health, never very strong, broke down under the strain. His doctors, believing that London pollution was the chief villain, advised fresh country air as a remedy, and Burney moved to King's Lynn, where he had been offered the post of organist at St. Margaret's Church. Though resigning himself to nine years of provincial exile in Norfolk, he never gave up his intention of returning to London.

The stay in Norfolk and the care of a growing family temporarily slowed his rise to prominence. After his return to London in 1760, he became reasonably prosperous as a fashionable music teacher, which might have continued to be his sole lot had higher ambitions not moved him. Teaching young ladies was his bread and butter; understanding and making sense of the origins and historical development of music engaged his deeper sympathies and intellectual interests. It was apparently in Norfolk that he first conceived the idea of writing the work that became *A General History of Music* and began to collect material for that purpose. Back in London, where he plunged into the world of concerts and operas while giving sometimes ten lessons a day, he continued his serious research in the newly opened British Museum, as well as in the libraries of Paris during brief visits there. He became a passionate book collector (his remarkable library, including many choice items on music, eventually grew to some 10,000 volumes). In 1769 he took his doctorate in music at Oxford.

Whereas literary men such as James Thomson or Samuel Johnson expected to conquer London by publishing a poem or staging a tragedy that would bring them to public notice, Burney had the interesting idea of exploiting the fashionable Grand Tour for his own musical ends. In 1770 and 1772 he traveled on the Continent to find out more about contemporary European music and gather materials for his magnum opus. He published two very readable, informative accounts of his musical tours, whose success was immediate. Second editions of *The Present State of Music in France and Italy* and *The Present State of Music in Germany, the Netherlands, and the United Provinces; Or, The Journal of a Tour through Those Countries, undertaken to collect Materials for a General History of Music* appeared in 1773 and 1775 respectively.[2] The two volumes established Burney's reputation as a musical scholar and man of letters. In May 1773 Dr. Johnson "pronounced him to be *one of the first writers of the age* for travels,"[3] and on 29 December of the same year he was elected a Fellow of the Royal Society. He was now "on the list of *Great Men*."[4]

The author of the *Tours* became known in London as a man to be reckoned with in matters of musical taste, one who corresponded with the philosophes Denis Diderot, Baron Paul-Henri d'Holbach, and Jean-Jacques Rousseau in France, and with musical scholars such as Padre Martini in Italy and Christoph Ebeling in Germany. His travel books revealed his acquaintance with dozens of contemporary composers and musicians, giving valuable biographical information and providing shrewd critical assessments, often spiced with telling anecdotes.

Burney's *General History of Music* (composed in rivalry with the music history of Sir John Hawkins) established his reputation as a leading music historian and is still quoted with great respect by musicologists.[5] The first volume was published in 1776, the second in 1782, and the last two in 1789. When his daughter Fanny published *Evelina* (1778) and *Cecilia* (1782) and was acclaimed England's best woman novelist, her success enhanced his own. Genial by temperament, highly clubbable, Burney was by this time on intimate terms with Dr. Johnson at Streatham; he was a respected member of The Club and a friend of Joshua Reynolds, Edmund Burke, James Boswell, Arthur Young, Sir Joseph Banks, Edmond Malone, and other celebrities. The son of an obscure dancing-master had become "the Great Doctor Burney."

His Memoirs and Their Destruction

In August 1782, shortly after finishing the second volume of his *History of Music,* Burney paused to look back at the first fifty-six years of his eventful life. While staying with his old friend Samuel Crisp in Chessington, he wrote a first draft of his memoirs, sketching an outline of his early career from his birth until his arrival in London in 1744 and perhaps until 1766, the year preceding his second marriage.[6]

That he continued working on his memoirs after 1782 is clear from the statement of his daughter Fanny, then Mme d'Arblay, that the manuscripts she later examined were "written in his own honoured hand, or copied by Sarah, Charles himself, little Molly, & some one other, whose writing I know not."[7] Sarah Harriet, Burney's daughter from his second marriage (b. 1772), was his amanuensis between 1788 and September 1798, when she ran away with her half-brother James. As she did not return until after July 1807, those parts of the memoirs copied by her must have been written either before 1798 or after 1807.

After Sarah Harriet left, Burney found another amanuensis in his servant Mary More, whom he had employed as a young girl in 1793 and whom he trained to be his secretary. She stayed with him until 1803, when she married a whitesmith by the name of Walker. She probably copied those parts of the memoirs written between 1798 and 1803.

The sections copied by "some one other" may have been transcribed by Molly's sister Rebecca, or "Becky," whom Burney hired in 1803 as "a successor to my invaluable secretary [but it] will be a long time ere she will be qualified to fill half of [Molly's] office. I send her to a writing-master every night to mend her hand wch is legible, but not yet settled."[8]

After Mme d'Arblay's departure for France in April 1802, Burney became more friendly with his son Charles, the classical scholar, who ran a school for boys at Greenwich. Charles was compiling a history of the stage; Burney supplied him with reminiscences of theatre life between 1744 and 1751,[9] and Charles would have been only too happy to transcribe those sections of his father's memoirs that dealt with the theatre, especially with Garrick.[10]

In December 1805 Burney set out to make a fair copy of his early drafts, and as he reread this fair copy in 1806–7, he made several additions to it. In November 1806 he mentions "a work of my own wch was begun [   ] years ago I do not expect to live to finish,"[11] and at an unspecified later date he wrote that "even in sickness and during the encreasing infirmities of uncommon longevity I planned new labours, and new editions of the old,"[12] possibly alluding to the memoirs. This is as much as we can gather about their composition.

Mme d'Arblay did not learn of their existence until after her return from Paris in the autumn of 1812, when her father

> put his Key into my hands, & pointed to the Pigeon holes in which were the packets he bid me to read to him. . . . The chief of our private time was given to his poetry, & to bits & scraps of his Memoirs, pointed out by himself—& which, taken separately, & selected, & apropos to some current subject, or person, read agreeably,—when read by Himself, &

consequently intermixt with anecdotes & recollections that rendered them interesting—as was every thing he ever related.[13]

Burney evidently expected that after his death Fanny would publish an account of his life based on the copious memoirs and letters he had left in manuscript. "I know it was his intention," she wrote, that

> it was certainly my business, if the Life *must* be printed, to prepare it for the press . . . & that Charles . . . was to take my place as to all the Manuscriptural possessions & decisions, had I continued in France, because, after me, he thought Charles the most acquainted with the press, & the most *au fait* as to the details of his life, from living most familiarly with him of late years, of any of his family.[14]

When Burney died in 1814, the practical Charles thought that a timely publication of the memoirs might be of "*pecuniary* value," and with this in view he handed the manuscripts to Mme d'Arblay. But "at the moment we lost our dear Father," she explained later,

> I was in too much affliction for any authorship faculties or calculations; but my internal opinion & expectations were That I had nothing to do but to revise & somewhat abridge his own Memoirs, which I thought would contain 3 Volumes in Octavo; & to select his Correspondence to the amount of 3 more, which would rapidly sell the whole, in chusing them from the Names of Garrick, Diderot, Rousseau, Dr. Warton, Dr. Johnson, Mr. Mason, Horace Walpole. Lord Mornington, Mr. Crisp, Mr. Greville, Mrs Greville Lady Crewe, Mr. Bewley, Mr. Griffith, Mr. Cutler, M^rs Le Noir Lord Macartney, Lord Lonsdale. Duke of Portland, Mr. Canning. Mr. Windham. Mr. Wesley. Mr. La Trobe. Mr. Walker.— Mr. Burke, Mr. Malone. Sr J. Reynolds. Mr Seward. Kit Smart. Mrs. Piozzi.[15]

This indicates that Mme d'Arblay wished to present her father as a literary man rather than a music historian, and also that she at that time saw her task chiefly as editor of the material he had left in manuscript.

In the autumn of 1814 she took the manuscripts with her to Paris, but Napoleon's sudden return from Elba prevented her from examining them; she was forced to flee to Brussels: "All my MSS—my family papers—my dear Father's Memoirs . . . all left in Paris, from my hurry of flight," she wrote in March 1815 from Brussels.[16] It was not until January 1816, three months after her return to England, that this "immense hoard of papers . . . chiefly MSS. &

Letters of my dearest Father" reached her; even then, some of Burney's correspondence was "left in Paris."[17]

On 22 September 1816 she wrote: "I have begun reading my dear Father's mss. What a Labrinth!—new information & new sadnesses!"[18] In March 1817 Mrs. Frances Whalley reported that Mme d'Arblay "is now engaged in arranging a variety of papers which old Dr. Burney left, chiefly consisting of his correspondence with literary characters of his time. But it will be two years at least before this mass can be assorted and prepared for the press."[19] On 14–15 June Mme d'Arblay wrote to Princess Elizabeth that she was "rummaging, sorting, selecting, preserving or destroying the innumerable mass of Mss. of every description left by my Father. He seems to have burnt nothing: things the most common & useless being hoarded with those that are most edifying, secret, or interesting."[20] On 27 July she noted in her diary: "Daily work at my dear Padre's MSS—his memoires—poems—odd papers."[21] On 24 January 1818 the Princess Elizabeth mentioned "the MSS. of [her] dear Father which she wished [her] to collect, & to precede by his Memoirs."[22]

Mme d'Arblay's diaries for 1819–20 contain numerous entries about her work on Burney's manuscripts, and six of these specifically mention the twelve notebooks of the memoirs: 7 May 1819—"Finished 2^d examination of Cahier 1st of MS. Memoirs de mon Pere"; 26 February 1820—"Ms 4th Cahier MS Mem. of my Padre"; 5 March—"MS. Mem. Dr. Burney"; 18 March—"MSS Memoirs Dr. Burney N° 4"; 27 March—"MS N° 9 Memoirs of Dr. Burney"; 21 April—"MS Memoirs of Dr Burney N° 12."[23]

It is not clear just when she changed her mind about how to edit her father's memoirs. Charles, who had himself copied parts of them and who was Burney's alternative choice as editor of his manuscripts, died unexpectedly on 28 December 1817. Had he lived, he certainly would have looked over her edition; left to herself, Mme d'Arblay began to have second thoughts.

Her brother-in-law, Charles Rousseau Burney, suggested that she write "a Biographical Preface,"[24] presumably to introduce the six volumes of letters and memoirs. On 3 July 1820 she wrote that she "should ere this have published a selection of the Correspondence, with Memoirs of the Life of my dearest Father—a task delegated to me by my family—& accepted as a *devoir*;—a *Tribute* to his honoured Memory."[25] Although the phrasing of this is ambiguous, it suggests that by this time she thought of writing her own "Memoirs of the Life of my dearest Father" instead of editing Burney's manuscript.

At last, after three years of "rummaging," she made up her mind to destroy the greatest part of the memoirs because she felt that they were "opening to the publick view a species of Family degradation to which the Name of Burney Now gives no similitude." In her letter to her sister Esther Burney of [25]–28 November 1820,[26] she gives her justification for an act that biographers of Dr. Burney have unanimously deplored:

> It was at Ilfracomb, in 1817. that my definitive disappointment took place. In reading the Memoirs *de suite,* with a red pencil in my hand,[27] for little erasures & curtailings, I soon, unhappily, discovered that they really were so UNLIKE all that their honoured writer had ever produced to the Publick, that not only they would not have kept up his Credit & fair Name in the literary World, if brought to light, but would certainly have left a cloud upon its parting ray—attended by a storm of disapprobation, if not invective, upon the Editor who,—for a fortnight's quick profit from his earlier established Celebrity, had exhibited her faded Father's faded talents.[28]—A FORTNIGHT, I say; because, the first curiosity satisfied, the Memoirs would have sunk to Waste, & have been heard of no more.
>
> All the juvenile Voluminous MSS. are filled with *literal* Nurse's tales,—such as, narrated by himself, were truly amusing, as his vivacity & quickness & ready Wit rendered every thing that passed his lips: but on paper, & *read,* not *recited,* they were trivial to poverty, & dull to sleepiness. What respected his family, mean while, was utterly unpleasant—& quite useless to be kept alive. The dissipated facility & negligence of his Witty & accomplished, but careless Father; the niggardly unfeelingness of his nearly unnatural Mother; the parsimonious authority & exactions of his Eldest half Brother; the lordly tyranny of his elder own Brother; the selfish assumingness of his Eldest sister,—& the unaffectionate, & Worldly total indifference of every other branch of the numerous race to even the existence of each other,—poor good Aunt Rebecca excepted— all these furnish matter of detail long, tedious, unnecessary,—& opening to the publick view a species of Family degradation to which the Name of Burney Now gives no similitude.[29]
>
> In coming to the epoch of Manhood, I had hoped to find some interesting details, & descriptions, relative to our dear & lovely own Mother: but—from whatsoever Cause, he is here laconic almost to silence. 3 or 4 lines include all the history of his admiration & its effects.[30] Whether these were recollections too melancholy for his Nerves, or whether the intensity with which he had once felt on this subject had

blunted his remnant Sensibility, I cannot determine—but he gives his whole paper at this time to enormous long paragraphs & endless folio pages, upon the City electioneering for organs & Concerts, & Stanley's rivalry, & Frasi,[31] & local interests of the day, now sunk from every memory, & containing Nothing that could either benefit or amuse a single Reader by remaining on record.

Then follow various Cahiers on Norfolk & Lynn, with some more agreeable style of Writing,[32]—but still upon people not generally known, nor ever described with circumstances that may create a running interest for them. All is detached, vague, & unknit into any consistence.

At last comes London; & Then all the great Names I have mentioned to you begin to occur: & here I had the full expectation of detail, anecdote, description, & conversation, such as to manifest these characters in the brilliant light of their own Fame, & to shew our dear Father the Carressed, sought, honoured & admired Friend of such a constellation; for SUCH he was, & as much LOVED & ESTEEMED as if he had been the Universal Patron of them all.—

But alas, what a falling off ensues!—He contents himself with *Naming* all these people, saying WHERE they met, mentioning the first day he made acquaintance with them; where they dined together—the Day, the Week—the Month, the Year—& then stops short, to go to some other date for some other such encounter. There is little more than Copying the minutes of engagements from his Pocket Books, made at the time his Memory was full & gay, & when he purposed dilating upon every Name & circumstance in his Memoirs, as he did, on the moment, in his discourse to his family or friends.

This is the General History of the Memoirs, 12 Volumes in number,[33] through which I have been Wading, painfully, laboriously wading;—for the hand is small sometimes to illegibility, & the Abbreviations are continual, & sometimes very obscure. Some of the Volumes I have read over 4 times, from different Copies, now of his own & now of some Copyist. When the latter has been *Sarah,* the *writing* is flowing & easy.[34] But—most elaborately, the dear indefatigable author wrote frequently the whole of every Cahier 3 times over him self; & my fear of missing any thing that might be recorded in one, & not in another, & my desire to ascertain whether there were any difference in the narrations, & any choice to be taken, induced me to hold it right not to destroy a line unexamined.

There are, you will be sure, many exceptions to this general *anathema,* but they are partial, & of so little Volume, compared with what is hopeless, that I have not stopt to enumerate, though I shall carefully preserve them.

So much for the Memoirs, which I have now perused through-out, with the most sedulous attention, & have gone over a second time, in marking & separating every leaf, or passage, that may be usefully, or ornamentally, Biographical. While all that I thought utterly irrelevant, or any way mischievous, I have committed to the Flames. Whatever admits of any doubt, or demands any Enquiry, I have set apart.

Two weeks after she mailed this letter, Mme d'Arblay noted a list of manuscripts: "All these have been finally Examined And Extracted The rest have been *Destroyed.*—Italian Tour Amplified—This 9th Decr 1820."[35]

Even after her destruction of the bulk of his memoirs, Mme d'Arblay still planned to edit her father's letters, as her diary for 1826 reveals.[36] In 1828, however, she discovered that judgments handed down in 1813 and 1818 prevented her publishing letters addressed to Dr. Burney,[37] and as publishers kept hinting that if her own account of her father did not come out, some outsider less qualified than herself might wish to publish one, she decided to abandon her original design of *editing* her father's manuscripts to become instead his official *biographer.*

Her own *Memoirs of Dr. Burney,* published in 1832, is a very poor substitute for what she destroyed. Written in prose of turgid preciosity very different from her early style, it made her father into a Sir Charles Grandison and from the time of its publication in 1832 elicited caustic critical comment. John Wilson Croker rightly took her to task for giving as much space to herself as to Dr. Burney, pointing out that as editor she should have presented her father's memoirs in substantially the form in which she found them.[38]

Croker could not have known of the fragmentary remains in Burney's hand; these came to the attention of critics only in 1950. Miriam Benkowitz, the first to compare the British Library fragments with Mme d'Arblay's *Memoirs,* says that Mme d'Arblay "chose to pervert or to eliminate nearly all the material her father had recorded as autobiography."[39] Roger Lonsdale, who made use of the fragments in his excellent biography of Dr. Burney, devotes to the memoirs an entire chapter, in which he analyzes Mme d'Arblay's frequent distortions and manipulations of the text and concludes that she "contrived to drain her father's personality of any colour."[40] Until now, however, such critical evaluations could be verified only by scholars who took the pains to examine these fragmentary remains in private and public collections on both sides of the Atlantic. The present edition is an attempt to restore the surviving half (or so) of the first volume of memoirs as he wrote them, so that the reader can judge Burney's own account of his early career.

The Surviving Fragments

Between 1817 and 1820, while she was sorting out Burney's papers, Mme d'Arblay compiled a twenty-nine page inventory of the various manuscripts in her possession.[41] On page 2 she lists codes that indicate her intentions with regard to the manuscripts. Three of these concern us here:

+   "investigated for further consideration"

o   "examined & destroyed"

⚹   "Examined & Amalgamated with others"

After a preliminary inventory, she wrote out (p. 17) a list of "MSS. de mon cher Père / in my possession / To arrange—preserve, or destroy" (here called List A), which gives a good idea of the extent of Burney's memoirs in 1817–20. The symbol preceding each entry represents her initial evaluation of the manuscript; that following, her final verdict.

+	1.	Ms. Book of his own Memoirs in his own hand, from the year 1726 to 1744.	o
⚹		2d Ms. Memoirs from 1729 to 1766[42]	o
⚹		3d Ms. Memoirs from 1776 to 1779	o
⚹		4th Private Memorandums general	o
⚹		5th Memoirs from 1743 to 1799	o
⚹		6th Continuation of 1765 to 1770	+
⚹		7th From 1771 to 1777	+
o	8	Crewe Hall 1797	o
⚹	9.	Continuation 1802 from p. 98	o

✳	10.	Mem: of 1808	o
✳	11.	Memoirs from beginning, & mixt N° 11	o
✳	12.	Memoirs MSS. unpaged & mixt	
✳	13.	Memoirs Fragments & odd morsels, sundries	
✳	14.	Memoirs from 1771. Return from Italy.	

It is evident that Mme d'Arblay originally meant to amalgamate most of these memoirs (except item 8) but on second thought decided to destroy them, except items 6 and 7 and perhaps 12–14, which have no "final verdict" symbols.

Page 18 of the register lists five volumes of Burney's poetry and badinage; page 19 (here called List B) reads as follows:

✳	1.	Copies of Letters unsorted	✳
	2.	Copies of Letters in his own hand	·✳
	3.	Ms. Copies, mixt, Memoirs	✳
	4.	Mss. & Copies, uncertain	✳
+	5.	Mss. Poetry unsorted	✳
	6.	Memoirs—Copies—Chinese	✳
	7.	MSS. Memoirs unsorted	✳
o	8[a]	MS notes on Rousseau's Confessions, Marble Bk	o
	8[b]	Interesting sundries, unclass'd, for Mem[rs]	✳
o	9.	Curious Adver[ts] & fragments	o
		Extracts from old Newspapers.	
	10.	Musical Fragments, undecided.	
	11.	Confused MSS de Mon Pere de toutes espèce	

List B shows that items 3, 6, 7, 8[b] (and possibly 11) contained parts or fragments of Burney's memoirs, and that these had not been destroyed, but "Examined & Amalgamated with others." She gives no final verdict on items 10 and 11.[43]

Just how full a record of his life his manuscripts contained is clear from

Burney's remark to his son Charles in 1806 that he would have no difficulty filling in the details of his life after 1760 because from that year on he had kept "records in my pocket books . . . to the present time, and c^d tell you where & how I spent every hour of my life."[44] Following her inventory of Burney's letters and correspondence, Mme d'Arblay lists (p. 23) his "Pocket Books in general from 1750 to 1813," specifically those of 1760, 1768, and 1800–1813. These were printed (Baldwin) diaries in which Burney entered daily memoranda about his engagements, dinners, lessons given to scholars, amounts of money received or paid out—matter-of-fact entries, very different from his memoirs. All are marked ○: "examined and destroyed."[45]

Although nine of the twelve notebooks of Burney's memoirs from List A were destroyed, other material from both lists escaped destruction. Most would have been from the "Confused MSS de Mon Pere de toutes espèce," "odd morsels, sundries," or "Memoirs MSS. unpaged & mixt." Approximately 158 fragment-sheets[46] of this material have been preserved: about 104 in the Berg Collection, 25 in the Osborn Collection, and 29 in the British Library (Add. MSS 48345, ff. 1–19, 22; Barrett Collection, Egerton MS 3700B, ff. 1–9). They probably derived from items 6, 7, and 12–14 of List A and items 3, 6, 7, 8[b], and possibly 4 and 11 of List B.

Burney's own introduction makes it clear that he considered his memoirs of great value to posterity, commenting that they "will be drawn up with too much sincerity and integrity to appear during the Author's life." Having closely observed men of all classes, from peasants to kings, he intended to display them

> in their respective situations, & to delineate their virtues, vices, and apparent degrees of happiness & misery . . .
>
> A book of this kind, though it may mortify & offend a few persons of the present age, w^d be read with avidity at the distance of some centuries by antiquaries & lovers of anecdotes, though it will have lost the piquancy of personality.[47]

But whatever Burney's intentions may have been when he wrote his introduction, he never achieved a fully realized whole from the various parts of his memoirs: some parts were evidently quite fully developed; others remained in draft. Of these he wrote:

> I have short records of the numerous invitations wth wch I was honoured at this time entered in my Baldwin pocket books, w^ch [having] serv'd as a ledger must be very dry & uninteresting without the mention of whom I

met at the [   ]al places, or recording the conversations, bons mots, or characteristic stories told by individuals, who struck fire out of each other, producing mirth & good humour:—when these short entries were made I had not leisure for details, & now memory will not supply them—yet there is a transient pleasure, perhaps a gratification of vanity, in the reminiscence of the company with wch I was allowed, indeed pressed to associate; but sh^d these memoranda be termed mes confessions, they, at the worst, c^d only be called *vain boasts* of notice & favours rec^d from eminent & worthy persons; not of transactions too corrupt & depraved to be termed *human frailties,* or *amiable weaknesses.*[48]

Burney's comments indicate that such memoranda were very different from the fully developed sections of his memoirs, which he took pains to revise, often several times.[49]

Lonsdale (1965, pp. 435–36) suggests that the memoirs took something like the following general outline: volume 1, 1726–66; volume 2, 1766–70;[50] volumes 3–5, the unpublished portions of the journal of his travels through France and Italy;[51] volumes 6–7, the years with Johnson and the Thrales. Later volumes (as Mme d'Arblay's List A shows) carried the memoirs at least to 1799 and possibly further.

The first volume, covering Burney's life from 1726 to 1766, is relatively well preserved; of the second volume only half a dozen fragments have survived.[52] What makes the first volume of special interest is the sparsity of firsthand information about the first forty years of Burney's life. His first extant letter is dated September 1751, when he was twenty-five, and only twenty of his letters written between that date and 1765 are known to have been preserved. From 1770 the account of his life in his own words is amply documented in the *Tours* as well as in his correspondence, which becomes more copious about this time. But for his early career, there is little except Mme d'Arblay's "edited" version of his memoirs and the fragments presented here.

The fragments give a substantially richer perspective on his youth than does Mme d'Arblay. They reveal in his own anecdotal style much more about his early interest in music and his involvement in the "low" theatrical world where he followed in his father's footsteps. They give glimpses of Vauxhall Gardens with its rakes and fiddlers, about whom he evidently liked to talk, for they were as significant a part of his experience as his acquaintance with Handel or, later, with the great figures of London society. Much of this his daughter prudishly omitted from her account as unworthy of the famous historian of music, friend of Garrick and Dr. Johnson, and father of the celebrated author of *Evelina*. Here in his own words, then, is something of his early life, different in tone from the domestic life in Poland Street and St. Martin's Street that Fanny Burney so vividly portrays in her early diaries. She knew only from hearsay the "low" world, never far from Grub Street and pantomimes, in which young Burney and his extraordinary ne'er-do-well father moved before she was born, and one feels that she excluded it as unworthy of "the Name of Burney."

Reconstruction

Evidence that the first volume of memoirs existed in a relatively finished state comes from Burney's holograph index (which precedes the text of the fragments in this book) and surviving fragment-sheets. The paginated index provides a rough outline of his early life as he himself saw it, from his birth and parentage to his "Return from Paris" in the summer of 1765. The index is not complete; the bottoms of its leaves have been torn off, resulting in six lacunae: missing are entries for pp. 10–14, 30–56, 68–75, 87–105, 119–36, and 148 to the end. Still, we are left with more than half of the total index entries for the years 1726–66. The pagination refers to the fair copy he began transcribing in December 1805 (hereafter called Nbk 1805) from earlier drafts.

No less than fourteen full sheets, thirty half-sheets, and three quarter-sheets of Nbk 1805 survive. The full sheets and top half-sheets are paginated, and the pagination corresponds to Burney's manuscript index. These sheets, now dispersed on both sides of the Atlantic, furnish about two-thirds of the fragments printed in this edition.

There are eleven full sheets and eleven half-sheets in the Berg Collection, New York Public Library, which provide full, partial, or variant text for Fragments 36, 42–44, 46–47, 66, 72, 74–81, 88, 89, and 98–107. Another seventeen half-sheets in the British Library (Add. MSS 48345, ff. 2–16) furnish full, partial, or variant text for Fragments 11, 14, 17–28, 30, 32–34, 47, 49–56, 59–61, and 63–64. The Osborn Collection at Yale University has three full sheets, two half-sheets, and three quarter-sheets, which provide text for Fragments 1–7, 38–39, and 69–70.[53]

Examination of these materials reveals that when Mme d'Arblay went through Burney's text between 1817 and 1820, she scored through phrases, revised Burney's tone and syntax, and sometimes obliterated whole passages. Then, presumably, she ripped the volume down the spine and tore its sheets in half (or in quarters) before consigning much of it to the flames. This would explain the half- and quarter-sheets among the surviving pages.[54]

Other fragments besides the remains of Nbk 1805 have survived, even though Mme d'Arblay marked them for destruction. These additional manuscript sources, which account for some thirty-five fragments or variant texts in the present edition, are described in the headnote to the textual notes that follow the appendixes.[55]

Burney's index served as a guide for our reconstruction of the first volume. Sometimes both index heading and corresponding text exist and sometimes one but not the other. For cases in which text exists but an index heading does not (for example, where there are lacunae in Burney's Index), Lonsdale's meticulous and well-documented biography (1965) has been a useful guide.[56] Burney also kept a notebook of inserts to be added to the fair copy. This is a special case, for in its surviving sheets we have Burney's intended additions to text that is missing.

In the process of sorting the fragments, transcribing them from the original manuscripts, and placing them in proper chronological order, we were sometimes able to bring together widely separated fragment-sheets to form a continuous narrative.[57] Where variant texts exist, preference has invariably been given to the fuller and richer version; the variant is listed in the textual notes.[58] In a few cases a text that is continuous in the original manuscript has been split for chronological reasons—for example, Fragments 18 and 87: the first refers to events that occurred in the early 1740s, whereas the second brings Burney's account to the 1760s. Otherwise, an attempt has been made to follow Burney's own ordering, with the exceptions of Fragments 40 and 88, both of which appear to have been placed later in Burney's fair copy. Again, they were assigned their present place for chronological reasons (see textual notes). Occasionally, we have inserted a "Bridge" between two fragments in order to incorporate all of Burney's own index headings and to fill some gaps in the story, where other sources make it possible to do so.

Of the 117 fragments in the present edition, 103 are taken from Burney's original manuscripts; eleven from previously printed sources, such as his *History of Music,* when they refer specifically to matters of autobiographical interest (these may be recognized by an italic heading);[59] two (Fragments 41 and 68) and part of a third (Fragment 84) from Mme d'Arblay's *Memoirs* (which, as they are not in Burney's own words, are printed in italics). Fragment 102, although transcribed by Burney for his memoirs, consists chiefly of an autograph letter of Garrick.

In the interest of continuity, a few passages from letters in which Burney reminisces about his early days have been included. Our guiding principle has been to give an account of Burney's early career in his own words. For this reason, too, his own additions and revisions (he often crossed out a word and replaced it with a better one) have been silently incorporated into the text, and only a few significant variants are listed in the textual notes.

As our purpose has been to recover Burney's own account, Mme d'Arblay's corrections and deletions have been disregarded; this frequently required pains-taking decipherment of Burney's text through her revisions and attempted obliterations.[60] Since a record of her constant interference would have made the apparatus almost impossibly complicated, her revisions are described in the textual notes in general terms only ("lightly" or "heavily scored," "obliterated," and the like).

Conjectural readings are placed in angle brackets ⟨ ⟩; editorial insertions appear in square brackets [ ]; indecipherable material is indicated by empty square brackets; and text that Mme d'Arblay intended to obliterate is restored in half-brackets ⌐ ¬.

Annotations, Appendixes, and Textual Notes

To make up for missing text, our annotations are as full as possible and, again, quote Burney in his own words whenever possible, using letters, published works (such as the *History of Music* and the *Commemoration of Handel*), and especially his articles in Rees's *Cyclopaedia,* which he was finishing at about the time he set out to revise his memoirs. These articles, like the memoirs, are full of reminiscences and anecdotes, which often illuminate the text of the fragments. His evaluations of contemporary musicians, with many of whom he was on intimate terms, are also given in his own words, but his often erroneous dating has been corrected in the light of modern scholarship.

Where we have only Burney's index entries, his own works were often of great help in our efforts to elucidate their meaning and are frequently quoted in our notes. In one case (see Fragment 38, note 8) where only a part of Burney's manuscript is extant, the quotation from Rees supplies the rest, which suggests that Burney sometimes consulted his memoirs while composing articles for Rees.

Appendix A offers editorial comment on Burney's second wife's dowry.

Appendix B consists of excerpts from his articles in Rees and manuscript sources; these reveal his delight in anecdote.

The textual notes give the source(s) of each fragment, record significant variants, and briefly describe the nature of Mme d'Arblay's editorial interventions. Sources of letters quoted in the annotations and bridge passages can be found in *A Catalogue of the Burney Family Correspondence 1749–1878* (*Cat. Corr.*) and in *Letters of Dr Charles Burney,* to be published by Oxford University Press, beginning in 1988 (annotations to this edition of the *Letters* will also include references to later fragments of Burney's MS memoirs).

The text reproduces Burney's spelling and punctuation, except that in the interest of typographical clarity we have omitted the period that Burney habitually placed under the raised letters of abbreviations.

1. See Burney's autobiographical sketch (BL Add. MSS 48345 f.22ᵛ; quoted in Lonsdale 1965, p. 21).

2. Edited in 1959 by Percy A. Scholes as *Dr. Burney's Musical Tours in Europe,* these two volumes are hereafter referred to as the *Tours.*

3. *ED,* 1:222.

4. "You laugh at your poor acquaintance, and he laughs at himself (he was always a *gigler* you know) when you tell him of his being on the list of *Great Men*" (CB to Mrs. Crewe, 8 Aug. 1773, Berg).

5. The numerous references to CB in *New Grove* are a good indication of this.

6. "Began Augᵗ 1782," wrote CB at the top of the fair copy of his "Introduction," adding, "Trans. Decʳ 26. 1805. Commenced" (Osborn). In April 1806, in answer to his son Charles's query about theatrical events in the 1740s, he said that he "had written down in 1782 all I cᵈ then remember of dramatic transactions during these times, from 1744 to 1751, when I went to Lynn" (see Bridge: Frags. 61–62).

7. *JL,* 12:700–701.

8. Just how much he had appreciated "little Molly" is evident from the fact that on 28 Oct. 1804 he stood "god-father to my ex-

cellent old Servant Molly More's now Mrs. Walker's little girl" (Diaries, Berg). To Rebecca, who never married, he left thirty guineas in his will (Scholes 1948, 2:263). Both were still alive in 1819 (*JL,* 9:142).

9. CB to Charles Burney, 16 and 19 April 1806 (Comyn), and n. 6, above.

10. CB's major collection of material on eighteenth-century theatre and on Garrick is preserved in the British Library (see BL Catalogue under "Burney, Charles, DD").

11. CB to John Belfour, 12 Nov. 1806 (Osborn). The figure for the number of years is illegible.

12. An undated loose sheet in Burney's hand (Osborn).

13. *JL,* 11:186.

14. *JL,* 13:700.

15. *JL,* 11:187.

16. *JL,* 8:65; see also pp. 70, 83, 109, 279, 336.

17. *JL,* 9:43. The remainder was brought back to England in October 1817 by her ailing husband, Alexandre d'Arblay.

18. *JL,* 9:218.

19. *JL,* 10:512n.

20. *JL,* 9:428.

21. *JL,* 10:937.

22. *JL,* 10:859.

23. We owe these references to Joyce Hemlow, who has examined Fanny's unpublished diaries (Berg). These, like Burney's pocket Baldwin diaries, give a rather dry list of daily activities.

24. *JL,* 12:701.

25. *JL,* 11:163.

26. *JL,* 11:188ff.

27. Some of Mme d'Arblay's corrections in red pencil occur in the fragments preserved in the British Library (e.g., Add. MSS 48345, f. 2ʳ) but most of her corrections and obliterations were made in ink.

28. It is amusing to read this comment by a woman sixty-eight years old writing to her seventy-year-old sister. Mme d'Arblay's *Memoirs of Dr. Burney* appeared in 1832, when she herself was eighty—whereas Burney began his memoirs at the age of fifty-six, when he was at the height of his powers (see Lonsdale 1965, pp. 433, 440).

29. This paragraph no doubt reveals Mme d'Arblay's true motives for destroying Burney's memoirs and some of his more compromising letters.

30. As Lonsdale 1965 (p. 438) points out, "This statement is manifestly untrue, for at least two pages were devoted to Burney's courtship of Esther Sleepe and later passages described her popularity at Lynn and death in 1762." See Frags. 49–50, 69, 93.

31. See Frags. 54–56.

32. Most of these were destroyed.

33. Perhaps items 1–7, 9–12, and 14 from List A (see below). She does not seem to include here the bundles of "odd morsels, sundries," etc., mentioned in Lists A and B. A fragment in Berg, which mentions Burney's introduction to the Thrales in 1776, is headed "to vol. vii. p. 19."

34. Only one specimen of Burney's memoirs transcribed by Sarah Harriet has survived, and this deals with post-1769 events, not included in this edition. Burney employed Sarah Harriet as an amanuensis to write letters when he was ill, and there is an extant transcript in her hand of part of his *Tours* (Lonsdale 1965, p. 99, n.5).

35. In her "register raisonné" (see n. 41), p. 23. There is, however, an entry in her diary for 29 Dec. 1820: "MSS. Last Pocket Book de mon Pere" (Berg), which shows that she examined it after the rest were destroyed.

36. 7 Jan. 1826: "MSS. 1789 Lettres *à* mon cher Pere"; 28 Feb.: "MSS à mon Pere—95," etc. (Berg). At this point, only letters are mentioned, as the bulk of his memoirs had been destroyed.

37. Mme d'Arblay to Esther Burney, 6 and 16 Feb. 1828 (Berg). See also *JL,* 12:700; for an explanation of the judgments, see *JL,* 12:701 n.13.

38. "Madame d'Arblay's Memoirs of Dr. Burney," *Quarterly Review* 49 (1833): 97–125.

39. "Dr. Burney's Memoirs," *RES* 10 (1959): 257–68.

40. Lonsdale 1965, p. 450.

41. Preserved in Berg, where it is described as a "Holograph notebook: register raisonné." It contains lists not only of CB's but of her own manuscripts and letters.

42. A scrap of paper in CB's hand (Barrett, Egerton 3009, f. 14) refers to a "List of books and Papers in wᶜʰ memoranda are made of my progress through life, from cradle to decreptitude— / Nᵒ I blue from 1726 to 1743 / II from   to 1766 / III Johnsoniana & Bons Mots." Items I and II no doubt correspond to Mme d'Arblay's first two items, which she destroyed. Part of item III is preserved in Barrett (Egerton 3700B, ff. 1–9).

43. The "confused MSS" probably included "Conjugal Remembrances of my dear Father," which Mme d'Arblay mentions in her (unpublished) diary for 24 Feb. 1820. These are also missing.

44. CB to Charles Burney, 19 April [1806] (Comyn).

45. Nevertheless, some survived and are preserved in Berg; the longest, for 1796, is complete. They are valuable for an understanding of eighteenth-century musical life and have proved useful in annotating the forthcoming edition of Burney's letters.

46. The term "fragment-sheet" is used here to denote the physical object, a sheet or scrap of paper with text on recto and verso, to distinguish it from our numbered "fragment," which is usually text taken from either recto or verso of a fragment-sheet.

47. Frag. 1.

48. Berg.

49. For Mme d'Arblay's dishonest interpretation of Burney's comments authorizing her destruction of almost the entire body of the memoirs, see Lonsdale 1965, pp. 442–43; and Frag. 1, n. 1.

50. Burney indicated that the present Frags. 112 and 113 were to go to vol. 2, pp. 11 and 16 respectively. They both deal with events of 1767, which suggests that the second volume opened with an account of that year.

51. These have been since published as *Music, Men, and Manners in France and Italy, 1770,* ed. H. Edmund Poole (1969; rpt. 1974) from the original manuscript in the British Library (Add. MSS 35122).

52. Frags. 111–17.

53. Frags. 115–17 in Osborn probably come from the 1805 redaction of vol. 2.

54. Only two sheets of the introduction survive intact. Full sheets in Berg are also torn in half and consist of matching tops and bottoms.

55. There are, of course, many post-1769 fragments, but these do not concern us here. There are no index entries for Frags. 111–17, which are all that we know to have survived of vol. 2.

56. The fact that some of the top half-pages are paginated also helped in restoring CB's order in sections for which there are no index headings. See textual notes to Frags. 98–106.

57. See, e.g., textual notes to Frags. 34 and 47. An amusing instance occurs in an account covering late June 1803, not in this volume. In a fragment-sheet (BL, Add. MSS 48345 f. 20^v), Burney talks of Dr. North, who "had as much ready wit as Geo. Selwyn, and much more good"; another fragment-sheet in the Berg Collection in New York begins: "humour. Music at L^y Clarges's," etc. Only now has Mr. North's "good humour" been recovered.

58. See textual notes to Frags. 18, 31, 40, 45–46, 70, 72, 89, and 96.

59. See Frags. 10, 15, 35, 48, 57–58, 67, 82–83, 86, and 91. They are headed in italics to distinguish them from those taken from the original manuscripts.

60. We have also disregarded passages that she quotes as deriving verbatim from Burney's manuscript (*Mem* 1:9, 19, 129–33, 155; 2:168–71). The surviving manuscripts show that even here she tampered with her father's text.

Memoirs of Dr. Charles Burney

Burney's Index to the
Fair Copy of His Memoirs

[half-sheet torn away]

The opening page of the 1805 redaction of the
memoirs, indicating Burney's second thoughts
and Mme d'Arblay's revisions and deletions.
Courtesy of the Osborn Collection.

Text of the Fragments

Introduction

If the Life of an humble individual on whom no Splendid Appointments, Important Transactions, or Atrocious Crimes, have called the attention of the public, can afford amusement to the friends he leaves behind, without being offered, either as a model to follow, or a precipiece to shun, the writer's intention will be fully accomplished. But there is no member of society, who, by diligence, talents, or conduct, leaves his name and race, a little better than those from which he sprung, is, perhaps, not totally without some claim to attention, on the means by wch such advantages were atchieved.

My life, though it has been ⌐not without its⌐ tissue of toils, parsimony, sickness, & sorrow, has yet been so much more pleasant & prosperous than I had a title to expect, or than many others with higher claims have enjoyed, that its incidents when related may perhaps help to put mediocrity in good humour, and repress the pride, and over-rated worth, and expectation of indolence.

⌐Whether anecdotes & memorandums concerning so insi[g]nificant an individual deserve to be written, or whether these will ever merit any more than the private perusal of my own family and intimate friends, will be left to their decision. They will be drawn up with too much sincerity and integrity to appear during the Author's life.⌐

Perhaps few have been better enabled to describe faithfully & exactly, from an actual survey, the manners & customs of the age in wch he lived, than myself: ascending from those of the most humble cottagers, & lowest mechanics, to the first Nobility, and most elevated personages in the kingdom, with whom circumstances, situation, & accident, at different periods of my life, have rendered me familiar. Oppressed and laborious husbandmen, insolent & illiberal Yeomanry, overgrown Norfolk Farmers, generous, friendly & hospitable Merchants, Men of business & Men of pleasure, Men of Letters, Artists, Men of Science, Sportsmen & country Squires, dissipated and extravagant voluptuaries, Gamesters, Ambassadors, Statesmen, & even sovereign princes I have had an opportunity of examining, in almost every point of view. All these & more it is my intention to describe in their respective situations, to delineate their virtues, vices, and apparent degrees of happiness & misery, ⌐as well as the person and manners of Men of rank, learning, talents & abilities, wth whom I have lived, corresponded, or been in some way connected.⌐

A book of this kind, though it may mortify & offend a few persons of the present age, w^d be read with avidity at the distance of some centuries by antiquaries & lovers of anecdotes, though it will have lost the piquancy of personality.[1]

My Grand Father, James Macburny, who by the letters wch I have seen of his writing, and circumstances concerning him wch I remember to have heard from my Father and Mother,   *My Grand Father*[2] was a gentleman of a considerable patrimony, at great Hanwood, a village in Shropshire, who having received a good education, in the latter years of his life was appointed Steward to the Earl of Ashburnham,[3] & had a house in Privy Garden, White Hall. In the year 1727, he walked as Esquire to one of the Knights, at the coronation of King George the II.[4]

My Father, James, born likewise at Hanwood, 1675, was well educated both in school learning & accomplishments. He was a day   *My Father*[5] *&* Scholar at Westminster School, under the celebrated   *Dr Busby* Dr. Busbey,[6] while my Grandfather resided at White Hall. I remember his telling a story of the severe chastisement he rec^d from this terrific disciplinarian for playing truant after school hours, instead of returning home. My Grandfather, who had frequently admonished him in vain, not to loiter in the Street, lest he sh^d make improper and mischievous acquaintance; finding no attention was paid to his injunctions, he, without manifesting any anger, or telling my father the subject, gave him a letter addressed to the Revd Dr Busby, wch he delivered with ignorant chearfulness on his entrance into School. The Doctor, when he had perused it, called my father to him, and in a very mild & seemingly good humoured voice, said; "Burney, can you read writing?" Yes, Sir, answered my father with great courage and flippancy. Then read this letter aloud, says the Doctor. When my father, with an audible voice, began: "Sir, my son, the bearer of this letter, having long disregarded my admonitions against his stopping to play with idle and corrupt boys, in his way from school"—here my father's voice fell & faltered—"Go on," says his master, "you read very well:" "I am sorry to be under the necessity of entreating you to—to—to cor—" here he threw down the letter & fell on his knees;—crying out—"indeed Sir, I'll never do so again! pray forgive me!" "Oh you read perfectly well" the D^r again tells him; "pray finish the letter." And making him pronounce aloud the words—"correct him", complied with my Grandfathers request in a very liberal manner.

Whether my father was intended for any particular profession, I know not; but during his youth, besides his school learning, he acquired several talents as accomplishm^ts wch in the course of his life he was obliged professionally to turn to account. He danced well, performed well on the Violin, and was a portrait painter of no mean talents. ⌐He likewise wrote a fine hand, and was a good [   ].⌐7   *his education*

During the reign of Queen Anne, he had the place under governm^t of licencer of the Hawkers & Pedlars, wch he lost on the accession of George the first.

Notwithstanding the *Mac,* wch was prefixed to my Grandfather's name, and wch my father retained for some time, I never c^d find at what period any of my ancestors lived in Scotland or Ireland, whence it must have been derived.[9] My Father and Grandfather were both born in Shropshire, and never were in Scotland or Ireland.   *drops the Mac[8]*

Very early in his life, my father lost the favour of his sire, by eloping from home & marrying a young actress of Goodman's fields theatre by whom he had a very large family. My Grand-father's affection, alienated by this marriage, and disapproving his conduct, perhaps, in other respects, to the usual [   ] of old age, added that of marrying his female domestic, to whom, and to a Son, Joseph, the consequence of this marriage, he bequeathed, at his decease, all his possessions, wch were very considerable.[11] This son, however, was not more pru-dent than my father; for he contrived, early in life, to dissipate his patrimony, and subsisted many years in Norfolk, by teaching to dance.[12] I visited him in 1756 in a tour to Yarmouth. He lived then at Ormsby, a beautiful village near that town, [with his wife,] a large Family of beautiful Chil-   *his first Marriage[10]*   *My Grandfather's 2^d Marriage*   *His Son, Jo—by that Marriage*   *Joseph's imprudence* dren, an elegant Villa and garden,[13] & [*he appeared, at that time, in perfectly restored & easy circumstances*].[14]

1. When Mme d'Arblay was revising CB's memoirs, she added disingenuously at the bottom of the page, as if CB were writing: "Had health, spirits, & native vigour favoured the execution of this project, no memoirs of the times, or none but Boswells Johnson would have contained equal instruction with Entertainment—but, alas, they all failed in its execution."

2. James MacBurney II (c. 1653–1723) of Great Hanwood, Shropshire, married c. 1677 Mary Evans (1649–1713), daughter of the local rector, Nehemiah Evans, from whom he inherited an estate at Hanwood. According to Worcester Mem., p. 1, "he studied portrait painting as an amateur, with considerable success; having received instructions from [Thomas] Murray [1663–1734], an eminent Painter at that time"; if so, he probably took lessons from Murray in the 1690s. "A very good portrait" of him "painted by Murray" was in the family in 1899. A photographic reproduction is in the extra-illustrated copy of Mme d'Arblay's *Diary and Letters* in the National Portrait Gallery, London (shelf-mark B.I.1 14) from the original owned in 1926 by "the late Colonel H. Burney, Wavendon Towers." James MacBurney's will, dated 24 Jan. and 25 March 1723, was proved 18 April 1723 (PRO/PROB 11/590). It shows that shortly before his death he lived at "Dowgate Hill London."

3. John Ashburnham (1687–1737), 3rd Baron Ashburnham; cr. Viscount St. Asaph and Earl of Ashburnham, 1730; M.P. for Hastings, 1710; Gentleman of the Bedchamber to the Prince of Wales, 1728–30. CB's grandfather could not have become his "secretary" (Worcester Mem.) before 1710, when John Ashburnham succeeded his brother William as 3rd Baron. MacBurney mentions in his will

"one Bond or Obligation from the Right Hon[ble] John Lord Ashburnham" dated 8 May 1719 and "also the sum of Fifty pounds out of the Moneys due to me by the Right hon[ble] John Lord Ashburnham."

4. CB made a slip here: James MacBurney had died four years earlier, in March or April 1723. According to Worcester Mem., the coronation was that of George I in 1714, and "the Knight" was John Ashburnham himself.

5. James MacBurney III (d. 1749) was born in May 1678. As "he seem'd to have a greater inclination for the study of painting, than any other occupation his Father had him instructed by [Michael] Dahl [1656–1743], a famous Painter born at Stockholm. He likewise gave him a good education in other respects, as it is thought, he originally intended him for a Physician; but as that profession required much more application and steadiness, than he was possessed of, it was soon given up. . . . His life was a succession of gaieties and troubles & the number of places he appears to have liv'd at, proves the unsteadiness of his conduct" (Worcester Mem., p. 2).

6. Richard Busby (1616–95), headmaster of Westminster School from 1638, whose rule by the birch became proverbial. The incident CB relates occurred about 1690.

7. "The varieties, & eccentricities of this Gentleman's life, might, if collected together, make an entertaining history, to *any* who were not sufferers by his volatile, & improvident conduct. It might at least afford an excellent moral lesson on the happy effects of prudence & application, where exertions are necessary for the support of a family; but his ready wit, & great flow of spirits, made him always an acceptable guest; & he found it

more to his taste and disposition, to shine at a convivial meeting, than to study his real advantage. The consequences of which were, that as his health declined in his Old Age, his circumstances kept pace, and his family were left to lament, that his talent for pleasantry, & love of sociability, overcame his prudential care, either for himself or them" (Worcester Mem., p. 8).

8. About 1726, the year of CB's birth, his father took the "great liberty with the family name" of dropping the "Mac" and was "after this period call'd *Burney* alone. His particular reason for this alteration has not been preserved" (Worcester Mem., p. 5). Lonsdale (1965, p. 2) conjectures that his reasons may have been similar to those which, CB says, led Charles Macklin the actor to change his name from McLaughlin—"to get rid not only of its *Paddy* appearance but of its harshness."

9. According to Worcester Mem., p. 1, CB's great-grandfather James MacBurney came to England "from Scotland in the year 1603, with King James I." A "Portrait by [George] Jameson [1587–1644] in dress of a warrior" was in the Burney family ("Burney Pedigree" drawn by the author of Worcester Mem. in the extra-illustrated copy of Mme d'Arblay's *Diaries and Letters*). The portrait is not listed in John Bullough's monograph *George Jameson The Scottish Vandyke* (1885), which contains a "Catalogue of his Works so far as well Authenticated."

10. "In 1697, when only in his 19th year, he married Miss Rebecca Ellis [1681–pre-1720], a genteel and handsome young lady, then in her 16th year, who brought him 15 children, 9 of whom lived" (Worcester Mem., p. 2). The Goodman's Inn Fields Theatre did not open until 1729; perhaps CB was thinking of the Lincoln's Inn Fields playhouse, which was in use from 1695 to 1714

before being rebuilt (note in *ED*, 1:xvi). In 1729 James MacBurney was engaged in the newly opened Goodman's Inn Fields Theatre, which led to young CB's being sent from Chester to Condover (see Bridge: Frags. 1–2).

11. The grandfather's first wife, Mary, died in 1713. Both he and she were buried in New Chapel, Petty France, Westminster. The "domestic" whom he married after 1713 is called Martha in his will; she was "probably a Welsh girl." At his death "the bulk of his fortune . . . was supposed to be about £8000" (Worcester Mem., p. 4). He left "all the moneys in Gold and Silver" to her and to his son Joseph by her. To his other son, James (CB's father), he left half of his furniture and the "remainder of the estate"; to his grandson Edward (b. 1698), a surgeon, £1000; and to his grandson Thomas (b. 1707), dancing-master, £40. For Joseph Burney (d. October 1781), who was "remarkably handsome," see Millican. "There is a very good portrait of him in the family painted by Dahl" (Worcester Mem., p. 4).

12. Millican shows that Joseph was often in financial trouble and, having wasted his and his wife's money, spent some time in prison for debt. He evidently left Ormsby for King's Lynn, where he was buried 7 Oct. 1781 (St. Margaret's Parish Register, Burials).

13. Joseph married on 2 March 1741/2 Theodosia Bayley of Ormsby, and had by her three daughters—Theodosia (b. 1742), Martha (b. 1746), Jemima (b. 1748), and two sons—Hugh Lloyd (b. 1744?) and Joseph (b. 1750). He and his wife had to relinquish their "elegant Villa" in 1764, eight years after CB visited them, apparently because of Joseph's debts (Millican).

14. Added by Mme d'Arblay, who discarded the sheet on which CB completed the sentence.

BRIDGE: FRAGMENTS 1–2

*My father obliged to
use his
accomplishments pro-
fessionally*[1]

*His company much
sought*

His first Wife dies—

*Marries Mrs Anne
Cooper
Who had captivated
Wicherly*[2]

*Levelling—its conse-
quences*[3]

Weaver[4]

*Pranks by him & my
father*

Birth of the Author[5]

On 31 October 1729 the new theatre of Goodman's Inn Fields opened in Ayliffe Street under Thomas Odell's management, and Burney's father, engaged as actor, left for London.[6] His theatrical activities there obliged him, before he left Shrewsbury, to send the three-year-old Charles to Nurse Ball (Frag. 2, n. 2) and Burney's then six-year-old brother Richard (b. June 1723) to "a small school" in the village of Condover, four miles from Shrewsbury, "where they were so happy that the remembrance remain'd with them during life" (Worcester Mem., p. 5). "I lived in a village myself till I was 12 years old, & remember every face, superstition, proverb . . . as well as if I had quitted my nurse & Shropshire Village but 6 months" (CB to Thomas Twining, 10 May 1804, Osborn). His brother Richard "in his early youth had a passion for drawing, wch he manifested on every wall wth chalk, and every scrap of paper he c^d get at" (Berg). "One of the first toasts I was taught to drink in my adolescent State was, 'a health to the Barley mow!'" (CB to Richard Cox, 7 [Jan.] 1796, Lloyds). He recalls "the familiar manner in wch the sexes treated each other in the *hops* I had seen in my early youth, in a village, where these *ballets* were literally *Country dances,* not *Contre-danse,* as the French pretend" (CB to Edmond Malone, 9–10 Nov. 1806, Bodleian); and that "when I was a boy in Shropshire though November was sometimes gloomy & provoked nervous people to *hang* & *drown*; yet the *whole* month was seldom in fault—I remember the finest weather for field sports imaginable, I have been a hunting, shooting and cour[s]ing, & sat [munching] cold meat & bread & cheese in a Gravel or Marl pit wth great luxury—But, December, in whose iron reign expires the checkered Year as my friend Kit Smart sung, was rugged & the Reaking & Welsh mountains were cover'd wth Snow" (CB to Frances Fermor, [? Aug. 1807], Osborn). He also recalls that "in adolescence, I was made a friend to insects & animals, by my father assuring me that they were not machines: but had feeling, & suffered pain, like human creatures if maimed or wounded. After this I never spun a cock chafer, pulled the wings & legs off flies—impaled butterflies, or with pleasure worms, & magots, nor c^d see bull or ⟨badger⟩ baitings—or Cocks thrown at, or even armed wth spurs for fight. These early moralities are necessary for children of the best natural disposition, who never think of right & wrong till told 'to do as they w^d be done by'" (CB to Edward Miller, 17 Sept. 1799, Comyn).

About 1757 Burney revisited Condover with his wife, and according to Worcester Mem. (p. 5) the thirty-one-year-old music teacher "(who had an excellent poetical genious) on paying a visit at the place, when he was grown up, wrote some verses upon his sensations, & the alterations he perceived, much in the stile of Goldsmith's 'Deserted Village [1776];' but was written many years before that composition." Burney's verses are not known to be extant, though they were "still in preservation" in 1899 when "Memoranda of the Burney Family" (Worcester Mem.) was written.

At seventy-one Burney passed through Shrewsbury but did not go to Condover, "not having my ⟨poor⟩ brother with whom to strole ab^t, there was no one with me to partake of the melancholy pleasure of visiting poor Nurse Balls habitation, and grave" (CB to Mme d'Arblay, [22–24] July [1797], Berg; to Susan Phillips, 26 Oct. 1797, Barrett).

Fragments 2–7 give glimpses of his childhood at Condover.

1. On 30 Oct. 1718 we catch a glimpse of him as actor in *Love for Love,* in Lincoln's Inn Fields: "Ben—Burney, who never appear'd on this Stage before" (*London Stage,* pt. 2, 2:512), but then his name disappears from the stage records for eleven years, and we are left to speculate about how he did "use his accomplishments professionally." See Frag. 1, nn. 5, 7.

2. MacBurney's first wife, Rebecca, died

before 1720, "but of what complaint she died, or where she was buried is not known;—but in the year 1720, which must have been very soon after her death, he was again married (when . . . in his 42ᵈ year), [this time] to Miss Ann Cooper [c. 1690–1775], a young lady of Shrewsbury, daughter to a Herald painter. She had a small fortune, & had received an offer of marriage from the celebrated Wycherly the Poet. At this time Mr. James M.B. was by profession a Painter" (Worcester Mem., pp. 3–4). She may have had some Welsh ancestry, as CB later humorously refers to his "Welsh blood" (CB to Christoph Ebeling, 15 July 1773, Osborn). Photographic reproductions of a very handsome portrait of "James MacBurney" by Dahl and of his second wife Anne Cooper are in the extra-illustrated copy of Mme d'Arblay's *Diary and Letters*. It is possible that these are the portraits of Joseph Burney and his wife (see Frag. 1, n. 11).

3. Though the meaning is not clear, the preceding entry on CB's father and the following on Weaver suggest that the passage may have dealt with the effect Puritans had on dancing in England. In his article "Dance" in Rees, CB writes: "The descendants of the original inhabitants of our island, the Cambro-Britons, in our own memory, on Sundays used to be played out of church by a fiddle, and to form a dance in the church-yard at the conclusion of the sermon . . . but however harmless the practice may originally have been, it has, we believe, been totally discredited and abolished by the dissenters and methodists."

4. John Weaver (1673–1760) was a dancing-master whose title to fame is that he introduced to England the art of pantomime, "the first entertainment that appeared on the English Stage, where the Representation and Story was carried on by Dancing Action and Motion only." He wrote several essays on mime (listed in the *Dictionary of National Bi-*

ography), the most important of which was *An Essay towards an History of Dancing* (1712); see Lonsdale 1960. "Mr. Weaver," writes CB, "besides his professional knowledge, was a man of infinite wit and considerable learning, who, after retiring from the capital, ended his days in Shrewsbury, where he had established a boarding-school of great reputation, and continued teaching to dance till he was 90 years of age" ("Choreography" in Rees). For his teaching young CB to dance, see Frag. 14.

5. CB and Susanna Burney were twins, born "in *Raven Street,* where I first gave my mother cause to make wry faces," on 7 April 1726 (O.S.). CB was baptized on 5 May in St. Mary's Church, Shrewsbury. Susanna died at age eight (Scholes 1948, 1:4; Lonsdale 1965, p. 2; CB to Thomas Twining, 1 Jan. 1798, Folger). "These are the last children of Mr. James M.B. 9 were living by the first wife, & 4 by the second, he had therefore (with the 7 that died) 20 children!" (Worcester Mem., pp. 4–5). See also the genealogical chart of the Burney family (*Cat. Corr.,* facing p. xvi). CB's godfather, "from whom I had the name of Charles," was Charles Fleetwood (d. 1747?), James MacBurney's boon companion "in his better days" and later manager of Drury Lane (CB to Charles Burney, 19 April 1806, Comyn; Frag. 20 and n. 2).

6. *London Stage* (pt. 3, 1:13–123) details his career at Goodman's Inn Fields. On 5 Nov. 1729, six days after the theatre opened, he played Ben in Congreve's *Love for Love*; on 1 Dec., Obadiah in Sir Robert Howard's *The Committee*; on 16 Dec., Fondlewife in Congreve's *The Old Batchelor*; on 10 Feb. 1730, Sir Avarice in Henry Fielding's *The Temple Beau*; and on 28 May, Modely in James Ralph's *The Fashionable Lady*. On 3 June, *Othello* was staged for his benefit, and his son Thomas danced in the afterpiece, *The Shepherd's Holiday*. On 19 June he played Purser in Shadwell's *The Fair Quaker of Deal*. During the

summer, when Goodman's Inn Fields was closed, he performed Goody Tyler in *Wat Tyler and Jack Straw* at Bartholomew Fair (31 Aug. 1730). During the winter season he again acted Modely; on 14 Feb. 1731, Dorcas in Christopher Bullock's *The Cobbler of Pres-* *ton*. His last recorded performance was Oba-diah on 18 March 1731. He probably left Goodman's Inn Fields when Giffard replaced Odell as manager, and returned to Shrews-bury. See also Highfill, 2:425.

FRAGMENT 2

Condover, 1729–38

Wars, and helped the [   ] Victories. And this wa[   ] [a]rithmetic that was [   ] as I afterwards ma[   ] from stolen moments [   ]-dance.

My father's numerous[1] [   ] made it necessary to ⟨learn⟩ [   ] man-ner possible. To N[urse Ball][2] [   ] paid for my board, and a [   ] for my cloaths & educati[on.[3] . . . As I gained] a footing with the village[rs of Condover, both male and] female, I formed many aff[ectionate] [   ] spent my time very pleasantly [at various games] such as hide & seek, draw br⟨ea⟩ [   ] [be]tween two apple trees, qui[te] [   ] Foot-ball, Bandy, prison b[ars][4] [   ] only I felt no want of dign[ity] [   ]

1. Perhaps "numerous children." Fragments 2–7 derive from sheets torn in six and the resulting scraps are irregularly shaped, which accounts for the large number of lacunae.

2. Elleanor Ball née Brown (c. 1680–1743). On 28 Sept. 1699 she married Andrew Ball, and was buried on 2 May 1743 (*Register of Condover,* pp. 157–58, 223, 229). CB fondly recalls "her long Stories," and how she "used to say . . . Well, but 'if I sh^d tell you till tomorrow'[''] (CB to Mme d'Arblay, 9 Oct. 1806, Berg), and "her great proverbial Wisdom" in such sayings as " 'twas a sorry bird who bewrayed his own nest" or "Sue a beggar, & catch a louse" (CB to Elizabeth Allen Burney, 8 Dec. [1790], Barrett; to Charles Burney, 20 Oct. 1809, Osborn). See also Frag. 5, n. 2.

3. Moll Flanders paid £5 a year to the governess of her son in London, but country rates were probably lower.

4. "Bandy," a ball game played with bent sticks, like field hockey; "prison-bars," a boys' game in which "the players are divided into two parties who occupy distinct demar-cations, 'bases,' 'homes' or 'dens,' the aim of each side being to make prisoner by touching any player of the opposite side who runs out from his enclosure" (*Oxford English Diction-ary*). The latter is now sometimes called "British bulldog."

FRAGMENT 3   Condover, 1729–38

[th]at they were utterly [   ] with unkindness and [   ] [   ]me, that
there was no [   ] [   ]ght of them. And on [   ] [accomm]odated
myself to my [   ] [sub]mitting to every ignoble [   ] on me: so that if
instead [   ] [pa]id £4 a year to me as [   ] [I wor]ked harder for her
than I [   ] ⟨in⟩ carrying the dinner and [   ] to Andrew Ball, my
Nurse's [husband]¹ [   ] [pi]tching, or felling timber; when [   ] to
wᶜʰ she had no right, from the [   ] the year round in carrying [   ]
[w]ell, for the use of the house [   ] in my nurse's [   ]

    1. Andrew Ball died four years before his
wife and was buried 22 Feb. 1739. See Frag. 2,
n. 2.

FRAGMENT 4   Condover, 1729–38

    [   ] hemp-yard, in gleaning wit[h] [   ] stones for mending the
roads (sh[   ] [   ] established) Weeding in the pa[   ] the crows from the
grounds of [   ] to all this & more I not only submi[tted] [   ] was
devoid of the lofty s⟨p⟩ [   ] who called himself a gen[tleman] [   ]
daughter and only child,¹ m[   ] [   ] [after]wards lived and worked [am-
bi]tion was to be bound Apr[entice] [   ] a trade by wᶜʰ I might [   ]
being taken home by m[y] [   ]
    My amusements, ho[wever] [   ] [occu]pations and ideas, thou[ghts]
[   ] those of playing with

    1. This refers no doubt to Andrew and   "who called himself a gen[tleman]" was
Nurse Ball's only daughter Elinor, b. 21 July   probably Andrew Ball.
1700, a year after their marriage. The man

FRAGMENT 5   Condover, 1729–38

    [   ] now from [   ] ⟨t⟩hem to make regular remittan[ce] [   ]
[perh]aps the number of miles be[tween] [   ] ⟨carrier⟩ of ⟨stock⟩ payment.¹

w^th [   ]tly upbraiding me, and [   ] of my father & mother's [   ]
unpleasant to my care, had [   ] of people, whom she had [   ]
[fam]ily was known, ⟨had some⟩ [   ] [ra]re compassion, and others
[   ] of flippancy, some [   ] [chil]dren with wch I amused [   ] &
sometimes bestowed [   ] [n]urse had altered for me in her bills. and to
[   ] ideas of a neglected [   ] from absent parents [   ]²

1. This may refer to young CB's walking four miles from Condover to Shrewsbury and back, when he went to visit his family.

2. Nurse Ball was evidently a substitute for CB's "unnatural mother." Mme d'Arblay, who destroyed her father's reminiscences of his childhood because they were "filled with *literal* Nurse's tales" (see editors' introduction), nevertheless prints "the favourite couplets which the good nurse Ball most frequently sang to him at her spinning wheel; and which he especially loved to chaunt, in imitating her longdrawn face, and the dolorous tones of her drawling sadness":

Good bye, my dear neighbours! My
  heart it is sore,
For I must go travelling all the world
  o'er.
And if I should chaunce to come home
  very rich,
My friends and relations will make of
  me mich;
But if I should chaunce to come home
  very poor,
My friends and relations will turn me
  out of door,
After I have been travelling, travelling,
  travelling, all the world o'er.

CB "quitted" her, "as he always protested, with agony of grief" (*Mem.*, 1:5).

FRAGMENT 6   Condover, 1729–38

age. Roger Gwyn, who [   ] who kept the only Ale [house . . . in the]
town,¹ had, by some mi[sfortune] [   ] been rendered a cripple: [   ]
used to ride ab^t as his [   ] an active sharp boy, w[ho] [   ] his Esquire.²
Indeed I wa[s] [   ] when I attended my Chev[alier] [   ] as Sancho,
on some occas[ions]

Another of my favourite [pastimes was ringing] [   ] Indeed I had
hardly strength [   ] entirely, or make one in a
[   ] and jangle, and the Clark [   ] [hav]ing   *Fond of ringing*³
palsey, was very gla[d to send me] chiming to church, & at [   ] This
indeed was so profitable a [   ]

1. Roger Gwynn (1686–1742), innkeeper, died soon after CB left Condover and was buried 12 Dec. 1742. The alehouse was probably "The Horseshoe" on the Hereford road.

See *Register of Condover,* pp. 142, 190, 228; *Victoria County History: Shropshire,* 8:33–34.

2. CB wrote "Equerry" above "Esquire."

3. "The ringing of bells," writes CB, "though now a recreation chiefly of the lower class of people, is a very curious exercise. . . . In ringing, the bell, by means of a wheel and rope, is elevated to a perpendicular: in its motion to this situation, the clapper strikes forcibly on one side, and, in its return downwards, on the other side of the bell, producing at each stroke a sound. The music of bells is altogether melody; but the pleasure arising from it consists in the variety of interchanges, and the various succession and general predominance of the consonances in the sounds produced. . . . In England, the practice of ringing is reduced to a science; and peals have been composed, which bear the names of the inventors" ("Ring" in Rees; for a more complete discussion, see "Change-Ringing" in *New Grove*). CB later wrote an "Epigram on Ringers," which is listed in the Index to his Poet. Nbk, though the verses are missing; he also had in his library "The Art of Ringing, with Peals, MS" 1668 (*Cat. Mus.,* no. 994). The twelfth-century church of St. Andrew and St. Mary at Condover had at the time five bells, the minimum number required for change-ringing. Rhyming rules for ringers, dated 1744, are on a tablet in the tower (*Victoria County History: Shropshire,* 8: 55).

FRAGMENT 7   Condover, 1729–38

[was] my first Music-Master.[1] [   ] & a good ear, my progress [was admired in the] [   ] whole parish. I was [   ] & *sol-fa'd*—kept [   ] [   ]ing in 3 & 4 different parts, so much [   ] men, that I was elevated [   ] or Cantor, and used not only [   ] sh^d sing, but [   ] off the tune.

Still more of Psalm singing[2]

[Satu]rday what we

At ab^t 12 or 13 [an end was put to my *ru*]*ral felicity,* by my father [who by taking me] away [from Condover] and placing me at [   ] [Shrewsbu]ry, not in order to learn Music [   ] deign to try whether I had [   ] to be [   ] school, ⟨for⟩[4]

Go to the free sch. Salop[3]

1. As CB says later (Frags. 9, 10) that his first music master, in the true sense of the word, was Baker, we can only speculate about who introduced him to music at Condover. Scholes (1948, 1:6–7) suggests that CB had some instruction from the local village parson, the Rev. George Luellyn or Llewellyn (d. 3 Aug. 1739), whom CB describes "from my own knowledge" as a rector of Condover,

where I was nursed and spent the first twelve or thirteen years of my life; during which time Mr. Luellyn constantly resided there.

This gentleman, who was a lively

Welshman and a man of wit and taste in the arts, was so much attached to the Stuart family, so fond of Music, and so active in all his pursuits, that he was often called by the Whigs, "a Jacobitical, musical, mad Welsh parson."

Luellyn had been acquainted with Purcell, and in 1702 supplied Dr. Blow with thirty "additional songs" to the "second, and more correct edition" of *Orpheus Britannicus* (*Hist. Mus.*, 3:495 and n.; Mercer, 2:394 and n., where CB also describes his Dutch taste in gardening).

2. His fondness for psalm-singing, however, did not outlast his youth. For CB's later critical attitude to the singing of psalms in church, championed by Mason in his *Essay on Church Music* (1795), see CB to William Mason, 8 June 1795 (Berg); and "Psalmody, Parochial" in Rees.

3. By 1739, CB was attending the Free School at Shrewsbury. No registers of its pupils have been preserved, nor is CB's name entered in the book "in which Hotchkiss, the headmaster, recorded some of his scholars" (Lonsdale 1965, p. 3; for a photograph of the school, see Scholes 1948, 1: pl. 1). Later in his MS memoirs CB mentions a wig he used to wear "at school, when it was the fashion for boys to have their heads shaved, perhaps for cleanliness, and convenience in puerile deeds." He adds that he "had never worn a wig since" (Berg).

4. When CB revisited Shrewsbury in July 1797, he remembered "how different were my ideas of this Town 60 years ago, on leaving Condover! I thought it then heaven upon *yearth,* and its buildings the most splendid on its surface," not the "narrow, dirty, irregular & ill-built streets" which he noticed in 1797. He also mentions "the Severn, where I narrowly escaped drowning more than once," and "the Free School, where I was flogged" (*Mem.,* 3:244–45; CB to Charles Burney, 19 Aug. 1797, Comyn; CB to Susan Phillips, 26 Oct. 1797, Barrett; CB to Thomas Twining, 1 Jan. 1798, Folger; Frag. 8).

BRIDGE: FRAGMENTS 7–8

A King's Scholar at Chester[1]

Great Frost[2] *&*
Cadman[3]

Wilcox, Mapletoft,
Henchman[4]

Flogged for
prompting[5]

Lose my place but not
my Honour[6]

1. Having left the school at Shrewsbury, CB, age thirteen, "went to his father at Chester & on [25 Dec. 1739] was entered a Kings Scholar in the Grammar School" founded by Henry VIII (BL, Add. MSS 48345, f. 22ʳ), on the nomination of John Prescott (1691–1767), Prebendary of Chester 1715, Rector of Waverton 1716, Treasurer of the Charity School 1739–40. On 9 Dec. 1746 Prescott was deprived of the prebend by the Bishop "for immoralities" (Burne, pp. 190, 207–8).

CB's father had returned from Dorset about 1738 and "spent the last years of his life at Chester." "Lord Cholmondeley [1702/3–70], who was his great friend & Patron," had "procured him the place of Surveyor of Window lights, which he occupied till the time of his death" in June 1749 (Worcester Mem., pp. 5, 8; BL, Add. MSS 48345, f. 22ʳ).

2. The frost "which began the 26th" of Dec. 1739, shortly after CB's arrival in Chester, continued through Jan. 1740 and "grew more severe than has been known since the unbearable Winter of 1715–16; so that many who had lived at *Hudson's Bay,* declar'd they never felt it colder in those Parts" (*GM,* 10: 35).

3. Robert Cadman (1712–40), a tightrope walker in Shrewsbury, "performed several feats on the rope fixed from the top of the spire to a tree in a field over the Severn. He attempted to slide down the rope across the river, but it snapped and he fell and was dashed to pieces"; the accident occurred on 2 Feb. 1739 (Scholes 1948, 1:9). Cadman was buried at St. Mary's Church two days later (Fletcher 1911, p. 357). CB, who was then thirteen, might have been on a visit to see his brother James; he probably witnessed the ac-

cident. See Frag. 12 and n. 1.

4. Charles Henchman (1671–1741), headmaster (1714–41) of the King's school that CB attended, and John Mapletoft (d. 1761) were both Prebendaries of Chester Cathedral. In 1737, together with John Prescott (n. 1, above), they summoned CB's music teacher Edmund Baker (Frag. 9, n. 1) to reprimand him for refusing to sing an anthem, which he was obliged to do, though he claimed that organists were exempt from singing anthems (Burne, pp. 190–91, 195). Wilcox has not been identified. He may have been Thomas Wilcocke, in 1746 chaplain of the Hospital of St. John the Baptist (Chester City Record Office A/B/4/118ᵛ).

5. Mme d'Arblay (*Mem.,* 1:6) paraphrased the incident as follows:

He was frequently heard to declare that he had been once only chastised at school, and that not for slackness, but forwardness in scholastic lore. A favourite comrade, who shared his affections, though not his application or his genius, was hesitating through an ill-learnt lesson, and on the point of incurring punishment, when young Burney, dropping his head on his breast to muffle his voice, whispered the required answer.

"Burney prompts, Sir!" was loudly called out by a jealous or malevolent fellow-student: and Burney paid the ignoble tax at which his incautious good nature, and superior talents, were assessed.

6. This no doubt refers to the preceding anecdote and may suggest that CB was demoted in class.

FRAGMENT 8   Chester, early 1740s

Fisher Tench, a dancing-master at Chester, being in a stall of the Cathedral
when one of the Choirmen began to roar the Anthem:
"I will sing unto the Lord"[2]—said, loud enough to be   *Fisher Tench*[1]
heard by me, among the King's scholars of the Free-school—"You *may* sing to
the Lord if you please; but I'll be hanged if you shall sing to me"—& hastened
out of Church. This so tickled my fancy, that I fear I laughed rather inde-
corously—for w^ch—on one of the other boys turning informer, I was flogged
next day.

1. Fisher Tench (bur. 24 June 1784) married Margaritta (1717–94) in 1750 or earlier.
Three of his sons—Tarleton, Thomas, and
Richard—died between 1751 and 1756 (Far-
rall, pp. 193–94, 197, 505, 508–9, 540, 552).

2. Psalm 104, "I will sing unto the LORD

as long as I live," set to music by Dr. William
Croft. It is listed in *A Collection of Anthems
used in the Cathedral Church at Chester and
most Cathedral Churches in England* (1782),
p. 18.

FRAGMENT 9   Chester, early 1740s

The first Music he learned was of Mr Baker the Organist of the Cathedral,[1]
who being distressed for an assistant during a fit of the Gout, taught to play a
Chant on the Organ before he knew his Gammut or the names of the keys. And
this single chant, the first in Dr Boyce's 1st Vol. of
Cathedral Music,[2] was all that he was able to play to the   *Sing at Chester Con-*
Choir during his master's first fit of the Gout. Between   *certs & play the Org.*
that and another fit he learned his Gammut and a few   *without knowing my*
more chants, and a couple of Handel's opera songs,   *notes*
Dove sei,[3] & *Gode l'alma*,[4] wch he performed without knowing a word of Italian
or hardly a note of Music.[5] But so indulgent was the audience, composed of the
first people of Chester and its neighbourhood, that he was not only much
applauded, but sent for to Shrewsbury, to sing at his brother's concert;[6] who
finding he c^d make him useful not only as a singer but as his deputy at St Mary's
church, pressed his father to let him remain at Shrewsbury to pursue his musical
studies regularly.[7]

1. Edmund Baker (bur. 5 Feb. 1765), organist of St. Chad's, Shrewsbury, came to Chester in 1727, where he was appointed "Organist & teacher of the singing boys" and became "the first real professional organist that Chester Cathedral had since the Restoration" (Bridge 1913, pp. 41–47). For his skirmishes with the prebendaries in 1737, see Bridge: Frags. 7–8, n. 4; and for the charge against him that he was not teaching the choristers properly, see Burne, pp. 194, 200–202, 208. Baker "had been a scholar of Dr Blow, & was said by my father, who remembered Purcell, Blow, & the principal organists of their time, to have played the organ in the style of his Master & his contemporaries; & it was as near as possible [to] what you call *simple Music*" (CB to William Mason, 8 June 1795, Berg). Baker was in fact a pupil of Arne, not of Blow (*New Grove*, 3:488).

2. "The Preces" and "Chant for the Psalms" by Thomas Tallis appear on pp. 1–2 of William Boyce's first volume of *Cathedral Music* (1760), in which "Mr. Charles Burney" figures among the subscribers. "I will send *your choir* this very chant, the oldest and the best that is still in use," CB wrote later to the Rev. Samuel Hoole (23 Oct. 1804, Osborn).

3. "Dove sei amato bene" from *Rodelinda* (1725). "The favour of this air extended into the country, where it was heard with indulgence at a concert fifteen years after its performance; when, without knowing how to construe, or even pronounce the words, I had been taught to sing it by the organist of Chester, at fourteen years old" (*Hist. Mus.*, 4:299n; Mercer, 2:731n).

4. "Gode l'alma consolata" from Handel's *Ottone* to a libretto by Nicolò Haym, first performed 12 Jan. 1723. This opera contains another "Dove sei," different from that in *Rodelinda* (n. 3, above).

5. "I began Music late," CB commented to Hoole (n. 2, above), "my eldest daughter was a better player at 7 y^{rs} old than I was at 17; but early players were then Phenomena."

6. James Burney IV (1710–89) was CB's half-brother, son of James MacBurney III by his first wife. He succeeded Dr. William Hayes (Frag. 16, n. 3) as organist of St. Mary's Church and held the post for fifty-four years. In 1758 he married Ann Wood (c. 1688–1772), daughter of Basil Wood of White Abbey. At his death in 1789 he bequeathed £60 for a clock and chimes for St. Mary's Church (Scholes 1948, 1:15n). See Frag. 16. Later in life CB remembered "going to sing at Jemm's concert [at] Shrewsbury" with his father, and how on their way from Chester they "lay . . . at the George Inn" at Whitchurch (CB to Susan Phillips, 26 Oct. 1797, Barrett).

7. Mme d'Arblay writes: "It was . . . in age only that Mr. James Burney was his brother's senior or superior; from him, therefore, whatever could be given or received, was finished almost ere it was begun, from the quickness with which his pupil devoted himself to what he called the slavery of conquering unmeaning difficulties in the lessons of the times" (*Mem.*, 1:7–8).

FRAGMENT 10 Chester, 1741

When HANDEL went through Chester, in his way to Ireland, this year, 1741,[1] I was at the Public-School in that city, and very well remember seeing him smoke a pipe, over a dish of coffee, at the Exchange-Coffee-house; for being extremely curious to see so extraordinary a man, I watched him narrowly as long as he remained in Chester; which, on account of the wind being unfavourable for his embarking at Parkgate, was several days. During this time, he applied to Mr. Baker, the Organist, my first music-master,[2] to know whether there were any choirmen in the cathedral who could sing *at sight*; as he wished to prove some books that had been hastily transcribed, by trying the choruses which he intended to perform in Ireland. Mr. Baker mentioned some of the most likely singers then in Chester, and, among the rest, a printer of the name of Janson,[3] who had a good base voice, and was one of the best musicians in the choir. At this time Harry Alcock,[4] a good player, was the first violin at Chester, which was then a very musical place; for besides public performances, Mr. Prebendary Prescott[5] had a weekly concert, at which he was able to muster eighteen or twenty performers, gentlemen, and professors. A time was fixed for this private rehearsal at the *Golden Falcon*,[6] where HANDEL was quartered; but, alas! on trial of the chorus in the Messiah, *"And with his stripes we are healed,"*—Poor Janson, after repeated attempts, failed so egregiously, that HANDEL let loose his great bear upon him; and after swearing in four or five languages, cried out in broken English: "You shcauntrel! tit not you dell me dat you could sing at soite?"—"Yes, sir, says the printer, and so I can; but not at *first sight*."

1. Handel went to Dublin early in Nov. 1741, taking with him the score of *Messiah*, composed between 22 Aug. and 14 Sept. 1741. CB no doubt heard in Chester the first rehearsal of parts of the oratorio. For an account of Handel's stay in Dublin in 1742, see Henry Quin to CB, 16 July 1788 (Comyn); and "Quin" in Rees.

2. See Frag. 9, n. 1.

3. Peter Jeynson or Joynson (d. 1764), printer, was made freeman of Chester on 9

Aug. 1732 (Bennett, p. 293). He had joined the choir of Chester Cathedral in 1731, was admitted to full membership in 1738, and in 1743 was admonished for poor attendance at church, though he remained in the choir until his death (Burne, pp. 200–204).

4. Unidentified.

5. See Bridge: Frags. 7–8, n. 1.

6. An engraving of this old tavern is reproduced in Scholes 1948, 1:15, pl. 2.

FRAGMENT 11

[Worsdale[1] sang some airs with] all the dignity and florid style (as [I suppose) was ever heard in a] serious Italian Opera Singer, and a part in Lampes serious opera of Amelia.[3] And sung

Lampe[2]

many humorous songs between the Acts, particularly, "Young Roger came tapping at Dolley's window,"[4] &c, with great humour & comic effect.

But young Shuter,[5] who had attended M^r & Mrs Lampe as a footboy at Preston, and who now served them in that capacity at the Golden Falcon[6] at Chester was such a pickle, and contrived to mount the Stage in the absence of Worsdale, and took him off so exactly, that he rec^d even more applause than Worsdale himself, for wch he w^d have been horse-whipped, had the painter caught him.[7]

At Chester, the great hall of the Blue-coat Hospital was fitted up for an Opera-house,[8] and the performances pleased very much, particularly those who had never heard an Italian Opera, among whom none were, perhaps, more delighted than myself. The music I thought charming,   *Drag. Wantley*[9] and think so still for the time in wch it was composed.
The humour of the drama, from the old ballad of *Moore of Moore hall,* written by Harry Carey, is admirably supported [by Lampe's music.][10]

1. James Worsedale (1692?–1767), a colorful denizen of Grub Street who dabbled in painting, poetry, music, and dramatic composition as well as acting. He was a crony of Henry Carey (see n. 2, below), who dedicated one of his poems "to his Dear Friend, Jemmy Worsedale." According to Mrs. Pilkington, he seems to have been well versed in all the subterfuges of the underworld of letters of his day (see Pilkington, passim). Pope employed him in his sparrings with "the unspeakable Curll."

2. John Frederick Lampe (1703–51), German-born bassoonist and composer who came to England c. 1724, was engaged as a bassoon player in the orchestra of the King's Theatre and later as composer at the Haymarket Theatre. In 1738 or 1739 he married Isabella Young, daughter of Charles Young, organist of All Hallows, Barking-by-the-Tower. As Isabella's sister Cecilia (c. 1711–89) had married Thomas Arne in 1737, Lampe became Arne's brother-in-law. The two sisters were professional singers.

"In 1741," writes CB, "Lampe and his wife and sister, with Sullivan the singer, the two

Messings, and Jemmy Worsedale, went to Preston Gild, and afterwards to Chester, where they performed the *Dragon of Wantley,* the Dragoness, Amelia, &c. I happened to be at Chester school when this company arrived there, and frequently heard them perform" (*Hist. Mus.,* 4:662 and n.; Mercer, 2:1007 and n.). CB considered Lampe "a truly ingenious man, well versed in the theory of the art, with a most happy turn for humour, without buffoonery, in his comic operas; and, moreover, a man of probity, with great simplicity of manners, and possessed of a kind and benevolent heart" ("Lampe" in Rees). Lampe was a friend of Henry Carey (c. 1689–1743), poet and playwright, illegitimate grandson of George Savile, the famous Marquess of Halifax. He set to music a number of Carey's librettos (see nn. 3, 9, 10, below).

Daniel Sullivan (fl. 1741–48), alto singer, acted on 2 Feb. 1743 as Moore in Lampe's *Dragon of Wantley* (n. 9, below). *London Stage* lists his performances and songs between acts until 18 April 1748. His song "Gentle Parthenissa," set to the words of Richard Steele and performed 15 April 1743, is in BL, shelf-marks G.313.(92); G.315(139); 157.1.7.

Frederick Messing and his brother (fl. 1740–63), horn players and violinists, came to England "about the year 1740" and "were the first who pretended to perform in all keys" on "*chromatic* horns" ("Horn" in Rees). According to Fitzpatrick (pp. 102–3), who lists their public performances, they were probably natives of Erzgebirge and the first of "the Austro-Bohemian school of playing to reside in England for any length of time."

3. "This opera, written by Harry Carey, was first performed March 13th, 1732, in the principal character of which, Miss ARNE, afterwards so celebrated as a tragic actress by the name of Mrs. CIBBER, first appeared on the stage, as a singer. The Music which, according to the advertisement, was 'set in the Italian manner,' having been much applauded, was soon avowed by Lampe, and Miss Arne's performance interested every hearer" (*Hist. Mus.*, 4:655; Mercer, 2:1001).

4. Composed by Henry Carey, it was known in its published versions as "Roger's Courtship."

5. Edward Shuter (1728?–76), actor of humble origin, was then in his teens. After some practice with country companies and the customary experience of poverty and privation about which he liked to joke, he made his debut on 8 July 1744 as Catesby in *Richard III.*

6. See Frag. 10, n. 6.

7. In *Hist. Mus.* (4:662n; Mercer 2: 1007n), CB words the anecdote differently: "Shuter, then a boy of about twelve or fourteen years old, was a livery servant to Lampe, and a special Pickle, who took off all the performers, and among the rest, Worsdale, so well, in Carey's song of 'Young Roger came tapping at Dolley's Window,' that it was with difficulty he was prevented from breaking his bones."

8. The Blue-coat Hospital, founded in 1700 as a charity school for boys and erected in 1717, is a fine Georgian building. In CB's time its premises were rented for public performances such as the one here mentioned.

9. "The year 1737 was rendered memorable at Covent-Garden theatre by the success of the burlesque opera of the 'Dragon of Wantley,' written by Carey, and set by Lampe, 'after the Italian manner.' This excellent piece of humour had run twenty-two nights, when it was stopped, with all other public amusements, by the death of her majesty queen Caroline, November 20th; but was resumed again on the opening of the theatres in January following, and supported as many representations as the 'Beggar's Opera' had done, ten years before. And if Gay's original intention in writing his musical drama was to ridicule the opera, the execution of his plan was not so happy as that of Carey; in which the mock heroic, tuneful monster, recitative, splendid habits, and style of music, all conspired to remind the audience of what they had seen and heard at the lyric theatre, more effectually than the most vulgar street tunes could do; and much more innocently than the tricks and transactions of the most abandoned thieves and prostitutes. Lampe's music to this farcical drama was not only excellent fifty years ago, but is still [c. 1802] modern and in good taste" ("Lampe" in Rees).

10. Carey, in his dedication of the farce to Lampe, calls attention to his own low burlesque style and continues: "Your Musick, on the other hand, is as grand and pompous as possible, by which Means the *Contrast* is the stronger, and has succeeded accordingly." "The Twelfth Edition" of *The Dragon of Wantley,* "with Additions," dated "Pall Mal, Jan. 3, 1738," is prefaced by "An Excellent Ballad Of a most Dreadful Combat, fought between MOORE of Moore-Hall, and the DRAGON of Wantley" (pp. 7–13), which suggested the plot of the farce, probably

taken from Thomas d'Urfey's *Pills to Purge Melancholy* (1719 ed., 3:10) or from *Collection of Historical Ballads* (1727). In "A Critical Remark" (p. 6), Carey attributes it to "the late Mr. Rousillon" and comments: "This Ballad does not properly fall under the Denomination of Historical, it having been ever look'd upon as a Criticism or Ridicule upon *St. George, The Seven Champions, Guy of War-wick,* and several other Songs of the like Nature, and is the same to Ballads of Chivalry, as *Don Quixote* is to Books of that kind." (For a discussion of the topical allusions in the ballad, see Percy, 3:244–52). After the success of this burlesque Carey wrote a sequel, *Margery; or a Worse Plague than the Dragon* (first produced 9 Dec. 1738)—hence CB's name for it, "the Dragoness."

BRIDGE: FRAGMENTS 11–12

In the summer of 1797 Burney revisited Chester, "one of my Alma Maters, where I had not been for 40 years."[1] "This City" he writes, "is extremly curious in many things not to be found elsewhere—such as the Walls *round* the Town— the Rows, or colonades, *in* the Town—The Castle at the *Top* of the Town—& The Cascade of the whole river Dee, *beneath* the Town, &c—Ld Falmouth[2] . . . offered to shew me Chester—but L^d help his Lordship!—I c^d have shewed him a thousand things of wch he knew nothing—& though I say it, I was a very *pretty* & useful *Cicerone,* both at Chester & Shrewsbury, to . . . our Company." Two years later he recommends Chester to his son: "You will find it a curious & venerable old Town, like no other in the Kingdom—You must see its zone, *the Town Walls,* wch are kept in perfect repair, & in summer serve as a Mall for idle pedestrians. The *Rows*—or species of Piazzas, through wch upstairs or down, you may walk under Cover through all the principal Streets in the City—The *Cathedral* & *first Organ* I ever touched, & free-school, where I have been frequently *touched* in my turn—See likewise the *Bridge-Cascatella* near it—the *Castle,* & sumptuous *Prison,* that will make you wish to inhabit it, externally, at least, more than any of the Royal Palaces" (CB to Charles Burney, 19 Aug. 1797, Comyn; and 25 Dec. 1799, Osborn. See also CB to Susan Phillips, 26 Oct. 1797, Barrett; and to Thomas Twining, 1 Jan. 1798, Folger).

1. He had been there last on a visit "in 1758, with your poor dear Mother" (CB to Susan Phillips, 26 Oct. 1797, Barrett).

2. George Evelyn Boscawen (1758–1808), 3rd Viscount Falmouth 1782, the youngest son of CB's friend Mrs. Boscawen.

FRAGMENT 12   Shrewsbury, 1742–43

[On my return to Shrewsbury] what was my surprise
and horror, to see my once happy play-mate Dick the   *Run away to*
Barber,[2] who among the liveried tribe had become a   *Shrewsbury*[1]
profligate fine gentleman, & intoxicated with Ale and Village Importance, had
enlisted for a soldier! When entering into all the debaucheries of the Military of
Petty France,[3] he had not been six months in the Capital, before he merited by
his ill conduct 100 Lashes for his first offence, as a specimen of the discipline to
wch he had subjected himself.

Soon after this, I made another melancholy discovery on the parade. *Billy
Cope,*[4] son of the widow Cope, a respectable woman, who, with *his* assistance,
carried on her husband's [b]usiness as a miller, on the old Stone-bridge, at
Shrewsbury. He was so diligent, civil, and tidy a young man, with so interesting
a face and figure, that he was pointed to by all the mothers in the neighbourhood as a model for their sons. But in [an e]vil hour, being inveigled into an alehouse by a recruiting party at Meal, a village [a] mile from Salop, and made
drunk, he enlisted for a soldier; and though I only knew him by figure and
character, I was shocked to see him on the parade among the soldiers, and to
hear, that in despair at having ruined his mother, and without the least hope of
ever gaining his liberty, he had taken to drinking, and had undergone the same
discipline as Dick the Barber.

The discovery of these dire effects of ill conduct in young people awakened,
at the time, very serious reflexions in *myself,* and operated more powerfully,
perhaps, upon my mind, than even Hogarths admirable lesson given in the
Good and Bad 'prentice (wch I believe was not then published) could have
done.[5]

---

1. CB's stay at the Chester Free School
terminated on 27 March 1742 (Lonsdale 1965,
p. 5). The reason may have been that when he
visited Shrewsbury to sing at his half-
brother's concert, James "pressed his father
to let him remain at Shrewsbury to pursue
his musical studies regularly" (Frag. 9), but
as his family at Chester objected, CB simply
ran away to Shrewsbury, where he became
James's apprentice. Much later CB wrote:
"When I left the Town . . . there was not a

single housekeeper of any kind of consequence that I did not know" (CB to Susan
Phillips, 26 Oct. 1797, Barrett). In a fragment
in the Berg collection, CB adds:

> Shrewsbury is totally altered since I was
> there in 1743–4 [in fact, 1742–4]. The
> Water Lane & the remains of the old
> Blockhouse, where goods used to be
> lodged for the Barges or Boats that go to
> Bridgenorth, Gloucester & Worcester are

not what they used to be—much of the precipices over wch poor Cadman attempted to fly is planted—the rest of the Walk to the new Bridge must be often overflowed. But near the exit of the ⟨River⟩ there are large flag stones crampt wth iron.

The old Stone Bridge had on one side of it habitable houses like old London Bridge, but the new, built of Brick by Gwynn opens at the bottom of the Wild-Cop.

2. Not identified. CB, now about sixteen, had played with him three years earlier in Shrewsbury.

3. A street in the parish of Westminster, so called from the number of French who settled there; CB's grandparents were buried there (Frag. 1, n. 11).

4. Perhaps William Cope, who died 15 Nov. 1783 in the Shrewsbury county jail. Another William Cope died 12 July 1752 at the infirmary (Fletcher 1911, pp. 489, 393).

5. Hogarth's *Twelve Prints, call'd Industry and Idleness: shewing the Advantages attending the former, and the miserable Effects of the latter, in the different Fortunes of two Apprentices* was published 15–17 Oct. 1747. See Paulson, 2:61.

FRAGMENT 13   Shrewsbury, 1742–43

[I never] rested till I borrowed the B^k, transcribed all the 6, & practiced them night and Day. The Quantity of Music I copied at this Time, of all kinds, was prodigious, & my activity & diligence surprised every body. For besides writing, teaching, tuning and playing for my Brother, at my *momens perdus,* I was educating myself in every way I was able. With copy books I improved my writing so much, that my Father w^d not believe I wrote my Letters myself. I tried at least to keep up the little Latin I had learned.[1] Practiced both the Spinet & Violin many hours a day, wch with reading, transcribing Music & poetry, attempts at Composition, and my brother's affairs filled up every hour of the longest day.[2] Indeed I had a great passion for angling, & whenever I c^d get time to pursue that sport, I ran no risk of losing my time if the Fish did not bite, for I had always a book in my Pocket, wch enabled me to wait with Patience their Pleasure.[3]

Studies and amusem^ts there

The aerial Castles I now built, & The plans I formed

1. In the Chester Free School, "where I hic, haec, hoc'd it" (CB to Susan Phillips, 26 Oct. 1797, Barrett).

2. "This he did with great diligence dur-

ing 2 or 3 years, dipping into composition, by scoring authors of the first rank, setting songs, making bases to trebles, & trebles to bases for voluntaries till he c^d write & play in

two parts—learned the Violin, to tune instruments, transcribe music neatly, teach
scholars for his brother—played a little on
the German Flute, and learned a little
French" (autobiographical sketch, BL, Add.
MSS 48345, f. 22ʳ). For a description of a
manuscript specimen of young CB's musical
activities, see Frag. 19, n. 5.

3. CB later bought Izaak Walton's *Compleat Angler,* edited by Sir John Hawkins
(*Cat. Misc. Lib.,* no. 1942). But if he appreciated Hawkins's passion for angling, he did

not share his future rival's antiquarian taste
for Elizabethan music; see Lonsdale 1965, pp.
190–91.

CB recollected another pleasure at this
time: "There is at Shrewsbury a famous
plum-pie, called a Symnel of wᶜʰ the crust
covered with saffron is so hard that it cannot
be broken but will preserve the fruit within in
all climates uninjured to the furthest part of
the world—" (CB to Rosette Burney, 19
[Jan.] 1806, Burney-Cumming; and *Mem. of
Metastasio,* 3:193n).

FRAGMENT 14   Shrewsbury, 1742–43

[Among the] ⟨verses⟩ I liked were Prior's, wᶜʰ I borrowed; & not being rich
enough to purchase even a 2ᵈ hand Set I transcribed the whole two Volˢ
entirely.[1] And from a borrowed Shakespear, I made extracts of such passages as
I was most delighted wᵗʰ long before the Beauties of Shakespear were published.[2]

   In the height of Summer, I robbed my sleep of a few hours in order to meet
some other boys at a Bowling-green: and used to tie a string to one of my great
toes, wᶜʰ I put out the window of my room, by wᶜʰ I was waked as soon as it
was light, by an apprentice at next door.

   The Old friend of my father, Mʳ Weaver, now near 90, still continued to keep
open his boarding School wᵗʰ the assistance of the beautiful Mʳˢ Weaver & his
daughters;[3] taught to dance, & had an annual Ball, at wᶜʰ his Scholars, besides
the Minuet, Rigadon, and L'Ouvre, performed figure & pantomime dances
such as in the beginning of the century he had invented as Ballet Master in
London.[4] In remembrance of my father he gave me lessons, & allotted me a part
in a wooden shoe dance at one of his balls.[5]

   Of all my young Acquaintance at this time, the dearest and most affection-
ately beloved, was Tommy Woodington, a youth of exactly my own age[6]

---

1. Prior's *Poems on Several Occasions* (1707)
came out in two volumes in 1725 (4th ed.,
1742). Later, when he was less poor, CB purchased two sets of Prior's *Poems* (1709, 1741;

see *Cat. Misc. Lib.,* nos. 1453–54).

2. *The Beauties of Shakespear: regularly selected from each play . . . illustrated with explan-
atory notes and similar passages from ancient*

and modern authors, ed. W. Dodd, was published in two volumes in 1752 (2d ed., 1757). This early familiarity stood CB in good stead later, when he printed a selection of passages from Shakespeare that refer specifically to music (*Hist. Mus.,* 3:334–44; Mercer, 2:268–76). His letters also contain frequent quotations from Shakespeare and Prior.

3. In 1743 Weaver was seventy years old, not ninety (see Bridge: Frags. 1–2, n. 4). After the death of his first wife, Catherine (d. Sept. 1712), he married Susannah (1700–1770), whom CB would have known when she was in her early forties. Their daughters were Dorothy (bapt. 20 Jan. 1720); Elizabeth, who married John Williams on 22 Jan. 1737 and John Poole on 19 Feb. 1751; and Jane, who married Ephraim Furber on 1 Oct. 1751. See Fletcher 1911, p. 300; Fletcher 1918, pp. 872, 1015, 1139, 1145, 1223, 1330.

4. According to CB, Weaver, who "wrote at Sir Richard Steele's request, the three spectators on dancing, Nos. 67, 334, and 370,

translated, at the request of Mr. Isaac, another eminent dancing-master, from the original of M. Feuillet, this then new art of dancing by notation, to which all the dancing-masters of eminence subscribed; and we remember it in general use even in the country, among the professors of the Art" ("Choreography" in Rees). Lonsdale 1960 suggests that though *Spectator* no. 67 has been attributed to Eustace Budgell and no. 370 to Steele, CB's attributions may be right, as he had the information directly from Weaver.

5. "The wooden-shoe dance" was "Mars and Venus, with Vulcan's discovery and imprisonment of the lovers in a cage . . . in which our own juvenile vanity was highly exalted by being honoured with a part" ("Choreography" in Rees).

6. Not identified. The Thomas Woodington who was "bur. 2 May 1804, aged 71" was born in 1733 and would have been seven years younger than CB (Fletcher 1918, p. 1666).

FRAGMENT 15   Shrewsbury, 1742–43

I remember, very early in my musical life, to have heard one of the town waits,[1] at Shrewsbury, *vamp a base*[2] upon all occasions, he being utterly unable to read any one that was written; and as my ears were seldom much offended by the dissonance, I suppose that, by habit, he contrived at least to begin and end in the right key, and was quick in pursuing accidental modulation.[3]

[Vivaldi's] *Cuckoo Concerto,*[4] during my youth, was the wonder and delight of all frequenters of country concerts; and *Woodcock,*[5] one of the Hereford waits, was sent far and near to perform it.

1. "Attendant musicians on great personages, mayors, and bodies corporate, generally furnished with superb dresses, or splendid cloaks" ("Waits" in Rees; see also Bridge 1928).

2. Improvise a bass or basso continuo part.

3. For CB's own burlesque use of such dissonant "clattering of knives, forks, spoons, and plates," often practiced by the

town-waits during "a city-feast" (*Hist. Mus.*, 3: 102n; Mercer, 2:88n), see Frag. 83.

4. Vivaldi's concerto for violin and orchestra, RV335 (Ricordi ed., vol. 487). CB considered Antonio Vivaldi (1678–1741) "among the light and irregular troops," together with Albinoni, Alberti, and Tessarini

(*Hist. Mus.*, 3:561; Mercer, 2:445).

5. Thomas Woodcock (d. 1750?), brother of the well-known flutist Robert Woodcock, "kept a coffee-house at Hereford." He was "an excellent performer on the violin, and played the solos of Corelli with exquisite neatness and elegance" (Hawkins, 2:826).

FRAGMENT 16

Shrewsbury, 1742–43

my distress for Voluntaries on the Org. made extempore made me sensible of its use. My Brother had a very good finger, & what he attempted, wch was neither very brilliant nor elaborate he executed neatly.[1] He had however, no application for the slavery of conquering difficulties in the Lessons of the Times; & his want of Licence as well as fancy prevented his Voluntaries from rising above poverty & common-place. The Celebrated Felton, from Hereford,[2] & after him the 1st Dr Hayes, from Oxford,[3] came to Shrewsbury on a Tour while I was studying so hard without Instructions or example, and struck & stimulated me so forcibly by their performance on the Organ as well as encouragem^t that I went to work with an ambition & fury that w^d hardly allow me to eat or sleep. The 1st

Felton, Hayes & Matteis

Movem^ts I put together in order to play as Voluntaries were Centos, or bits & scraps from such music as I c^d get at of grave movem^ts the least likely to be discovered. Then I used to play a treble extempore to a base, & a base to a treble, of easy movements in corelli, valentini, or albinoni.[4] But after I had heard Felton, & Mr. afterward Dr Hayes, I used to write down movements in imitation of their Style, & even passages in two parts,

---

1. James was noted for his "extemporaneous voluntaries in the lighter manner of Handel's organ concertos, on whose admirable school his taste was formed, and the brilliant execution of his fingers on the echo stops, will not be forgotten" (Owen/Blakeway, 2:226).

2. The Rev. William Felton (1715–69) was ordained priest on 11 Aug. 1742 by the Bishop of Hereford, and on 3 Feb. 1743 became a vicar choral and sub-chanter of Hereford Cathedral. CB later called him "a dilettant[e] musician, above the common class of gentlemen performers. He was a good organ-player, and had a neat finger and powerful hand for common divisions, and the rapid multiplication of notes. As a composer he imitated Handel's organ concertos, and produced three sets, in which there were two concertos that were thought worth playing in London by Stanley at the Castle Concert, and Butler at Ranelagh. Two of his airs with

variations, were long the pride of every incipient player on the harpsichord in town and country" ("Felton" in Rees. See also *Hist. Mus.,* 4:664–65; Mercer, 2:1008–9; and for an anecdote of Handel's view of Felton, *Commen.,* pt. 1, pp. 32–33n).

3. William Hayes (1708–77) "began his career early in life, as organist of St. Mary's in Shrewsbury [1729–31], being the first appointment to the office, after the erection of an instrument in that church, by Harris and Byefield" ("Hayes" in Rees). In 1731–34 he was organist of Worcester Cathedral but resigned to become organist and master of the choristers at Magdalen College, Oxford. On 14 Jan. 1742 he succeeded Richard Goodson as professor of music at the university; he took his Mus.D. in 1749. CB calls him "a very good organ-player" and praises his canons, catches, and glees. "His canon of 'Let's drink and let's sing together,' is perhaps the most

pleasant of all those laboured compositions which go under the name of canons."

4. For CB's views on Arcangelo Corelli (1653–1713), composer and violinist, see *Hist. Mus.,* 3:550–59; Mercer, 2:437–44; and "Corelli" in Rees. He lists Guiseppe Valentini (c. 1680–post-1759) "among other composers, *à dozzina*," who "published, in Holland, nine different works for violins . . . but they have been long since consigned to oblivion, without any loss to the public, or injustice to the author" (*Hist. Mus.,* 3:549–50; Mercer, 2: 437). CB's early admiration for Tomaso Albinoni (1671–1751) also waned. He calls him "an excellent performer on the violin" but merely lists his compositions without evaluation (*Hist. Mus.,* 3:560; Mercer, 2:445). According to Hawkins (2:678), Albinoni's works "at length became so familiar in England, that many of the common fiddlers were able to play them."

FRAGMENT 17   Shrewsbury, 1742–43

In going to attend Matteis[1] for my lesson on the Violin at his house a considerable distance from my brother's, I met with an accident that distressed me very much. Being ashamed to carry my fiddle through the streets in an ostensible manner,[2] I cut a slit in the lining of my coat, and carried it unperceived. But in passing by the Cross on a market day, during the time when a poor bear was at the stake, and a great croud of Spectators assembled, I c[d] not help stopping, to see how the bear defended himself; when Ursa Major breaking loose, put the mob to flight in such a panic, that they tumbled over each other, and over me among the rest; when smash went my instrument into shivers!—so here's another "story of the *Bear* & *Fiddle*," besides that in Hudibras.[3]

1. Nicola Matteis (d. 1749?), violinist and composer, learned the art from his father. Between 1700 and 1737 he was a member of

the court orchestra at Vienna and composed ballet music for the court opera house there; many of his MSS are still preserved in the

Court Library (Scholes 1948, 1:17). Accord-ing to CB, Matteis "must have returned to England soon after Mr. North's *Memoirs of Music* were written; as I remember to have seen him at Shrewsbury, where he was settled as a language master as well as performer on the violin, in 1737. I afterwards learned French, and the violin of this master, who continued at Shrewsbury till his decease, about the year 1749. He played Corelli's solos with more simplicity and elegance than any performer I ever heard" (*Hist. Mus.*, 3:516n; Mercer, 2: 410n; and "Matteis" in Rees).

2. Carrying a fiddle in one's hand was looked down upon in England; see Frag. 102, n. 6.

3. See Samuel Butler, *Hudibras,* pt. 1, canto 1, lines 674ff.; and Hogarth's engraving illustrating the incident (Paulson, 1:pl. 47).

Character of L^y Tankerville

This L^y was the daughter of Sr Jno Ashley of the Abbey foregate, Shrews-bury.[1] She manifested a passion for Music very early in practicing on the German Flute wch was then little known in the country.[2] Sr Wm Fowler Bar^t of Shrewsbury[3] & this lady were the only performers on that instrum^t then that obtained or deserved the least notice. But Miss Ashley practiced the Harp^d likewise and took lessons of my Brother the Shrewsbury Org^t She used to have little Matteis, the language master & 1st Violin of the place to accompany her. She was an *espiegle* in her younger days, loved mischief; & finding Matteis timid & helpless in the slightest distress or danger, insisted during summer on taking her lesson in an old and lofty Oak tree, in the middle of wch she had a seat & desk formed for her accommodation, and another tottering seat & desk for poor Matteis, who was so terrified and nervous that he c^d not stop a note in tune.

This Lady in 1742 was married to Lord Ossulston, afterwards Earl of Tanker-ville. I was in Shrewsbury at the time & saw the Wedding at St Julian's Church.[4]

---

1. Alicia Astley (1718–91), third daughter and co-heir of Sir John Astley (d. 1772) of Pat-shull, co. Stafford, by Mary née Prynce, of Shrewsbury. Sir John owned and occupied the New Hall, Abbey Foregate, Shrewsbury. CB could have become acquainted with her through his half-brother James the organist (Frag. 9, n. 6), whose wife's grandmother, Margery Astley, was daughter of Sir Walter Astley (d. 1652); see Owen, p. 261.

2. The German side-blown flute (*flûte traversière*) was introduced to London c. 1705 by the French flutist Jean-Baptiste Loeillet. In 1707 Jacques Hotteterre published *Prin-*

cipes de la flûte traversière, ou flûte d'Alle-magne, the earliest treatise on the flute in the new form, which was pirated in London for many years in such imperfect translations as *The Modern Musick-master* (1731).

3. Sir William Fowler (b. 1708?) of Har-nage Grange succeeded as 3rd Baronet in 1731 and died c. 1746, having embarked for Cal-cutta on board an East India ship, which was lost at sea.

4. The marriage took place on 23 Sept. 1742 (*GM,* 12:546; Scholes 1948, 1:6). In the BL version of this episode Mme d'Arblay comments: "(Q.) She took Lessons at 7 a.m. the morn apres." Charles Bennet (1716–67), styled Lord Ossulston, had returned from army service in the West Indies. In 1753 he succeeded his father as 4th Earl of Tanker-ville. In *Mem.,* 1:9, Mme d'Arblay gave 1738 as the date of the marriage and, assuming that CB was then only twelve, gratuitously added the following sentence as if CB were writing: "I remember leading off with a choral song, or hymn, by her direction, to chaunt her out of St. Julian's Church. I was then quite a boy." Scholes (1948, 1:6, 13), who corrects her information, nevertheless uses it to point up CB's abilities "as a public vocalist" in his boy-hood. The truth is that CB, then sixteen years old, merely "saw the Wedding" (see textual note).

FRAGMENT 19 Chester, 1743

place; sometimes I had thoughts [of becoming musical] manager of a strolling company of players, [composing exer](-cises) to teach and accompany the Actors in their Songs. Not as an Actor or Singer myself: for I always felt a repugnance to exhibiting myself on a public Stage. In this critical time of my life, my father, who I believe, loved me very affection- *Return to Chester* ately, encouraged me to return to Chester; and my *in 1743* Mother, whom I had most offended by my flight, seeming to have forgotten it, I went back to them in the summer or autumn of the year 1743.[1]

I then went to work immediately on my arrival in resuming my studies: I found only an old Spinet by Keen with short 8ths to practice on.[2] It was the property of my eldest sister,[3] who had made such little use of it, after my elopement, that it was in a deplorable condition; but I was able to take it all to Pieces, new string it, repair the jacks, furnishing most of them with new tongues and bristles, and regulating the touch.[4] After *Alcock, Whiteman* wch I was incessantly at it, either practicing or compos-ing;[5] except when I went to practice with, and accompany, Whiteman,[6] the successor of Harry Alcock, as first violin player of Chester. Whiteman was a very

1. The heavily crossed-out line originally read: "ab^t the beginning of the year 1743." Summer is more likely; see the beginning of Frag. 20.

2. Stephen Keene (c. 1640–post-1719) was a maker of virginals, spinets, and harpsichords who lived in 1693 in Threadneedle Street (Boalch, p. 80). The short octave was a special arrangement of the keys. As the lowest chromatic tones were almost never needed in early keyboard music, they were omitted from the keyboards of early organs and harpsichords. CB mentions spinets "by Keen and Slade, in queen Anne's time, with the long keys of ebony and the short of ivory" ("Spinet" in Rees).

3. Ann or Nancy (b. 1722), the eldest of CB's father's children by his second marriage, was then twenty-one.

4. One reason why CB took such pains in repairing Nancy's spinet was that by then he had "had some lessons on the Harp^d of Mr Orme" (BL, Add. MSS 48345, f. 22^r). Edward Orme (1716–77) was elected organist of Chester Cathedral 25 June 1765, after the death of Edmund Baker (Frag. 9, n. 1). His portrait is reproduced as a frontispiece to Bridge 1913. "Mr Orme left his books to Mr Bailey, the present Org^t of Chester—who lent me a chest full of such as I wished to examine, when I was writing my Hist^y"(CB to J. C. Walker, 20 Sept. 1803, Osborn).

5. On his return to Chester, CB "was inflamed with a rage for composition, & attempted by himself Lessons, Sonatas, Songs, & Concertos till the autumn of 1744" (BL, Add. MSS 48345, f. 22^r). This was a continuation of his musical activities in Shrewsbury (Frag. 13, n. 2). A holograph manuscript dated 1744 (BL, Add. MSS 39957) gives an idea of the repertory he was studying: it consists of three suites of lessons by John Christopher Smith, two concertos by Handel, one solo by Arne, and twelve sonatas by Geminiani, copied from printed scores. Folio 16 is an elaborate duplication of the Geminiani title page:

SONATE

A

VIOLINO e BASSO

COMPOSTE DA

FRANCESCO GEMINIANI

OPERA IV

Stampate in Parigi 1739.

trascritte nella Citta di

CHESTER MDCCLIV

Dal Carlo Burney giovane di 18 anni.

[Grant, p. 340]

CB had evidently also transcribed Geminiani's *Concerti grossi*, Opus 2 and Opus 3, published in 1732: "Before I was 18 I scored Geminiani's 2 sets of Concertos, for improvement in Counterpoint, & I remember when he was about to print them in score, with new *readings*, he borrowed my MS which he never returned" (CB to Thomas Twining, 14 Dec. 1781, Osborn. See also *Hist. Mus.*, 4:644; Mercer, 2:993).

6. A resident violinist and oboe player. "On 23 Apr. 1751 the Chester *Courant* advertised a concert for the benefit of Mr Orme at which the overture of 'Alfred' and a violin solo by Mr Wightman will be performed. . . . Another Concert took place the next day for the benefit of Mr. Wightman, and a third Concert on April 27th for the benefit of Mr. Parry (Harpist to Sir Watkin Williams Wynn), so that we may certainly say Chester was still the 'musical place' that *Burney* had described" (Bridge 1913, p. 48).

BRIDGE: FRAGMENTS 19–20

At home "we were merry, & laughed as loud as the Burneys always do, when they get together and open their hearts; tell their old stories; & have no fear of being *Quizzed* by interlopers. It was so in my poor dear old fathers time, & my boyish days—when my brother Thomas from London or James from Shrewsbury came on a visit to Chester, we used, old & young, Male & female, to sit up all night—not to drink, but to laugh *à gorge deployée*" (CB to Mme d'Arblay, 29 Oct. 1799, Osborn; for CB's half-brother Thomas, see Frag. 25, n. 3).

FRAGMENT 20   Chester, Summer 1743

It was during the summer of 1743 that the celebrated Dubourg, an old acquaintance of my father, and state composer, and Master of the band in Dublin, coming through Chester in his way to London   *Dubourg*[1]
[and] hearing that my father was an inhabitant of
Chester, called on him. They talked over old times, having often met at Mr Fleetwood's in his better day.[2] Seeing a Spinet in the room, he asked who made use of it; when he was told that I was a young & humble musical student, who wd be supremely happy cd he hear him (Mr Dubourg) touch the Violin, he was so obliging as to send for his instrument; and I had the honour of accompanying him in the 5th Solo of Corelli,[3] without ever having had a Master in thorough-base. I was very proud of being able to acquit myself tolerably in this first trial of my skill, for I never had accompanied a great player before. His performance gave me infinite pleasure; being in form, style and execution superior to any player on the Violin that I had heard before.[4] Dubourg was a man of wit, who had been admitted into good company without, as well as with, his fiddle. He gave me his variations to Jack Latin[5]

1. Matthew Dubourg (1703–67), "a very eminent performer on the violin . . . was the natural son of the celebrated dancing-master, Isaac, and had instructions on his instrument by Geminiani, soon after his arrival in England, 1714." Dubourg's fame as a soloist in London procured him in 1728 "the appointment of composer and master of his majesty's band in Ireland. He resided several years in that kingdom afterwards," and in this function he composed birthday odes for Dublin Castle from 1728 to 1764 ("Dubourg" in Rees; *Hist. Mus.,* 4:650–51; Mercer, 2:998). CB relates an anecdote about Dubourg and Handel, who in 1742 attended Dubourg's performance in Dublin. Indulging in a ca-

dence of extraordinary length, Dubourg "wandered about in different keys a great while, and seemed indeed a little bewildered, and uncertain of his original key . . . but, at length, coming to the shake, which was to terminate this long close," made Handel cry out: "You are welcome home, Mr. Dubourg!" (*Commem.*, pt. 1, p. 27n).

2. Charles Fleetwood (d. Aug. 1747) came into possession of a landed estate of £5,000 when he was twenty-one but lost it and turned a sharper. From 1734 to 1745 he was manager of Drury Lane, staged expensive pantomimes and raree-shows, some of which caused riots among the spectators (Frag. 29, n. 1) and led to his replacement late in 1745 by Lacy. For the "strange, profligate, unprincipled, swindling, gay, winning, fascinating Charles Fleetwood," see Davies 1780; Dibdin; Buss; and Highfill, 5:297–301. He was

CB's godfather (Frag. 1, n. 20).

3. From Corelli's *Sonate a violino e violone e cimballo . . . Opera quinta* (Rome, 1700).

4. "I saw him at Chester in 1744, and had the pleasure of accompanying him in the fifth solo of Corelli, which he performed in a manner so superior to any one I had then heard, that I was equally astonished and delighted; particularly with the fulness of his tone and spirit of his execution" (*Hist. Mus.*, 4:651; Mercer, 2:998).

5. "Jacky Latin" is a Scottish folksong: see Crawford, pp. 17–18; the tune is printed in Burns, no. 80. Dubourg's variations on the tune have not been traced. In 1789 Dubourg's "innumerable solos and concertos" were "in the possession of one of his disciples, and of some of them the composition is excellent" (see n. 4, above).

FRAGMENT 21   Chester, August 1744

[I practised then] repeating passages, and "trying confusions" in melody and harmony, so different from country dances & street tunes, I remember my mother's maid asking one of my sisters: "What is [it] Master Charley was playing? is it tunes, or Consorts of music?"

In August of 1744, M^r and Mrs Arne arrived at Chester from Dublin,[1] where he had been engaged as composer & Concert Master,
& she as principal singer. Arne had succeeded Handel, *Arne—*
who had had his Oratorios performed in Dublin, when driven thither, according to Pope, by the goddess of Dulness.

> Arrest him, Empress; or you sleep no more!—
> She heard, & drove him to the Hybernian Shore.
> Dunciad. b^k IV.   [lines 69–70]

Mr Arne had carried over with him, as singers, besides Mrs Arne, the eldest of A[n]thony Young's 3 daughters, all singers: Cecilia, Isabella, & Esther;[2] Mrs Arne had been taught by Geminian.[3]

1. Thomas Augustine Arne (1710–78), who was to play an important role in CB's career, had married Cecilia Young, the celebrated singer. He and his wife went to Ireland in 1742. Arne's last performance in Dublin took place on 6 June, and he traveled back to England in August. As the *General Advertiser* of 4 Sept. 1744 announced his arrival in London on 3 Sept., his stay in Chester must have occurred late in August 1744 (information from Arne's biographer John A. Parkinson). See Scholes 1948, 1:19–20; Lonsdale 1965, pp. 9–14. For CB's assessment of Arne, see *Hist. Mus.*, 4:655–57; Mercer, 2: 1001–2; "Arne" in Rees; Frags. 22–24, 27, 29–31, 47, 60, 62; Bridge: Frags. 34–35, and 61–62. Cecilia Young's first recorded performance was on 4 March 1730 at Drury Lane. She had "good natural voice and fine shake" and "had been so well taught, that her style of singing was infinitely superior to that of any other English woman of her time" (*Hist. Mus.*, 4:653–54; Mercer, 2:1000). For CB's fuller assessment, written after her death, see CB to Mr. and Mrs. Barthélémon, 21 Oct. 1789 (Osborn).

2. CB made a slip in this part of the draft: Cecilia (c. 1711–89) married Arne 15 March 1737. Isabella married Lampe in 1738 (Frag. 11, n. 2); and Esther, c. 1762, a Mr. Jones who kept a music shop in Russell Street. Cecilia and Isabella sang, sometimes together, at Covent Garden and elsewhere. Their father appears to have been, not Anthony, but "Charles Young, organist . . . son of Anthony Young, a musician and music-seller in St. Paul's churchyard, commonly called Tony Young" ("Young" in Rees). CB evidently mistook the daughters' grandfather for their father.

3. Francesco Geminiani (1687–1762), violinist and composer, pupil of Corelli, came to England in 1714 but "was seldom heard in public during his long residence. . . . His compositions, scholars, and the presents he received from the great, whenever he could be prevailed upon to play at their houses, were his chief support." Among his theoretical works the *Art of Playing the Violin* (1748) was "infinitely superior to . . . any other book of the kind." CB goes on to say: "Geminiani, with all his harmonical abilities, was so circumscribed in his invention, that he was obliged to have recourse to all the arts of musical cookery, not to call it quackery, for materials to publish . . . he transformed Corelli's solos and six of his sonatas into concertos, by multiplying notes, and loading, and deforming, I think, those melodies, that were more graceful and pleasing in their light original dress" (*Hist. Mus.*, 4:641–45; Mercer, 2:990–94).

FRAGMENT 22   Chester, August? 1744

Musicorum et [cantorum]
Magna est distantia
Isti dicunt, illi sciunt
Nam qui facit quod non sapit
Definatur bestia.

Between a singer & musician
Wide is the distance & condition;

The one repeats. The other knows
The sounds which harmony compose,
And he who acts without a plan
May be defin'd more beast than man.[1]

The songs in Comus, in the first Alfred, in the blind beggar of Bethnel Green,[2] in Shakespear's plays, such as "Blow, blow thou winter's wind;["] "To keep my gentle Jesse," The Cuckoo[3] &c had arrived at Shrewsbury, and been sung by my brother and his scholars, before I quitted that town; but when I heard them sung by Lowe[4] & Mrs Arne, under the direction, & to the accompaniment of the author, my delight was inexpressible. Yet in hearing none was my pleasure so complete, as in that admirable national song, for the first time, "When Britain first at Heav'n's command—or *Rule Britannia*,"[5] wch I thought the most pleasing air to English words, wch our national music c^d boast. And I have not changed my opinion since.

1. CB translated these "old Monkish Rhymes mighty neatly" from Guido di Arezzo's prologue to *Antiphonarium* when he was preparing the second volume of *Hist. Mus.* He showed them to Mrs. Thrale, who transcribed them in her diary on 1 March 1779, saying, "They will contribute to egayer les Choses" (*Thraliana,* 1:371). They were later printed in *Hist. Mus.* (2:80–81; Mercer, 1: 463–64), where CB notes that they derive from Boethius (*De Musica* I.xxxiv), who was the first to point out the distinction between a musician, "who can examine, judge, and give reasons for what is done," and a singer, "the mere practician [who] hears it without understanding it" ("Boethius" in Rees).

2. The masque *Comus,* with Milton's text rewritten by John Dalton, was first performed with great success at Drury Lane on 4 March 1738. *Alfred,* though never as popular as *Comus,* was staged in a bewildering number of versions: at Cliveden House near Maidenhead, the seat of the Prince of Wales, on 1 Aug. 1740; then revised by Arne "after the manner of an oratorio" in March 1740 (Frag. 29, n. 2). CB probably refers to the latter as "the first Alfred" to distinguish it from an-

other version, performed 23 Feb. 1751, with CB's own music (Frag. 60). See Fiske, pp. 224–29. *The Blind Beggar of Bethnel Green,* by Robert Dodsley, had been set to music by Arne and produced at Drury Lane on 3 April 1741.

3. "Blow, blow thou winter's wind" and "The Cuckoo" are two of the three songs that Arne set to music for the performance of *As You Like It* at Drury Lane on 20 Dec. 1740. "The Cuckoo," CB says, "was constantly encored when sung by Mrs. Clive" (*Hist. Mus.,* 2:411n; Mercer, 1:685n). "To keep my gentle Jessy" is one of two songs he wrote for a production of *The Merchant of Venice* first performed at Drury Lane 14 Feb. 1741.

4. Thomas Lowe (d. 1 March 1783), "a stage singer, with an exquisite tenor voice," had made his debut at Drury Lane in autumn 1740 and evidently stopped at Chester with the Arnes in 1744. "His first profession," writes CB, "was that of a gold and silver-lace" Spitalfields weaver, "and he began music too late to read it as a language, so that he learned the songs, which he performed in public, by his ear to the end of his life. He stood, however, very high in the favour of lovers of

English ballads, particularly those of Dr. Arne at Drury-lane and Vauxhall, composed expressly for his voice and bounded abilities. He was the rival of Beard, and gained as much applause by the sweetness of his voice, through all his ignorance, as Beard, a regular bred musician, brought up in the king's chapel, could do by his knowledge of music, humour, and good acting." However, "Low was profligate, extravagant, and unprincipled; which rendered the latter part of his life disgraceful and wretched. From acquiring unbounded applause, and an income of more than 1000*l*. a year, he was reduced to the lowest state of indigence, and degraded into a chorus singer at Sadler's Wells, Cuper's Gardens, and even a ballad-singer in the streets" ("Low" in Rees).

5. Composed to the words of James Thomson for the masque of *Alfred* (n. 2, above) and first published in 1741. It was heard in London on 20 March 1745 at Drury Lane at a benefit for Mrs Arne; during the Jacobite uprising of 1745 it became a loyalist song (Frag. 29, n. 2). CB refers to it several times in his correspondence, especially in the 1790s, always with great admiration.

FRAGMENT 23

Chester, August? 1744

⟨dated⟩ my compositions, he said he was glad that I had as[c]ertained the chronology of these studies, as I sh^d be ashamed of them sometime hence, if ever I learned counterpoint regularly.[1] And told my father it was pity so industrious a youth, with such a disposition for the art wch I was studying, sh^d not be placed under an eminent Master in London, who w^d regulate my studies and give my talents fair play. This struck my father and myself very forcibly; but as we supposed that it w^d be attended with an enormous expence, to send me to London, to pay a first-rate Master, and for board, lodging, & cloaths, nothing further passed on the subject, till, at a second visit,[2] Mr Arne spoke out, and said he would take me to town as an apprentice, for £100 premium, & exempt my father from all further expence.

This proposal we sh^d have eagerly embraced, if the £100 c^d [have been furnished][3]

1. One day while waiting for Arne, CB met Filippo Palma, "a Neapolitan singing-master," who "was so ignorant of counterpoint, that he . . . condescend[ed] to ask a young apprentice to Dr. Arne to furnish a base; and yet he touched the harpsichord in so original and seemingly masterly a manner, that this apprentice would have given the world to exchange all his knowledge in counterpoint for signior Palma's 'Toccatini'" ("Palma, Filippo" in Rees; Scholes 1948, 1: 31–32).

Arne at this time may have used his violin solo in E major "as a test of young Burney's abilities." The original in Arne's hand is in BL, Add. MS 39957, f. 34, among "Harpsichord solos transcribed by Dr. Charles Burney at Chester." It has been edited by John A.

Parkinson in the Musica de Camera Series, no. 80, Oxford, 1979; see Parkinson, p. 902).

2. Arne's second visit to the Burney house could have taken place within a day or two of the first.

3. Mme d'Arblay wrongly states that "to this proposal Mr. Burney senior was induced to consent" (*Mem.*, 1:11). Lonsdale (1965, pp. 8–9) calls attention to the poverty of CB's father at this time and suggests that "Arne eventually agreed to take Burney to London without insisting on any payment." See Frag. 24.

FRAGMENT 24

Chester, August? 1744

& I could play on the Violin, Tenor, & Harp^d well enough to be admitted into an Orchestra, or an Organ-loft, as an assistant; all these circumstances considered, Arne foresaw that I sh^d be a more profitable than expensive part of his Family.

My father & I, dazzled by the Idea of avoiding expence in going to the Capital; of being instructed by a Master of the first abilities and fame among the natives of our Island; and of hearing all the great performers and compositions of other countries, made no objection to the length of the tutelage, & total dependance on a master, who if avaricious, selfish, sordid, and tyrannical, might render the best part of my life slavish & miserable.[1] The bargain however was struck, the Articles *bound apprentice till* drawn, and covenants exchanged in a legal & regular way.[2]

1. CB is here voicing a view of Arne's character as he was later to experience it (see Frag. 31), one amply confirmed by Mrs. Pilkington's son, John Carteret, who had previously been an apprentice to Arne: his apprenticeship came to an end when he stole and "pawned some of [Arne's] music books," whereupon "Mr. Arne, his Wife, and Lo[w]e were beating me for three hours to make me confess what I had done." Young Pilkington was "locked in, in order to be sent to Newgate next day" but managed to break the lock and run away. The letter in which he wrote this account to his mother is dated "Edinburgh, Sept. 16, 1744," about the time when Arne engaged CB as a new apprentice, although the Pilkington incident probably happened in Feb. or March 1738, when "they were rehearsing *Comus*" (see Pilkington, pp. 287, 290–92).

2. These involved an apprenticeship of seven years, without payment of the £100 Arne had originally asked. According to the *General Advertiser* of 4 Sept. 1744, when CB set out for London with Arne, "the party travelled on horseback, Mrs. Arne on a pillion behind Burney." CB stayed in the Arne household, "next door to the Crown" in Great Queen Street, Lincoln's Inn Fields. Scholes (1948, 1:22, pl. 3) reproduces an engraving of the house.

FRAGMENT 25 London, Autumn 1744

know the power of instinct [or at] least of memory,[1] I wrote a letter to him dated Chester, wch I carried myself in the character of his brother Charles's particular friend, a Mr Arnold (30 years before *one Arnold* was talked of)[2] desiring him to shew this friend the humours of London, and to do him every act of kindness in his power: "as I had a very particular affection for him, and regarded him as an *alter idem*." He rec^d me therefore, as his brother's particular friend, very kindly, and was very assiduous in initiating me in the pleasures of the Capital.

This brother lived with a half brother, the 2^d son of my father by his first wife.[3] My own brother (Richard) carried the rites of hospitality so far as to present me to the brother with whom he lived, and begged of him to ask me to dinner. This invitation distressed me very much, and put the pseudo char[a]cter wch I had assumed in danger of being discovered sooner than I wished: as this half brother had been at Chester on a visit to my father during my first residence there,[4] and in all probability w^d recognize me at the first glance.

1. Before he left for London, CB decided to play a trick on his elder brother Richard, with whom he had spent six years in Condover as a boy. Richard must have left Condover earlier than did CB, perhaps in 1735, when he was twelve and CB nine years old. Richard went to London, where he became apprenticed to his half-brother Thomas (n. 3, below). As the two brothers had not met since then, CB wondered whether Richard, now twenty-one, would recognize him (he was eighteen) after nine or ten years' separation.

2. The well-known Dr. Samuel Arnold (1740–1802), composer and CB's fellow musical graduate, was at this time only four years old. The "Arnold" mentioned here is a fictional name devised by CB to test Richard's "power of instinct" or at "least of memory."

3. Thomas Burney (b. 1707) began his career as a dancer in the theatre. A great number of his performances between 1726 and May 1732 are listed in *London Stage*. At thirty-seven, he "was settled in London, and was an eminent Dancing Master." Richard, who (c. 1734–35) became Thomas's apprentice, "was treated with great severity" by his half-brother, yet he managed to "improve himself on the violin" and "taught himself french." Later Thomas became "tired of the life he led, and determined to try his fortune by emigrating to America," while Richard inherited his thriving business (Worcester Mem., pp. 5–6), but this occurred after the incident CB is narrating.

4. In 1741, when CB was fifteen.

FRAGMENT 26   London, Autumn 1744

In this manner I played the *Incognito* for near a month. Whenever my brother Richard called on me in Queen Street,[1] he hitherto had only asked if the young gentleman from Chester was within, without naming me; but calling one day when I was out, he desired the servant to tell Mr Arnold, that Mr Richard Burney had called upon him. Mr Arnold! says the maid, there is no one of that name here. No! says my brother; why what is the name of the young gentleman who came up to town with Mr Arne from Chester? Oh that's Master Charles Burney. This discovered the plot, & blew me up, without powder.

My brother was in a great rage with me for the imposition, & with himself for being the dupe of such a barefaced deception: recollecting then, that I had talked of Charles & the family in such a way as none but a branch of that family c^d know. And he was so angry with both himself and me, that he did not soon forget the trick I had played him.[2] Perhaps he thought it was a bit of

1. Arne's house in London, where CB stayed with his master (Frag. 24, n. 2).

2. According to *Worcester Mem.* (p. 6), Richard, "having very narrowly escaped the effects of the smallpox, which he had to a dangerous degree . . . received as much pleasure as his situation would allow, in the Company of his Brother Charles, who at this time came up to London to be a Pupil under Dr. Arn."

FRAGMENT 27   London, Autumn 1744

[On his return to London Arne was] immediately engaged at Drury Lane Theatre as composer of Songs, Dances and Act tunes, at a salary of £3 a week; & Mrs Arne as principal Singer, at the same salary.[1] And there being at this time no vacancy in the Band, I was employed as a supernumerary Violin or Tenor, occasionally, in pantomimes or musical pieces, when some of the performers in the orchestra were wanted on the stage, as Chorus singers; or behind the scenes in serinades, processions and other musical purposes, for stage effect. And for this I was not in Salary, but p^d by the night; only ^s5 each time: To wch I had no claim, nor did I consider myself degraded by the meanness of the pay, as there were others, much my seniors, who performed on similar occasions on the same terms. What I was most interested[2]

1. Of Mrs. Arne, CB wrote after her death: "I never had forgotten the good soul's kindness to me during my residence with Dr Arne; when, It is not too much to say, I profitted more in my studies by the advantage of accompanying her in her vocal exercises, than by any instructions wch the D^r had leisure to give me. . . . As long as I remained under the same roof, I tried every thing in my power, and not unsuccessfully, to contribute to domestic harmony, so necessary to the welfare of the whole family, as well as the comfort of individuals. And I did flatter myself, If I had continued longer wth them, the union w^d have been of longer duration" (CB to Mr. and Mrs. Barthélémon, 21 Oct. 1789, Osborn).

2. "I was at the House every Night, with Arne," wrote CB later. "My God-father Mr Fleetwood was still manager, from whom I had the name of Charles; but shut up, & sculking for debt. Lacy's name had not yet been heard" (CB to Charles Burney, 19 April [1806], Comyn). Shortly after CB's arrival the Drury Lane actors, led by Garrick and Macklin, seceded from Fleetwood's unprincipled management, while Fleetwood himself "was dying, excruciatingly, of a generalized gout, confined to his house for fear of arrest, and in arrears to all his players" (Nash, p. 192). For James Lacy, see Appendix B, n. 22.

FRAGMENT 28

heard him. The Harpsichord was played [by] Burges,[1] who had a very neat finger that never failed him in the common passages of wch his concertos were composed. The elder Cervetto, the worthy Hebrew to whom the galleries had given the cognomen of *Nosey,*[2] had not been long in England; he was a Venetian & knew the fingerboard of his instrument, and composition, very well; but he had not that firm vocal tone for which his son[3] became so justly celebrated. Hebden,[4] a Yorkshire man was first Bassoon & second Violoncello. Bennet,[5] an eleve of Dr Pepusch,[6] played the Tenor, & occasionally, was a Chorus singer & figurante in processions. He knew the Laws of counterpoint very well, but had not a spark

1. Henry Burgess the younger (fl. 1738–65), harpsichordist, organist, and composer. He was one of the original subscribers of the Royal Society of Musicians (28 Aug. 1739) and, according to a playbill advertising a concerto of his composition at Cuper's Gardens in the summer of 1741, "as promising a genius and as neat a performer as any of the age" (Highfill, 2:418).

2. Giacobbe Bas(s)evi Cervetto (1682?–1783), Italian composer of German-Jewish origin (his name probably deriving from "Hirschel"—little stag), arrived in London in 1738 and was solo cellist at Drury Lane, where he later succeeded Garrick as manager; see *Hist. Mus.,* 4:660, 669; Mercer, 2:1005, 1012. "He was an honest Hebrew," writes CB, "had the largest nose, and wore the finest

diamond ring on the fore finger of his bow hand. . . . Another remarkable circumstance in the history of the elder Cervetto . . . is, that he extended his existence to 100 years complete, with the character, not only of a good musician, but a good man" ("Cervetto" in Rees).

3. James Cervetto (1747–1837), "who, during childhood surpassed his father in tone and expression on the violoncello; and who in riper years, was as much noticed at the opera for his manner of accompanying recitative, as the vocal performers of the principal characters for singing the airs" ("Cervetto" in Rees). For a performance by the son and father a Burney musical soirée on 15 Nov. 1768, see *ED*, 1:32.

4. John Hebden (fl. 1741–49) was "well known in London, in the middle of the last century, as a performer on the bassoon and violoncello of the second class. He was more a useful than an ornamental player on both these instruments. At Vauxhall he was second on the bassoon, where Miller was the first; and at Drury Lane, where Cervetto was first violoncello, Hebden was second; yet he often played concertos on the bassoon at benefit concerts with considerable applause" ("Hebden" in Rees; CB adds that he "was totally ignorant of composition").

5. Perhaps John Bennet (fl. 1744–72), who played in Aug. 1744 at Mulberry Garden, Clerkenwell. He is listed in Mortimer as a "Tenor [horn player] to the Queen's Band, Organist, and Teacher on the Harpsichord" (Highfill, 2:34). He may be identical with the John Bennett (1725?–84) who in April 1752 succeeded CB as organist of St. Dionis Backchurch (*New Grove*, 2:496).

6. For Dr. Pepusch, see Frag. 35.

FRAGMENT 29   London, 1744–45

Ld Falkland's treatm^t of the savages who broke the Harp^d at D. L.[1]

Mar. 20th this year (1745) My Master Arne had Alfred the Great, of his own composition, performed for his benefit, "after the manner of an Oratorio."[2] It was repeated [o]n April 3^d & 24th & May 23^d at Drury Lane; but so ill attended, that there was not company sufficient to pay the expences, & his performers, vocal & instrumental, consented to accept, at the end of the season, of half pay.[3]

I had a fair score to make, & to transcribe all the Voice-parts, teach many of them, attend rehearsals to correct the books, & to go into the City to the printers of news-papers, wth advertisem^ts In doing this, & more, I sh^d have had great pleasure, had my master been prosperous. Some of the music I thought very good; but all was ill performed, except Mrs Arne's part of the Queen Ellendy[,] the choruses thin and the contrast between the force of Handel's genius, and that of his band, was too manifest not to be soon discovered by the public.

1. Lucius Charles Cary (c. 1707–85), 7th Viscount Falkland 1730. On 17 Nov. 1744, riots broke out at Drury Lane, caused by Fleetwood's new policy of adding pantomimes as afterpieces and raising the price of admission. When the spectators loudly protested, Fleetwood hired "bruisers" from among the actors; they were "armed with bludgeons and clubs to menace the audience," who "raised the greatest uproar" (see Victor 1:41–46; *London Stage,* pt. 3, 2:1130–33; YW, 18:538–39; Nash, p. 198; and Green, pp. 18–19). "It was then," writes CB, "that I saw Lord Falkland beckon the Ruffian who jumped on the Harpsichord, broke all the strings, and stamped on the belly of the Instrument till he broke it into shivers—'Sir! Sir!' calls out my Lord from a side box above the pit, as if he wanted to tell him of something else that he c^d destroy in punishm^t of the Managers—the Glasses and sconces were all broken already—the benches torn up & hurling on the stage—and when the *Gemman,* the friend of our friend Kirckman, who occasioned the Want of a new Harp^d for the playhouse, approached Ld Falkland, & stood on Tiptoe, holding his head as high as he c^d to hear what his Lord^p had to say, he gave him *such* a violent slap on the face as was heard & applauded by every lover of peace and order in the house. The *chap* blustered and vowed vengeance when he c^d get at him. But his Lord^p was suffered to go peaceably to his Carriage without being put to the trouble of treating his other cheek in a similar manner. . . . I remember very well that the riots & their ruinous consequences lasted a full fortnight" (CB to Charles Burney, 16 and 19 April 1806, Comyn). For Jacob Kirckman see Frag. 41, n. 2, and Appendix B. CB intended this anecdote to go to "Vol. 1, top of p. 39," which is not extant.

2. This revised *Alfred,* first performed at the Smock Alley Theatre, Dublin, on 10 March 1744, was now given with great pomp in London; it was then that *Rule, Britannia!* was first heard in London, "in imitation of those [odes] formerly sung at Banquets of Kings and Heroes"; see Scott, pp. 385–97.

3. The prices for this performance were raised by a shilling and sixpence: "Mrs Arne hopes humbly the Town will not be offended at this small advance of the Price, this performance being exhibited at an extraordinary expence, with regard to the number of Hands, Chorus singers, building the stage, and erecting an organ; besides all other incidentals as usual." When it was repeated on 3 April, Arne "being inform'd that some persons have objected to the small addition of Prices," decided to charge normal prices "notwithstanding he performs at above £70 Expence" (*London Stage,* pt. 3, 2:1161, 1164; only the first two performances are listed, not those of 4 April and 23 May).

FRAGMENT 30   London, March–April 1745

[can]nonade,[1] when the Enemy more alert than the French, discharged the first Cannon, wch so terrified Pepin, that he faints away; when awaking from his trance, he, in very solemn tone, asks those around him:

"Where am I? is this Elysium wch I see,
And you my friends still follow me?

Inform me—did that dreadful ball
Which killed your Monarch, kill you all?"[2]

This is all that I can remember of this abortive piece, and almost all that was allowed to be said or sung, for I have forgot whether it was lyrical or declamatory. God forgive me! but I believe it was written by my Master; it was performed for his benefit.[3] (The play wch preceded this farce was Venice preserved, in wch Mrs Cibber played Belvidera.)[4]

During l[e]nt, 1745, by a letter from my Master to Handel, I was admitted into his Oratorio band to play the Tenor; attended rehearsals sometimes at his house in Brook Street, and sometimes at Carlton-House.[5]

---

1. This fragment refers to *King Pepin's Campaign. A Burlesque Opera, of Two Acts,* by William Shirley (fl. 1739–80), performed on 16 and 19 April 1745 at Drury Lane (published 1755). Act II, sc. ii shows the French camp near Menin. King Pepin, determined to take the town, throws "the first Fascine," but as "*a Cannon fires at a Distance . . . he falls flat on the Stage*:

> *Marg.*   How dreadful do the
>   Cannon roar!—
> *Const.*   Alas! our Monarch is no
>   more!—

2. Is this Elysium which I see?
   And where my Friends still follow
      me!—
   Inform me; did the fatal Ball
   That kill'd your Monarch, kill ye all?
   [Ibid.]

3. The farce contains three choruses and thirteen airs. Arne, whose benefit night it was, composed a duetto, a trio, and a "Ballad, in Parts," for it.

4. Susannah Maria Cibber (1714–66), the celebrated tragedienne, was Arne's sister. For a lively account of her life and tribulations, see Nash. Belvidera—in Otway's tragedy, which preceded the farce—was one of her great roles. She also sang "Gentle Shepherd" in Shirley's burlesque afterpiece.

5. Carlton House was the seat of the Prince of Wales. "As I first arrived in London in the year 1744," writes CB, Handel "did bestride our musical world like a Colossus. . . . In 1745, I performed in his band, sometimes on the violin, and sometimes on the tenor, and by attending the rehearsals, generally at his own house in Lower Brook-street, and sometimes at Carlton-house, at the desire of his constant patron the late prince of Wales, father to his present Majesty, I gratified my eager curiosity in seeing and examining the person and manners of so extraordinary a man, as well as in hearing him perform on the organ. He was a blunt and peremptory disciplinarian on these occasions, but had a humour and wit in delivering his instructions, and even in chiding and finding fault, that was peculiar to himself, and extremely diverting to all but those on whom his lash was laid" (*Hist. Mus.*, 4:662, 667–68; Mercer, 2:1007, 1009–10). Handel's lash fell on young Burney as well; see Frag. 57. In *Commem.*, CB quotes many of Handel's comments, imitating his heavily accented English: e.g., finding the house half empty in the spring of 1745, he said, "Nevre moind, de moosic vil sound de petter" (pt. 1, p. 29n).

FRAGMENT 31 London, 1744–46

It grieves me that gratitude does not oblige me to speak with more reverence of him as my Master;[1] but the truth is, he was so selfish & unprincipled, that finding me qualified to transcribe music, teach, & play in public, all wch I c^d do before I was connected with him, he never wished I sh^d advance further in the Art. And besides not teaching or allowing me time to study & practice, he locked up all the B^{ks} in his possession,[2] by the perusal of wch I c^d improve myself; particularly The Lessons of Scarlatti & Handel, & Madrigals of Palestrina, of wch last he never w^d let me see the score, but of a Sunday Night, when Mrs Arne, Mrs Cibber, Miss Young,[3] himself & I used to perform them in Queen Street, he was at the trouble of drawing out a Tenor part for me to sing by, lest in doing it for myself, I sh^d improve by examining how the several parts were constructed. Of these 3 authors by this means I was but the more eager to be possessed; wch ere I left him, by the assistance of Fr^{ds}, I was enabled to do.[4] Indeed rather than not turn my small abilities to some lucrative acc^t he w^d have me employed in teaching, or playing any Instrument, at any place or price. Sometimes I played the Violin, and sometimes the Tenor, for Handel, in his oratorios.[5] & was employed at Drury Lane as a supernumerary Tenor at ^{s}5 a Night, whenever he c^d take Bennet[6] from the Orchestra to sing in the Choruses on the Stage. But these were only my Evenings amusem^{ts}—in the morning Winter & Summer, when he had no Scholars to send me to, I was constantly employed as a Copyist of his own Compositions, either for the Playhouse or Vaux-Hall; & this under pretence that Norton, Lowe & Simpson,[7] the Copyists for those places were not to be trusted with his precious Scores.[8]

1. The MS of Frag. 40 ends: "It may seem strange & ungrateful in me not to have spoken with more respect and regard of My Master Arne, than I have hitherto done, but I had too much reason to complain of his selfishness." The present fragment is taken from a draft of CB's article on Arne for Rees; understandably, he did not print this section (Lonsdale 1965, p. 13).

2. One reason Arne kept his manuscript scores locked up was no doubt that his previous apprentice had stolen some and pawned them (see Frag. 24, n. 1).

3. Esther Young was one of Mrs. Arne's two sisters. CB became acquainted with Mrs. Cibber, Arne's sister, in April 1746 (Frags. 30, n. 4; and 34, n. 10).

4. A transcript of "Palestrina—Madrigale, Motteti e Salmi a 5 Voc. *in score* MS" is listed as item 395 in *Cat. Mus.* In 1814 it was sold for the high sum of "£12.6" to "Bartleman."

5. CB may have been one of the string players at the rehearsal of the *Occasional Oratorio* in Handel's house on 7 Feb. 1746 (Deutsch 1955). "After my first arrival in London, 1744," writes CB, Handel "seldom was absent from the benefit for Decayed Musi-

cians and their Families; and I have sometimes seen him at the Play houses, the Opera,
and at St Martin's church, when the late Mr.
Kelway played the organ" (*Commem.*, pt. 1,
p. 34).

6. See Frag. 28, n. 5.

7. Ferdinand Norton, musician, died at

High Wickham, Bucks., in December 1772
(*GM*, 43:47). Redmond Simpson (d. 23 Jan.
1787) is listed in Mortimer as "Haut boy, one
of the Queen's Band, *Brewer-street, Golden
square*." For Lowe, see Frag. 22, n. 4.

8. For a continuation of this character of
Arne, see Frag. 62.

FRAGMENT 32   Elsham, Autumn 1745

But Arne's apprentice spent the autumn of 1745 very pleasantly in Lincolnshire at Willm Thompson's Esqr at Elsham near Brig,[1] where he became
known to several great Families who honoured him with their countenance &
friendship as long as they lived.[. . .]

Page to Queen Caroline,[2] and was [known to possess a] correct ear, by w^ch
he sung with a pleasing voice, [and   ] English songs that were in favour,
& fragments of opera songs, "as he was a constant auditor in the ^s5 Gal^y of the
Haymarket Theatre." When I arrived at Elsham, I found there, besides M^r T.
and his Lady, his brother, Mr Robt Thompson,[3] M^r Le Grand,[4] and 5 or 6
young Ladies of the neighbourhood. I had the honour of being introduced to
the acquaintance of all the families that visited at Elsham: such as the Pelhams,[5]
the Andersons,[6] the Gores,[7] & the Carters. Four of the Miss Gores, and Miss
Molly Carter[8] were inmates. Miss Philly Gore,[9] a great beauty, & Miss Carter,
very young, intelligent and handsome, though very pleasing, did not discover
herself to be possessed of so large portion of wit, as that for wch she has since
been so justly celebrated.

I continued here during the month of Septr Octr and part of Novr and never
passed my time more pleasantly in my life. It was one continued series of mirth,
amusement & festivity.[10]

1. William Thompson of Muckamore
died in 1754. His will, dated 31 March, was
proved 2 Sept. 1754 (Vivian H. King, MS
genealogical table of the families of Thompson and Carter, 1914, BL shelf-mark LR 270.
b.15).

2. Not identified.

3. William Thompson (n. 1, above) had

married Elizabeth Blain. His brother Robert
is not listed in the genealogical table of the
Thompson family.

4. Not identified. Mme d'Arblay, in her
paraphrase of the passage, calls him "Billy Le
Grand" (see n. 10, below).

5. Charles Pelham (c. 1679–1763) of
Brocklesby, Lincs.; M.P. for Great Grimsby

1722–27, for Beverley 1727–34, 1738–54; married Anne (d. 8 March 1739), daughter of William Gore, in June 1714. After his death in 1763 his estates went to his grand-nephew Charles Anderson (d. 1823), a subscriber to *Hist. Mus.,* who assumed the name Anderson-Pelham; cr. Baron Yarborough 1794.

6. Sir Edward Anderson (d. 3 May 1765) of Broughton, Lincs., three miles from Brigg, married first Mary Harvey, by whom he had two sons and three daughters; second Frances Batty, by whom he had a son and two daughters. A "David Anderson" is listed among the subscribers to *Hist. Mus.* For genealogies of the Pelhams and the Andersons, see Maddison, 1:19–24; 3:765–66.

7. Charles Gore (d. 7 Dec. 1754) of Horkenstow, Lincs., father of Charles, Jr. (1729–1807).

8. Probably Mary Carter (d. 1812), daughter of Thomas Carter (d. 1765) of Robertstown and Rathnally. She later corresponded with Lady Mount Edgecumbe, Edward Jerningham, and Horace Walpole (YW, 9:95 n.23), and in her old age with CB (Lonsdale 1965, p. 472).

9. Sister of Charles Gore, Jr. (n. 7, above).

10. Mme d'Arblay gives the following paraphrase of this fragment: "Miss Molly Carter, in her youth a very pretty girl, was, in the year 1745, of a large party of young ladies, consisting of five or six Miss Gores, and Miss Anderson, at William Thompson's Esq., in the neighbourhood of Elsham, near Brig. Bob Thompson, Mr. Thompson's brother, Billy Le Grand, and myself, composed the rest of the set, which was employed in nothing but singing, dancing, romping, and visiting, the whole time I was there; which time was never surpassed in hilarity at any place where I have been received in my life" (*Mem.,* 1:19).

FRAGMENT 33   Elsham, Autumn 1745

[La Francesina][1]

-sing and useful to me: as She was of the Italian School, & had sung in several of Handel's Operas, with her fine shake & execution sufficient to sing *Sweet bird! Myself I shall adore, The morning Lark to mine accords his notes,* & all Handel's songs wch were expressly composed for the *Francesina's* Warble.

But before I left Mr Thompson's seat in Lincolnshire, the Rebellion broke out in Scotland, & put all London and a considerable part of the Nation into confusion[2]

1. Elizabeth Duparc (d. 1778?), "a very pleasing female Italian singer, and a beautiful woman, arrived in England in 1736, in order to sing in the opera established by the nobility and gentry against Handel." Later, however, she sang "for Handel at the end of his opera regency in Lincoln's-inn-fields, 1740, in the little drama of "Imeneo," or Hymen, and in 1741 in "Deidamia," the last opera which he composed, and in which she had an air at the end of the first act, "Nascondi l'usignol," composed in a light airy

style, suited to the active throat of the Fran-cesina. It was for the natural warble of this singer that Handel composed his English airs of execution, such as "Sweet Bird," in Mil-ton's Penseroso, "Myself I shall adore," and "The morning lark to mine accords his throat," in Congreve's Semele, &c. Though the Francesina came hither as second wom-an, and had not a voice sufficiently powerful for a first woman's part in a large theatre, having quitted the opera stage, she attached

herself to Handel and was the principal sing-er in his oratorios during many years" ("Francesina" in Rees; *Hist. Mus.*, 4: 434; Mercer, 2:829).

2. The Young Pretender landed in Scot-land on 2 Aug. 1745, but the news that "re-bellion broke out in Scotland" became wide-spread only after he defeated Sir John Cope on 20 Sept. at Prestonpans and threatened Edinburgh Castle.

FRAGMENT 34 London, September 1745–June 1746

During the following season, beginning Sept^r [1]745 & ending in June 1746, Mrs Cibber was not engaged at either Theatre. But when the public subscrip-tion for the families of soldiers who might fall during the rebellion, was carrying on at Guild-Hall, Mrs Cibber offered to play Polly in the beggar's Opera on three different Nights, for the aid of this benevolent fund.[1] Some very malicious Letters concerning Mrs Cibber's being a Roman Catholic appeared in the news-papers—[a]nd were well answered.[2] Though Mrs Cibber's ⟨m⟩other[3] was a bigoted Catholic & Jacobite, [I], who lived in the family, and coming out of Shropshire, was a bit of a Jacobite myself, can answer for Mrs Cibber being a truly loyal and good subject. Her proposal for three performances of Polly in the Beggars Opera having been accepted she played it at Covent-Garden,[4] Novr 14th 16th & 17th Mrs Pritchard[5] acted Lucy, Hippisley[6] Peachum, & Lowe Mackeath.

Mrs Cibber had never acted Polly before; and was plunged into a violent quarrel wth Mrs Clive ab^t the part, several years previous to this period.[7] The latter Lady to whose appearance & disposition the part naturally belonged, then peremptorily refused to accept of it. However, her stomach came down at last, and a few year[s] after, 1745, she *did* look & act the part admirably.[8]

On the 12th of April 1746, Mrs Cibber, the celebrated actress, Mr Arne's sister, who had been in France, & had not appeared on any stage in England for 9 years,[9] was prevailed on by her brother to play the part of Monimia in the Orphan for his benefit, which as soon as advertised, there was such a demand for boxes, that it was found necessary to lay pit and boxes together; & I never afterwards, saw the Theatre more crowded, or a more splendid au[dience][10]

1. Susannah Cibber had suggested to Garrick in October 1745 that he play with her for the benefit of a benevolent fund; but as he was off to Ireland, she placed a notice in the *Daily Advertiser* on 7 Dec. "offering to play Polly in *The Beggar's Opera* to benefit the Veteran's Scheme" (Nash, pp. 212–16).

2. Catherine or "Kitty" Clive née Raftor (1711–85) had made her debut on the stage in 1729. She was enraged that Susannah Cibber "stole" the role of Polly from her and placed an anonymous letter in the *Daily Advertiser* on 9 Dec. in which she called Mrs. Cibber's proposal "a Jesuitical Stroke of a Papist Actress in Pursuit of Protestant Popularity," warning readers that "her whole family are, in the strict sense, Roman Catholick." Mrs. Cibber answered this the following day in the same paper, stating that she was indeed of the Romish persuasion, but that was "a private matter" and "she was unswervingly loyal to the present royal family and its line" (Nash, pp. 215–16).

3. Anne Arne (d. 1757) was a midwife and a Roman Catholic who raised her children in her faith, attending the mass at the Sardinian embassy chapel in Lincoln's Inn Fields (Nash, pp. 13–15). "I remember seeing a board with her Name & profession upon it among her Chattels during my first arrival in London," wrote CB in a draft of his article on Arne (Frag. 31). It was she who told young CB that she had heard "God Save the King" during the Glorious Revolution sung for the Catholic James II (CB to Sir Joseph Banks, 29 July 1806, BL, Eg. 3009, f. 13).

4. The dates that follow should read "Dec^r" rather than "Nov^r."

5. Hannah Pritchard née Vaughan (1711–68) had made her debut in 1733 and became one of the stars in Garrick's galaxy, though Dr. Johnson called her "a vulgar idiot."

6. John Hippisley (d. 1748), actor and playwright, who excelled in comic parts, as his ugly face always elicited laughter from the audience.

7. This famous quarrel about who was to play Polly took place in 1736, before CB's arrival in London. *The Beggar's Opera* was finally performed, with Kitty Clive as Polly, on 31 Dec. 1736 before a riotous audience; the quarrel between the two actresses was burlesqued in *The Beggar's Pantomime*, in which Kitty Clive and Mrs. Cibber appeared as Madam Squeak and Madam Squall (Nash, pp. 94–103).

8. On 3 Dec. 1745 Kitty Clive played Lucy, voluntarily relinquishing the role of Polly to her protégée, Mrs. Vincent (Highfill, 3:350).

9. This is an odd slip on CB's part. Mrs. Cibber had resumed her acting career on 22 Sept. 1742, before CB came to London, and had never been in France.

10. "The demand for Places [was] more than Double what the Boxes will contain." Mrs. Arne also sang three opera songs (*London Stage*, pt. 3, 2:1232). "The page was played by *Master Arne* (Michael, his natural son by his mother's maid). I perfectly remember the pains that were taken by Mrs Cibber as well as his father in teaching Michael to speak, and to act, and to sing: for his father wrote and set a song (almost baudy) for him in character—I remember how grand a benefit it was—and my Master's extravagance *there upon* . . . it was then that my acquaintance wth Mrs Cibber began" (CB to Charles Burney, [23 April 1806], Comyn). Michael Arne (c. 1740–86) was then five or six years old. Mme d'Arblay mentions Mrs. Cibber's Sunday evenings at her "house in Scotland yard," where young CB "found himself in a constellation of wits, poets, actors, authors, and men of letters" (*Mem.*, 1:14).

BRIDGE: FRAGMENTS 34–35

"Old Mrs Arne the Mother of Dr Arne & Mrs Cibber . . . assured me at the time (1746) that 'God save the King' was written & sung at the time for King *James,* in 1688, when the Prince of Orange was hovering over the coast; she said she had heard it sung, not only at the playhouse, but in the Street[1]—Her Son, Mr Arne, composer to Drury Lane Theatre, at the desire of Mr Fleetwood, the Patentee, Harmonized this loyal Song for the Stage—and he made a Trio of it for Mrs Cibber, Beard, & Reynolds,[2] with instrumental accompanim^ts without knowing the Author of the words or original melody. And it continued to be sung and called for a full year after the suppression of the Rebellion. I, then a pupil of Mr Arne, was desired by some of the Covent Garden singers with whom I was acquainted and who knew that I was a bit of a Composer, to set parts wch I did utterly ignorant who wrote the words or set them to Music"[3] (CB to Sir Joseph Banks, 29 July 1806, BL, Eg. 3009, f. 13).

1. For Anne Arne, see Frag. 34, n. 3; for a full discussion of the controversial origins of what later became the national anthem, see Scholes 1954.

2. John Beard (c. 1717–91), tenor, made his debut in 1737 and sang at both Drury Lane and Covent Garden (see Frags. 61, n. 3; and 83, n. 3). Henry Theodore Reinhold (1690–1751), German bass who, after his arrival in London, sang in various works by Handel, made his last recorded appearance in CB's *Alfred,* 23 Feb.–9 March 1751. He died two months later on 14 May (*New Grove,* 15:724–25).

3. For CB's later involvement in the controversy about the authorship of "God Save the King," see CB to Charles Burney, 8 Feb. 1799 (Coke).

FRAGMENT 35   London, 1746

[Dr Pepusch][1]

About the year 1746, I was so fortunate, at the late Dr. Arne's, as to be introduced to his acquaintance, of which from his great reputation for science, I was very ambitious. The first time I had the honour to play to him, I ventured to attempt a very difficult lesson of Scarlatti; and when I had done, he both flattered and frightened me extremely, by saying: "pray young man play me that *bagatelle* again."[2] What a great man must this be, thought I, who calls a lesson that has cost me such immense labour to execute, a *bagatelle*! But it was neither a fugue nor a canon.

In one of my visits to this venerable master,[3] very early in my life, he gave me a short lesson which made so deep an impression, that I long endeavoured to practise it. "When I was a young man, said he, I determined never to go to bed at night, till I knew something that I did not know in the morning."

1. Johann Christoph Pepusch (1667–1752), composer of German origin, came to England about 1704 and took his Mus.D. in 1713. In 1728 Pepusch "was very judiciously chosen by Gay, to help him to select the tunes for the "Beggar's Opera," for which he composed an original overture upon the subject of one of the tunes ('I'm like a skiff'), and furnished the wild, rude, and often vulgar melodies, with bases so simple and excellent,

that no judicious contrapuntist will ever attempt to alter them for the theatrical purpose for which they were originally designed" ("Pepusch" in Rees). CB had "frequently the advantage of shewing his exercises in composition to Dr. Pepusch, Rosengrave, and Geminiani" (*EM*).

2. See Frag. 43.

3. Pepusch was then seventy-nine years old.

FRAGMENT 36   London, mid 1740s

I've been at dear Vaux-Hall—[and heard   ][1] wch I believe was never sung there; but it was popular, and excited curiosity in the public to see so charming a place. John Worgan (afterwards Dr Worgan) was his successor in 1745.[2] He was then very young, & a dull & timid extempore player, feeling his way, & modulating in his preludes to Handel's Organ Concertos, from Palestrina's Madrigals, in little more than common Chords in plain counterpoint. He afterwards, however, became an excellent Fughist, a neat player of Scarlatti's Lessons,[3] and a perfect master of the touch of the Organ. But his style of composition was not pleasing; his melody was often uncouth, never graceful; and his harmony & modulation, like that of his master Roseingrave[4] are too studied and unnatural to please the public, or even connoisseurs of good taste.

1. Although the manuscript is torn here, the song CB heard was almost certainly "Green-Wood-Hall: or Colin's Description (to his Wife) of the Pleasure of Spring Gardens. Made to a favourite Gavot from an Organ Concerto compos'd for Vauxhall" [1742],

by Thomas Gladwin (c. 1710–c. 1799), harpsichord player and organist. He was in 1739 one of the original subscribers of the Royal Society of Musicians and is listed in Mortimer as living in South Audley Street.

2. John Worgan (1724–90), organist at

Vauxhall, at St. Mary Axe (c. 1749), St. Botoloph's (1753), St. John's Chapel, Bedford Row (1760); Mus.D. 1775, Cambridge. About 1744 he "succeeded Mr. Gladwin in playing the organ at Vauxhall Gardens" (*Hist. Mus.,* 4:665; Mercer, 2:1009). "He learned the rudiments of music of his elder brother" James (1715–53), "who had likewise an organist's place in the city, and played the violoncello in the Vauxhall band. Their scholars on the harpsichord were very numerous, particularly within Templebar; and John, as an organist and opener of new organs, rivalled Stanley. He was a very studious man, and dipt very early into the old ecclesiastical composers of Italy. . . . His constant use of the organ at Vauxhall, during the summer, ranked him with Stanley and Keeble; and his enthusiasm for Scarlatti's lessons, with which he was impressed by Roseingrave, rendered him equal to Kelway in their execution" ("Worgan" in Rees). CB had in his library "*Worgan's* Select Organ Pieces, Nos. 1, 2, 3 and 4, and Preludes" (*Cat. Mus.,* no. 846). See CB to Twining, 24 Feb. 1782,

Osborn; and for Worgan's biography, *Musical Quarterly Review* 5 (1919): 113.

3. For Worgan's reverence for Domenico Scarlatti, see Appendix B.1.

4. Thomas Roseingrave (1688–1766), organist and composer, "who pointed [Worgan's] attention to the pure harmony and modulation of Palestrina, and organ-fugues of Handel." Young CB "prevailed on him once to touch the organ at Byefield's, the organ builder," and used "frequently to visit him at Mrs. Bray's, Hampstead, where he resided. His conversation was very entertaining and instructive, particularly on musical subjects"; however, "his intellects in the latter part of his life, being somewhat deranged, rendered his character so singular that he merits some notice for his eccentricities, as well as professional abilities." See "Roseingrave" in Rees; *Hist. Mus.,* 4:263–66; Mercer, 2:703–6, which also provide amusing anecdotes of Roseingrave's encounter with Domenico Scarlatti and the results of a luckless love affair.

FRAGMENT 37

to empty benches the 2ᵈ Night,[1] and never arrived at a 3ᵈ.

After the battle of Culloden,[2] all was joy and hilarity among loyal subjects, and the Duke of Cumberland[3] never appeared in a Theatre without being saluted with

> "He comes! He comes! the Hero comes,
> Sound, sound the trumpet, beat the drums."[4]

The season at Vaux Hall was very prosperous, and songs of triumph were sung every night. The King went thither several times in person, and the prince and princess of Wales, his present Majesty's illustrious Parents,[5] very frequently.

However, the *Bucks* of those days, were rather more riotous than the libertins and men of spirit of the present times. One Night after the performance in Spring gardens was over Mr Arne, Mrs Arne, her sister Miss Young, and myself being just sat down to supper on the 1st floor of a lodging house by the water side, we were alarmed at a loaded plug coming through the window & falling in the middle of a codling pie and cream wch broke the dish and splashed us all over—Mr A. & I instantly descended with hearty intentions to discover & chastise the ruffians who had been guilty of the outrage. When in issuing forth, who shd we meet at the door but Sr Chas Sedley[6] and Capt. Harvey[7] drunk, and in a fury to find one of the waiters who had refused to give them any more wine, and who in pursuing they thought had taken shelter in our lodging house; we assured them that no such had entered the house; and invited them upstairs to partake of our supper; and they accepted the invitation and eat some cold meat & fragments of our broken pye. These gentlemen being so drunk and riotous that they were refused more wine, wch enraged them so that they broke the lamps, beat not only the waiters, but Mr Dawson the rich glass manufactur[er][8] of Lambeth and Cook the Poet,[9] friends of Tyers the Proprietor of the Gardens,[10] for remonstrating with them for the ravages they were committing; then driving Mr Tyers from the bar took possession of it, got wine & glasses from one of the terrified waiters, got astride on the bar and drank bumpers hand to fist, the bottle in one hand & the glass in the other, till seeing one of the waiters run by who had affronted them, they quitted the bar & pursued him to the water side, where they thought they had kennelled him in our apartments

a Bill was filed against these bacchanalian gentn By Mr Dawson & the poet Cook for assault & battery wch cost them £1500.

Poor Tyers durst not appear in this prosecution, though his losses were very considerable—in the destruction of bottles, glasses, & Lamps; but he feared offending the Corps of Bucks; and Sir Chas Sedley was one of the most agreeable and pleasing men in the kingdom, except during these fits of inebriety. I lived much in his set afterwards, & never loved any man of fashion more sincerely; he was a natural English character; frank, open, and full of wit and pleasant humour. He was very handsome in his youth, always extremely fond of Music, & the best gentleman performer on the German Flute, of his time. I had not the honour of knowing Capt. Harvey; but he had so many friends and admirers, that amidst all his madcappery he must have had inherent good qualities to ballance his poliçoneries.

1. CB may be referring to a revival of John Dennis's *Liberty Asserted; or, French Perfidy Displayed,* performed at Covent Garden on 23 and 25 April 1746, but more probably to the *Occasional Oratorio* by Handel, in the rehearsal of which he assisted on 7 Feb. 1746 but

which ran for three, not two, nights: 14, 19, and 26 Feb. 1746. See Frag. 31, n. 5; for Handel's comment on playing to a half-empty house, see Frag. 30, n. 5.

2. 16 April 1746.

3. William Augustus, Duke of Cumberland (1721–65), son of King George II, commanded the English forces that defeated the Young Pretender.

4. Opening lines of Henry Carey's song for three voices from *Britannia,* an entertainment sung at Goodman's Inn Fields Theatre on 11 Feb. 1734 on the occasion of Princess Anne's marriage to the Prince of Orange. For printed scores of this popular song, see BL, shelf-marks G.308 [112]; H.1994.a [45]; H. 1652.ww.3).

5. Frederick Louis (1707–51), Prince of Wales, on 26 April 1736 married Augusta (1719–72), daughter of Frederick II, Duke of Saxe-Gotha.

6. Sir Charles Sedley (1721?–78), 2d Baronet of Nuthall, near Nottingham, succeeded his father in 1730; educated at Westminster (1732) and Oxford (1739); M.P. for Nottingham 1747–54, 1774–78. In 1765 he was indirectly involved in a duel between his friend William Chaworth and Lord Byron (*AR,* 8: 208–12).

7. Probably Augustus John Hervey (1724–79), second son of John Lord Hervey (Alexander Pope's "Sporus"). He had a reputation for "madcappery." In 1744, while lieutenant in the Royal Navy, he privately married Elizabeth Chudleigh and sailed for the West Indies, returning to England in Oct. 1746; the event CB mentions probably occurred after this date. He was captain in the navy 1747–75 and won much admiration for his vigorous support of Admiral Byng. The other, less likely, candidates are Lord John's brothers: Henry Aston Hervey (1701–48), who in 1735 became captain of the 1st Dragoon Guards but left the army in 1742; or his younger brother Felton Hervey (1713–73).

8. John Dawson (b. 1708?), "of the Plate Glass-house, near Vauxhall." He died 23 Dec. 1761 (*GM,* 31:604; Barker/Stenning, 1:253).

9. Thomas Cooke (1703–56), Grub Street writer whose translation of Hesiod (1728) earned him the nickname of "Hesiod" Cooke and a place in Pope's *Dunciad* (2:130). He also wrote for the stage, songs for Vauxhall, and a libretto for one of Rich's harlequinades.

10. Jonathan Tyers had leased the Spring Gardens at Vauxhall and opened them on 7 June 1732. See Frag. 38, n.1.

FRAGMENT 38

London, 1745–50

[Tyers,[1] who had established Vaux-]Hall gardens, as a place of public entertainment & ⟨evening⟩ retreat in summer from the dust & heat of the capital, was a man of strong parts & good taste, with a considerable portion of Wit. Of his origin I know nothing, but that he must have had some patrimony to have enabled him to live in the great world, with wch he seemed well acquainted, & to set such an expensive & complicated machine a-going. He seems in his youth to have been very well acquainted with Con: Philips,[2] and I have heard him describe his first interview, and subsequent scenes with that Lady, in a very lively manner. He had established a weekly meeting, a kind of club of Wits, at the Royal Oak, before I was acquainted with him; consisting of Mr Dawson of Lambeth above-mentioned;[3] Harry Hatsel,[4] equally witty, corpulent, sensual, and profligate, with Falstaff; Moore, author of Fables for the female sex;[5] Cook, the translator of Hesiod;[6] & Harry Fielding[7] had been among them before my time.

Mr Tyers was very powerful in conversation; but his liberality, taste, and resources in variety of expedients in laying out, and[8]

1. Jonathan Tyers (d. 1767) had obtained in 1728 a lease of the Spring Gardens at Vauxhall, which he opened as Vauxhall Gardens in 1732 and in 1752 became proprietor. He was an enterprising manager. Johnson took him off as "Tom Restless" in *Idler* no. 48, while Fielding in *Amelia* praised his "truly elegant taste" (see n. 7, below).

2. Teresia Constantia Phillips (1709–65), celebrated courtesan, known as "Con. Phillips," apparently started her career at age twelve with "Thomas Grimes," the future 4th Earl of Chesterfield. In 1748 she published her memoirs, *An Apology for the Conduct of Mrs. Teresia Constantia Phillips* (3 vols., 1748), which had run through four editions by 1761. They were edited by Paul Whitehead, whose services she is said to have remunerated "in kind" (*Dictionary of National Biography*).

3. See Frag. 37, n. 8.

4. Henry Hatsell (d. 1762), bencher of the Middle Temple, was the son of judge Sir Henry Hatsell (1641–1714).

5. Edward Moore (1712–57), having failed as linen-draper, turned to literature. His *Fables for the Female Sex* came out in 1744. He later turned to playwriting and in 1753 became editor of the *World,* a satirical weekly.

6. See Frag. 37, n. 9.

7. As Martin Battestin informs us, Fielding's friendship with Tyers, Moore, and Cooke went back to the 1730s. Fielding pays a handsome tribute to Tyers in *Amelia,* IX.ix. For his friendship with Edward Moore, see Battestin's edition of *Tom Jones,* pp. 729–30n. CB's statement here appears to be the only evidence for Tyers's "club of Wits."

8. "His taste, liberality, and spirit," writes CB, evidently drawing on his manuscript memoirs, "in supporting and ornamenting this elegant place of amusement with paintings by Hogarth and Hayman; an excellent band of music; an orchestra in the form of a temple in the open air, with an organ equal in size and workmanship to many of the most noble instruments of that kind in our churches; and a constant succession of ingenious exhibitions; rendered it a public place more attractive, admired, and imitated by foreigners, than any one our country could boast. In every part of Europe a nominal Vauxhall has been established; nor was there a theatre on the continent thirty years ago [in the 1770s], with scenery and ball[e]t pantomimes, without an attempt at representing Vauxhall" ("Tyers" in Rees).

FRAGMENT 39   London, 1745–50

a Rotunda for wet weather, in wch he employed Hayman to paint Lord Clives victories & conquests in India.[1] He contrived the representation of a Cascade without water, with wch the public has been amused, between the acts of the Music,[2] near 60 years: And every year some new specimens of his taste & invention were exhibited, to vary the entertainment of his paradisaical place.

Before I leave it, I must relate an instance of *good luck* that happened to the fat & facetious Harry Hatsel, one of Tyers's club of wits, who calling one very hot summer's morning on Mr Arne, in the way of visit, at his apartm^ts in Marble Hall, a spacious old mansion in ruin, wth an extensive garden totally wild, neglected and tempting with no forbidden fruit; but Mr Arne being from home, I did the honours, & took him into the garden, or rather desert,[3]

1. Francis Hayman (1708–76), later one of the founders of the Royal Academy, began as a scene-painter for Fleetwood, the proprietor of Drury Lane, and is best known for the series of pictures ornamenting the alcoves at Vauxhall, which he and Hogarth painted (for a list, see Leslie/Taylor, 1:327–31).

2. According to CB, Tyers "began with a small band of wind-instruments only, before he erected an orchestra, and furnished it with an organ; but in the summer of 1745, to render it still more attractive, he added, for the first time, vocal to his instrumental performances. Here the talents of many of our national musicians were first displayed and first encouraged; here Collet and Pinto on the violin, Snow on the trumpet, Millar on the bassoon, Worgan on the organ, &c. annually increased in merit and favour. Here Messrs. Arne, Lowe, and the elder Reinhold sung during many years, with great applause, Dr. Arne's ballads, duets, dialogues, and trios, which were soon after circulated throughout the kingdom, to the great improvement of our national taste. During this first summer, his little dialogue of Colin and Phoebe, written by the late Mr. Moore, author of 'Fables for the Female Sex,' was constantly encored every night for more than three months successively" ("Tyers" in Rees).

3. The conclusion of the anecdote, which related the ludicrous "misfortune . . . at Marble Hall" (Frag. 45) of Harry Hatsell (Frag. 38, n. 4), is unfortunately missing.

FRAGMENT 40   London, mid 1740s

[Garrick]

I, of course, availed myself of this [   ] privilege as often as I could, particularly when *he* acted,[1] whom I saw either from the Orchestra, or from behind the scenes. And such were his spirits at this time, that he c^d put off tragedy and put on comedy, like a garment, at his pleasure. One night I remember, after the most afflicting scenes of king Lear,[2] when the curtain was let down, peeping through one of the slits at the spectators all in tears, using their handkerchiefs, as frequently to their noses as eyes, he says—yes, yes, my dears. you have it, &, mopping his fingers, ran into the green-room. From some such flow of spirits as this, we may perhaps account for Dr Johnson's severe speech, wch he is said to have made when Garrick complained of him & Dr Sumner[3] talking and laughing so loud while he was acting in tragedy, that it destroyed his feeling: "No, no Davy (says Johnson) Punch never feels."[4]

In diverting children, wch Garrick was very fond of doing, he used to take off the old puppet-show *Punch,* placing himself against a wall, seeming to speak through a comb, & to be moved by wires. Nobody talked such pretty nonsense, as our great Roscius, to children & lap-dogs.[5]

At this time, when the house was much crowded, gentlemen were allowed to stand behind the scenes, & between the acts to go into the green-room. One gentleman particularly was noticed by Mrs Woffington,[6] who took an enormous quantity of snuff, wch was travelling ⟨post⟩ from his nostrils to his mouth, without his checking its current with his handkerchief. Woffington, giving Garrick a jog, whispers, "did you ever see anything so beastly! Why now nobody dares tell this filthy gentleman to blow his nose"—Yes, says, G. I dare—Upon wch he calls out aloud to the whole company.—"Come! I'll make a proposal."—When all stared at him, curious to hear his proposition—"Let us all blow our noses." Woffington ran out of the room screaming with laughter—& I was obliged to follow her in order to enjoy the burst of laughter wch the proposal provoked, & never knew whether the gentleman felt its force, or still gave the snuff as free a passage as ever.

One night when Garrick & Quin acted together at Drury Lane in the first part of Henry the IVth, Garrick in Hotspur & Quin in Falstaff,[7] while the K^t was trying to lift the dead Hero on his shoulder to demand the reward for killing him, he asks G. in a whisper if he'll sup with him at the Bedford head?[8] when G. says, *sotto voce,* "it is not in my power, I have promised to sup with Woffington".—"Oh, Oh, you have?" when, putting both knees on his chest, & pressing on him with all his weight till in as loud a whisper as became a dead man, G. says—"O God! you'll kill me—I ha—ve not promised!—I'll do—o whatever you order me!"—[9]

By using my privilege of being behind the curtain and in the music-room, I saw & heard of many curious scenes & incidents wch were concealed from the public.

Mrs Clive, the best comic actress, perhaps, that ever trod our stage,[10] was perhaps the worst singer, except in songs of humour such as The Life of a beau—The Cuckoo[11]—and the songs in the part of Lucy in the Beggar's opera, wch her mimicry and humour rendered extremely entertaining. But wth a bad voice, out of tune, and a total ignorance of Music, her singing was detestable. Arne & she had probab[l]y had a quarrel before he went to Ireland;[12] for she refused to sing his Music. And when he new set the Tempest,[13] and she undertook the part of Ariel, he sent her the beautiful and characteristic air: "Where the bee sucks there suck I"—she sent it back untried, and employed Defesch, a good contrapuntist, but a dull composer[14] to set all the songs in her part.[15] After I left Mr Arne (long before he received his degree of Doctor in Music at Oxford)[16] he found his profits as a composer so small, by the constant failure of his Oratorios, that on the death of Gordon,[17] he accepted the place of first Violin to the D.L. band. When one night Mrs Clive having undertaken a song in wch she was imperfect: as she was given to be out of time as well as tune; at a hitch, she calls out loud to the band, "why dont the fellows mind what they are ab^t?" At the end of the Act Arne went up stairs in the name of the whole band to remonstrate against her insolence, when the only satisfaction he obtained, was a slap on the face. In return, he literally turned her over his knee and gave her such a manual flagellation as she probably had not received since she quitted the nursery; but as a proof that she had made a good defence, he came back without his wig, all over blood from her scratches, & his long point ruffles torn & dangling over his nails.[18]

1. CB must have seen Garrick soon after his arrival in London, when "his Master, then only Mr Arne . . . procured him a station in the Orchestra of Drury Lane" (BL, Add. MSS 48345, f. 22^r). At the end of the 1744–45 season Fleetwood sold Drury Lane to Lacy; on 9 April 1747 Garrick became Lacy's partner in the management. As a supernumerary member of the Drury Lane band, CB heard much backstage gossip.

2. Garrick played Lear at Drury Lane fifteen times between 24 Oct. 1744 and 25 Jan. 1750. CB probably refers to one of the following performances: 30 Oct., 14 Nov., or 23 Dec. 1747 (see Oman, p. 107).

3. Robert Carey Sumner (1729–71), headmaster of Harrow and friend of Dr. Johnson.

4. A simpler version of this anecdote ("Punch never feels") appeared in "Apophthegms, sentiments, &c," Johnson's *Works* (1787), 11:206. Five years later Murphy recorded it as part of a conversation at which he, not Sumner, was present, in his *Essay on Johnson's Life and Genius* (1792); see *Johnsonian Misc.* 1:457. "It may have been on one of these occasions when he was wringing hearts

as Lear that Mrs Clive, who had just emerged from one of her standing fights with her manager, was heard to announce to the wings, 'Damn him! he could act a gridiron!' " (Oman, p. 107). Mme d'Arblay describes Garrick's manner of acting "as if his face, and even his form, had been put into his own hands to be worked upon like Man a Machine" (*Mem.*, 1:170). Diderot later advocated this sort of "method acting" in his *Paradoxe sur le comédien* (1773).

5. "How many pities that he has no children," exclaims Fanny Burney, "for he is extremely, nay passionately fond of them" (*ED*, 1:150). She recounts how in the 1760s Garrick used to amuse the Burney children in CB's house in Poland Street. He would invite them to "Mrs. Garrick's box in the theatre," and then imitate "to Dr. Burney" their reactions there: "first the amazement; next, the indignation; and lastly, the affright and disappointment. . . . In these various changes, Mr. Garrick altered the expression of his features, and almost his features themselves" (*Mem.*, 1:169–70; see also Oman, pp. 268–69).

6. Margaret or "Peg" Woffington (1713?–60) came to London from Dublin in 1740 and soon became one of the city's leading actresses. She played with Garrick and became his mistress in 1742. Garrick proposed to her, found her unfaithful, and in the spring of 1745 broke off the affair, though both continued to act at Drury Lane.

7. Late in 1746 James Quin (1693–1766), who excelled in the role of Falstaff, persuaded Garrick to support him as Hotspur. There were five performances of *Henry IV, Part I* at Covent Garden (not at Drury Lane as CB states) between 6 and 13 Dec. Garrick fell ill after the fifth performance and never acted Hotspur again, as it did not suit his character (see Davies 1784, 1:224–27; Davies 1780, 1: 100–101).

8. "No joke ever raised such loud and repeated mirth, in the galleries, as Sir John's labour in getting the body of Hotspur on his back. . . . Quin had no difficulty in perching Garrick upon his shoulders, who looked like a dwarf on the back of a giant" (Davies 1784, 1:273–74). The anecdote is mentioned in a slighter form (Quin saying audibly to all in the wings, "Where shall we sup to-night?") in Parson (pp. 130–31).

9. This amusing elaboration by CB is a bit suspect, as Garrick's affair with Peg Woffington had cooled off by the spring of 1745 (see n. 6, above).

10. For Kitty Clive, see Frag. 34, n. 2. She was highly temperamental, "a mixture of combustibles," wrote Tate Wilkinson (3:41–45), who saw much of her behind the scenes.

11. "Life of a Beau" is a song from *The Coffee-House,* by Henry Carey (Drury Lane, 26 Jan. 1738). For "The Cuckoo," see Frag. 22, n. 3.

12. Arne and his wife went to Ireland toward the end of 1742 and returned in the autumn of 1744.

13. Performed 31 Jan. 1746 at Drury Lane, with Arne's music for the masque "Neptune and Apollo," and the song "Where the bee sucks."

14. Willem De Fesch or Defesch (1687–1757?), Dutch composer, came to England after 1731. Although his numerous songs were published first in single sheets, then in a collected edition issued by Walsh (c. 1752), Mr. John A. Parkinson informs us that he has never seen any of these Shakespeare settings by De Fesch and doubts whether they were ever published. CB remarks elsewhere that De Fesch was "a voluminous composer, but his productions were in general dry and uninteresting" (*Hist. Mus.*, 4:672; Mercer, 2: 1015).

15. "Which was a greater loss to the public, than disgrace to Dr. Arne," adds CB in

print, "who was as superior to Defesch in genius, as Mingotti was to Clive in the art of singing. Yet so little do we know our own powers, that though she was a most admirable and original actress in such comic parts as Nell in 'The Devil to Pay,' and Mrs. Heidelberg, in the 'Clandestine Marriage,' she never was so happy as when she played lady Townley, and was attempting to sing fine serious Italian songs: though she had neither ear, voice, nor knowledge of music, so that had Defesch's songs been less dull than they usually were, they would never have been sung into public favour by Mrs. Clive" ("Defesch" in Rees).

16. Arne received his Mus.D. at Oxford on 6 July 1759. CB left him in Sept. 1748 (Frag. 47).

17. Mr. Gordon (fl. 1736–45), violinist. CB says that Gordon "in the year 1744 played the first violin in Drury-lane play-house. He was a young man, born in Norfolk, who had travelled to Italy for improvement. He was very near-sighted, and always played in spectacles. He succeeded [c. 1736] Charke, had a strong hand, good tone, and was well fitted to his station. He generally played a concerto in the second music, as was then the practice, which was very attractive" ("Gordon" in Rees). For his brother John (fl. 1744–73), the violoncellist, see ibid.; and Highfill, 6:275–76. For Richard Charke, see Appendix B.

18. The fragment ends with CB's comment on Arne's selfishness (see Frag. 31, n. 1). Elsewhere, CB writes: "Arne, when composer in salary at Drury-lane theatre, composed very pleasing and appropriate act-tunes to many of the stock plays, which never were printed, but preserved in MS. in the archives of the old theatre; but we suppose that the strains of Orpheus or Amphion might be as easily recovered as these compositions" ("Entr'acte" in Rees).

FRAGMENT 41

London, Summer 1746

This gentleman[1] *one morning, while trying a new instrument at the house of Kirkman, the first harpsichord maker of the times,*[2] *expressed a wish to receive musical instruction from some one who had mind and cultivation, as well as finger and ear; lamenting, with strong contempt, that, in the musical tribe, the two latter were generally dislocated from the two former; and gravely asking Kirkman whether he knew any young musician who was fit company for a gentleman.*

Kirkman, with honest zeal to stand up for the credit of the art by which he prospered, and which he held to be insulted by this question, warmly answered that he knew many; but, very particularly, one member of the harmonic corps, who had as much music in his tongue as in his hands, and who was as fit company for a prince as for an orchestra.

Mr. Greville, with much surprise, made sundry and formal inquiries into the existence, situation, and character of what he called so great a phenomenon; protest-

ing there was nothing he so much desired as the extraordinary circumstance of finding any union of sense with sound.

The replies of the good German were so exciting, as well as satisfactory, that Mr. Greville became eager to see the youth thus extolled; but charged Mr. Kirkman not to betray a word of what had passed, that the interview might be free from restraint, and seem to be arranged merely for shewing off the several instruments that were ready for sale, to a gentleman who was disposed to purchase one of the most costly.

To this injunction Mr. Kirkman agreed, and conscientiously adhered.

A day was appointed, and the meeting took place.

Young Burney, with no other idea than that of serving Kirkman, immediately seated himself at an instrument, and played various pieces of Geminiani, Corelli, and Tartini, whose compositions were then most in fashion. But Mr. Greville, secretly suspicious of some connivance, coldly and proudly walked about the room; took snuff from a finely enamelled snuff-box, and looked at some prints, as if wholly without noticing the performance.

He had, however, too much penetration not to perceive his mistake, when he remarked the incautious carelessness with which his inattention was returned; for soon, conceiving himself to be playing to very obtuse ears, young Burney left off all attempt at soliciting their favour; and only sought his own amusement by trying favourite passages, or practising difficult ones, with a vivacity which shewed that his passion for his art rewarded him in itself for his exertions. But coming, at length, to keys of which the touch, light and springing, invited his stay, he fired away in a sonata of Scarlatti's, with an alternate excellence of execution and expression, so perfectly in accord with the fanciful flights of that wild but masterly composer, that Mr. Greville, satisfied no scheme was at work to surprise or to win him; but, on the contrary, that the energy of genius was let loose upon itself, and enjoying, without premeditation, its own lively sports and vagaries; softly drew a chair to the harpsichord, and listened, with unaffected earnestness, to every note.

Nor were his ears alone curiously awakened; his eyes were equally occupied to mark the peculiar performance of intricate difficulties; for the young musician had invented a mode of adding neatness to brilliancy, by curving the fingers, and rounding the hand, in a manner that gave them a grace upon the keys quite new at that time, and entirely of his own devising.[3]

To be easily pleased, however, or to make acknowledgment of being pleased at all, seems derogatory to strong self-importance; Mr. Greville, therefore, merely said, "You are fond, Sir, it seems, of Italian music?"

The reply to this was striking up, with all the varying undulations of the crescendo, the diminuendo, the pealing swell, and the "dying, dying fall," belonging to the powers of the pedal, that most popular masterpiece of Handel's, the Coronation Anthem.[4]

This quickness of comprehension, in turning from Italian to German, joined to the grandeur of the composition, and the talents of the performer, now irresistibly vanquished Mr. Greville; who, convinced of Kirkman's truth with regard to the harmonic powers of this son of Apollo, desired next to sift it with regard to the wit.

Casting off, therefore, his high reserve, with his jealous surmises, he ceased to listen to the music, and started some theme that was meant to lead to conversation.

But as this essay, from not knowing to what the youth might be equal, consisted of such inquiries as, "Have you been in town long, Sir?" or, "Does your taste call you back to the country, Sir?" &c. &c., his young hearer, by no means preferring this inquisitorial style to the fancy of Scarlatti, or the skill and depth of Handel, slightly answered, "Yes, Sir," or "No, Sir;" and, perceiving an instrument not yet tried, darted to it precipitately, and seated himself to play a voluntary.

The charm of genuine simplicity is nowhere more powerful than with the practised and hackneyed man of the world; for it induces what, of all things, he most rarely experiences, a belief in sincerity.

Mr. Greville, therefore, though thwarted, was not displeased; for in a votary of the art he was pursuing, he saw a character full of talents, yet without guile; and conceived, from that moment, an idea that it was one he might personally attach. He remitted, therefore, to some other opportunity, a further internal investigation.

Mr. Kirkman now came forward to announce, that in the following week he should have a new harpsichord, with double keys,[5] *and a deepened bass, ready for examination.*

They then parted, without any explanation on the side of Mr. Greville; or any idea on that of the subject of these memoirs, that he and his acquirements were objects of so peculiar a speculation.

At the second interview, young Burney innocently and eagerly flew at once to the harpsichord, and tried it with various recollections from his favourite composers.

Mr. Greville listened complacently and approvingly; but, at the end of every strain, made a speech that he intended should lead to some discussion.

Young Burney, however, more alive to the graces of melody than to the subtleties of argument, gave answers that always finished with full-toned chords, which as constantly modulated into another movement; till Mr. Greville, tired and impatient, suddenly proposed changing places, and trying the instrument himself.

He could not have devised a more infallible expedient to provoke conversation; for he thrummed his own chosen bits by memory with so little skill or taste, yet with a pertinacity so wearisome, that young Burney, who could neither hearken to such playing, nor turn aside from such a player, caught with alacrity at every opening to discourse, as an acquittal from the fatigue of mock attention.

This eagerness gave a piquancy to what he said, that stole from him the diffidence that might otherwise have hung upon his inexperience; and endued him with a courage for uttering his opinions, that might else have faded away under the trammels of distant respect.

Mr. Greville, however, was really superior to the mawkish parade of unnecessary etiquette in private circles, where no dignity can be offended. . . . He grew, therefore, so lively and entertaining, that young Burney became as much charmed with his company as he had been wearied by his music. . . .

This meeting concluded the investigation; music, singing her gay triumph, took her stand at the helm; and a similar victory for capacity and information awaited but a few intellectual skirmishes, on poetry, politics, morals, and literature,—in the midst of which Mr. Greville, suddenly and gracefully holding out his hand, fairly acknowledged his scheme, proclaimed its success, and invited the unconscious victor to accompany him to Wilbury House.[6]

1. Fulke Greville (c. 1717–c. 1804), of Wilbury, Wilts., son of the Hon. Algernon Greville, 2d son of the 5th Baron Brooke. After attending Winchester 1728–33 and Oxford (matric. 3 Jan. 1733/4, Brasenose College), he went on a Grand Tour. He was M.P. for Monmouth 1747–54. In 1756 he published *Maxims, Characters, and Reflections*: "Several of the former are pretty; all the latter . . . absurd," wrote Horace Walpole to Henry Seymour Conway (YW, 37:460).

Sometime in the summer of 1746, the twenty-year-old CB became acquainted with Greville, an event that turned out to be a milestone: it introduced CB for the first time into high society. Mme d'Arblay's account, given here, is touched up by the art of the *romancière* but is almost certainly based on portions of her father's memoirs that she destroyed.

2. Jacob Kirckman (1710–92), "an excellent harpsichord maker" of Swiss extraction, came to England in the 1730s, married the widow of his employer Tabel, and set up a shop in Great Pulteney Street East, where this encounter took place. For CB's anecdotes about him, see Appendix B.

3. In his letter to Katherine Raper, 12 April 1776 (Berg), CB elaborates on "my Evolutions of Fingering." He recommends a young scholar "keeping her Hands *round*, wch can only be done by the Thumbs constantly hanging over the Keys." See "Fingering" in Rees, which shows that CB derived other aspects of his technique from Couperin's *L'Art de toucher le clavecin* (1717); and Frag. 84, n. 9.

4. The first of four anthems composed for the coronation of George II in 1727, published in the first collected edition by Walsh, c. 1743. For CB's account of it, see *Commem.*, pt. 2, pp. 26–27. Mme d'Arblay here indulges in a novelist's fancy: the harpsichord on which CB was performing had no pedals, hence no swell.

5. I.e., two keyboards. Boalch (p. 84) says: "It is possible that Kirkman made one or two harpsichords reaching down to the C below his usual bottom F." More than 150 of Kirckman's harpsichords have survived.

6. Wilbury House in Wiltshire—designed and built in 1710 by auditor William Benson, who sold it c. 1740 to Greville—was set in an estate "of 2000 to 3000 acres" and "about 7 miles in extent, surrounded by a plantation, and 4 miles of it enclosed by an oak paling." Perhaps the first venture of the Inigo Jones revival, it foreshadowed a new type of country house, the villa. Greville added single-storey wings, each containing a room with rococo drops of musical instruments and pendant medallions of classical heads, as well as other decorations. It is described in Campbell (1:51–52), and in two copiously illustrated articles in *Country Life* (see Tipping; Hussey), from which the information above is taken. CB fondly recollected memories of his early days at Wilbury House when he revisited it almost half a century later (CB to Frances Crewe, 8 Oct. 1792, Osborn; Frag. 44, n. 14).

BRIDGE: FRAGMENTS 41–42

"I may be said to have been in the great world ever since I went first to Wilbury with Mr Greville, wch is now near 60 years—," Burney later wrote, "& though only a Musician, I was never sent to the 2^d table, nor was I any *gene* to the company wth whom I had the honour of dining . . . I have never lost one friend by a *quarrel,* except M^r G[reville].—There must have been something very inoffensive at least, in my conduct and manners among my betters abroad & at home, to be so countenanced—But I shall get into Puffing, wch I always hated in myself & others—& therefore . . . I shall drop the subject" (CB to Lady Crewe, [Oct. 1807], Osborn).

FRAGMENT 42

[Character of Fulke Greville]

He had not only made the tour of Fr. and Italy, but knew the manners of the court, & higher circles in his own country: Architecture, Sculpture, Painting, Music and Poetry. Add to this the fame he had acquired as the best & most graceful gentleman Tennis player; as driving a set of bay horses, many of wch were fit for hunters, but all had some blood in them, and two or three had been in training for the Turf; one of wch he used as a road horse, when he did not chuse to enter his carriage; but however he travelled, he was attended by his two servants on horseback, wth each a Fr. Horn on his shoulder, on wch they played well wherever he stopt, either to dine or sleep. All these were striking and dazling circumstances to young ladies; but he had such a passion for the Turf & for play, as alarmed the fathers. He had lost considerable sums at Whites[1] and at Bath, and had 14 running horses in training, 6 or 7 of wch had the honour of the Godolphin Arabian for their sire.[2] He set off with a pack of hounds, a man Cook, and while a bachelor he frequently gave dinners to large parties of persons of the highest rank & fashion. All this had happened before he honoured me with his notice, & had, I believe, materially injured his fortune, & obliged him to mortgage & sell several of his estates.[3]

1. White's Chocolate-house in St. James's Street was the resort of men of fashion for high play. On 5 Sept. 1741 Horace Walpole wrote to Mann that Fulke Greville "lost near fifteen thousand pounds to Janson [Henry Janssen], you know, a professed sharper" (YW, 17:126).

2. One of the three famous ancestors of the British thoroughbreds, the Godolphin Arabian (c. 1723–52) was actually a Barb, imported from France. For an account of him and his equally famous offspring, see *Encyclo-*

paedia Britannica, 11th ed., 13:720–21. A print of him by Stubbs in the British Library is reproduced in Parker (p. 135).

3. Later, CB gave a more critical account of his stay with Greville. He spoke of "the full use he had of my Time as an equivalent for his Money—of the sacrifices I made of all kind of Business in order to attend him in Town & Country, without ⌐wages or even Cloaths, except now and then one of his old Coats⌐" (CB to Samuel Crisp, 21 Jan. 1774, Berg).

FRAGMENT 43   Wilbury, Autumn 1747

In the Autumn of 1747, I went again with M[^r] G[reville to] Wilbury; where I met with Mr Crisp,[1] a man of infinite taste in all the fine Arts, an excellent Scholar, & who having resided many years in Italy, & being possessed of a fine tenor voice, sung in as good taste as any professed opera singer with the same kind of voice, I ever heard. Mr Boughton[2] who played a good fiddle, & who had been a constant attendant at the Opera in Handel's time, being extremely partial to him & the old Italian School; the disputes & partialities of these two Gentlemen were of singular service to me: I had no harpsichord Music with me but Handel's organ concertos,[3] wch I had transcribed at Shrewsbury; except a concerto or two of my master Arne's, the only music he ever taught me. But Mr Greville, of the same school and party as Crisp, made me a present of the two first books of Scarlatti's lessons, published by Roseingrave,[4] of w^(ch) I had never heard more than the one above mentioned and w^(ch) I had transcribed and learned by stealth, after hearing Mr Arne play it in the dark. This was the lesson I played to Dr Pepusch, when he was on a visit at Mr Arne's. w^(ch) he called, to my great astonishment, a *bagatelle*;[5]—but it was neither a Canon, nor a Fugue. And Mr Boughton, the father of Sr Boughton Rous, & of Lady Templetown,[6] a sensible & accomplished country gentleman, to support his musical principles, & make head against Scarlatti, & the Italian School, made me a present of Handel's two books of Lessons;[7] w^(ch) obliged me to practice both, & to admire the merit of both in a total[ly] different way: Scarlatti fanciful, capricious, wild, & full of new effects & passages; Handel rich in regular harmony, masterly in design, original, grand & new in the style of his youth, even in Italy. These were my exercises, and practice of a morning before the family was up; and my exhibitions of an evening, alternately, to the Abetters of the two schools.[8] But besides lessons, I had to play & hum a great deal of vocal music, w^(ch) Mr Greville had brought from Italy, and both Mr Crisp & Mr Greville who had heard it sung in Italy by great singers, with their voice & advice, gave me a good notion how to express it on the harp^d. Mr Boughton did the same by Handel's best opera and oratorio songs that were then in print: so that my studies

1. Samuel Crisp (1707–83), only son of Samuel Crisp (d. 1717) and Florence née Williams (d. 1719), admitted to Eton in 1718. About 1735 he went on a Grand Tour and spent some time in Italy, where he perhaps met Fulke Greville, who on his return invited him to Wilbury House. His tragedy *Virginia* was produced by Garrick on 25 Feb. 1754 without success. Fanny Burney, later Crisp's favourite correspondent, portrays him "as a *diletante,* both in music & in painting," who made himself something of a laughing stock at Wilbury House by prefering his "favourite pieces of Bach of Berlin, Handel, Scarlatti" to hunting (*Mem.,* 1:48–55). His portrait by Edward Francesco Burney is reproduced in *HFB,* pl. 1.

2. Shuckburgh Boughton (1705–63) of Poston Court, Herts., married Fulke Greville's eldest sister Mary, by whom he had three sons and three daughters.

3. Handel had published a set of organ concerti (Opus 4) in 1738 and a second set (Opus 5) in 1740.

4. *Forty-Two Suits of Lessons for the Harpsichord by Sig^r Domenico Scarlatti,* printed in two volumes, large quarto, by John Johnson at the Harp and Crown (*RISM,* 7:S1191), was edited by Scarlatti's great English admirer, Thomas Roseingrave.

5. This meeting with Dr. Pepusch probably occurred in 1746 (see Frag. 35).

6. Charles William Boughton Rouse (1747–1821), M.P., was the second son of Shuckburgh Boughton (n. 2, above), whose third daughter, Elizabeth, married in August 1769 the Hon. Clotworthy Upton (1721–85), cr. 1776 Baron Templetown.

7. Handel's *Suites de pièces pour le clavecin* came out in two volumes, the first published in 1720, the second in 1733.

8. In his manuscript sketch of a history of

instrumental music in England, CB wrote: "Our Music for keyed-Instruments has particularly occupied my attention for many years. I think few sudden & general Changes of style have escaped me. Till the publication of Handel's Harp^d Lessons, Concertos & Fugues for the Organ, we had no Music of that kind in England; & these Pieces were so masterly, new, & pleasing, that nothing else was listened to with equal Pleasure or imitat[ive]ly for near 50 years. The Lessons indeed of Domenico Scarlatti, were so wild, fanciful, difficult & eccentric as to be truly inimitable; and this was the only original Genius, who had no *Issue*; & who formed no School, & whose property was out of the reach of free-booters, Pilferers or Counterfeits. Next to these the more natural & ele-gant Style of *Alberti* captivated the Public, & was our object of imitation to every Smatterer in Composition throughout Europe. And I can recollect no general Revolution brought ab^t in the music of keyed-Instruments till the bold & Powerful Pieces of Schobert shewed the use of the Pianoforte & Pedal of the Harp^d & pointed out the means of imitating the light & shade of an Orchestra, & the Contrast & effect of a numerous band in the execution of Symphonies. This style continues still in favour on those instruments and as it is that of modern overtures, & full Pieces for Violins & wind-Instruments in general, wch can easily be adapted to their use, it will probably continue to enjoy equal longevity" (Mus. Nbk, pp. 246–47).

FRAGMENT 44

Wilbury, Autumn 1747

[Among the company at Wilbury House, I met a man] of infinite wit and pleasantry, Duke Hamilton, whose manners and character were not to be copied, but avoided;[1] M^r ⟨Streets⟩,[2] Mr Young of Dunford,[3] a strong marked character, for swaggering, meanness & lying, Mr Harris of Salesbury, the most amiable, learned, & worthy of men, who then lived the recluse life of a man of letters.[4] Mr Greville carried me to him very soon after my first arrival at Wilbury. This autumn[5] I saw the Dutchess of Queensbury;[6] & her singularities & humours, in saying everything that came uppermost, & treating the whole world as greatly her inferiours: Lord Talbot, a manly, bold, & robust character, somewhat too rough for a courtier, to all but the ladies.[7] These were chiefly dayly visitors; but with the inmates, M^r and Mrs Boughton & Crisp, I enjoyed tranquil study & practice in a morning, & their conversation and encouragement in performing the works of their favourite authors in the evening.

Mr Crisp had brought from Rome to England the first large Piano forte that was ever constructed, even at Rome. It was made by an English Monk of the name of Wood,[8] and I believe a present to his friend Mr Crisp, of whom Mr G. purchased it for 100 Guin[e]as. The touch was very imperfect, and mechanism clumsy; so that nothing but slow movements c^d be executed upon it. However [in] slow pieces, such as the dead march in Saul,[9] Arne's march in Zara,[10] and a very few pathetic strains in Italian operas, it had a magnificent & new effect in the Chiar'oscuri of wch with a little use it was capable. Experience was necessary to the performer upon it—wch by living in the house and trying effects and discovering the degree of force or delicacy of touch it was capable of, I gained considerable credit in showing it off.[11] And afterwards, when Plinius had rendered his Lyrichord[12] ready for exhibition & had constructed a *Piano Piece*,[13] as he called it, in imitation of Mr Greville's large P.F. he solicited me to display its powers to the public. But then I had other employm^ts wch I liked better than that of a shew-man.[14]

1. James Hamilton (1724–58) succeeded his father in 1743 as 6th Duke of Hamilton. Walpole (YW, 20:155, 302–3, 339) describes him in 1752 as frequently "popping out of bagnios and taverns," "hot, debauched, extravagant," and so violently in love with Elizabeth Gunning that at a masquerade "while he was playing at pharaoh . . . he saw neither the bank nor his own cards, which were of three hundred pounds each. He soon lost a thousand." After he married her in Feb. 1752, he became "the abstract of Scotch pride" and would "drink to nobody beneath the rank of earl."

2. Not identified. The name is barely legible.

3. Probably Edward Young (fl. 1747–59), whose family held the Manor of Little Durnford from 1548 to 1795. His wife Lucy (d. 1757) was perhaps a friend of James Harris (n. 4, below), who had leased land at Durnford in Salisbury in 1743 and later used the Prebendal House as a summer residence (information from Canon Cyril Witcomb).

4. James Harris (1709–80), classical scholar of Salisbury Close and Durnford, enjoyed a great reputation for erudition, though Dr. Johnson called him "a prig and a bad prig" (Hill/Powell, 2:225n; 3:245; 5:377). He encouraged concerts and the annual musical festival at Salisbury, and adapted words

to selections from Italian and German composers (published in two volumes by Joseph Corfe, the Salisbury organist). In 1744 he published *Three Treatises* (on art; on music, painting, and poetry; on happiness) and later *Hermes* (1751), which contained "his ingenious 'Essay on Music,'" in which he "illustrates his precepts and reflexions almost exclusively from Handel; but keeping pace with the times in the refinement of melody, without injuring harmony, Jomelli and Sacchini became his favourite composers: the first for rich harmony and grand new effects; the second for grace, pathos, and delicacy" ("Harris" in Rees). CB, who owned his works (*Cat. Misc. Lib.*, nos. 756–61), later met him in London (*ED*, 1:216) and corresponded with his daughter Louisa Margaret Harris (see his letter to her of [post 18] Jan. 1809, BL, Add. MSS 48345, ff. 43–44^v).

5. 1747.

6. Catherine née Hyde (d. 1777), Prior's "Kitty," married 10 March 1720 Charles Douglas (1698–1778), 3rd Duke of Queensberry. Her beauty and eccentricity made her notorious in the world of fashion, while her wit and kindness of heart won her the friendship of Gay, Swift, Pope, and other literary men. Her seat at Amesbury was close to Wilbury House.

7. William Talbot (1710–82), 2d Baron

Talbot, later (1761) cr. Earl Talbot, had eloped with Lady Frances, Duchess of Beaufort, in 1742. Walpole (YW, 17:453, 486) comments on "how she and Lord Talbot knew each other beside every green hedge." Elizabeth Pitt, sister of Lord Chatham, had been his mistress.

8. Not identified. All that is known of this instrument is the information given by CB here and in his article "Harpsichord" in Rees.

9. "This most happy and affecting movement, which has retained its favour near half a century," writes CB, "is so simple, solemn and sorrowful, that it can never be heard, even upon a single instrument, without exciting melancholy sensations" (*Commem.*, pt. 2, pp. 32–33). Handel's oratorio *Saul,* composed to a libretto by Charles Jennens, was first performed at the King's Theatre on 16 Jan. 1739. The dead march occurs in Act III. The original score is in the Royal Music Library (BL, R.M. 20.g.3).

10. Aaron Hill's *Zara,* to which Arne composed incidental music, had been produced at Drury Lane on 12 Jan. 1736. Arne's slow march survives in *The Compleat Tutor for the Hautboy* (published by J. Simpson, c. 1746; there were several subsequent editions).

11. "The tone of this instrument was . . . superior to that produced by quills," adds CB in his article "Harpsichord" in Rees, and the instrument "remained *unique* in this country for several years."

12. Roger Plenius (1696–1774) of South Audley Street, London, had patented in 1741 "the lyrichord, tuned by weights," and later "made a piano-forte in imitation of that of Mr. Greville. Of this instrument the touch was better, but the tone very much inferior" ("Harpsichord" in Rees). For "a description of the nature and construction of the lyrichord," see *General Magazine of Arts and Sciences,* Aug. 1755; and Boalch, pp. 120–21.

13. "Piece" in the sense of "contrivance," "specimen of handiwork" (*Oxford English Dictionary*).

14. The memories of Wilbury stayed long with CB. In 1800, after revisiting the place, he described it in a letter to Greville's daughter: "Wilbury, though sadly burnt up, looked very elegant & beautiful yesterday. And the trees & plantations, of wch I so well remember the planting more than 50 years ago, are grown. . . . The drive to the house, through the bordering wood, is charming. Lord bless me! There I saw many of the Pictures, and I believe all the Casts from antique statues, wch I so long since found there—In the Hall, wch is fitted up rather tawdrily, there is some ordinary sculpture over the Chimney, instead of the view of Stone-henge. But the Gial'antique table is there still—& the verd-antique in the drawing-room, on the left [of] the Hall. We dined in the room much enlarged, where the Japan bed whilom stood. All the space in front of the House . . . is now well wooded . . . & indeed, in riding round the domain, it has more the appearance of a *Ferme orné* than a Chateau or Villa . . . there is little alteration, I find, in the Garden or back grounds. But the ensemble strikes me as still in excellent taste" (CB to Frances Crewe, 23 Aug. [1800], Osborn).

BRIDGE: FRAGMENTS 44–45

"Handel, Geminiani & Corelli were the sole Divinities of my Youth," wrote Burney in 1781, "but I was drawn off from their exclusive worship before I was

20, by keeping company with travelled & heterodox gentlemen, who were partial to the Music of more modern composers whom they had heard in Italy. And for songs, those of Hasse[,] Vinci, Pergolesi, Rinaldo di Capua, Leo, Feo, Selli[t]i, Buranello, with a few of Domenico Scarlatti, won my heart, & weaned me from the ancient worship. However, at all times in my life I honoured an elaborate & learned composition for the Church whatever its age & country, & at all spare hours I was scoring pieces of Bird, Morley, Luca Marenzio, Stradella; and studying Palestrina, Steffani's admirable Duets, with Cantatas by old Scarlatti, Gasparini, the Baron D'Astorga, & Marcello" (to Thomas Twining, 14 Dec. 1781, Osborn). "Handel's compositions for the organ and harpsichord, with those of Scarlatti and Alberti, were our chief practise and delight, for more than fifty years" (*Hist. Mus.*, 2:510; Mercer, 2:405).

FRAGMENT 45   Bath, November 1747–February 1748

[At Bath]

After hunting for near a month & visiting & being visited by his neighbours, M[r] G. went to Bath & took me with him.[1] Here I got great Credit by playing Scarlatti lessons to Lord Holdernesse,[2] Lord Cowper,[3] & the 2 M[r] Franks's,[4] pas[s]ionately fond of Music. A bad old Harp[d] was hired of Chilcot organist of the Abbey;[5] Linley was then his apprentice.[6]

I saw the humours of high or rather deep, play, at hazard, & the private E O[7] table; Duke Hamilton,[8] Lord Chesterfield,[9] L[d] Waldgrave,[10] Lord Montford,[11] Sir Hugh Smithson,[12] M[r] Greville &c were usually of these Parties. Guineas were there in plenty, bank notes but few. I have seen 1000 G[s] in one heap, and Lord Holderness tired of winning small sums cr[i]ed out E [   ] little. No individual durst say dun; but 2 or 3 professed gamesters clubbed stakes and eased his Lord[p] very soon of his golden incumbrance. The chief Music at Bath was now at the Pump-room of a morning; I can remember no evening concerts, nor any other Music in the Ball rooms than Minuets & Country dances. I saw the tyranny of the Master of the ceremonies Beau Nash, wth his white hat under his arm and open breast, the coldest day in Winter;[13] I used to get up early in Pierpoint Street to see the great Lord Bolinbroke carried in a chair to the Pump room for privacy,[14] before the rest of the company was assembled.

D[r] Twisden the Bishop of Raphoe,[15] was now at Bath, and generally rode out in a morning on the Hills with Ld Holderness and Mr Greville; I then used to be mounted and ride out with them, when it frequently happened that races were run to some certain point by the Peer, the Bishop & the Commoner wch to me was very good sport, particularly one morning, when the goal was a Haystack in a distant field, between wch there was a five-bar gate to leap, in attempting wch the Prelate's horse did not clear the gate, but got intangled between the two upper bars transferring all the impetus intended for clearing the gate, to the rider, the B^P was hurled into the Air & seemed to fly into the next field while his horse remained stationary; wch was quite as good a joke to me as Harry Hatsels misfortune had been at Marble Hall.[16] I thought I sh^d never compose my muscles again: to see a B^P try to leap a 5 bar gate and fail! was a joke at my time of life, a far ridere a morto.

From Bath Mr G. went to London, & I returned to my Master Arne & the Playhouse where though I was not a regular member of the Orchestra

1. According to the *Bath Journal*, "Mr. Greville" arrived on 2 Nov. 1747.

2. Robert D'Arcy (1718–78), 4th Earl of Holdernesse, later secretary of state, had arrived on 12 Oct. He developed a great passion for opera early in life. Walpole (YW, 18:130–31) describes "a magnificent *repas*" he gave late in 1742 to opera singers; in 1743 he managed the London Opera with Lord Middlesex. In May 1744 he was appointed ambassador to Venice but left the post 23 Aug. 1746 (Horn, pp. 84–85). CB later dedicated his first published composition to him (Frag. 52, nn. 1, 2).

3. William Cowper (1709–64), son of the Lord Chancellor, succeeded as 2d Earl Cowper in 1723; was Lord of the Bedchamber 1733–47; and received an honorary D.C.L., Oxford, in 1728. He arrived in Bath on the same day as Greville (n. 1, above).

4. Naphtali Franks (1715–96), of Mortlake, Surrey, later (1764) F.R.S., became one of the leading members of the Great Synagogue in London (*GM*, 66 (1796): 968; and Roth, pp. 62–64, 299). "Mr. and Mrs. Franks," according to the *Bath Journal*, arrived in Bath on 26 Oct. 1747. A "Mr. Franks.

Chester," perhaps the William Franks elected F.R.S. on 8 March 1781, subscribed to *Hist. Mus.* See also Frags. 58, 107.

5. Thomas Chilcot (d. Nov. 1766), organist of the Abbey Church in Bath from 1733 until his death.

6. Thomas Linley (1733–95), "an eminent music professor and organist, long resident at Bath," was then a boy of fourteen. Later, "having a large family of children, in whom he found the seeds of genius had been planted by nature, and the gift of voice, which, in order to cultivate, he pointed his studies to singing, and became the best singing master of his time.... He was not only a masterly player on the organ and harpsichord, but a good composer, as his elegies and several compositions for Drury-lane theatre evinced" ("Linley" in Rees). For his daughter Elizabeth, see Frag. 115, n. 3, and Appendix B.6.

7. "A game of chance, in which the appropriation of the stakes is determined by the falling of a ball into one of several niches marked E or O respectively" (*Oxford English Dictionary*). "EO" stands for "even and odd." The game was apparently introduced to Bath by Beau Nash (n. 13, below) to evade the Act

of Parliament of 1739 that made games of hazard "with numbers thereon" illegal. See Gadd, pp. 80–81, which reproduces Thomas Rowlandson's cartoon "E.O. or the Fashionable Vowels" (1781).

8. See Frag. 44, n. 1.

9. Philip Stanhope (1694–1773), 4th Earl of Chesterfield, was in Bath from c. 15 Feb. to 9 March 1748 (*Letters,* ed. B. Dobrée, 1932, 3:1099–1119).

10. James Waldegrave (1715–63), 2d Earl Waldegrave, Lord of the Bedchamber to George II (1743), was to become in 1751 governor of the young Prince of Wales, later George III, and to play a prominent part in politics as an independent man known to possess the confidence of the king.

11. Henry Bromley (1705–55) of Horseheath, co. Cambridge; M.P. for Cambridgeshire 1727–41; cr. Lord Montfort, Baron of Horseheath, 9 May 1741.

12. Hugh Smithson (1715–86), 4th Baronet of Stanwick, Yorks., 1729; High Sheriff of Yorkshire 1738–40; M.P. for Middlesex 1740–50; Earl of Northumberland 1750. In 1740 he had married Elizabeth, only daughter and heiress of Algernon Seymour, Baron Percy, and on 12 April 1750 by Act of Parliament assumed the name and arms of Percy. Later, as Duke of Northumberland, he was to play a prominent part in the political life of the 1760s and 1770s. He arrived in Bath on 26 Oct. 1747 (*Bath Journal*). Walpole charged Smithson, considered the handsomest man of his day, with "sordid and illiberal conduct at play" (Walpole *Memoirs,* 1:418–20), a failing which is alluded to in "A Tale" published with *The Rolliad,* where "the Duke divides a small unclaimed sum with the waiter at Brooks's" (*Dictionary of National Biography*).

13. Richard Nash (1674–1762) had become "the King of Bath" early in the century. He said he wore his immense creamcoloured beaver hat to prevent its being stolen. He was a regular frequenter of gaming tables and after 1745, when more stringent regulations were passed, made large sums, evading the law by the invention of new games (see n. 7, above).

14. Henry St. John, Viscount Bolingbroke (1678–1751), approaching his seventies and crippled with "Rheumatic pains," arrived in Bath on 4 Jan. 1748 (*Bath Journal*; see also Sichel, 2:581–82).

15. The Rt. Rev. Philip Twysden (1714–52) of Peckham, Kent—M.A., D.C.L., Oxford, 1745—was nominated Bishop of Raphoe on 28 Feb. and consecrated 29 March 1747 (Powicke/Fryde, p. 362). According to the *Bath Journal,* he arrived on 12 Oct. 1747.

16. See Frag. 39, n. 3.

FRAGMENT 46   London, 1747

About this time,[1] Mr Greville's attachment began with Miss Fanny Macartney, in A[r]gyle Buildings. Mr Macartney,[2] a gentleman of an ancient Irish family, with a great estate in that kingdom, had, at this time, four daughters & two sons. The eldest daughter[3] had a fortune settled upon her by a relation, independant of her father, & lived in Ireland, where, in the time of Lord Harcourt's Lieutenancy,[4] she became an active politician; and afterwards a well-known public character at Bath. The eldest son, Major Macartney,[5] was no less distinguished for eccentricity of character than his eldest sister. He was long regarded as a *Buck of the first head,* among the young men of the world, and a profligate among the women. Coute Macartney, the second son, was the cotemporary and friend of Gray at Eton, of whom he had M.S. copies of the Church Yard & Eton College, wch he read to his sisters long before they were printed or known to the public.[6] This young gentleman, who was intended for the church, was an excellent scholar, had an admirable taste in literature, and was as regular & amiable in his conduct and character, as his brother was wild and profligate.

Miss Catherine Macartney[7] had a mind and taste in literature, highly culti-vated. There was no work of the higher classes of merit in English or French wch she had not read, nor no subject or species of writing, wch it became a female to study wch she was not able to discuss, without pedantry or arrogance, in a playful and pleasing manner.

Character of Miss Macartneys

Miss Fanny Macartney,[8] the third daughter of Mr Macartney, had early distinguished herself among her friends by her taste in poetry, & other accomplishments; and has been distinguished by Mr Horace Walpole (late Lord Orford) for her personal charms, under the character of *Flora,* in his poem entitled The *Beauties* of St James's, in verses unworthy of the grace and beauty she possessed.[9]

This most amiable, pleasing, as well as beautiful young Lady, had captivated Mr Greville, who from birth, fortune and figure, had fair pretensions to an alliance with any family in the kingdom, & was looked up to by the fathers as such from his family & fortune, and by the daughters for his personal appearance. I had been recommended to her as a master to teach her accompanyment, & the compositions of her favorite composers, Alberti,[10] Scarlatti, & Pergolesi.[11] During the courtship, it was the pleasantest business I had to do. The Ladies, Miss Kitty, Miss Fanny, & Miss Molly Macartney,[12] were all accomplished, fond of Music, & great readers. There was a pleasantry and playfulness in the conversation of them all, that was new to me, who had then been intimately acquainted wth so few ladies of family & fashion. Miss Molly Macartney, of whom I have hitherto said nothing, was beautiful in face & figure, had a small impediment in her speech, something like what the French term *parler gras,* wch so far from being disagreeable, harmonized with her face, manners, and resources for conversation, & was more agreeable than the contrary.

Mr Greville from a romantic

Mr *Greville Marries*
Miss Fanny
*Macartney*¹³

1. In 1747.

2. James Macartney (1692–1770) of Belfast (Eton 1706–7; Trinity College, Dublin), son of James Macartney, Justice of the Queen's Bench in Ireland, married Catherine Coote in 1715.

3. Alice Macartney was still living in 1789, unmarried, with her sister Catherine (see Lodge, 7:91).

4. Simon Harcourt (1714–77), 1st Earl Harcourt, was appointed Lord Lieutenant of Ireland on 9 Oct. 1772 and resigned 25 Jan. 1777.

5. Francis Macartney (d. 1759), M.P. for Blessington 1749.

6. Coute Macartney (1729–48) was not Thomas Gray's contemporary at Eton but was there in 1742 when Gray, not far away at Stoke Poges, composed his major poems. On 5 May 1743 Macartney matriculated at University College, Oxford (B.A. 1746/7). There is no evidence that during his stay at Eton the thirteen-year-old saw the manuscript of Gray's *Elegy*; it may not yet have been composed. It was published on 15 Feb. 1751, and as young Macartney died 20 May 1748 in Dublin, he could not have copied it out from the printed text. It seems more likely that while at Oxford he saw Gray's *Eton Ode,* which had been printed by Dodsley at the end of May 1747, and being an Etonian himself, copied it out and passed it among his sisters later in 1747. CB, recollecting the events after forty or fifty years, no doubt remembered that Coute Macartney was circulating a poem by Gray in manuscript, and probably added the *Elegy* to the *Eton Ode.*

7. See n. 3, above.

8. Frances Macartney (c. 1730–89), later godmother of Fanny Burney. CB later wrote that "the beautiful, charming & accomplished Mrs Greville, whose counsel, conversation, & love of literature, formed young Burney's character, rendered his abode in the family at once delightful & useful to him during the rest of his life" (BL Add. MSS 48345, f.22^v). Her "Ode to Indifference" was much admired, and some of her occasional verses were preserved by her daughter Frances Crewe in the "White Album" of Crewe Hall (a partial transcript by Charles Parr Burney is in Osborn). Her "little Novel," which she sent to Fanny in MS, has been discovered by Betty Rizzo, who is preparing her biography.

9. How pretty Flora, wanton maid,
   By Zephyr woo'd in noon-tide shade,
   With rosy hand coquetly throwing
   Pansies, beneath her sweet touch
      blowing;
   How blithe she look'd, let FANNY
      tell;
   Let Zephyr own it half so well.

Walpole had written these verses in July 1746; see Lewis *Walpole,* p. 26. Later, Fanny Greville was to appear as Flora in her husband's *Maxims, Characters, and Reflections* (Frag. 41, n. 1).

10. Domenico Alberti (c. 1710–40), "a Venetian *dilettante,* gifted with genius and an exquisite taste. . . . At a time when there was little melody in harpsichord lessons, he brought about a revolution in the style of playing that instrument, by giving a singing treble to a rapid base, composed of chords

broken into groups of semiquavers, which it was so easy to imitate" that it became known as 'Alberti's bass' ("Alberti" in Rees). See Frag. 43, n. 8.

11. The fame of Giovanni Battista Pergolesi (1710–36), "this exquisite composer" and "child of taste and elegance," reached England in the early 1740s, especially after the performance of his *Olimpiade* at the King's Theatre, 20 April 1742; its first air, "Tremende oscuri attroci," "was sung at concerts by Frasi for ten years at least, after the run of the opera was over" (*Hist. Mus.,* 4:448, 551–57; Mercer, 2:840, 919–24). CB probably taught Fanny Macartney accompaniments to Pergolesi's vocal compositions, which he praises for their "clearness, simplicity, truth, and sweetness of expression," as Pergolesi's sixteen lessons for the harpsichord (now considered spurious) were not published until 1771 and 1778 (*New Grove,* 14:400).

12. Mary Macartney (d. 28 May 1765) on 2 June 1761 married William Henry Lyttelton (1724–1808), 1st Baron Lyttelton of Frankley (second creation). She died in Jamaica, where she accompanied her husband, who was governor there 1760–66.

13. Greville married Fanny Macartney, who was then of age, early in 1748 "in a somewhat melodramatic manner." To add a romantic touch to the event, he eloped with her, and asked CB and the Misses Macartney to assist at the clandestine ceremony. On his return from the wedding to beg pardon of his father-in-law, he was greeted with the sarcastic remark, "Mr. Greville has chosen to take a wife out of the window, whom he might just as well have taken out of the door" (*Mem.,* 1:59). Lonsdale (1965, p. 20) points out that "the fact that Greville asked Burney to give the bride away at this clandestine marriage indicates the confidence and esteem which he reposed in the young man."

BRIDGE: FRAGMENTS 46–47

Mme d'Arblay tells how the Grevilles often acted at home "sundry proverbs, interludes, and farces, in which young Burney was always a principal personage. In one, amongst others, he played his part with a humour so entertaining, that its nick-name was fastened upon him . . . that of a finical, conceited coxcomb, a paltry and illiterate poltroon; namely, Will Fribble, Esq., in Garrick's farce of *Miss in her Teens.* Mr. Greville himself was Captain Flash, and the beautiful Mrs. Greville was Miss Biddy Bellair; by which three names, from the great diversion their adoption had afforded, they corresponded with one another during several years." She prints Burney's verse letter in the character of "WILLIAM FRIBBLE. ESQ. To Her Who Was Once Biddy Bellair," and adds that during his stay with the Grevilles he also became acquainted "with Dr. Hawkesworth, Mr. Boone, and Mr. Cox" (*Mem.,* 1:60, 113–14, 59).

Goes to London
en famille

FRAGMENT 47   London, 29 September 1748

However, in 1748, he [Fulke Greville] had been so accustomed to have me
with him at a stated sum for my time to Mʳ Arne, that
he wished to appropriate me to himself entirely, by   *Released from my*
purchasing the remaining three years of my time.[1] And   *apprenticeship*
this being proposed & negotiated at a period when my Master was out of Cash,
the transfer of my Indenture was concluded at Michaelmas, this year for £300;
when I was entirely domesticated with Mʳ Greville, and accountable to him for
my time, wᶜʰ I spent very pleasantly, particularly after his marriage with the
charming Miss Fanny Macartney, whose person, good taste & sweet temper
illumined all her steps wherever she trod.[2]

Mʳ Greville, soon after I left Arne, on Garrick making some difficulties in
granting me leave of absence when he wished to take me with him out of Town,
made me resign my place in the D.L. band[3]

1. In September 1744 CB had bound himself apprentice to Arne for seven years.

2. Later CB confided to Mrs. Greville's
daughter: "You know, I was called the *Youth,*
long after you were born [1748]. *My Lady*
gave me that appellation, to steer clear of the
too high title of young Gentleman, or too
degrading address of boy, or young man"
(CB to Frances Crewe, [2]5 July 1794, Osborn).

3. The last sentence indicates that after his
release from Arne's apprenticeship CB remained a member of the Drury Lane band
(Frag. 27). The resignation probably occurred during the 1748–49 season, when
Greville wanted CB to stay with him at Wilbury.

FRAGMENT 48   London, 6 February 1749

I know not what Sir John Hawkins means by the *cold reception* of I R E N E.[1] I
was at the first representation, and most of the subsequent. It was much
applauded the first night, particularly the speech on *to-morrow.*[2] It ran nine
nights at least. It did not indeed become a stock-play, but there was not the least
opposition during the representation, except the first night in the last act, where
Irene was to be strangled on the stage, which *John* could not bear, though a
dramatick poet may stab or slay by hundreds. The bow-string was not a
Christian nor an ancient Greek or Roman death.[3] But this offence was removed

after the first night, and Irene went off the stage to be strangled.—Many stories were circulated at the time of the author's being observed at the representation to be dissatisfied with some of the speeches and conduct of the play, himself; and, like la Fontaine, expressing his disapprobation aloud.[4]

1. CB's "Esteem & veneration" for Dr. Johnson began in "the year 1747 when I read your Plan of your Dictionary . . . I eagerly seized the opportunity of Subscribing to you as Shakespear's Editor" (CB to Samuel Johnson, 14 Oct. 1765, Hyde). On 6 Feb. 1749 he attended the first performance of *Irene* at Drury Lane; Sir John Hawkins, in *The Life of Samuel Johnson* (1787), says that it "was received with cold applause" (pp. 198–202). For a comprehensive account, see Clifford, pp. 1–14.

2. Act III, sc. ii.

3. According to Dr. Adams, all went well "till it came to the conclusion, when Mrs Pritchard, the heroine of the piece, was to be strangled upon the stage, and was to speak two lines with the bow-string round her neck. The audience cried out '*Murder! Murder!*' She several times attempted to speak;

but in vain. At last she was obliged to go off the stage alive" (Hill/Powell, 1:196–97). *John* is no doubt a pun on John Bull and Sir John Hawkins.

4. Several unauthenticated anecdotes relate to the unsuccessful performance of La Fontaine's opera *Astrée* (28 Nov. 1691). In one, La Fontaine, attending a performance, found the opera badly done and asked who had written it. He was reminded that he himself was the author, to which he replied that that didn't make it any better. See *Oeuvres de Jean de la Fontaine*, ed. H. Régnier, 1921, 1:cxl–cxlii). CB probably found the anecdote in La Harpe's *Cours de littérature* (pt. 2, 9: 164), which he reviewed in *Monthly Review* 33 (Dec. 1800): 449–66. La Harpe had wrongly thought the anecdote concerned La Fontaine's *Daphné*.

FRAGMENT 49   London, Spring 1748

⟨Chester⟩ with Mr Arne to learn composition. This brother, lately married,[1] being possessed of several great schools, and advancing rapidly in his profession, hired a great house in Hatton Garden,[2] in wch there was a large sky-light parlour that he fitted up as a Ball Room; in this, on leisure evenings, he gave a dance to young people of his own age, some of whom had been his scholars. This custom began before I quitted Arne; and my brother never failed to give me notice of these meetings, nor I of availing myself of his kindness, when I was not copying Music, or employed in the Orchestra at Drury Lane, or the *Oratorio.* Among the females of nearly my own age, whom I used to meet at my brother's private balls, there were many pretty girls, but no one to whom I was so frequently engaged as a partner, as to Miss Esther Sleepe,[3] the daughter

My own courtship
& Marriage

of Old Sleepe,⁴ the ⟨head⟩ [of the City waits] and furnisher of bands for municipal [festivities, and Mʳˢ Sleepe,] the daughter of a M. Dubois,⁵ [who] ⟨kept⟩ a Fan Shop in Cheapside

1. Richard (Frag. 25, n. 1) had married in 1745 "an amiable young Lady of the name of Humphreys, whose Mother, (report says) was descended from the family of Dudley Earl of Leicester." She was twenty-five, he twenty-two. After his half-brother Thomas left for America, Richard, who inherited his business, found "himself tolerably well settled, with good prospects before him" (Worcester Mem., p. 7).

2. After the birth of two boys, James (11 Dec. 1746) and Charles Rousseau (Dec. 1747), to whom CB stood as godfather, "Mr. and Mrs. Burney removed from Fetter Lane, to a good & airy house in Hatton Garden.... There is a picture of them in the family, taken about this time, the faces by Gainesborough (kit cat size) which were reckoned excellent likenesses. The drapery, & other parts were finish'd by an inferior artist" (Worcester Mem., p. 7).

3. Esther Sleepe (1725?–62) appears to have been baptized on 1 Aug. 1725 at St. Vedast, Foster Lane, as daughter of Richard Sleepe (n. 4, below). For her identification as daughter (b. 9 May 1723) of James Sleepe, see *HFB*, pp. 4 n.3, 492. In 1747 she took the unusual step for a woman of applying to be a freeman of the Company of Musicians, which she was granted on 7 Aug. 1747 but lost eight days after her marriage, when the privilege was conferred on CB (Dawe, pp. 12–13, 85; Frag. 50, n. 4). According to Worcester Mem. (p. 7), she was "a Lady of great strength of mind, possessing a taste for literature, with an engaging manner, & much beauty" (see Frag. 50, n. 2).

4. Richard Sleepe, freeman of the Company of Musicians, who married Esther Wood in 1705, was buried 23 March 1758 in the churchyard vault, parish of St. Michael Le Querne (Boyd's "Index to Middlesex Mar-

riages"; information kindly supplied by Joyce Hemlow). He was a leader of the City waits, the Lord Mayor's band. In 1739 he was ordered to "add two trumpets to his band of music" and on 25 Oct. 1739 was "paid £4 for the City musick at laying of foundation stone of Mansion House" (Dawe, p. 12).

5. Probably Pierre Du Bois (d. 1747?), Esther Sleepe's grandfather, of a French Huguenot family of merchants who came to England early in the seventeenth century and lived in Threadneedle Street. He probably lived at No. 43 in the Poultry (Frag. 51, n. 4). The fact that Parisian makers of musical instruments, who had no company of their own, often became members of the company of Fan-makers (Scholes 1948, 1:52) may explain his connection with Richard Sleepe (n. 4, above).

His daughter probably anglicized her name to Wood before she married Richard Sleepe in 1705 (n. 4) and became the mother of CB's first wife. She had been "from some unknown cause—probably of maternal education . . . brought up a Roman Catholic," and both Fanny and Susan describe her as "a real fine lady, of other days." She was acquainted with Esther's and CB's plans, and CB "loved his mother-in-law as sincerely as if she had been his mother-in-blood" (*Mem.*, 1:78–81; *HFB*, p. 5). In 1732 she gave a delicately stitched needlework sampler covered with aphorisms to her daughter Esther, then nine years old, with the following dedication in cross-stitch: "Esther Sleepe is my name and in my youth wrought the same & by this work you may plainly see what care my parents took of me. November the Last in the year 1732" (*HFB*, p. 5). It was sold at Sotheby's, 19 Dec. 1960. The sampler could, of course, have been worked by the child from a prepared pattern.

FRAGMENT 50   London, June 1749

[I] gave up my own opinion & judgement to her whenever they differed from her sentiments, wch was very seldom.[1]

Neither I nor my lovely sweet heart met with any opposition to our union, as there was no fortune on either side; we only waited for Mr Grevilles consent, as I thought myself accountable to him for my conduct as well as for my time. But having talked to him of my attachment to Miss Sleepe & described her person & manners, I, at length, shewed him and Mrs Greville a picture of the sweet girl in Miniature, painted by Spencer.[2] Mr Greville was so struck with her beauty, that without my hinting a wish to complete our union till the full time of my apprenticeship was expired,[3] he cried out, "why don't you marry her?"— when I eagerly said—"*may* I?"—We lost no time; (the Marriage Act was not then even in contemplation) but the next day had the Gordian knot tied at May-Fair; where a Hymenæal priest had always, as in the Fleet, a parental witness ready to make a present of a bride.[4]

Mr Greville was at this time preparing to go to Italy with his Lady and infant daughter[5] & to remain on the continent for some years, & it was always intended that I sh^d make a part of his

1. One problem which the young couple faced was Greville's tempting offer to CB to accompany him to Italy. Fanny gives a long romanced account of the debates between CB and Esther Sleepe on the subject (*Mem.,* 1:73–81) without revealing the true reason for their difficulties, the fact that Esther was pregnant. CB did not want to leave her alone in London, but Esther "would listen to no project that might lead him to relinquish such solid friends, at the very moment that they were preparing to give him the strongest proof of their fondness of his society." Matters came to a head when their daughter Esther was born on 24 May and baptized 25 June 1749, shortly before CB was to set out with the Grevilles for Italy. This led to the scene here described by CB.

2. Gervase Spencer (d. 1763), miniaturist, charged £3 in his early days for a portrait. CB wished to have Esther's miniature so "that he

might bear her resemblance next his heart" if he went with the Grevilles to Italy (*Mem.,* 1:75). In his will he appropriately bequeathed the miniature, "admirably painted by Spencer just before our Marriage," to his daughter Esther (Scholes 1948, 2:271). In 1970 the original was owned by Miss Stella M. Alleyne. It is reproduced in *HFB*, facing p. 53.

3. CB's contract with Arne, which was now in Greville's possession (Frag. 47), would have expired in 1751.

4. They were married on 25 June 1749 (Armytage, p. 137). The fact that little Esther was born a month before their marriage might account for their wedding taking place at St. George's Chapel, which was well-known for the performance of clandestine marriages; i.e., marriage ceremonies without license, publication of banns, or parental consent.

5. Frances (later Mrs. Crewe) was bap-

tized 28 Nov. 1748, and CB stood proxy for the Duke of Beaufort as her godfather (Lonsdale 1965, p. 20). The Grevilles set out for Italy shortly after CB's marriage. On 17 May 1749 Walpole wrote to Horace Mann at Florence: "You are to have . . . Mr Greville and his wife, who was the pretty Fanny Mccartney" (YW, 20:58). As CB's father died at this time

(June 1749; see Bridge: Frags. 7–8, n. 1), CB probably went to Chester to attend the funeral before he married Esther. Christopher Smart, who in July sent condolences "for the loss of your Father," did not know whether CB was still "in the Kingdom" or with the Grevilles in Europe (Lonsdale 1965, pp. 26–27).

FRAGMENT 51

London, July 1749

*Candidate for an
Organist's place*[1]

I thought I had gained a great point & ensured my election, by ha[v]ing obtained the favour and vote of Sr Joseph Hankey, Alderman of the Ward, & his Brother Sr Thomas.[2] Sr Joseph certainly procured me many votes among his trades people & dependants, though he lost me many others, as he was not popular in the parish. The election was long suspended, by a vestry dispute, whether it was to be by open poll or holding up of hands, or by ballot. There was a paper war, counsel, learned in the law, consulted on both sides[3]—and I shall leave them for a while to settle this point, & go

*Patronised by
Sr Jos. Hankey
in the City*

back a little to relate what I sh^d have ⟨to⟩ld previous to my marriage, & ceasing to reside with Mr Greville.[4]

The notice with which I was honoured by the Earl of Holdernesse[5] at Bath, in 1746, did not end so abruptly as Bath acquaintants usually do: his Lord^p desired I w^d call upon him in London, wch I did not fail to do, and I was not only

*And Lord Holdernesse
in Westm^r*

always let in by the Porter, but desired by my Lord to repeat my visits, wch soon were rendered flattering, by his detaining [me] ⟨with only⟩ himself and Lady Holdernesse.[6] I used to

---

1. After the departure of the Grevilles for Italy, CB began to look for a new job. On 3 July 1749, a week after his marriage, he paid the necessary fees to become a freeman of the Musicians' Company (Frag. 49, n. 3). This

was requisite to his candidacy for the place of organist at St. Dionis Backchurch in Fenchurch Street, left vacant by the death on 17 July of the organist Philip Hart (see Edwards; Scholes 1942).

2. Sir Joseph Hankey (d. 28 June 1769) was a prominent London banker. Originally a haberdasher (Master of Haberdashers 1737–38), he was elected alderman for Longbourn Ward on 1 Feb. 1737; became senior alderman ("Father of the City") 1758–69; was knighted 4 Aug. 1737. He was treasurer in 1749, vice-president 1749–54, and president 1754–63 of the Honourable Artillery Company; president of St. Thomas's Hospital 1751–69. With his brother Thomas (knighted 1745) he founded a bank at the sign of the Three Golden Balls in Fenchurch Street (Beaven, 1:171, 253, 2:xxvi, 127, 197; Price, pp. 72–73).

3. The "paper war" was between the champions of the secret ballot (one man, one vote) and the open poll according to the varying rates the voters paid. The big bankers (such as Sir Joseph Hankey) as big rate-payers championed plural voting power (Scholes 1948, 1:50). For a fuller account of the election, gathered from the Vestry Minutes, see Edwards; Scholes 1942.

4. After Greville left for Italy, CB and Esther moved to the Fan Shop in the Poultry (Lonsdale 1965, p. 23), the home of Esther's mother (Frag. 49, n. 5). The Church Rate Books of St. Mary Cole, Cheap Ward, show that "Esther Sleep," proprietor of "No 43 Poultry," paid the rent of £24 from Easter 1747 to Easter 1749, and "Charles Berney" the same rent from Easter 1749 to Easter 1750. The remuneration "for the scavenger" went up from 3s. 6d. in 1747 to 16s. in 1750 (Guildhall Library, MS 11 316, vols. 142, 145, 148, 154, 160; information kindly supplied by Joyce Hemlow).

5. See Frag. 45, n. 2.

6. Mary née Doublet (1720–1801), daughter of Francis Doublet, Member of the States of Holland, married Lord Holdernesse at The Hague in Nov. 1742. Mme d'Arblay adds: "Many notes of Lord Holdernesse still remain of kind engagements for meetings," even after 12 April 1771, when he was appointed governor to the Prince of Wales. Only one of these notes, dated 7 Jan. 1776, has been preserved (Osborn). "At Holdernesse House, the fine mansion of this earl, young Burney began an acquaintance . . . with Mr. Mason, the poet, who was his lordships's chaplain" (*Mem.*, 1:23–24).

FRAGMENT 52

London, Winter 1747–Spring 1748

> *Dedicate my Op. 1ma*
> *to him[1]*

put into the hands of an engraver & pu[b]lished in 1747.[2]

During my connexion with Drury Lane theatre, I became intimately acquainted with Oswald, the Scotish Orpheus,[3] the celebrated performer of old Scots tunes on the Violoncello, and maker of many more, w^ch, by his manner of playing them and keeping a Music-shop, on the pavement of St Martin's church-yard, turned to good account. The first two or three ballads I ever printed, issued from his shop.[5] I set

Acquaintance with Oswald, Honble & Rev. Mr Hume Thompson & Smollet[4]

to Music ab^t this time Thompson's ode on the Æolian Harp,^{6} wch was performed one morning at Lady Townshend's^7 to whom I had the honour of being introduced by the Honble & Revd Mr Hume, afterwards Earl of Hume,^{8} who had not only a passion for Music, but played well on the Violin. This most amiable & worthy divine was extremely partial to my first attempts at composition, & while I remained in London manifested his zeal for my prosperity in the most friendly & flattering manner, particularly during my canvas, and at my election for the Organist's place in the city. He gained me several votes, & on the day of election handed all the female electrices over the

Set Thompson's Ode on the Æolian Harp

1. *Six Sonatas for two Violins, with a Bass for the Violoncello or Harpsichord. Most humbly dedicated to the Rt. Honble. the Earl of Holderness. Opera prima. London. Printed for the Author by Wm. Smith in Middle Row, Holborn, and sold at Mr. Richd. Burney's in Hatton Garden* (*RISM*, 1:B.5054). "These being printed by subscription at my own expence, were never thrown into the shops, & the plates having been long lost, I fear a Copy can only be found by accident in a shop of old 2^d hand Music" (CB to ?, 24 Oct. 1797, BL, Add. MSS 48345, f. 41). Copies exist in the University Library, Cambridge; the Rowe Music Library, King's College, Cambridge; and the Faculty of Music Library, University of Toronto. Scholes had another, now in Osborn.

2. A slip for 1748. On 13 Feb. 1748, CB placed the following announcement in the *Daily Advertiser*: "In May next, will be publish'd by subscription Six Sonatas. . . . The Price to Subscribers will be a Guinea for the Large, and half a Guinea for the Small Paper, the whole to be paid at the Time of Subscribing." This edition was ready for delivery on 30 May 1748. "A second Edition" was advertised as "just publish'd" on 24 July 1748" (Scholes 1948, 2:340).

3. James Oswald (1711–79) began his career as a dancing-master at Dunfermline in 1734, from where he moved in 1736 to Edin-

burgh, where "he issued several collections of *Scots Tunes*." In 1741 he arrived in London and found employment with the music publisher John Simpson, probably as a sort of subeditor. In 1747 he set up his own music shop at 17 St. Martin's Lane. CB may have met him in June 1748, for the second edition of his *Six Sonatas* (published 24 July) is advertised as available at Oswald's shop (the first one, published 30 May, was not).

4. CB no doubt met Tobias Smollett (1721–71) through Oswald (n. 3, above) and his circle of Scottish friends, including John Armstrong, David Mallet, and James Thomson. Smollett had settled in London in 1744, and Oswald set to music at least four of Smollett's lyrics, including "The Tears of Scotland," composed after the battle of Culloden (Knapp 1931; Deutsch 1948). CB's acquaintance with Smollett cannot have been very close, for he believed that "The Tears of Scotland" had been written by Armstrong: "Oswald, who set this song to music, and published it, assured a friend of ours, still living, that he had it from Armstrong in his own hand-writing" (CB's article in the *Monthly Review* 16 (1795): 71, quoted in Lonsdale 1965, p. 30). For "Hume," see n. 8, below.

5. One of these ballads was entitled "Lovely Harriote. A Crambo Song, the

words by Mr. Smart. Set to music by Charles Burney. Printed by J. Oswald." See Scholes 1948, 2:342; Lonsdale 1965, p. 25.

6. CB probably got hold of Thomson's manuscript of "An Ode to Aeolus's Harp" through Oswald, who "passed for the inventor of the Aeolian harp," which Thomson describes in *The Castle of Indolence* (canto 1, st. 40). But as Oswald "was unable to read the account of it" in Kircher's *Musurgia Universalis* "written in Latin, Thomson gave him the description of it in English, and let it pass for his invention, in order to give him a better title to the sale of the instrument at his music-shop in St. Martin's Church-yard" ("Voice" in Rees; quoted in Lonsdale 1965, p. 29). Thomson's poem first appeared in print in May 1748 and in the same year in Dodsley's *Collection of Poems*, 4:129. CB's musical setting of it has not been located. Seward (2:375) relates that CB, visiting Thomson "one day at two o'clock in the afternoon,

found him in bed, with the curtains closed and the windows shut; and, asking him, why he remained so long in bed, was answered by him in the Scottish accent, 'Why, Mon, I had no motive to rise.'"

7. Etheldreda or Audrey (1703–88), daughter of Edward Harrison of Balls Park, Herts., in 1723 married Charles Townshend (1700–64), 3rd Baron Townshend of Lynn Regis, 3rd Viscount Townshend of Raynham. She was renowned for her lively tongue and malicious wit (see Sherson, passim).

8. Alexander Home (d. 8 Oct. 1786), admitted fellow-commoner at St. Catherine, Cambridge, 17 June 1737, was in holy orders until 1761, when he succeeded his brother as 9th Earl of Home. In 1759 CB was to dedicate to him *Six Sonatas for Two Violins and a Base, addressed to the Hon. and Rev. Mr. Home. Opera IV^{ta} Printed for John Johnson, opposite Bow Church in Cheapside* (*RISM*, 1:B.5056; Scholes 1948, 2:343).

FRAGMENT 53   London, 1750–51

I assisted him [Oswald] in the accompaniments to his melodies;[1]—afterwards I had a pleasure in working for him, by the sheet, as it amused me more than teaching. He obtained a patent for the sole publication of all Music composed, or pretended to be composed, by the dilettanti members of *the Society of the Temple of Apollo*.[2] Under this patent he published his own compositions, a Cantata & six songs of mine,[3] as well as whatever I afterwards composed for the Playhouse.[4]—He persuaded Mr Garrick that the members of this Society were gentlemen of taste and talents, who met to shew each other their compositions, & have them tried under the direction of two or three Masters to point out to them their mistakes in counterpoint. That some of the members had much original genius, & w^d compose for the stage any pantomime entertainment, musical farce, or even incidental songs in serious dramas: For wch they

Society of the Temple of Apollo

w^d want no money for themselves, all the remuneration they sh^d require w^d be some moderate gratuity for the Masters who [   ] Garrick listened to this very attentively,[5]

1. See Frag. 52, n. 4, and CB to Charles Burney, 8 Feb. 1799 (Coke).

2. Probably the copyright grant given to Oswald on 23 Oct. 1747 (Kidson). Later in his life CB wrote: "As I was formerly the *WHOLE Society of the Temple of Apollo*, I am now the whole Committee, Secretary, Clerks, & Porters, of the Ladies' Association for the Fr. Em. Clergy"(CB to Mme d'Arblay [30 Oct. 1793], Berg). Lonsdale (1965, pp. 30–32) points out that the Society of the Temple of Apollo in fact consisted of Oswald, who had the patent, and CB, who did most of the work in preparing the various scores for publication.

3. *Six Songs Composed for the Temple of Apollo. To which is added, A favourite Cantata set to musick by Mr. Chas. Burney, Opera II, Lib. I. London, printed for and sold by J. Oswald at his Musick shop in St. Martin's Church-yard in the Strand.* Copies in the National Library, Edinburgh, and in the Trinity College of Music, London. The cantata is Gay's *The Despairing Shepherd,* scored for two violins and a bass (Scholes 1948, 2:342).

4. See Frags. 59–61.

5. As Lonsdale (1965, pp. 31–32) points out, Garrick's ambition to stage Shakespeare's plays at Drury Lane was sorely tested in the summer of 1750, as the London public preferred the low burlesque and harlequinades offered by John Rich at the rival Covent Garden to "our *Lears,* and *Hamlets.*" For this reason "Garrick listened very attentively" to Oswald, who offered to supply music for the more popular entertainments, which would fill the coffers of Drury Lane. See Frag. 59, n. 2.

FRAGMENT 54

London, October 1749

Contested election for
St. Dionis Backchurch
& character of
constituents[1]

be out of a fresh jar, & not dry.

Another seeming to be no party man, perusing me from top to toe, and seeing how young & thin I was, says—"Young man I am afraid you are not equal to the great pipes, you may manage the little ones well enough, perhaps, but I fear the great ones will be too much for you."[2]

A third, to whom I was presented by the kind Mr Hume, takes him on one side, & whispers—"is he honest?"—meaning faithful to Paris & Chas the

Pretender. But Mrs Fletcher, the wife and shop-woman of a Butcher in Lead-enhall Market,[3] lamenting, though very civil to me, the loss of their late Organist, Mr Hart,[4] says, "he was a charming man, and used to make the Organ go round the church, & round the church!"—meaning the effect of the Swell.

However, after a long & tiresome struggle, I gained the election by at least 15 to one.[5] And I took a house in Fenchurch Street, to be near the Church & my new city friends, whom I ever found to be zealous, hospitable, & friendly.

After the great fire in Cornhill, wch happened ab^t this time, by which at least 200 houses were destroyed,[6] & the *Swan Tavern* among the rest, where the famous concert was held, under the direction of Stanley,[7] who played the Organ, Festing first Violin,[8] Froud principal 2^d [9] Weideman the German Flute,[10]

---

1. Here CB resumes the story of his election as organist of St. Dionis's Backchurch, Aug.–Oct. 1749 (Frag. 51, nn. 1, 3). Nine candidates presented themselves for the contest and "had to play, in alphabetical order every Sunday morning and afternoon, beginning July 30." In October, after the candidates had had their trial Sundays, the parish proceeded to the election (Edwards; Scholes 1942).

2. In July 1778 CB related this anecdote to Mrs. Thrale, who records it as having taken place shortly after his arrival in King's Lynn (*Thraliana*, 1:332).

3. Not otherwise identified.

4. Philip Hart (Frag. 51, n. 1), who had been appointed first organist to St. Dionis's Backchurch in 1724 and held the position for twenty-five years, "entertained little relish for those refinements in music which followed the introduction of the Italian opera into this country, for which reason he was the idol of the citizens, especially such of them as were old enough to remember Blow and Purcell" (Hawkins, 2:825). For a description of the organ at St. Dionis, built by Renatus Harris, see Scholes 1948, 2:318–19.

5. The election was held on 26 Oct. 1749 (the original "Poll Book" is in Guildhall MSS 11266). Of the six candidates, CB headed the list with fifty votes, Gilding (afterward organist of St. Edmund the King and Martyr,

Lombard Street) coming next with only four votes; Larkin had one, and the remaining three—Griffes, Rolfe, and Salmon—received none. The salary was £30, and the organist, to be chosen annually, was required to play at "two services on Sunday and on other usual Festivals, and to have no deputy but in case of sickness" (Edwards).

6. The great fire actually happened a year earlier, on 25 March 1748 in Exchange Alley. It "burnt with great fury for 10 hours, and consumed almost all the houses . . . among which were several noted coffee-houses and taverns, five book-sellers and many other valuable shops in *Cornhill.*—Some accounts make the number of houses destroy'd 160, but by the plan just published it appears to be no more than 80, and 14 or 15 damaged" (*GM*, 18:138).

7. John Stanley (1712–86), blind organist and composer, was "the conductor and soul of the Swan and Castle concerts in the city," which were established about 1740 (*Hist. Mus.*, 3:621; Mercer, 2:494). "As far as I was able to learn, when I first came to London in 1744, Jack James, & Stanley by their slight Cornet Pieces first introduced therin org. playing & execution wth the right hand on the org." (CB to William Mason, 8 June 1795, Berg).

8. Michael Christian Festing (c. 1680–

1752), violinist and composer, "was the leader and chief conductor of the musical establishment here [Ranelagh] from the time of my arrival in London till his death. This performer, with a feeble hand, little genius for composition, and but a shallow knowledge in counterpoint, by good sense, probity, prudent conduct, and a gentleman-like behaviour, acquired a weight and influence in his profession, at which hardly any musician of his class ever arrived. He led during many years at the opera, at Ranelagh, at the concert at Hickford's room, at the Swan and Castle concerts in the city, and often at Handel's oratorios. Nor was there a benefit concert for any English professor at that time without a solo on the violin by Mr. M. C. Festing" (*Hist. Mus.*, 4:668–69; Mercer, 2:1011–12).

9. This was probably Charles Froud (d. 1770), "organist of St. Giles church, Cripple-

gate," one of the original subscribers to the Royal Society of Musicians in 1739 (Highfill, 5:419). He attended William Caslon's Thursday concerts of Lunatics, "to whom, whenever he came, Mr. [John] Woolaston gave place, and played the second violin" (Hawkins, 2:807). In 1760 he composed a song, "The Lass of Broomhall Green" (*BUCEM*, 1:355); in 1763 he is listed in Mortimer as "Organist and Teacher on the Harpsichord. *King-Street, Bloomsbury.*"

10. Carl Friederich Weideman (d. 1782) "came to England about 1726. He was long the principal solo player, and composer, and master for the German flute. He was a good musician. . . . But in his productions for the German flute, he never broke through the bounds of that mediocrity to which his instrument seemed confined" ("Weideman" in Rees).

FRAGMENT 55   London, Winter 1749–50

dirty, said, in excuse, that they c^d not afford coach hire out of their salary. This occasioned an enquiry, a new pay master, and an open rupture between Sir Joseph & Stanley,[1] who had many zealous friends, fond of his person and performance. However, the break was irreparable, and without application I was appointed to supply his place at the Organ & Harpsichord;[2] wch I undertook with fear and trembling, being always extremely timid in public

King's Arms Concert in the City Appointed to play the Org. at it on a Quarrel between Sr Jos. Hankey & Stanly

playing; but more now than ever, as I was sure that however well I may acquit myself professionally, all Stanley's friends w^d be my enemies, & very unwilling to be pleased.

Luckily the first night[3] I did not chance to play a Concerto of Handel, or of Felton, wch Stanley had ever played, & in which *l'esprit de comparaison* w^d certainly not have been in my favour, as at least two thirds of the Audience were Stanley's intimate friends, cross & indignant at his dismission, though voluntary. I fortunately composed a concerto for the occasion,[4] in wch I had not

forgotten the sweetness of the Hautbois stop in the Adagio, wch by means of
the swell, and accompaniments of the [   ] happened to please, & acquired
me very great

1. After the destruction of the Swan, the City concerts were transferred to King's Arms Tavern, Cornhill. Sir Joseph Hankey (Frag. 51, n. 2) evidently had a good deal to do with the financing of these concerts, of which John Stanley was the musical "conductor and soul." We do not know the reason for the quarrel between the two: perhaps the musicians complained that their salaries were so low that they arrived all "dirty" for the performances, because they "could not afford coach hire out of their salary."

2. This probably happened in December 1749. Six weeks after his election as organist of St. Dionis, on 3 Dec. 1749, CB was elected member of the Royal Society of Musicians (Records of the Musicians' Company, Guildhall MSS 3091, 3098; cited by Lonsdale 1965, p. 23n); in the winter of 1749 he was "en-

gaged to preside at the harpsichord in a subscription concert then recently established at the King's Arms in Cornhill" (*Harmonicon,* 1832, p. 215, quoted in Scholes 1948, 1:52).

3. Scholes (1948, 1:53) prints an advertisement, with CB's name in it, for a benefit concert given on 26 Feb. 1750 "at the King's Arms Tavern (late the Swan) in Cornhill." This may be the concert CB mentions here, though there could have been an earlier one in Dec. 1749 or Jan. 1750. For Felton, see Frag. 16, n. 2.

4. "An Organ Concerto by Mr. BURNEY" was the second part of the "Concert of Vocal and Instrumental MUSICK" mentioned in n. 3, above. The score of this organ concerto is not known to have been preserved.

FRAGMENT 56   London, Winter 1749–50

⟨nor⟩ the execution [   ] bad, as my courage was frequently refreshed and invigorated by loud applause; particularly in the use of the swell, when left to myself at the pauses, *ad libitum.*

Besides this Concert, my acquaintance with Sir Joseph Hankey during the Election at St Dionis Back Church, procured me Frasi[1] for a scholar; & Frasi procured me Guadagni on his first arrival,[2] to accompany him in his studies, and assist him in the pronunciation of the English words in the parts given him in the Oratorios by Handel: and even the acquaintance of Handel himself; who used to bring an Air, or Duet, in his pocket, as soon as

Acquaintance wth Frasi—become her Master

composed, hot from the brain, in order to give me the time & style, that I might communicate them to my scholar[3] by repetition; for her knowledge of musical characters was very slight.[4] But this connexion with Frasi was attended with some unpleasant circumstances to me at the Castle Concert, where Stanley despotically reigned.[5] For when she had any new Italian songs to sing, from MS. copies, wch she had studied with me, she wished I sh^d be there to accompany her, though Stanley's memory was so astonishingly retentive that he knew all the favourite songs of Handel by heart, and c^d play even the 2^d violin parts to the works of Corelli and Geminiani. But when Sir Jos. Hankey propos[ed] [*half page missing*] going to set fire to Stanley's house,[6] thought it a very

Sir Jos. Hankey going to Burney's house[7]

violent measure, and advised the angry knight to moderate his wrath a little, & not burn a man's house down for so slight a cause.

1. Giulietta Frasi (fl. 1742–72), Italian opera singer, "came to England in 1743." "At this time [she] was young and interesting in her person, had a clear and sweet voice, free from defects, and a smooth and chaste style of singing; which, though cold and unimpassioned, pleased natural ears, and escaped the censure of critics. . . . She sang at Ranelagh, at the triennial meetings at Worcester, Hereford, and Gloucester; at the two universities, and in London at the Swan, King's Arms, and Castle concerts, at the concert at Hickford's Room, Brewer-Street, at all benefit concerts; and was the principal singer in Handel's oratorios during the last ten years of his life" ("Frasi" in Rees).

2. Gaetano Guadagni (c. 1725–92),

one of the most celebrated opera singers of the last century . . . first came into England with a company of burletta singers, brought hither by Croza, an adventurous impresario, in 1748, at which time there was no serious opera in meditation.

It was the first company of comic singers that tried its fortune in London. Guadagni, then very young, wild, and idle, with a very fine counter-tenor voice of only six or seven notes compass, performed the serious man's part in these burlettas, and was but little noticed by the

public; till Handel, pleased with his clear, sweet and full voice, engaged him to sing, in Samson and the Messiah, the fine airs which he had composed for Mrs. Cibber's sweet and affecting voice of low pitch. ("Guadagni" in Rees)

At the 26 Feb. 1750 concert, where CB performed an organ concerto (Frag. 55, nn. 3, 4) "signor Gaetano Guadagni, from the Opera House" sang "The Vocal Part." In the spring of 1750 Guadagni's impresario, Croza, "ran away, leaving the performers and innumerable tradespeople, and others, his creditors" (*Hist. Mus.*, 4:460; Mercer, 2:850).

3. At Frasi's apartments; see Frag. 57.

4. "It has been said that Sig^r Lovatini [Frag. 113, n. 1] who sung so well had no knowledge of Music, the same has been said of the Banti—but this assertion must not be understood too literally—They neither of them c^d sing at *sight,* or learn their parts without a Master to play them over, perhaps a thousand times. . . . I have frequently performed that office to very great singers" (CB to William Mason, 8 June 1795, Berg).

5. For the Castle Concerts, see *The Laws of the Musical Society at the Castle Tavern in Pater-Noster Row, Printed in the Year MDCCLI.* There is a copy in the Bodleian (see Scholes 1948, 1:23n).

6. The cause of Sir Joseph's second quarrel with Stanley is unknown; see n. 7, below.

7. Mrs Thrale gives the rest of the story as CB told it to her in 1777: "The Doctor told me a comical Story one Day of some Nobleman I forgot whom, who had long patronized Stanley the famous Organist, and in consequence of the favours granted, sent to him when he was to have a Concert at his House for Select Company on some Occasion, to request of him that some Person might be admitted whom Stanley did not approve of: the Musician therefore in a Spirit of Independence or Insolence or what you will—sent My Lord a Refusal, which he was that moment foaming with Passion over—when Mr Greville came in, and seeing his

Friend much agitated asked him what was the matter; Why that Scoundrel Stanley says he after all my kindness to him refuses me a Ticket I ask'd for—but I don't care, I'll go to **Burney's House** tomorrow;—where the D^r had a Rival Concert,—and that I know will *vex* him.—*Vex* him indeed! replies the other laughing, I think it would *vex* a Man to have his *house burnt.*—Vex him! in good Time! What a Passionate Creature you are now. To go *burn his house* or even talk of it for such a Trifle" (*Thraliana*, 1:218). Mrs. Thrale, who probably did not remember the story accurately, except for the pun, composed a punning rondeau "To *burn ye*." See Thrale *Autobiography,* 1:314–15.

FRAGMENT 57   London, 1748

Besides seeing HANDEL, myself, at his own house, in Brook-street, and at Carlton-House, where he had rehearsals of his Oratorios, by meeting him at Mrs. Cibber's, and, at Frasi's, who was then my scholar, I acquired considerable knowledge of his private character, and turn for humour.[1] He was very fond of Mrs. Cibber, whose voice and manners had softened his severity for her want of musical knowledge. At her house, of a Sunday evening, he used to meet Quin,[2] who, in spite of native roughness, was very fond of Music. Yet the first time Mrs. Cibber prevailed on HANDEL to sit down to the harpsichord, while he was present, on which occasion I remember the great Musician played the overture in *Siroe*,[3] and delighted us all with the marvellous neatness with which he played the jig, at the end of it.—Quinn, after HANDEL was gone, being asked by Mrs. Cibber, whether he did not think Mr. HANDEL had a charming hand? replied—"*a hand,* madam! you mistake, it's a *foot*,"—"Poh! poh! says she, has he not a fine finger?" "*Toes,* by G—, madam!"—Indeed, his hand was then so fat, that the knuckles, which usually appear convex, were like those of a child, dinted or dimpled in, so as to be rendered concave; however, his touch was so smooth, and the tone of the instrument so much cherished, that his fingers seemed to grow to the keys. They were so curved and compact, when he played, that no motion, and scarcely the fingers themselves, could be discovered.

At Frasi's, I remember, in the year 1748, he brought, in his pocket, the duet of *Judas Macchabaeus, "From these dread Scenes,"* in which she had not sung when that Oratorio was first performed, in 1746.[4] At the time he sat down to the harpsichord, to give her and me the time of it, while he sung her part, I hummed, at sight, the second, over his shoulder; in which he encouraged me, by desiring that I would sing out—but, unfortunately, something went wrong, and HANDEL, with his usual impetuosity, grew violent: a circumstance very terrific to a young musician.—At length, however, recovering from my fright, I ventured to say, that I fancied there was a mistake in the writing; which, upon examining, HANDEL discovered to be the case: and then, instantly, with the greatest good humour and humility, said, "I pec your barton—I am a very odd tog:—maishter Schmitt[5] is to plame."

When Frasi told him, that she should study hard, and was going to learn Thorough-Base, in order to accompany herself: HANDEL, who well knew how little this pleasing singer was addicted to application and diligence, says, "Oh, vaat may we not expect!"[6]

1. For CB's early encounters with Handel, see Frags. 10, 30, and 31, n. 5.

2. See Frag. 40, n. 7.

3. Handel's opera to a libretto by Metastasio (revised by Haym) was first performed at the King's Theatre on 17 Feb. 1728.

4. *Judas Maccabaeus* was first performed at Covent Garden on 1 April 1747.

5. John Christopher Smith (1712–95), musician of German origin, was "Handel's copyist, steward, and confidential countryman, who came over with him from Germany, and lived an inmate with him to nearly the time of his death. He used to engage and pay the performers in the oratorios carried on by Handel himself; and being a good musician, was the most correct copyist of his time" ("Smith" in Rees). See also CB to Fanny Burney, 2–4 Oct. 1792 (Berg).

6. "Had he been as great a master of the English language as Swift, his *bons mots* would have been as frequent, and somewhat of the same kind" ("Handel" in Rees). For another anecdote in the composer's colorfully accented English, see Frag. 30 n. 5.

FRAGMENT 58   London, 23 May 1750

Giardini[1] came to England in 1750. His first public performance in London, at which I was present, was at a benefit concert for old Cuzzoni,[2] who sung in it with a thin cracked voice, which almost frightened out of the little theatre in the

Hay-market, the sons of those who had perhaps heard her at the great theatre in the same street, with extacy. But when Giardini played a solo[3] and concerto, though there was very little company, the applause was so loud, long, and furious, as nothing but that bestowed on Garrick had ever equalled. I had met him the night before at a private concert, with Guadagni and Frasi, at the house of Naphtali Franks, Esq., who was himself one of the best dilettanti performers on the violin at that time;[4] and we were all equally surprised and delighted with the various powers of Giardini at so early a period of his life; when, besides solos of his own composition of the most brilliant kind, he played several of Tartini's, in manuscript, at sight, and at five or six feet distance from the notes, as well as if he had never practised anything else. His tone; bow; execution; graceful carriage of himself and his instrument; playing some of my own Music, and making it better than I intended, or had imagined it in the warm moments of conception;[5] and, lastly, playing variations,[6] extempore, during half an hour, upon a new but extraordinary kind of birth-day minuet, which accidentally lay on the harpsichord—all this threw into the utmost astonishment the whole company, who had never been accustomed to hear better performers than *Festing, Brown,* and *Collet!*[7]

1. Felice de Giardini (1716–96), violinist and composer, pupil of Paladini and Somis. For CB's later account of his "diabolical" character, see Appendix B.

2. Francesca Cuzzoni (c. 1698–1770), celebrated soprano, sang in London 1723–28 and again 1734–36. On her final visit a benefit was arranged for her on 23 May 1750 at the Little Theatre in the Haymarket. "I was at this concert myself, and found her voice reduced to a mere thread; indeed, her throat was so nearly ossified by age, that all the soft and mellifluous qualities, which had before rendered it so enchanting, were nearly annihilated, in her public performance; though I have been assured by a very good judge, who frequently accompanied her in private, that in a room fine remains of her former grace and sweetness in singing Handel's most celebrated songs, by which she had acquired the greatest reputation, were still discoverable" (*Hist. Mus.,* 4:308; Mercer, 2:737).

3. By Giovanni Battista Sammartini (1700/1–75), organist and composer, who "was one of Giardini's masters on the violin; and the first piece [Giardini] played in public, after his arrival in England, was a solo at the benefit of Cuzzoni, composed by San Martini of Milan" ("Martini, Giovanni Batista san" in Rees).

4. See Frag. 45, n. 4.

5. We don't know what CB's "own Music" was on this occasion, but Giardini evidently gloried in such improvised embellishments. While still at Naples, before his arrival in London, as a member of "the opera orchestra, he used to flourish and change passages much more frequently than he ought to have done. 'However,' says Giardini, of whom I had this account, 'I acquired great reputation among the ignorant for my impertinence; yet one night, during the opera, Jomelli, who had composed it, came into the orchestra, and seating himself close by me, I

determined to give the Maestro di Capella a touch of my taste and execution; and in the symphony of the next song, which was in a pathetic style, I gave loose to my fingers and fancy; for which I was rewarded by the composer with a—violent slap in the face; which,' adds Giardini, 'was the best lesson I ever received from a great master in my life.' Jomelli, after this, was however very kind, in a different way, to this young and wonderful musician" (*Hist. Mus.*, 4:522; Mercer, 2:896).

6. "Desiring me to accompany him on the violin, while he played" (Mus. Nbk, c. 97, sect. 2, p. 39).

7. For Michael Festing, see Frag. 54, n. 8.

Abraham Brown (fl. 1739–68), violinist, succeeded Festing at Ranelagh in 1752 (Highfill, 2:361). CB calls him "a performer who had a clear, sprightly, and loud tone, with a strong hand; but though he had travelled through Italy, he was ignorant of Music, and the pieces he played consisted of *notes, et rien*

que des notes: for he had no soul or sense of expression. He brought over a favourite solo of Tartini (the second in the second set, published by Walsh), with which alone he figured at all concerts, for at least six or seven years, without ever entering into Tartini's true style of playing it, or that of any performer of his school. Mr. Brown, however, had not the mortification either to feel or know his defects; but, on the contrary, was conforted with a full conviction of his superiority" (*Hist. Mus.*, 4:670; Mercer, 2:1012–13).

Richard Collet (fl. 1737–67), violinist, in 1739 one of the original charter members of the Royal Society of Musicians, was in 1745–48 leader of the band at Vauxhall Gardens (Highfill, 3:391–92). "His tone was full, clear, and smooth, and his hand strong," writes CB, "but having neither taste nor knowledge of Music, he always remained an inelegant player" (*Hist. Mus.*, 4:668; Mercer, 2:1011).

FRAGMENT 59   London, December 1750

I now began to be in fashion in the City, as a Master, and had my hands full of professional business of all kinds, scholars at both ends of the town, Composition, & public playing.

Establish an Interest in the City

In December this year, Oswald reminded me of the *Society of the Temple of Apollo;* and said, that Mr Garrick had sent him word that he sh^d give the dilettanti members something on wch to exercise their fancy very soon; a promise wch he fulfilled.[1]

The first employment that was assigned to this pretended *Society,*[2] was the pantomime entertainment of *Queen Mab,* planned by Woodward,[3] who delivered to Oswald, in writing, subjects for the tunes that were to paint the several scenes & events of the piece; in which Puck the Fairy had several Songs that were written by Garrick, and sent to Oswald for the Society to set, who delivered them to me.[4]

At this time, the best Chorister in any of the three Cathedrals was master Vernon, a scholar of Mr Savage, [master of the boys at] St Paul's, who was then our best[5]

1. For the reasons which caused Garrick to commission music from Oswald, see Frag. 53, n. 5.

2. As Lonsdale (1965, pp. 32–33) points out, when CB wrote this section of his memoirs, he forgot to mention some single songs he then composed for *Robin Hood. A New entertainment as it is perform'd at The Theatre Royal in Drury-Lane. The Musick composed by the Society of the Temple of Apollo,* which was staged as an afterpiece to *The Alchemist* on 13 Dec. 1750 (CB to ?, 24 Oct. 1797, BL, Add. MSS 48345, f. 41). For its publication, see Scholes 1948, 1:54, 2:340–41. For the libretto by Moses Mendez, see Fiske, p. 223. CB's three songs—"I'll sing you a song that shall suit you all round," "As blythe as a Linnet sings in the Green Wood," and "To an Arbor of Woodbine"—were printed by the Society of Apollo in single sheets in 1751 and reprinted in 1755–56.

3. Henry Woodward (1714–77), the great comic actor at Drury Lane and a friend of Garrick. Between 1749 and 1756 he wrote several interludes and pantomimes in which he acted the part of Harlequin.

4. At this point Mme d'Arblay adds in her own hand: "& I composed the whole Music of that Pantomime." Her statement is confirmed in CB's short autobiographical sketch, in which he adds that the pantomime "ran 60 nights the first season, and was revived almost every Winter for near 30 years after" (*EM*). See also CB to ?, 24 Oct. 1797 (BL, Add. MSS 48345, f. 41).

5. Joseph Vernon (c. 1739–82), later tenor and composer, was then eleven and a chorister at St. Paul's Cathedral under William Savage (c. 1720–89), Master of the Children, 1748. Vernon "was selected from among the choristers of that cathedral, in 1750, to perform the part of Puck the fairy in Queen Mab," and Savage "taught Vernon to sing the fairy's songs in the pantomime." When CB visited Savage during the rehearsals, "happening to call on him one morning while he was dressing, we found that he had three boys to wait upon him while he was washing his hands: one to bring in and hold the eure [ewer], one to present him the washball, and a third to hold the towel" ("Vernon" and "Savage" in Rees). *Queen Mab* was first performed at Drury Lane on 26 Dec. 1750 and ran continuously until 1 Feb. 1751. For its astonishing success and reception, see Lonsdale 1965, pp. 33–34. Scholes (1948, 2:341) lists two versions of CB's score—*The Comic Tunes in Queen Mab* and *The Songs of Queen Mab,* both "printed for J. Oswald" (one "publish'd by authority," the other "by permission of the Society")—and two copies of the *Overture.*

FRAGMENT 60   London, Winter 1750–51

[*Alfred* had been rewritten by] Mallet, and transformed from a masque of two acts to a regular Tragedy of five acts, with incidental songs, duets and Chorus.[1] Mr Garrick himself performed the part of Alfred, & Miss Bellamy[2] that of

Ellenda, his Queen. Miss Norris[3] was the principal female singer, Champness[4] the conjurer.

The Poet wanted the words of all the songs to be adapted to old Scotch tunes. I indulged him in 2 or 3;[5] but as Alfred was not a Scotsman, I thought it w^d be ridiculous to confine all the Songs to scotish melody. I therefore new set all the rest except "Rule Britannia," wch had been so happily set by my Master Arne,[6] that I very early in life thought it the most pleasing, and the best song that ever was produced by a native of England in our language. The whole nation has since been of my opinion, & it is now become a national Air, & will continue both words & Music in favour as long as our Naval Heroes continue to guard our country and to "rule the waves."

At the end of this season 1750, in coming home from a

1. Early in 1751 David Mallet, at Garrick's suggestion, rewrote the masque of *Alfred,* composed by Thomson and set to music by Arne (Frags. 22, 29), "to enlarge the design into 5 Acts, and make ALFRED, what he should have been at first, the principal figure in his own MASQUE" (Mallet's advertisement to *Alfred: A Masque. Acted at the Theatre-Royal, By His Majesty's Servant's. Price One Shilling and Sixpence.* 72 pp.—in BL, shelf-mark 841, ff. 55–56). CB set this version to music, except for two songs by Arne that were incorporated from the earlier version. It was performed at Drury Lane on Saturday, 23 Feb. 1751. This revised version "Compos'd by the Society of the Temple of Apollo" was advertised for publication on 28 March 1751 (*London Stage,* pt. 4, 1:239). For copies of the score, see *RISM,* 6:352 (O 161; listed under "Oswald, James," publisher of the print). For an evaluation of the two versions, see Fiske, pp. 224–29.

2. George Anne Bellamy (1727?–88), Irish actress, who had made her debut in London in 1742 or 1744. Her name "George Anne" was given her by mistake for "Georgiana."

3. Elizabeth Norris (b. 1730?), mezzo-soprano, made her debut at Covent Garden on 10 Dec. 1748 as Euphrosyne in *Comus.* In September 1749 she was engaged by Garrick

as a singer at Drury Lane and was the heroine in CB's *Robin Hood* (Frag. 59, n. 2). "Miss Norris sang in my Robin Hood, and Alfred," wrote CB. "She was a handsome Irish Girl brought over, &, I believe first *done over,* by Jemmy Worsdale. It was at *his* desire that I went to her lodgings at Tavistock Street to teach *her* the songs she had to sing—Macklin came in one day while I was with her, to teach her how to act and speak—I w^d have resigned her to Shylock [Macklin, so called from his favorite role], but he w^d not let me—and desired I w^d go on with my instructions—and after I had gone through 2 or 3 songs with her—he went away—saying, 'Mind what that gentleman says'" (CB to Charles Burney, 16 April 1806, Comyn). Her career was short; after 23 Oct. 1752 her name disappears from the advertisements (Fiske, p. 635), no doubt because she married Mr. Chitty (see Bridge: Frags. 61–62, n. 1).

4. This was Samuel Thomas Champness (d. 1803), who as a boy sang under the direction of Handel; his later career is mainly associated with singing in Handel's oratorios, for which his "full, deep, and majestic" voice was particularly fitted. His name is first recorded in the part of Benjamin in the oratorio of *Joseph and his Brethren,* performed at Covent Garden 2 March 1744 (Highfill, 3:149–51;

New Grove, 4:128–29; Frag. 109, n. 3).

5. The Scots tunes included "Pinkie House," of which a note in the score says, "The above Melody is Old, and suppos'd to be David Rizzio's." The attribution of this song to the Italian secretary of Mary Queen of Scots was exploded by Hawkins (Fiske, p. 227).

6. Two of CB's songs "are in the grand manner, notably 'Swell the Trumpet's boldest Note,' scored for trumpet, drums, and strings with good independent parts for the violin" (Fiske, p. 227). Fiske points out that CB replaced "Rule, Britannia!" with a patriotic finale, "We've fought, we have conquered": "There is nothing to be said for the vainglorious words, but the tune is rather good." Fiske also prints the score (pp. 225–26) and comments that some of CB's music, notably "Peace, thou fairest child of Heav'n," is inferior to Arne's setting, which was preferred.

On 26 Feb.—three days after the opening of the new *Alfred*—Arne, irritated by Garrick's staging of the play, published the following advertisement in the *Daily Advertiser*: "*To the Publick*: As Mr Arne originally composed the Music in the Masque of Alfred, and the town may probably on that account imagine the Music, as now perform'd, to be all his production, he is advised by his friends to inform the publick that but two of his songs are in that performance, viz.: the first song beginning *O Peace thou fairest child of Heaven*; and the Ode in Honour of Great Britain, beginning *When Britain first at Heaven's Command,* with the chorus, *Rule Britannia, Rule the Waves,* &c. which songs he submitted to be mix'd with the productions of others, to oblige the author of the poem. Tho. Aug. Arne" (*London Stage*, pt. 4, 1:238). The plural "others" suggests that Arne did not know that CB had composed the music for this version.

FRAGMENT 61   London, 23 February 1751

[On the opening night of *Alfred* I was obliged to give a] Concert in the City.[1] & I fear my performance there was not meliorated by my anxiety for the fate of my Offspring at Drury Lane. I hardly staid to play the final Chord of the last piece on the Organ, ere I flew out of the concert-room into a Hackney coach, in hopes of hearing some of my stuff performed (if suffered to go on) before it was finished; but neither the coachman nor his horses being in so great a hurry as myself, before I reached Temple bar, I took my leave of them, & "ran like a Lamp-lighter", the rest of the way to the Theatre; and in a most violent perspiration, clambered into the Shilling Gallery, where scarcely I c^d obtain admission, the rest of the House being extremely crowded,[2] wch did not diminish the sudorific state of my person. I entered luckily, at the close of an Air of Spirit, sung by Beard,[3] which was much applauded—This was such a cordial to my anxiety & agitated spirits, as none but a diffident and timid author, like myself, can have the least conception. The piece went on very prosperously for five nights,[4] when it

1. Probably at the King's Arms Tavern in Cornhill, where he had replaced Stanley as organist (Frag. 55).

2. The "new masque called Alfred" was played "before a very numerous and splendid audience" and "as it justly deserved met with great and Universal applause" (*Daily Advertiser,* 25 Feb. 1751).

3. Toward the end of Act III, sc. v: "The clouds break away; and on the edge of a rock, in full view, a spirit is seen amidst a blaze of light, who sings the following: From those eternal regions bright" (see Bridge: Frags. 34–35, n. 2). John Beard (Bridge: Frags. 34–35 n. 2) also sang CB's air "We've fought, we have conquer'd." For CB's comments on him, see Frag. 83, n. 3.

4. For eight nights in fact, between Saturday 23 Feb. and Saturday 9 March 1751, with average receipts of £160 to £180 a night. On Wednesday 6 March there was no performance, and the *General Advertiser* of that day reported that "some Gentlemen and Ladies" intended to hire the theatre for their performance of *Othello* "on Thursday," 7 March. "They applied therefore to the Author of the Masque now performing at Drury Lane, who, without hesitation, agreed that the run of *Alfred* should be interrupted for one night to oblige them." So the eighth and last performance of *Alfred* was "deferr'd till Saturday," 9 March 1751. The *General Advertiser* adds: "Some persons, it seems, continue still under a Mistake that this Masque is the same with the first draught of one formerly written under the same title: they need only, to be undeceived, look into the advertisement prefixed to that performance just now printed for A. Miller, in the Strand" (*London Stage,* pt. 4, 1:240). Later, CB wrote, "I earned the liberty of the Theatre in Drury Lane in the year 1751 by Music I composed for Queen Mab, Robin Hood, & Alfred" (CB to Charles Burney, 14 Feb. 1793, Berg).

BRIDGE: FRAGMENTS 61–62

In a letter to his son recalling "dramatic transactions . . . from 1744 to 1751," Burney mentions in particular "*Chitty* the Timber Merchant,[1] who kept Miss Norris the singer, was called *The Town,* and used to harrangue the Malecontents, standing on a bench in the Pit.[2] . . . Chitty was thinner & his face of a less roseate hue, than that of our friend Rogers.[3] And I remember Cox, a punning witty dancing-master[4] meeting him in the Piazza of Covent Garden and observing that "the *Town* was very *thin* for the time o' year" (Feb[y]). It was Miss Norris, Chitty('s) *Piece,* who lived with Arne's Piece[5] at Twickenham, & who in a very hot evening, stript among the bushes in what they thought a very private place, on the banks of the Thames, and went into the Water together; but having been spied by some boys who were bathing at a distance, they ran away with their cloaths—this gave birth to the song written by Mr Windham's Father[6]—

"The boys in the Thames
your conduct condemns
because that as how you can't swim."—&c

This event must have happened after I left Arne, & he had left his wife,[7] that he dared commit—*whoredom* so publicly. The song, "Tommy Arne, Tommy Arne It becomes your *consarn*"—was in the News-papers of the times"[8] (CB to Charles Burney, 16 April 1806, Comyn).

1. Perhaps Jacob Chitty, in 1763 "Turkey Merchant, *Ironmonger-lane*" (Mortimer, p. 19), or more probably Samuel Chitty (d. 4 Nov. 1768) "of The City Militia," who lived in "George Yard, near Paul's Wharf, Thames str." (*A Compleat Guide to All Persons who have any Trade or Concern with the City of London,* 1765, p. 133). Chitty was a crony of the actors Macklin, Foote, and James Dexter (d. 1788) and of Garrick's enemy Sir John Hill (1716?–75). In 1745 he evidently wrote a libel on Garrick: "Chitty's acknowledging the rudeness of it, must be a double shock to the *Orator*" (Garrick *Letters,* 1:57). James Boaden prints from Garrick's papers an undated satirical piece (written c. 1753–55) called "Chitty's Creed": "I believe in Mr. Charles Macklin, Mr. Samuel Foote, Dr. John Hill, Mr. R. [*sic*] Dexter, my wife, and myself . . . I believe [her] to be the sweetest singer, and *myself* to be the greatest critic, that ever England saw. I believe myself superlatively happy in taking Miss Betty Norris to wife, as I believe Miss Betty Norris superlatively honoured in having me for a husband. I believe, now my wife has left Drury-lane Theatre, that Garrick is the worst actor and manager that ever the stage was cursed with" (Garrick *Corr.,* 2:351). For Elizabeth Norris, see Frag. 60, n. 3.

2. This may be why Garrick called him "the *Orator*" (n. 1, above). CB refers perhaps to the riots that "happened in 1744, my first winter in London" (CB to Charles Burney, 19 April [1806], Comyn), for which see Frag. 29, n. 1. In a later account, CB associates Chitty with the Jan. 1763 riots at Drury Lane (CB to Edmond Malone, [23 Aug. 1810], Burney-Cumming) when he began to be known "by the Name of the *Town*," from "a set of young men, who called themselves the Town" (Genest, 5:14).

3. Samuel Rogers (1763–1855), the poet, who later corresponded with both CB and Charles Burney (*Cat. Corr.,* pp. 48, 269, 282, 289).

4. John George Cox (d. 29 March 1758), dancing-master and oboist in the King's Band, 1752 (Highfill, 4:19).

5. "Whose name no one knows." It probably was *not* Charlotte Brent (Appendix B, n. 28), Arne's "most promising pupil."

6. Col. William Windham (1717–61) of Felbrigg, father of the statesman William Windham (1750–1810). He was a close friend of Garrick and stayed at his house during his visits to London. For CB's account of him, see Bridge: Frags. 72–73.

7. Arne left his wife Cecilia in Dublin, where they had gone on a tour in 1755–56.

8. Windham's verses have not been

traced. It seems that the episode occurred
after 1756, "Mr W. being at Garricks & hearing
of the Nymphs misfortune" (CB to Edmond
Malone, [23 Aug. 1810], Burney-Cumming).
CB was intimate with Windham in Norfolk
"from 1756 to 1760" (Bridge: Frags. 72–73). In
December 1764, after the failure of Arne's
Guardian Outwitted, Windham's verses were
used as a model for another satire on Arne:

> Doctor Arne, Doctor Arne,
> It gives me *consarne*
> To hear that in Nature's despite,
> You have ta'en up the pen

Which your neighbours condemn
Because that *as how* you can't write. . . .

> The critics all *stares,*
> And the authors they *swears*
> It will ne'er go down with the *City,*
> Though *Fizgig* and *B—k*
> Will flatter the work,
> And it sure would have pleased Mr. *Chitty.*

This parody appeared in *St. James's Chronicle,*
18 Dec. 1764. See P. C. Roscoe, pp. 240–41.
The editors wish to thank Mr. John A. Parkinson for calling their attention to these
verses.

FRAGMENT 62   London, 1749–51

Garrick ignorant what his [Arne's] musical merit may have been[1] [h]ad such
an utter contempt for his vanity, and general Character, that he hardly ever
qualified him wth any other title in Private, than the *Rabscalion.* Indeed all the
managers knowing him to be a more regular bred attorney than Musician, took
care to tie him neck & heels in all contracts otherwise he w^d not have been kept
honest by his own principles & probity. But though he was selfish, mean &
rapacious after money, he spent it when acquired like a Child in gratifying his
vanity and incontinence. He never c^d pass by a woman in the Street, to the end
of his life without Concupiscence, or, in plain Engl. *picking her up,* if her look
was not forbidding, & impracticable. It has frequently happened in walking
home with my Wife of a Night, if we have by some accident been separated for a
few minutes, that she has been accosted by the D^r with that design, ere I c^d
overtake her or he know to whom she belonged.

1. In the manuscript this text is continuous with that of Frag. 31. It has been placed

here because it refers to an event that took
place after CB's marriage.

FRAGMENT 63   London, February–May 1751

Having had a very severe illness this Winter wch confined me to my bed for 13 weeks,[1] and having a consumptive cough, night sweats, and being in a manifestly tender state of health [I was made to] swallow medicines—All this rendered existence a heavy burthen, and I often wished its termination; indeed nothing checked that wish but the sight of my most kind and tender nurse, my dear & affectionate Wife, who administ[e]red all my medecins, sat up with me every night, & scarcely ever left me, but to quiet a fractious child who was just taken from nurse.[2] After a few of these miserable days, my excellent friend and patron, Mr Hume,[3] hearing that I was ill, and had had no physician, nor other medical assistance than that of an old city apothecary, sent Dr Armstrong[4] to me, who constantly refused a fee, a regulation which I afterwards found, had been agreed on between him & Mr Hume

I had so long admired Dr Armstrong's poetry, & liked him as a man whom I had frequently seen at Oswald's, that when he was coming to me, if any one had felt my pulse before I knew of his approach, and after his arrival, I am certain there w^d have been found a considerable difference in its vibration. The first thing he did, made my apothecary stare, and think him mad, by opening my bed curtains & lifting up the sashes, to cool my room, and allow me to breathe a pure[5]

1. CB "was seized with a violent Fever" (BL, Add. MSS 48345, f. 22^v) shortly after 23 Feb. 1751, when he rushed to see the performance of *Alfred* (Frag. 61).

2. James (b. 13 June 1750). Esther (b. 24 May 1749) was then over a year and a half old.

3. See Frag. 52, n. 8.

4. John Armstrong (1709–79), doctor and poet, after taking his M.D. degree at Edinburgh (1732), went to London, where he was appointed in 1746 physician to the Hospital for Lame, Maimed and Sick Soldiers. He was the friend of his poetical compatriots Mallet, Thomson, and Oswald. Before CB met him, Armstrong had published medical treatises and three didactic poems: *The Oeconomy of Love* (1736, rev. 1768), *The Art of Preserving Health* (1744), and *Benevolence* (1751). Thomson portrays him among his cronies who inhabited *The Castle of Indolence* (st. 60):

With him was sometimes join'd, in silent
        walk
    (Profoundly silent, for they never
        spoke),
One shyer still, who quite detested talk:
    Oft, stung by spleen, at once away
        he broke
To groves of pine and broad o'ershadowing
        oak;
    There, inly thrill'd, he wandered all
        alone,
And on himself his pensive fury wroke,
    Nor ever utter'd word, save when
        first shone
The glittering star of eve—"Thank Heaven!
    the day is done."

See Knapp 1944. CB's review article in *Monthly Review* 16 (Jan. 1795): 71–76, contains some reminiscences of Armstrong.

    5. Armstrong was a firm believer in pure country air. In *The Art of Preserving Health* (quoted in Scholes 1948, 1:64) he wrote of London pollution:

Fly the rank city, shun its turbid air;
Breathe not the chaos of eternal
   smoke. . . .

It is not Air, but floats a nauseous mass
Of all obscene, corrupt, offensive things.

FRAGMENT 64

London, Spring 1751

[Armstrong not] being able to bring my fever to a crisis or to intermit, he ordered me into the air, and I was carried in a litter to Canonbury house,[1] where he likewise attended me. In my passage thither, whenever the Chairmen stopt to rest me, & themselves, I had the exhilerating comfort of hearing passengers say—"Ha! poor soul! he's going to his long home!"

My fever, wch in London had been nervous & pulse sluggish was at first encreased by the fatigue of removal, in a few days abated, and I found myself much refreshed by a more elastic air.

In this old Royal Palace wch was one of Queen Elizabeth's Villas, now an humble lodging house, and a receptacle for convalescent citizens [, I became acquainted with] Mr Newbury,[2] the ingenious bookseller, the partner of Dr James in the disposal of his powders,[3] and the admirable contriver and writer of little books for children, some of wch he gave away to all good masters & misses, *only paying 3^d for the binding.* (The full price [   ]) This worthy person rented a considerable part of the old palace [   ] retreat for himself and family.[4]

---

1. A thirteenth-century manor in Islington, given by Henry VIII to Thomas, Lord Cromwell. In CB's time the large tower was let out in apartments. Samuel Humphreys, compiler of words for Handel's oratorios, died in lodgings there in 1738; Ephraim Chambers, editor of the *Cyclopaedia*, in 1740. Later (1763–64) Goldsmith lived there. In a draft fragment of his memoirs (BL, Add. MSS 48345, f. 17^r), CB mentions his "tender state of health" and adds, "here Canonbury house, Newbery & Smart." Christopher Smart lodged there in 1752–57 after CB had left for King's Lynn. For CB's relations with Smart, see Lonsdale 1965, pp. 25–28.

2. John Newbery (1713–67), the publisher of books for children, whom Goldsmith describes in *The Vicar of Wakefield* as a "red-faced, good-natured little man who was always in a hurry." CB mentions twice in his letters that he brought "Mr. Newbery & the Poet" Smart together (CB to Fanny Burney,

29 Oct. 1792, Berg; CB to Thomas Twining, 10 May 1804, Osborn). Newbery married the widow of his employer William Carnan (d. 1737); she helped to set him up as a publisher, and Smart married c. 1752 her daughter Nancy, whom he called "the girl with golden locks." For Newbery's publishing career, see Welsh; and S. Roscoe.

3. Robert James (1705–76), M.D. Cambridge 1728, inventor of a powder against fever, much in use throughout the century; he took a patent on it 13 Nov. 1746. It was sold by John Newbery in his bookshop. Newbery, in his humorous book for children called *Goody Two Shoes,* tells how the heroine's father "died miserably" because he was "seized with a violent fever in a place where Dr. James's powder was not to be had." When Goldsmith died from an overdose of the powder, John Newbery wrote to the *Morning Post,* 27 April 1774, in defense of the wonder drug (*Dictionary of National Biography*), which continued to be in great demand in the Burney family (for its composition, see *JL,* 1:68 n.2).

4. "Mr. Newbery had apartments in Canonbury House, then a sweet rural spot" (Sherbo, pp. 86–87), though it is not certain when he moved there. In 1752 he invited Christopher Smart and his wife to stay at Canonbury.

FRAGMENT 65 Islington, Summer 1751

[While at Canonbury] I listened by the advice of Dr Armstrong to [a] proposal from Sr John Turner,[1] member [for] Lynn Regis to accept of the place of Org^t at St Margaret's Church in that Borough [a]t a Sal^y of £100 a year, encreased to that sum from £20 a year as an encouragem^t [to] a regular bred musician of some character to come down from the Capital to instruct the children of the principal families [in] the town & neighbourhood in Music[2]

1. Sir John Turner (1712–80) of Warham, Norfolk, M.P. for King's Lynn 1739–74, and mayor 1737 and 1748. The Turners were one of the leading families in King's Lynn, which they represented in Parliament for some eighty years. For more on Sir John, see CB to Esther Burney, [c. 30 Sept. 1751] (Osborn).

2. CB left for King's Lynn in Sept. 1751, leaving his wife and family in London. For a more detailed account of his post as organist at St. Margaret's Church in King's Lynn, see his letters to Esther (n. 1, above) and to the Parish of St. Margaret's (Scholes 1948, 1:81).

BRIDGE: FRAGMENTS 65–66

*Reception at Lynn.
Mayor's Feast   By
whom visited &
patronised there*[1]

*Clergy & Physicians
finding me fond of
books civil &
friendly*[2]

*Dr Hepburne & the
Revd Mr Pyle*[3]

*Sir Jno Turner &
the Collector*[4]

*Opponents of S^r Jno
at a contested Election
my enemies on my
arrival*[5]

*Schools & Scholars in
the Country*[6]

1. In Sept. 1751, CB set out for King's Lynn "to feel his way, & know the humours of the place, & prices of Lodgings, provisions &c" (CB to Charles Burney, 20 Dec. [1799], Berg). The mayor then was William Bagge (1700–1762). CB's first impressions of the place were very negative (CB to Esther, [c. 30 Sept. 1751], Osborn). He rented at £12 a year "a pretty convenient house" in Chapel Street and later moved to High Street, where in 1753 he was assessed £10 13s 4d, but in 1759–60 only £7 (Hillen, 2:491–92).

Shortly after his arrival in Lynn, CB started a series of subscription concerts. Dr. A. H. Mann collected advertisements for these from two Norfolk newspapers. The *Ips-wich Journal* of 27 Jan. 1753: "Lynn Mr. Burneys subscription Concert on Thursday 8 Feb. at 6 o clock Tickets 3/—"; of 4 Aug. 1753: "Lynn. Mr Burneys subscription concert at the Town Hall Tuesday 28 Aug. at 7 o clock. Tickets 3/—"; of 19 Oct. 1754: "Coronation day of His Majesty. New Organ at St Margarets accompanied with other Instruments. 1st Violin Mr Fisher. Haut boy, Mr. Sharp. Organ Mr. Berney. Conclusion Handels Coronation Anthem." The *Norfolk Mercury* of 10 Sept., 18 Sept., 2 Oct. 1757: "Lynn Regis, Norfolk. On Tuesday the 11th October there will be a performance of Sacred Music In St. Margarets Church, which will begin precisely at 3 o'clock in the Afternoon, and in the evening there will be a Ball, at the Town Hall. Tickets to be had at Mr. Burneys House in High Street"; of 16 Sept. 1758: "Mr. Burneys Concert is held on Tuesday Oct. 17 at the Town Hall. He still lives in High Street" (this is first advertised for Oct. 10th); of 5 May 1759: "Lynn Regis. Mr Burneys Concert (and after it a Ball) will be held at the Town Hall, on Friday 8th June" ("King's Lynn Musical Events," Mann MSS 15, Norfolk Record Office). See Scholes 1948, 1:85–86 for three of these advertisements.

2. "When I went into Norfolk, in the autumn of 1751, I found but one person, (the Rev. Mr. Squires, a man of learning, and a general purchaser of new books) who knew any thing of [the *Ramblers*]," wrote CB in a note to Boswell's *Life of Johnson*. The Rev. Charles Squire (c. 1694–1752) was headmaster of Lynn School and rector of Congham and Little Massingham (Hill/Powell, 1:208 n.3; 6:369; CB to Edmond Malone, 6 Oct. 1803, Bodleian). One of the "physicians" with whom CB became friendly was William Bewley of Great Massingham (see Bridge: Frags. 68–69, n. 1).

Mme d'Arblay points out the importance in smaller towns of "the physicians; who, for general education, learning, science, and politeness, are as frequently the leaders in literature as they are the oracles in health; and who, with the confraternity of the vicar, and the superior lawyer, are so commonly the allowed despots of erudition and the belles lettres in provincial circles" (*Mem.,* 1:95).

3. These were, according to a historian of King's Lynn, "two of the most prominent characters in this town"; see Richards, 2:889. On 19 Dec. 1751 CB wrote to his wife (*Mem.,* 1:91) trying to entice her to come to Lynn:

> If 'tis meet to fee or bribe
> A Leech of th'Aesculapius tribe,
> We Hepburn have, who's wise as
>   Socrates,
> And deep in physic as Hippocrates.

George Hepburn (1669–1759) had settled in King's Lynn early in the century "as a physician; in which character he soon acquired high reputation, so as to be placed at the head of the profession for near if not quite half the century" (Richards, 2:1028–32, gives a long account of him). Thomas Pyle (1674–1756), divine and preacher, author of *Paraphrase of the Acts and Epistles, in the manner of Dr. Clarke* (1725). In 1701 the corporation of King's Lynn appointed him minister of St. Nicholas's Chapel, and in 1732 he exchanged his old living for the vicarage of St. Margaret's. He resigned this place in 1755 and retired to Swaffham, where he died on 31 Dec. 1756; see Richards 2:1012–23; and Pyle, pp. 1–2.

4. For Sir John Turner, see Frag. 65, n. 1. In his letter to his wife (n. 1, above), CB says: "Even Sir J. who is the Oracle of Apollo in this Country is extremely Shallow." Charles Turner (Frag. 69, n. 3), Collector of the Customs House and Alderman of Lynn, was Sir John's cousin.

5. Evidently the fierce animosities aroused by the hotly contested election of 1747 were still simmering in 1751. Sir John Turner, whose opponent was William Folkes, Esq., owed his victory "less to his own management, than to the favour and influence of the Walpoles." "At the close of the poll the numbers were—for *Walpole* 199; for *Turner* 184; for *Folkes* 131." Richards (2:947–52) quotes a racy account by Edmund Pyle of "the insults heaped on the T——r family" and the satirical plays staged by the candidates against each other. Two of the most violent opponents of Sir John Turner were "Dr. B——," nicknamed "Busy Body" and [John] Harvey the "Pothecary."

6. Mme d'Arblay writes: "He had immediately for his pupils the daughters of every house in Lynn, whose chief had the smallest pretensions to belonging to the upper classes of the town; while almost all persons of rank in its vicinity, eagerly sought the assistance of the new professor for polishing the educa-

tion of their females: and all alike coveted his society for their own information or entertainment" (*Mem.,* 1:94). One of these was Dorothy Robertson, daughter of the Lynn wine merchant Walter Robertson (Frag. 67., n. 5): "She was of a pleasing figure, with fine black expressive eyes, danced well, and also sang and performed well on the harpsichord;

no wonder, as she received instructions from Mr. Burney. He was a person held in the highest estimation for his powers of conversation and agreeable manners, which made his company sought by all the principal nobility and gentry of the neighbourhood" (Young, p. 23; Young arrived in King's Lynn in 1758).

FRAGMENT 66   Narford, early 1750s

[Sir Andrew Fountaine][1]

for prints for the *Tale of a Tub,* [   ] of the [   ] that celebrated Satire. He was much esteemed by dean Swift, and is often mentioned with regard in his journal to Stella.[2] He was vice chamberlain to Queen Caroline, when Princess of Wales; afterwards appointed Tutor to Prince William, & created K[t] of the Bath.[3] He was no practical Musician; but at Card[i]nal Ottoboni's he told me, that he had often seen and heard Corelli;[4] and at the time when I used to give lessons in accompaniment to a gentleman[5] near his charming place at Narford, he used to visit my eleve: and when we played any of Corelli's works, he said it gave him infinite pleasure, as it reminded him of his happiness at Rome, when at the Academie, or Concerti, of Cardinal Ottoboni.

1. Sir Andrew Fountaine (1676–1753), virtuoso and art collector, satirized by Pope as Annius, was a friend of Swift. In 1727 he succeeded Newton as Warden of the Mint and in 1732 retired to his seat at Narford, four and a half miles northwest of Swaffham— built at the beginning of the century and frescoed by Pellegrini—where he assembled a remarkable "ragoust of paintings, statues, gilding and virtù," coins, books, Palissy ware, Limoges, majolica, etc. See Ketton-Cremer 1957, pp. 177, 179, 184.

2. Swift's many references to Sir Andrew in his *Journal to Stella* show that he was on close terms with him in 1710–13: "dined with sir Andrew" and "spent seven shillings for my dinner like a puppy"; "play'd at Ombre with him" till "eleven this evening like a fool"; spent evenings with him "wretchedly punning"; drank punch with him, or "sauntered at china-shops and book-sellers; went to the tavern, drank two pints of white wine," etc. (Swift 1:43, 51, 53, 99, 303; 2:416).

The beginning of this fragment is unfortunately missing; it would have provided a clue to the eight original designs for *A Tale of a Tub,* which are still preserved at Narford Hall. "Inserted in the very fine large-paper copy of the *Tale* which Sir Andrew received in 1710" and evidently showed in 1751 or 1752 to CB, they are of much higher quality than Bernard Lens's engravings, which appeared in the printed edition: see the Guthkelch/ Nicholl Smith edition of the *Tale,* pp. xxv– xxviii. The editors state that there is nothing to indicate that they were done by Sir Andrew himself, who was not, according to Walpole, "a practising draughtsman." It is likely that they were sketched for Swift by the Venetian painter Giovanni Antonio Pellegrini (1675–1741), who between 1708 and 1713 did the frescoes in "a hall at Sir Andrew Fountain's at Narford in Norfolk," and "painted besides many such small pieces of history before he left England" (Walpole *Anecdotes,* 2:627–28).

3. Sir Andrew had been knighted in 1699. In 1725 he was appointed vice-chamberlain to Princess Caroline and tutor to Prince William, for whom he stood proxy when the prince was made a Knight of the Bath. On that occasion Sir Andrew was granted a patent (14 Jan. 1725) for adding supporters to his arms.

4. Corelli was patronized by Cardinal Pietro Ottoboni (1667–1740), an enthusiastic lover of the arts, who maintained Corelli in his palace. Sir Andrew had been several times at Rome collecting antiquities, and no doubt heard Corelli between 1701 and 1708 at the Cardinal's Monday concerts, which were considered the most interesting events in Rome's musical life.

5. Not identified.

BRIDGE: FRAGMENTS 66–67

Early in his stay in Norfolk, Burney became acquainted with the North family, descendants of Roger North (c. 1651–1734), whose informative manuscript "Memoirs of Musick, being some Historico-critticall Collections on that Subject," 1728, CB quotes in *Hist. Mus.* "He had an organ, built by father Smith, for a gallery of sixty feet long, which he erected on purpose for its reception, at Rougham, his family seat in Norfolk. This instrument, though entirely composed of wooden pipes, was spritely, and infinitely more sweet in its tone, than any one of metal that I ever heard" (*Hist. Mus.* 3:409n; Mercer, 2:322n. See also "Roger North" in Rees).

"North's Ms. Memoirs of Music were sent me by the late D[r] North, Canon of Windsor,[1] the son of the writer of those Memoirs, wth whom, & his older brother, Roger North[2] of Rougham in Norfolk, I long lived in friendship. The North family . . . were originally of Norfolk, and great lovers and patrons of Music . . . to the death of my friend D[r] North, who had a very curious collection of Music, & was himself a good Musician. . . . I have, *somewhere,* a transcript of the chief part of the Memoirs of Music" (CB to Edmond Malone, 30 June 1799, PML).[3]

1. The Rev. Montagu North (1712–79), D.D., installed Canon of Windsor 30 June 1775. One of his letters to CB is extant (31 May 1771, Osborn).

2. Roger North (c. 1703–71) attended school at Thetford in Norfolk, was admitted at Middle Temple in 1718 and at Trinity College, Cambridge, in 1720; he later married Jane, daughter of William Lake of Hitchin

(Venn, *Alumni Cantabrigienses*).

3. North's surviving manuscripts are now in the British Library and the library of Hereford Cathedral. Selections from them, including the "Memoirs of Musick," appear in *Roger North on Music,* ed. John Wilson (1959). CB's transcript, which he used in preparing vol. 3 of *Hist. Mus.,* is not known to be extant.

FRAGMENT 67

early 1750s

*Patronage of L^d
Orford at Houghton*[1]

during my 9 years residence at Lynn, in the neighbourhood of Houghton, where I was patronized and spent much time; and having the run of that noble collection,[2] I could not help availing myself of the privilege of having the key from the house-keeper to wander about the apartments alone with the Catalogue[3] in my hand, at my leisure. Add to this, that two of my best and most intimate Norfolk friends, John Davis Esqr. of Watlington,[4] and Alderman Walther Robinson of Lynn,[5] were excellent dillettante painters, with whom I often went to Houghton and profitted from their remarks—In short I had the collection so much by heart, that I acted the part of a *Cicerone* to some of my friends who came from London, and other parts of the kingdom to make the tour of Norfolk. And I may be said to have been at home, not only at Houghton Hall, but at Rainham,[6] at Sir Andrew Fountaine's,[7] at Halcombe,[8] Blickling,[9] Wolterton,[10] and Sir Harry l'Estrange's.[11] At all which places there was painting, sculpture architecture and antiquities to examine.

1. George Walpole (1730–91), nephew of Horace Walpole, was educated at Eton; half a year before CB's arrival in Norfolk he succeeded his father as 3rd Earl of Orford, 1 April 1751, and on 8 April 1751 as High Steward of Lynn. He inherited Houghton, one of the great Norfolk houses, which his grandfather, Sir Robert Walpole, the Prime Minister, had

had constructed (1722–35) according to designs by Kent and furnished with a famous gallery of pictures (Ketton-Cremer 1948, pp. 162–87). The young lord's "love of music" (CB to Lord Orford, 18 Sept. 1752, Scholes Papers, Osborn) evidently led to his patronage of CB. Orford in his last letter to CB, 8 Nov. 1791 (Berg), mentioned his attempt at an opera and described his "Houghton Band . . . of Half a Dozen tolerable Voices Pick'd from among⟨st⟩ the Soldiers of the Regiment." CB replied: "I am extremely glad to find that yʳ Lordᴾ still continues to honour Music with your attention & Patronage. My own Studies, in former times, were very much invigorated & benefitted by the good taste & encouragemᵗ I met with at Houghton" ([14–15 Nov. 1791], Berg).

2. The famous collection of paintings on which Sir Robert Walpole had spent over £100,000 was sold by Lord Orford to the Empress Catherine of Russia in 1777–79 for £40,555 (or, according to J. H. Plumb, £36,080; see YW, 24:441 n.15).

3. Horace Walpole's *Ædes Walpolianæ* (1743). Reviewing Horace Walpole's works, CB writes: "This edition of the catalogue is embellished with splendid portraits of the first Lord and Lady Orford, and with views and ground-plans of Houghton Hall, which we do not remember to have before seen, when visiting the pictures with that catalogue in hand" (*Monthly Review* 27 [1798]: 59–60). He also laments "the loss of so valuable an assemblage of pictures, equal if not superior to any private collection in Europe."

4. "John Davis, Esq." died 4 Sept. 1778 (*GM*, 48:439). See Frags. 79–81.

5. No doubt Alderman Walter Robertson (1703–72), Scottish wine merchant, who in 1740 married Alice Tayler (1708–72), widow of the wealthy Simon Tayler (Bradfer-Lawrence, pp. 163–64). He was mayor of King's Lynn in 1747 and 1761. In the King's Lynn rate-books the names Robinson and Robert-

son are both frequently spelled "Roberson"—hence CB's slip.

6. Raynham Hall, the seat of George Townshend. See Frag. 72, n. 1.

7. At Narford; see Frag. 66.

8. Holkham, near Wells, the seat of Thomas Coke of Norfolk (1697–1759), cr. 1744 Viscount Coke of Holkham and Earl of Leicester, who began rebuilding it in 1733 in the new Palladian fashion. According to Mme d'Arblay, CB and Esther visited its "superb collection of statues, as well as of pictures," but as there were "neither pupils, nor a Male chief, no intercourse beyond that of the civilities of reception on a public day, took place" (*Mem.*, 1:100).

9. Blickling, an old Jacobean house near Aylsham, was owned by John Hobart (1694?–1756), 1st Earl of Buckinghamshire.

10. Wolterton, also near Aylsham, was the seat of Horace Walpole's uncle, Horatio Walpole (1678–1757), 1st Baron of Wolterton. Ketton-Cremer (1957, pp. 171–202) quotes contemporary accounts of the great Norfolk houses.

11. Sir Henry L'Estrange (d. 2 Sept. 1760), of Hunstanton, fifteen miles from King's Lynn, "the last survivor of that ancient family." At his death "I was favoured with [the] collection" of musical "'fancies' which had been made for the L'Estrange family, in Norfolk, by the celebrated composer of Charles the first's reign, Mr. John Jenkins" (*Hist. Mus.*, 3:356 and n.; Mercer, 2:283 and n. See also CB to William Mason, 8 June 1795, Berg).

FRAGMENT 68   King's Lynn, early 1750s

Studies at Home—
readings with wife[1]

As he could wait upon his country pupils only on horse-back, he purchased a mare
that so exactly suited his convenience and his wishes, in
surefootedness, gentleness and sagacity, that she soon seemed   Read on horse-back,
to him a part of his family: and the welfare and comfort of   & teach myself Ital.[2]
Peggy became, ere long, a matter of kind interest to all his house.

On this mare he studied Italian; for, obliged to go leisurely over the cross roads with
which Norfolk then abounded, and which were tiresome from dragging sands, or
dangerous from deep ruts in clay,[3] *half his valuable time would have been lost in*
nothingness, but for his trust in Peggy; who was as careful in safely picking her way, as
she was adroit in remembering from week to week whither she was meant to go.

Her master, at various odd moments, and from various opportunities, had com-
pressed, from the best Italian Dictionaries, every word of the Italian language into a
small octavo volume; and from this in one pocket, and a volume of Dante, Petrarch,
Tasso, Ariosto, or Metastasio, in another, he made himself completely at home in that
language of elegance and poetry.[4]

His common-place book, at this period, rather merits the appellation of uncommon,
from the assiduous research it manifests, to illustrate every sort of information, by
extracts, abstracts, strictures, or descriptions, upon the almost universality of subject-
matter which it contains.[5]

It is without system or method; he had no leisure to put it into order; yet it is
possible, he might owe to his familiar recurrence to that desultory assemblage of
unconcocted materials, the general and striking readiness with which he met at once
almost every topic of discourse.

This manuscript of scraps, drawn from reading and observation, was, like his
Italian Dictionary, always in his great coat pocket, when he travelled; so that if
unusually rugged roads, or busied haste, impeded more regular study, he was sure, in
opening promiscuously his pocket collection of odds and ends, to come upon some
remark worth weighing; some point of science on which to ruminate; some point of
knowledge to fix in his memory; or something amusing, grotesque, or little known,
that might recreate his fancy.

1. On 19 Dec. 1751, CB sent a long verse epistle to Esther in London, in which he proposed to her an extensive reading pro-gram of modern classics after she joined him in Lynn: Pope, Swift, Addison, Bacon, Con-greve, Dryden, Milton, *Don Quixote,*

Hudibras, Locke, and Shakespeare. Mme d'Arblay printed the verses in *Mem.,* 1:91–94. For his more learned reading, see Frag. 69, nn. 4, 5. It was during his stay in Norfolk that CB "first conceived the idea of writing a *General History of Music,* and began reading and collecting materials there for that purpose" (*EM*).

2. Mme d'Arblay destroyed CB's original account but paraphrased it in *Mem.,* 1:107–9, from which this passage is taken.

3. Later, traveling from Berlin to Potsdam, CB noted that "the road . . . is through a deep running sand, like the worst parts of Norfolk . . . where there are no turnpikes" (*Tours,* 2:169).

4. The pigskin volume of 150 pages, entitled *Dizionario portativo Italiano ed Inglese. compilato da Carlo Burney per l'uso proprio di se stesso MDCCLVI,* is now in the Osborn Collection. Its title page is reproduced in Scholes 1948, 1:pl. 9. As Lonsdale (1965, p. 43) points out, CB was encouraged in his Italian studies by Vincenzo Martinelli (1702–85), author of *Lettere familiari e critiche* (London, 1758): "I lived much with Martinelli, and often met him at Houghton, while I lived in Norfolk— there I saw all his letters before & while they were printing. I had not been in Italy then, & picked his brains as much as I c^d ab^t Musical hist^y & anecdotes, as well as literature in general. He was an excellent critic in his own language & of great use to me in its accentuation, & in pointing out to me the ignorance of many composers in setting words" (CB to J. C. Walker, 2 Feb. 1801, Osborn). On 27 Feb. 1760 Martinelli wrote to CB from London, congratulating him on his progress in the language (Osborn).

5. In the BL (Add. MSS 48345, ff. 23–37) there is a small common-place book with quotations from unnamed sources in English, French, and Greek; on p. 36, CB wrote: "Mem^{dum} All the preceding extracts in this common-place book were made at Lynn Regis Norfolk, between the y^{rs} 1755 & 1760."

BRIDGE: FRAGMENTS 68–69

Bewley's character,
talents,
& friendship[1]

Mr Robinson's worth
& friendly zeal[2]

Mr Stephen Allen
from a foe
becomes a friend[3]

1. William Bewley (1726–83) settled in Great Massingham near King's Lynn in 1749 as a surgeon and apothecary. He became friendly with CB in the early 1750s, and although they met infrequently after CB's departure for London in 1760, they maintained a regular correspondence until the end of Bewley's life. CB's letter to Thomas Twining

of 6 Sept. 1783, the day after Bewley's death, gives a short character sketch of his friend: "He was born the same year as myself;— loved every thing that you & I love—Music—Books—fun—& had an *extent* & *depth* of Science that I have never met with. In Electricity he has made as many discoveries as Franklyn, & in fixt Air as Priestley: an excellent anatomist, of course, but for experimental philosophy, there was no end or limit to it, and with all this a humanity, & goodness of heart, & a simplicity of character, enlivened by natural & original wit & humour, which delighted every body who conversed with him." See also *Mem.*, 1:105–7. In a letter to CB dated 18 March 1763, Bewley recollects the happy times spent at Lynn with the Burneys: "My *debauches scavantes* with the Father, & my innocent nocturnal commerce with the contending Sultana's, the daughters!" (Osborn). The best published account of their friendship is in Lonsdale 1965, passim. See also Frag. 85.

2. See Frag. 67, n. 5.

3. Stephen Allen (1724–63), wealthy merchant of a prominent King's Lynn family, no doubt sided with the opponents of Sir John Turner on CB's arrival in King's Lynn and was CB's "enemy" because CB was patronized by Sir John. In 1749 he married Elizabeth Allen, who later became CB's second wife; see Frag. 69, n. 7.

FRAGMENT 69   King's Lynn, early 1750s

Wodehouse's[1] &c. At Lynn the most intimate & affectionate friends I had were Walther Robinson,[2] Ald^n, Chas Turner, Collector of the Customs,[3] and Mr Stephen Allens. At all these houses I used to dine once a week & often my Wife, who never failed being invited to all evening Parties though no card-player. But she had a most agreeable turn for conversation; entered into the humours of her company; seasoned her conversation with agreeable wit & pleasing manners; wch with the beauty of her person occasioned her more invitations than she chose to accept: as she was very domestic, had a young family on her hands, generally one of them at her breast, and when we c^d spend an evening at home, we had a course of reading: history, voyages, poetry, and science, as far as Chambers's

Wife's reception everywhere, & the mutual friend^p and attachment of her, Mrs Allen & D. Young

Dict^y,[4] the French Encyclopédie,[5] & the Philosophical transactions, wch set her greatly above the generality of Lynn ladies; for few of them were readers, except Mrs Stephen Allen, and Miss Dolly Young,[6] to whom I was so partial, that I thought no three such females could be found on our Island. They read every thing they c^d procure. This congeniality of taste brought on a close intimacy & friendship between them, wch lasted till the termination of their several lives. Mrs Allen, a beautiful woman who had educated herself, & by her passion for reading had acquired the superficies of general literature in a superior degree to the[7]

1. Armine Wodehouse (c. 1714–77), of Kimberley, M.P. for Norfolk 1737–68, succeeded as 5th Baronet in 1754. The Wodehouses were a leading Tory family in Norfolk, and Sir Armine, though "nervous and irascible in temperament," was on good terms with George Townshend (Frag. 72), the Whig M.P. for the county (Namier/Brooke, 3:652).

2. See Frag. 67, n. 5.

3. Charles Turner (d. 1792), cousin of Sir John Turner, freeman (by gift) of King's Lynn 1737, Collector of Customs and Alderman at Lynn; elected Mayor in 1759 and again in 1767. "An extremely unpopular official, & the chief cause of the wane of his family's influence in Lynn" (Bradfer-Lawrence, p. 160).

4. *Cyclopaedia, or an Universal Dictionary of Arts and Sciences,* compiled by Ephraim Chambers, was issued in 1728 by subscription (5th ed., 1746).

5. In the earlier Osborn fragment, CB adds "to the 1st Edit. of wch I was so extravagant as to subscribe." Diderot's prospectus for the *Encyclopédie* appeared in November 1750; the first volume was published in July 1751 and delivered to the subscribers in August. The second appeared in January 1752, and the third in November 1757. The last volume (18) came out only in 1765, when there were 4,250 subscribers.

6. Dorothy Young (c. 1721–1805). The Stanley Public Library at Lynn has a copy of her *Translations from the French by D. Y.,* Lynn, printed for the author by Whittingham, 1770. "Dr. Charles Burney, 6 copies" figures among the subscribers (Scholes 1948, 1:75). It includes a translation of Diderot's *Fils naturel*; in 1770, CB gave a copy of it to Diderot (*Tours,* 1:316). Dorothy Young "was not only denied beauty either of face or person, but in the first she had various unhappy defects, and in the second she was extremely deformed," writes Fanny, who commends her "patience": "Her feelings were so sensitive, that tears started into her eyes at every thing she either saw or heard of mortal sufferings" (*Mem.,* 1:97–98).

7. Elizabeth Allen (1728–96), daughter of Thomas Allen of King's Lynn and Mary née Maxey, married Stephen Allen on 22 May 1749. "She was the most celebrated beauty of Lynn," writes Fanny. "She had wit at will; spirits the most vivacious and entertaining; and, from a passionate fondness for reading, she had collected stores of knowledge which she was always able, and 'nothing loathe' to display" (*Mem.,* 1:97–98). Mrs. Thrale in 1778 rated her, out of 20, "'Worth of Heart' 10; 'Conversation Powers' 7; 'Person Mien & Manner' 0; 'Good humour' 17; 'Ornamental knowledge' 9" (*Thraliana,* 1:331). A fine kit-cat portrait of her is in the possession of Dr. Raymond Paul Martin, Montreal.

FRAGMENT 70

[Snetzler,[1] a] worthy man & excellent workman, had, during his Apprenticeship, worked at the celebrated Organ at Harlem, in Holland; and introduced several Stops into the Lynn Organ, from that renowned instrument, particularly the *Dulciana* stop, of wch the tone is extremely sweet & delicate. It is now introduced as a solo stop *New Organ*[2]— in all our best Chamber Organs, and has this advantage over the reed Stops, that it stands in tune as well as the open diapason, wth wch it is in unison.[3]

After the new Lynn Organ was finished, wch had been two years in building, lovers of Music in Summer time used to come from Cambridge, Norwich, Yarmouth & Bury, to hear it.[4]

Soon after it was opened, however, when I[5]

parson Davil's aversion to Voluntaries[6]

Cram them down his throat

1. Johann Snetzler or Schnetzler (1710–85), Swiss organ builder, came to England in 1746 or 1747. For the fine organ he built in 1754 for St. Margaret's, according to CB's specification or a specification approved by him, see Hillen (2:493–97) and Scholes (1948, 2:319–20). "Snetzler's success in England probably owed much to Burney's high opinion of his abilities" (*New Grove*, 17:427).

2. For the old seventeenth-century organ built by George Dallam, which CB found on his arrival in King's Lynn, see CB to Esther Burney, [c. 30 Sept. 1751] (Osborn). "As the wooden pipes were so worm-eaten as to fall to pieces when taken out to be cleaned," CB recommended in 1754 that another organ be installed. Byfield "having had an application from the corporation of Lynn Regis, in Norfolk, to build them a new organ for St. Margaret's church . . . wished very much to persuade them to purchase the instrument made by Harris, which had been a second time excommunicated; but being already in possession of an *old* organ, they determined to have a new one; and by the advice of the author of this book, employed Snetzler to construct one, which he did very much to his own credit and their satisfaction" (*Hist. Mus.*, 3:438n; Mercer, 2:345n).

John Byfield (d. 1774) and John Harris (fl. 1726–43), son of Renatus Harris, were organ builders who carried on business in Red Lion Street, Holborn. For an account of the difficulties the church wardens encountered in attempting to dispose of the old organ, see Dr. A. H. Mann's "King's Lynn Musical Events" (Mann MSS 15, Norfolk Record Office; substantially reproduced in Scholes 1948, 1:77–79).

3. In another fragment CB wrote: "A new

Org. was given by the Corporation of Lynn to the Church of St Marg[a]ret the 1st year of my arrival, made by Snetzler it cost 180 ⟨l.⟩, is an excellent instrument and was the 1st in wch a ⟨Borduun⟩ or double-stop, and a Dulciana were introduced into this country, wth w^[ch] I am acquainted" (BL, Add. MSS 48345, f. 17^v). The Bourdon is a soft or moderately loud stopped flue stop of droning or buzzing quality. The organ at King's Lynn "had a Bourdon, to CC, of metal throughout, except the two lowest notes which were of wood" (Scholes 1948, 2:319). The Dulciana is a gentle small-scale inverted conical stop, first used in Austria. CB saw one in the great Haarlem organ, constructed in 1738 (*Tours*, 2:232). It was introduced to England by Snetzler (*New Grove*, 13:789).

4. "After this I had fr[e]quent concerts of sacred music chief[ly] from Handel's Oratorios in the ⟨ch⟩[urch]" (BL, Add. MSS 48345, f. 17^v). CB's first concert on Snetzler's organ was advertised on 9 March 1754 in the *Ipswich Journal*: "LYNN. The new Organ made by Mr. Snetzler of Oxford Road, London, for St. Margaret's Church, will be opened on Sunday, March 17 by Mr. Burney" (Scholes 1948, 1:79).

5. The missing text probably mentioned a malfunction. In a letter to J. W. Callcott (14 Jan. 1803, Osborn), CB wrote: "Snetzler put a reed Stop in the Lynn Org. under my eye, wch he called a *Fr. Horn.*—it was a louder and coarser kind of Hautboy."

In 1778, CB told Mrs. Thrale that he "was shewing off the Instrument in all its Variety of tones: it had 31 Stops, & was eminently excellent. One of the Corporation after listening attentively says to his Companion:— Brother Clark, your Daughter learns to play at Top of the Musick—can You tell me when he will come to the *Flats & Sharps*" (*Thraliana*, 1:332–33).

6. Rev. John Daville (fl. 1747–68), of Wigan Hall, is listed among the freemen of King's Lynn in 1747–48 and 1768 (*Lynn Magazine*, 1768, p. 86; Richards, 2:931). Like Mason, Daville preferred psalm singing to brilliant extemporizing on the organ. For CB's vigorous championship of voluntaries in church service, see CB to Mason, 8 June 1795 (Berg).

FRAGMENT 71   mid 1750s

among whom Mr Warner's 2 sons from Walsingham[2] were of considerable use one on the Violin and one on the Violoncello. It was at the Ball, after one of these Concer[ts] that the enlevem^t of Miss Audry T. happened by Capt. O.[3]

Fakenham Concerts & Balls[1]

1. These were no doubt held at the Red Lion, Fakenham, " a sorry house" and "an indifferent inn" where visitors to Lord Townshend's seat at nearby Raynham stopped overnight (Ketton-Cremer 1957, pp. 182, 192). The Bradfer-Lawrence Collection in the Norfolk Record Office (Bradfer-Lawrence, VI b [1]) has a list of "the Subscribed to Fakenham Concert for the Year 1753" with the following rules:

—That every Subscriber pays to the Steward half a Guinea. The First Concert be in April 1753 which shall be advertised

—That Every such Subscriber have then two Tickets delivered to him . . .

—That any Subscriber may admit any Gleman or Lady by a Ticket, Signed by himself Such Subscriber being answerable to yᵉ Steward, for half a Crown for every such Ticket

—That any Subscriber may admit a Performer without yᵉ Ticket being paid for

—That all Persons (not Performers) be seated & silent during yᵉ Performance

Among sixty-odd signatures, one clearly recognizable is that of W. Windham. According to the *Norfolk Mercury,* 7 Oct. 1758, "It appears that the Concert at Fakenham was altered from Wednesday 18ᵗʰ to Thursday 19ᵗʰ because Mr. Burney's concert being on the 17ᵗʰ and his voluntary on the organ on the 18ᵗʰ." For CB's voluntaries at St. Margaret's, see Frag. 70, n. 6.

2. Lee Warner (d. 17 Dec. 1760), of Walsingham Abbey, Norfolk, whom CB calls one of his close friends in Norfolk (BL, Add. MSS 48345, f. 22ᵛ), had three sons: Henry Lee (b. 1722) matriculated 30 June 1741 at St. John's College, Oxford; John Lee and Thomas Lee (both b. 1737) matriculated 19 March 1755 at Christ Church, Oxford. CB probably refers to the last two. Walsingham is five miles north of Fakenham.

3. The Hon. Audrey Townshend (d. 1781), sister of CB's patron George Townshend (see Frag. 72), was "a great coquette"; in Nov. 1756 she caused a scandal by eloping with Capt. Robert Orme (d. 1790), Braddock's aide-de-camp in America. According to Sherson (p. 300), Orme was "a handsome young officer in the Coldstreams . . . came from a good old Devonshire family, was known as an honest and capable man and a fine soldier, and made a favourable impression wherever he went. But my Lady Townshend had destined her beautiful daughter for Lord George Lennox. She never forgave her, and the Orme children got little or nothing at her death." The problem was that Orme was a married man and "poor Mrs. O. *run mad,* and gone in to the bedlam" (YW, 9:188 n.8; 20:495 n.5). On 13 Nov. 1756 the Rev. Edmund Pyle, who did not like the Townshends, wrote: "I suppose you've heard that Lord Townshend's daughter is run into Flanders with a married man (Capt. Orme) to whom she has given £14,000. She is with child—&, besides all her other infamy, has gone off deeply in debt to all sorts of tradespeople. The common wish expressed in town on this incident, was, would to God all the family were gone out of the nation!" (Pyle, p. 272).

Lord Townshend.[1]

His Lordᵖ was so innocent a shot in his younger days, that he cᵈ shoot at a Norfolk covey of birds as numerous as a flock of Pidgeons, without hurting one of them; but then he used triumphantly to say to the birds—"yes, yes,—you *may* go, but you *have* it."

on his return, being asked what he had killed?—why, says he, "I can't say that I have absolutely killed any; but I have frightened them most damnably."

The late Lord Orford,[2] a manly, active character, though fond of sporting of every kind, yet in hunting he was not fond of an awkward leap. And upon seeing him one day ride boldly after the Whipper-in, who took a very difficult leap over a hedge & double-ditch, I said to Ld T. then only Colonel T.[3]—Will my L^d venture to take that leap? No, no, says he—*he's only going to look for an objection.*—wch his L^p soon finding, he galloped to a gate at 1/2 a mile's distance, wch stood "so invitingly open," that he even preferred it [to] the honour of breaking his neck.

This most amiable, spirited, and worthy nobleman (Ld O.) however, more than 40 years after, broke his back in the field, by throwing himself off a runaway horse, in coursing![4]

Ld T. seeing himself surrounded by pickpockets in a mob at the door of the House of Lords, where he was waiting for his Carriage, he pulled out his watch & holding it up, he says to the pick-pockets—"my lads! 'tis only a metal watch, & not worth y^r trouble."

During the life of his father,[5] when he was only Col. Townshend, at his hunting Seat near Fakenham in Norfolk, he used to have his Children by L^y Ferrers, his 1st Lady,[6] brought in after dinner during the dessert, while the servants dined: when George the eldest son (afterwards Earl of Leicester)[7] usually took to sulk, & w^d not say a word, or do a thing he was desired—when the Col. clapping his hand on his head, cries out—"there's a fine boy for you—not only like his father but like his Grandfather." *The whole Townshend family & Lady Ferrars, always honoured*

Happening in the autumn of 17[87] to stop at Stockdale the bookseller's in Piccadilly,[8] Ld T. being in the shop, asked me if I had seen the papers that morn^g—& on my answering in the negative, he s^d — ["]Why, they say there, that the King has made me a Marquess"[9] ["]I am glad of it my Lord, I had hoped that y^r L^p w^d have had that honour conferred on you long ago.["] ["] It is unsolicited, if true, says he—but folks will say, that my son & I are playing at *leap frog.*"

His son on the death of his mother was Baron Ferrers of whom Ld T. then only a viscount, took place, till the baron, by being created Earl of Leicester, leaped over his father's head—but when *he* became a marquis it was the Son's turn to dowk[10] again.

On my enquiring after his Sons[11] many years ago, he said: "My boys have all left me: every boy is a patriot till he gets into the sunshine of St James's."

1. The Hon. George Townshend (1724–1807) of Raynham Hall, Norfolk. During his career in the army he saw action at Dettingen, Fontenoy, Culloden, and with Wolfe at Quebec; later, as M.P. for Norfolk (1747–64), he was a great advocate of the militia bill. In 1764 he succeeded as 4th Viscount Townshend. His subsequent political career with his brother Charles (1725–67) was marked by a series of quarrels and disagreements, and his "disposition to ridicule" showed itself in his masterly caricatures. See Herbert M. Atherton, "George Townshend, Caricaturist," *Eighteenth Century Studies* 4 (1970–71): 437–46. Ketton-Cremer 1957 (facing p. 66) reproduces a mezzotint portrait of "The Honble Colonel Townshend," after a painting by Thomas Hudson. For his wife and sons, see nn. 6, 7, 9, below; for CB's later association with him, when Townshend was Governor of Chelsea College, see CB to Rosette Burney, 23 July [1796], (Burney-Cumming); and *Mem.,* 3:363–64.

2. See Frag. 67, n. 1.

3. George Townshend was promoted to colonel in May 1758, so the event took place during the last two years of CB's stay in Norfolk.

4. He died 5 Dec. 1791. This last sentence is a later addition. Lord Orford's death has been variously attributed to a fall from a horse or to a relapse into mental disorder following the death of Martha Turk, his long-time mistress. See also CB to Susan Phillips, 28 Nov. 1791 (Lewis).

5. Charles Townshend (1700–1764), 3rd Viscount Townshend, styled Lord Lynn, M.P. for Great Yarmouth 1721–23. He was, according to Horace Walpole, as wrongheaded as his son, and madder, and in 1757 the two "engaged in a paper-war against one another, about the militia" (YW, 21:138; 30:142; 35:286).

6. Lady Charlotte Compton (d. 14 Sept. 1774), *suo jure* Baroness Ferrers, daughter of James Compton, 5th Earl of Northampton, married George Townshend 19 Dec. 1751. She bore him four sons and four daughters.

7. The Hon. George Townshend (1755–1811) was then only four or five years old. On his mother's death he succeeded to the Barony de Ferrers, and on 18 May 1784 was cr. Earl of Leicester. Later Master of the Mint (1790–94) and joint Post-Master General (1790–99).

8. John Stockdale (1749?–1814), bookseller, opened his shop opposite Burlington House in Piccadilly in 1781. CB could not recall the exact year, so he left the last two digits blank. The year was 1787; see n. 9, below.

9. George Townshend was created Marquess Townshend of Raynham on 31 Oct. 1787; the news was announced in the *London Gazette* on 27 Oct. 1787. Far from being "unsolicited," the marquisate was one of his lordship's long-standing ambitions.

10. Dialect for "duck." The sequence of the "leap frogging" between father and son was as follows: father succeeded as 4th Viscount 12 Mar. 1764; son succeeded mother as Baron de Ferrers in 1774, cr. Earl of Leicester 18 May 1784; father cr. Marquess 31 Oct. 1787. The last leap came at the father's death, in 1807, when the son succeeded as 2d Marquess.

11. Apart from George (n. 7, above), Lord Townshend's sons were the Rt. Hon. John (1757–1833), M.P. for Cambridge University 1780–84, Westminster 1788–90, and Knaresborough 1793–1818; the Rev. Frederick Patrick (1767–1836), Rector of Stiffken with Morston, Norfolk 1792–1836 (Venn, *Alumni Cantabrigienses*); and Charles Patrick (d. 27 May 1796).

BRIDGE: FRAGMENTS 72-73

In his brief autobiographical sketch (BL, Add. MSS 48345, f. 22) Burney mentions, among the men he had met in Norfolk, Col. William Windham (Bridge: Frags. 61–62, n. 6), father of the statesman William Windham. In 1810 he answered Malone's queries "on the subject of the eldest Mr Windham's face":

"It was more round than that of his Son, & in general less grave (except when conversing wth females) nor do I remember that he was pitted with the small-pox. I think, nay I am certain, that he was not so tall as his Son, but rather of a middle height, and more lusty & muscular; but active & dextrous at all manly exercises in his younger days, as I have heard: for I did not know him personally till he was past his middle age.

"After I was resettled in London, I saw little of him. During my intimacy wth him & Col. Townshend in Norfolk from 1756 to 1760, I discovered that he had very precise & just notions concerning good Music of the Italian best school, though he had never been in Italy; but this he may have acquired at Geneva,[1] as well as Rousseau . . . it seems to me as if the late Mr W. had no great reverence or partiality for the memory of his Father—perhaps from thinking that he had not used his mother well. When I told him that the Verses—'Tommy Arne, Tommy Arne &c[']'[2] were written by his Father, he was very unwilling to beleive it. And when I spoke of his Plan of discipline for the Norfolk Militia,[3] of his excellent drawings for the Evolutions of the common men—& of the great knowledge in Tacktics he was allowed to have, my eloge was heard with great coldness & indifference" (CB to Edmond Malone, 23 [Aug. 1810], Bodleian).

In a later note to Malone, written on the same day, Burney adds to the character of the elder Windham "his natural turn for humour, very much resembling that of Garrick, who never gave such an answer as was expected to common questions unless he was in comp^y with Foot, Johnson, or some of his known enemies. Mr W. certainly loved a bit of the *black* [humour], like his fr^d Davy & Swift" (Burney-Cumming).

---

1. Col. Windham traveled in 1741 in Switzerland. His *Letters from an English Gentleman to Mr. Arland, giving an Account of a Journey to the Glaciers or Ice Alps of Savoy* (1744) is one of the earliest printed accounts of Chamonix and Mont Blanc.

2. See Bridge: Frags. 61–62, n. 8.

3. He helped Colonel Townshend raise the Norfolk militia. His *Plan of Discipline composed for the Use of the Militia of the County of Norfolk* was published in 1760.

FRAGMENT 73   King's Lynn, 1750s

Underwood, Town-Clerk of Lynn[1] Having offended Alderman Holley[2] a proud & Passionate Man, he rec[d] a challenge from him to meet & give him satisfaction with sword or pistol w[ch] he left to his choice. Underwood a lawyer & conveyancer, instead of accepting the challenge thought it more prudent to solicit a conference & try to appease him without bloodshed. He therefore called on his enraged antagonist, and addressed him in the following manner: ["]I am very sorry, M[r] Alderman that I have offended you, & I beg your pardon: if that will not be sufficient satisfaction for the offence (turning round, he says) pray Sir kick—consider my wife & family."[3]

1. Robert Underwood was granted in 1727–28 the freedom of King's Lynn and on 29 Sept. 1729 succeeded Robert Bradfield as Town Clerk. He died 23 Jan. 1767; his will was proved at the Consistory of Norwich in 1767 (*GM,* 37:48; *Norfolk Record Society,* 1969, 38:181). His son, the Rev. Benjamin Underwood, was granted the freedom of King's Lynn in 1766–67 (Bradfer-Lawrence, pp. 172, 192).

2. Benjamin Holley, whose will is dated 16 Jan. 1750 (Norfolk PRO). His daughter Alice married first Simon Tayler (d. 1738) and in 1740 Walter Robertson (see Frag. 67, n. 5). The Holleys were one of the half-dozen

wealthy families who controlled the affairs of King's Lynn. In 1929 a genealogy of the family was in the hands of the Rev. George H. Holley, M.A. of Holme-next-the-Sea (Bradfer-Lawrence, pp. 155, 163).

3. In writing this anecdote CB was no doubt aware of "The Phantom Duel" of 1759—when his friend and patron Col. George Townshend challenged Thomas Coke (Frag. 67, n. 8)—in which "the resort to arms was avoided by common sense, by an ability to compromise, even by a due perception of the ridiculous" (Ketton-Cremer 1957, pp. 151–68).

FRAGMENT 74   Narborough, mid 1750s

[Major Mackenzie][1]

of Sir Henry,[2] its first Lord, by Major Mackenzie; & his Lady[3] being very fond of Music, and a pretty good performer on the harpsichord, hearing that I was just come from London wished to receive some lessons from me, if I w[d] come once a week or once a fortnight, dine at Narborough, and remain there all night, as it was 14 miles dis[t]ance from Lynn, & too far to come & go in one day.

I obeyed the summons, and was so pleased wth my reception, & with the Major & his Lady, that had I been rich, I w^d have paid for admission, instead of receiving money for my journey & instructions.

The history of this accomplished & matchless pair is so singular as to merit a record.

1. William Mackenzie (d. 12 March 1770), major in the army, was a lineal descendant of the Scottish earls of Seaforth, whose estates were forfeited in 1716.

2. Not identified.

3. Mary (d. 12 Feb. 1813), daughter of Matthew Humberston, Lincs., sister of Thomas Humberston (c. 1730–55), M.P. for Brackley. She married Major Mackenzie sometime before 1745; they had two sons and four daughters (Mackenzie, pp. 331–32).

FRAGMENT 75   mid 1750s

cut them with their scymeters, & have deprived them of all command of their horses. Ld M. fearing that Agnue w^d behave ill in the battle,[1] desired Mackenzie to admonish that *cheeld,* to behave like a Mon, & remember, that there were no other North Britons in this Army, except they three, & that by cowardice, he w^d not only disgrace himself, but his country. His answer to this admonition was, "by Gode I feel that I conna feeght! but G–d—n me if I run awaw!" However, after the first panic was over, & the battle begun, he fought like a dragon.

Returning home after the termination of this war with the Turks, the Major married Miss Humberston,[2] a most amiable and accomplished lady of an old family, & with a considerable fortune; but who, by the death of

1. The context is not clear. It may refer to some engagement in the War of the Polish Succession 1736–39, perhaps the bloody battle of Krozka, fought on 23 Aug. 1739, in which the Austrian army under Field Marshal Count Georg von Wallis was defeated by the Turks, who were commanded by the Grand Vizier Al Haji Mohamed (*GM,* 9: 441). Mackenzie and his fellow Scotsmen probably served in the Imperial army. "Ld M." may be Kenneth Mackenzie, Lord Fortrose (d. 19 Oct. 1761), father of Kenneth (Frag. 77, n. 1; Mackenzie, pp. 316–28). "Agnue" has not been identified.

2. Her father, Matthew Humberston (b. 1705) of Lincoln, died 3 Jan. 1735/6. According to Paul (7:510, 513), she was his heiress.

FRAGMENT 76

set sail for Macow,[1] [   ] Island, whither she brought, *herself,* to the Major, the first news of her recovery; & her first child was born in China. They returned to Europe before the rebellion in 1745, wch being broke out in Scotland, & he being among the regulars in the royal Army, encamped on a wet & marshy soil, he lost the use of his limbs so entirely, that, though one of the most manly, graceful, & fine figures I ever saw, he was as much unable to stand, or go alone, as a child of six months old: and though every means were tried wch the most able Physicians, Surgeons, & Anatomists c^d suggest, for the restoration of his strength, he remained a cripple to the end of his life.

Mrs Mackenzie when I first had the honour of attending her, had not been long out of the straw,[2] & was

1. No doubt "Macao."

2. The eldest son, Thomas Frederick (1753–83), later Colonel of the 100th Highland Foot Regiment, on coming of age assumed his mother's maiden name Humberston and in 1779 purchased the estates of his chief and kinsman Kenneth Mackenzie (Frag. 77, n. 1) for £100,000. The younger son Francis (1754–1815) inherited his brother's estates and on 26 Oct. 1797 was created

Lord Seaforth, Baron Mackenzie of Kintail, co. Ross. After his brother's death he would have become 9th Earl of Seaforth but for the attainder of William Mackenzie, 5th Earl of Seaforth, in 1716. He later became lieutenant-general and from 1800 to 1806 governor of Barbados. There were also four daughters: Frances Cerjat, Maria Rebecca, Elizabeth, and Helen (Mackenzie, pp. 331–45).

FRAGMENT 77

life wch he [Major Mackenzie] was obliged to lead, ⟨&⟩ have [heard] him, in reading an agreeable novel, wish that it w^d last during the remainder of his life. He was perfectly acquainted wth the hist^y & state of European nations; had a philosophic and speculative turn, &, with the conversation of his charming consort, he submitted to his calamity with the utmost resignation & good grace. I never saw a happier couple. The head of his family was Lord Fortrose, who married Lady Caroline Stanhop[e], he was afterwards Earl of Seaforth, upon whose demise the title was extinct.[1]

I cannot leave this family w^thout recording a piece of heroism performed by Mrs Mackenzie in their solitary ⟨old⟩ Castle, during the absence of the Major, when there were female servants only in the House. In going upstairs to her chamber [one] Night after supper, she heard somebody sneeze in the case of a large clock on

1. Kenneth Mackenzie (1744–81), cr. Baron Ardelve and Viscount Fortrose in 1766, and in 1771 Earl of Seaforth, all in the peerage of Ireland. On 7 Oct. 1765 he married Caroline (1747–67), first daughter of William Stanhope, 2d Earl of Harrington. When CB wrote this, he was not aware that the Seaforth title had been revived in the United Kingdom in 1797, when Francis Mackenzie was cr. Lord Seaforth, Baron Mackenzie of Kintail (Frag. 76, n. 2).

FRAGMENT 78   mid 1750s

whether as a thief or a lover, or [   ] out. Mrs Mackenzie, however, treated her in the same ⟨manner⟩ as she had done the inhabitant of the Clock-case; obliging her, as she loved her life, to proceed to the door, without daring to look back, & locked it on them both. And this most intelligent and firm-minded lady, so far from being robust and masculine, had the softest & sweetest toned speaking voice I ever heard, & a person perfectly feminine & delicate!

This Lady, whom I have always revered, is, I hope, still living. 1806.[1]

1. The year before his own death, CB copied out from the *Morning Post* of 15 Feb. 1813, "On Friday 12th inst. at Hadley in the county of Herts died Mrs Mary Humberston Mackenzie, Widow of the late Major Mackenzie, and Mother of Lord Seaforth." Mme d'Arblay added that CB, then eighty-seven, had "the grateful intention of writing a character of a favourite friend & Patroness" (Osborn).

FRAGMENT 79   Watlington, 1750s

[John Davies[1]], one of the Gentlemen of superior learning and intellects wth whose notice I was particularly honoured during my residence in Norfolk, [was] the lineal descendant of Sir John Davies, the eminent Lawyer and Poet, author of *Nosce teipsum*[2] or the original nature and immortality of the Soul; and the discovery of the true causes why Ireland was never entirely subdued; a work full of curious information concerning Ireland, & still in high repute.[3] This

Gentleman attached me to him the first time I saw him, though he only sent for me to tune his Harpsichord; but we soon became so intimately acquainted, that he desired I w^d dine with him & spend the day once a fortnight all the year round; and it was one of my most pleasant engagements. He was a widower, *d'un certaine age,* had never had the small pox, and had lived in constant fear of it; so that he rarely ventured to come to Lynn, at the distance of only 4 Miles from his seat.[4] He was a man of a powerful

1. For John Davies, see Frag. 67, n. 4. He lived at Watlington, six miles south of King's Lynn.

2. Sir John Davies (1569–1626), poet, appointed in 1606 Attorney General for Ireland, author of *Orchestra, or a Poeme of Dancing* (1596) and *Nosce Teipsum* (1599). A manuscript copy of the latter, with dedicatory verses "to my honourable patron and frend Ed. Cooke, Esq, her M^ties Attorney Generall," is preserved at Holkham Hall, Norfolk.

3. *A Discoverie of the Trve Cavses why Ireland was never entirely Subdued, nor brought vnder Obedience of the Crowne of England, vntil the Beginning of his Maiesties happie Raigne* (1612). John Davies gave his Elizabethan ancestor's Irish papers to the historian Thomas Carte (*Dictionary of National Biography*).

4. Between 1754 and 1756 the outbreaks of smallpox at King's Lynn were so serious that it was necessary to close the graveyard at St. Margaret's: "the hours for burial were extended from 8 a.m. to 9 p.m.; although funerals were conducted elsewhere, the tolling of the small bell at St. Margaret's was insisted upon; and it was decided to recover payment for the observance by applying, if necessary to the Spiritual Court" (Hillen, 2:492–93); see also Pyle, pp. 28, 44, 108, 131, 203).

FRAGMENT 80   1750s

[   ] the Master himself; & he [   ] divination, that connoisseurs who [   ] and seen the original said that his draperies were so well imagined, that if they had not been told the contrary, they sh^d have supposed he had seen the picture.[1]

He had taught himself Music, of wch he was very fond; but having no opportunity of hearing good performers in the country, & fearing to visit the capital, I was astonished to hear how well he played, wth respect to a[c]curacy of execution, such works as had been in favour early in the last century: such as the first Alberti, Tessarini,[2] Albinoni, & Vivaldi. These he played by memory, for he was so nice as to neatness & precision of execution, that, by dint of repe[ti]tion, in practicing them, they were fixed so firmly in his memory, that he had no other employment for

1. John Davies was an "excellent dilettante painter" (Frag. 67) and no doubt discussed painting when CB visited him.

2. Carlo Tessarini (c. 1690–post-1766), violinist and composer. "His style was light and flimsy, compared with that of Corelli and Geminiani," writes CB in Rees, "but his concertos not being very difficult, were much played in country concerts in our own memory, with those of Alberti, Albinoni, and Vivaldi. . . . He lived . . . in the perpetual labour of publication; but his productions would now be as difficult to find as those of Timotheus and Olympus." See also *Hist. Mus.*, 3:510, 560; Mercer, 2:405, 445.

FRAGMENT 81   1750S

Mr Davies's house fronted the London road from Lynn; but his garden & grounds were very near the river Ouse, and extremely damp & Fenny; yet such were his reflexion and good taste, that by draining, planting, & laying out his grounds, he had concealed the defects of his situation, and made his place, for summer time, both elegant & pleasing. In his pleasure garden, after dinner, we used to walk & philosophise. I never met with a more sound understanding. & it seemed to me a loss to our country, that his fear of the small pox prevented his being in Parliament, or filling some important station, where his great & enlarged mind might have had room to expand.

The family of Keene was formerly a witty race at Lynn. Mrs Keene, the mother of Sir Benjamin[1] & the Bish^p of Ely,[2] was still living when I went thither. Mr Keene, her

1. Sir Benjamin Keene (1697–1757) of King's Lynn, envoy extraordinary and plenipotentiary to Portugal and Spain 1745–48, 1750–57. His mother was Susan Rolfe, wife of Charles Keene (1674–1759)—merchant, alderman, and (in 1714) mayor of King's Lynn—whom she had married 13 Aug. 1696 (Pedigree of the Keene Family, Norfolk Record Office, Bradfer-Lawrence Collection 45).

2. Edmund Keene (1714–81), D.D., younger brother of Sir Benjamin, Master of Peterhouse, Cambridge, 1748; Bishop of Chester 22 March 1752, and of Ely 22 Jan. 1771.

BRIDGE: FRAGMENTS 81–82

Burney's stay in King's Lynn was lightened by periodic trips to London: "But during those nine years, though Norfolk was my home, I visited London every winter, in order to rub off rust and revive friendships" (*Hist. Mus.*, 4:452; Mercer, 2:843, see also Frag. 84). During these visits he evidently made arrangements to have a number of his sonatas published (Scholes 1948, 2:343), doubtless to keep his name alive in a city to which he had always planned to return. An amusing versified account of one his journeys from King's Lynn to London is in Berg.

FRAGMENT 82   London, Spring 1758

[Meets Dr Johnson]

Soon after this,[1] Mr. Burney, during a visit to the capital, had an interview with him in Gough-square, where he dined and drank tea with him, and was introduced to the acquaintance of Mrs. Williams.[2] After dinner, Mr. Johnson proposed to Mr. Burney to go up with him into his garret, which being accepted, he there found about five or six Greek folios, a deal writing-desk, and a chair and a half. Johnson giving to his guest the entire seat, tottered himself on one with only three legs and one arm.[3] Here he gave Mr. Burney Mrs. Williams's history, and shewed him some volumes of his Shakespeare already printed,[4] to prove that he was in earnest. Upon Mr. Burney's opening the first volume, at the Merchant of Venice, he observed to him, that he seemed to be more severe on Warburton than Theobald.[5] "O poor Tib.! (said Johnson) he was ready knocked down to my hands; Warburton stands between me and him." "But, Sir, (said Mr. Burney,) you'll have Warburton upon your bones, won't you?" "No, Sir; he'll not come out: he'll only growl in his den." "But you think, Sir, that Warburton is a superiour critick to Theobald?"—"O, Sir, he'd make two-and-fifty Theobalds, cut into slices! The worst of Warburton is, that he has a rage for saying something, when there's nothing to be said."—Mr. Burney then asked him whether he had seen the letter which Warburton had written in answer to a pamphlet addressed "To the most impudent Man alive." He answered in the negative. Mr. Burney told him it was supposed to be written by Mallet.[6] The controversy now raged between the friends of Pope and Bolingbroke; and Warburton and Mallet were the leaders of the several parties. Mr. Burney asked him then if he had seen Warburton's book against Bolingbroke's Philosophy? "No, Sir; I have never read Bolingbroke's impiety, and therefore am not interested about its confutation."

1. CB wrote up this episode himself; at his direction Boswell placed it (in his *Life of Johnson*) after Johnson's letter to CB, dated 8 March 1758. This suggests that CB first met Johnson late in the spring of 1758. CB wrote later that he then "had the Honour to wait on you, in Gough Square with a subscription of 5 Guineas for 5 Copies of your Shakespear on the behalf of Mr Greville" (CB to Samuel Johnson, 14 Oct. 1765, Hyde).

2. The blind Anna Williams (1706–83), Johnson's friend and companion.

3. Northcote's account of Johnson's lodgings in Gough Square also mentions "an old crazy deal table, and a still worse and older elbow chair, having only three legs" (Hill/Powell, 1:328 n.1).

4. Johnson had issued his proposals for an edition of Shakespeare in June 1756, and CB was zealous in obtaining subscribers to it at King's Lynn (CB to Samuel Johnson, 26 March 1757, Berg; *Mem.*, 1:124; Chapman,

1:111–13; Lonsdale 1965, p. 52).

According to Bernard Bronson, who discusses CB's account in his introduction to Johnson's *Works* (New Haven, Conn., 1968), 7:xxi: "We need not take the reminiscence *au pied de la lettre*." The plays CB saw "need not have been in the form of volumes," but rather of individual plays in proof. The edition was not to be published until 1765. *The Merchant of Venice* appears at the end of the first volume (pp. 385–488).

5. Recent investigation has shown that Johnson, in preparing his edition, used Warburton's text (1747) and that of the 1757 Theobald edition. See Evans; and Eastman.

6. For notes on *A Familiar Epistle to the Most Impudent Man Alive* (1749) and Warburton's *A View of Lord Bolingbroke's Philosophy: in Four Letters* (1754), see Hill/Powell, 1:329 n.2, 330 n.1. David Mallet (1705?–65) had been employed by Bolingbroke to write this pamphlet.

FRAGMENT 83   [1758?]

In 1769[1] I set for Smart and Newbery Thornton's burlesque Ode on St. Cecilia's Day.[2] It was performed at Ranelagh in masks, to a very crowded audience, as I was told; for I then resided in Norfolk. Beard[3] sung the salt-box song, which was admirably accompanied on that instrument by Brent,[4] the Fencing-master, and father of Miss Brent, the celebrated singer;[5] Skeggs[6] on the broomstick, as bassoon; and a remarkable performer on the Jew's-harp.— "Buzzing twangs the iron lyre." Cleavers were cast in bell-metal for this entertainment. All the performers of the old woman's Oratory, employed by Foote,[7] were, I believe, employed at Ranelagh on this occasion.

1. The date of this anecdote, which CB furnished as a footnote to Boswell's third edition of his *Life of Johnson* (1799), has been much disputed. It seems that Boswell's printer made an error in one or both of the last

digits. Lonsdale (1965, pp. 67–68, 485–90) gives a comprehensive summary of the problem of dating; he correctly dismisses 1769 as impossible—since John Beard retired from the stage in 1767—and suggests 1760 or 1763.

Additional evidence in Highfill (see n. 7, below) indicates that the date of this performance was probably 1758.

2. Bonnell Thornton (1724–68) published his burlesque "Ode on St. Cecilia's Day, adapted to the Antient British Musick: the Salt Box, the Jew's Harp, the Marrow Bones and Cleaver, the Hum Strum or Hurdy-Gurdy" in 1749. It was reprinted in May 1763 and performed at Ranelagh on 10 June. According to the *St. James's Chronicle* for 9–10 June, the musical setting for this revival was attributed to Arne. Dr. Johnson, who saw this revival, "praised its humour and seemed much diverted with it" (Hill/Powell, 1:420).

3. John Beard (see Bridge: Frags. 34–35, n. 2; Frag. 61, n. 3), "an energetic English singer, and an excellent actor . . . knew as much of music as was necessary to sing a single part at sight, and with a voice that was more powerful than sweet, he became the most useful and favourite singer of his time, on the stage, at Ranelagh, at all concerts; and in Handel's oratorios, he had always a capital part; being by his knowledge of music the most steady support of the choruses, not only of Handel, but in the odes of Green and Boyce" ("Beard" in Rees).

4. Charles Brent (1693–1770), counter-tenor and fencing master, sang the role of Hamor in Handel's *Jephtha* at Covent Garden and Micah in *Samson* in Feb.–March 1752 (Highfill, 2:314).

5. For Charlotte Brent, see Appendix B, n. 28.

6. *London Stage* lists his "first appearance" at Covent Garden on 6 May 1757, when he sang *A Solo on the Broomstick,* which he had composed. He also wrote with Mr. Massey "an additional scene" for *Galigantus* (28 Dec. 1758) and *Britannia's Triumph* (30 April 1760), both at the Haymarket.

7. Samuel Foote (1720–77), actor and playwright. *The Old Woman's Oratory* was a theatrical parody first staged by Smart and Newbery in Dec. 1751 and repeated at the Haymarket 18 May and 1 June 1758. It also featured "performances on the salt-box, Jew's harp, broomstick and other burlesque instruments" (Lonsdale 1965, pp. 487–88). If Highfill (2:314) is correct in stating, in his article on Charles Brent, that the performance of Bonnell Thornton's burlesque *Ode on St. Cecilia's Day* was in 1758, it is likely that the performance with CB's musical setting took place in that year. For an example of *Katzenmusik* or *charivari,* see Hogarth's engraving of the *Industrious Prentice* (reproduced in *New Grove,* 4:157).

FRAGMENT 84

At the head of Lord Orford's table was placed, for the reception of his visitors, a person whom he denominated simply "Patty;"[1] and that so unceremoniously, that all the most intimate of his associates addressed her by the same free

Lord Orford's character & constant patronage & regard

appellation. . . .[2] The table of Lord Orford, then commonly called Arthur's Round Table,[3] assembled in its circle all of peculiar merit that its neighbourhood, or rather that the country produced, to meet there the great, the renowned, and the splendid, who, from their various villas, or the metropolis, visited Haughton Hall.

Mr. Burney was soon one of those whom the penetrating peer selected for a general invitation to his repasts; and who here, as at Wilbury House, formed sundry intimacies, some of which were enjoyed by him nearly through life.

Yet though he [Burney] loved & respected the persons with whom he lived and passed his time very agreeably finding his family increasing, having 6 Children,[5] he was ambitious of a larger field of action in order to provide for his children & rise in his profession above the rank of a country organist; he therefore in the year 1760 ventured on speculation, to quit his provincial establishment and try to bear the fatigues and air of London.[6] But this was not done so rashly as many thought: when he quitted London it was for want of health, and in hopes of returning thither whenever his health w^d allow it. He therefore spent 3 weeks or a month in London every winter, to keep up his acquaintance, and prevent professional rust.[7] And when he did return his eldest daughter of only 7 years old was the best harpsichord player of her age, except the Frederica that had ever been heard in London.[8] This sample of his method of teaching[9] procured him scholars and a great boarding-school in Queen Square Bloomsbury[10]

Norfolk patrons & friends still living[4]

1. Martha Turk (c. 1737–91), called "Patty," Lord Orford's mistress. Mme d'Arblay adds, in her paraphrase of CB's text, that those "who might conclude from this degrading familiarity, that the Patty of Lord Orford was 'every body's Patty,' must soon have been undeceived, if tempted to make any experiment upon such a belief" (*Mem.*, 1:102).

2. For Lord Orford, see Frag. 67, n. 1. In the text not reproduced, Mme d'Arblay balanced his "liberal cast" and "the frank equality with which he treated all his guests," with his "moral defects," "as dangerous to the neighbourhood" as Sir Robert Walpole's "nefarious maxim, 'that every man has his price.'"

3. In his letter to Lord Orford of 17 April 1791, CB prides himself on being one of those who "had formerly the honour of being admitted to Prince Arthur's *round table*" (Berg).

4. CB probably mentioned here Lord Townshend (Frag. 72); John Hayes (c. 1708–92), whom he had met at Houghton and who became one of his lifelong friends (*Mem.*, 1:102–3); Christopher Anstey (1724–1805), the poet, "my old Houghton friend" (CB to Charles Burney, 8 Feb. 1799, Coke); Edward Miller (1730–1807), historian of Doncaster, who was CB's pupil in Norfolk and remained his correspondent; and perhaps old "Alderman Cary at Lynn [who] in his 86th year—when I asked him how he did . . . told me he was pretty well—'but, odd rabbit it! I don't know how it is—I can't walk so well a[s] I used to do'" (CB to Mme d'Arblay, 9 Oct. 1806, Berg). He had also met in Norfolk John Albert Bentinck (1737–75), the "scientific Musical fr^d of mine" (CB to Mme d'Arblay, 18 July 1799, Berg) and "Sir Jacob Astly," Baronet (d. 5 Jan. 1760) of Melton Constable (BL, Add. MSS 48345, f. 22^v), but these were no longer living when he set

out to write his memoirs.

5. Esther and James were born before Sept. 1751, when CB left for Lynn. Born in King's Lynn were Fanny (13 June 1752), Susan (7 Jan. 1755), and Charles (4 Dec. 1757). The sixth, Charlotte, was born on 4 Nov. 1761, after CB's return to London. Two boys called Charles, one born on 3 June 1751, the other in 1753?, died in infancy (*HFB*, pp. 6–7; Scholes 1948, 1:84n). In Dec. 1758 or Jan. 1759 another child was born who no doubt died soon after its birth; see Mrs. Greville to Esther Burney, 30 Jan. 1759 (Osborn).

6. According to Mme d'Arblay (*Mem.*, 1:133), CB's last act in 1760

in relinquishing his residence in Norfolk, was drawing up a petition to Lord Orford to allow park-room in the Haughton grounds, for the rest of its life, to his excellent, faithful mare, the intelligent Peggy; whose truly useful services he could not bear to requite, according to the unfeeling usage of the many, by selling her to hard labour in the decline of her existence.

Lord Orford good-humouredly complied with the request; and the justly-prized Peggy, after enjoying for several years the most perfect ease and freedom, died the death of old age, in Haughton Park.

7. In 1755 CB also visited Bristol with his wife (Lonsdale 1965, pp. 48–49), and in 1756 he made a tour of Yarmouth, during which he visited his half-brother Joseph at Ormsby. About 1757 he revisited Condover (Frag. 1, n. 13; Bridge: Frags. 1–2).

8. On 23 April 1760, when nine years old, Esther performed with several other young players at the Little Theatre in the Haymarket; "as there were several children at that time in London of uncommon proficiency on different instruments, a concert was made for them . . . in which they severally displayed their talents; Baron and Schmeling on the violin; Miss B. on the harpsichord, and Cervetto on the violoncello" ("Mara" in Rees). See Scholes (1948, 1:98), who prints the advertisement for the concert from the *Public Advertiser*. Cassandra Frederick or "Frederica" (1741?–post-1779) had made her debut on 10 April 1749 at the Haymarket Theatre as "a Child of Five years and a half old," when she performed "on the Harpsichord several lessons of Scarlatti and other Great Masters, and also a Concerto of Mr. Handels," though Lord Shaftesbury said she was eight. In 1758 she was engaged as a singer by Handel for his oratorio season, and later married Thomas Wynne (*New Grove*, 6:812–13; Highfill, 5: 402).

9. For CB's teaching method, see Frag. 41, n. 3. He also designed a card for use in teaching thoroughbass (music pl. 5 in Rees).

10. The boarding school was run by Anne Elizabeth Shields or Sheeles née Irwin; in 1735 at St. Dionis Backchurch she married John Shields, who had two academies, one at or near Chessington. The school in Queen Square was in existence in 1749 when it was known as Shields and Gamber school. It might have existed earlier, for their son James was baptized at St. George the Martyr in Queen Square on 24 Feb. 1738/9. According to Holborn rate-books, Gamber and Shields had a house in Queen Square from 1752 until 1763. After this date the entries mention only Shields, which appears as late as 1774. Queen Square was well known for boarding schools. About 1750 Mrs. Dennis founded her famous "Ladies' Eton" there (information kindly supplied by J. Swift, Librarian of the Metropolitan Holborn Public Library; see also *JL*, 11:273 n.6).

FRAGMENT 85   London, Autumn, 1760

Take a House in
Poland Street[1]

See the young King
proclaimed
in Leicester fields[2]

About this time D[r] Burney related to D[r] Johnson and his friends at Streat-ham the partiality w[ch] his writings had excited in a friend of D[r] B. M[r] Bewley,[3] well known in Norfolk by the name of the *Philosopher of Massingham*; who while the Ramblers were publishing, & long before the author's fame was established by subsequent works, had conceived such a reverence for him, that he urgently begged D[r] B. to give him the cover of the first letter he had rec[d] from him, as a relic of so estimable a writer. This was in 1755.[4] In 1760, when D[r] B visited D[r] J. at the Temple, where he had then Chambers,[5] he happening to arrive there before he was up: & being shewn into a room where he was to breakfast, finding himself alone, he examined the contents of the appartment to try whether he c[d] undiscovered steal anything to send to his friend Bewley as another relic of the admirable D[r] Johnson. But finding nothing better to his purpose, he cut some bristles off his hearth broom, & inclosed them in a letter to his country enthusiast, who rec[d] them wth due reverence.[6] The D[r] was so sensible of the honour done him by a man of Genius & Science to whom he was an utter stranger, that he said to D[r] B. "Sir! there is no man that has a speck of modesty but must be flattered wth the admiration of such a man. I'll give him a set of my lives, if he will do me the honour to accept of them."[7] In this he kept his word; & D[r] B. had not only the pleasure of gratifying his friend with a present more worthy of his acceptance than the segment from the hearth-broom, but soon after of introducing him to D[r] J. himself, in Bolt court, with whom he had the satisfaction of conversing a considerable time, not a fortnight before his death;[8] which happened in S[t] Martin's Street during his visit to D[r] B. in the house where the great S[r] Isaac Newton lived & died before.[9]

L[d] Sandwich's full
bottomed Wig.[10]

1. The Burneys probably left King's Lynn for London in Sept. or early Oct. 1760. Fanny, who was eight years old, remembers Po-land Street, off Oxford Road, as amid "fields, gardeners' grounds, or uncultivated suburbs"; it was within walking distance of

Queen Square. CB "had successively for his neighbours, the Duke of Chandos, Lady Augusta Bridges, the Hon. John Smith and the Miss Barrys, Sir Willoughby and the Miss Astons" (*Mem.,* 1:134). For the latter, see Frag. 104, n. 10; for CB's landlord Keane Fitzgerald, Frag. 106, n. 4. Another neighbour, not mentioned by Fanny, was George Mackenzie, 3rd Earl of Cromarty, who played a prominent part during the Scottish rebellion, was sentenced to death, and then pardoned; he died 28 Sept. 1766 in Poland Street (*Dictionary of National Biography*). His grand-nephew Kenneth Mackenzie (d. 1796) attended a Burney musical evening 15 Nov. 1768 (*ED,* 1:32).

2. George III was proclaimed king on 26 Oct. 1760 "about noon . . . first before Saville house, where the officers of state, nobility, and privy counsellors, were present, with the officers of arms, all being on foot; then the officers of arms being mounted on horseback, the like was done at Charing-cross; within Temple-bar; at the end of Wood-street, in Cheapside; and lastly, at the Royal Exchange with the usual solemnities. The archbishop of Canterbury, the duke of Leeds, and lord Falmouth, attended the procession into the city" (*AR,* 3:141). CB also attended the funeral of George II at Westminster Abbey on 11 Nov. 1760, where he heard "the Burial Service, set by Morley" (*Hist. Mus.,* 3:105; Mercer, 2:92).

3. See Bridge: Frags. 68–69, n. 1. This visit probably occurred late in 1760 after his definitive return to London from King's Lynn, though it could have taken place in the spring, when CB visited London to attend Esther's performance (Frag. 84, n. 6). On 27 Oct. 1790, CB wrote to Fanny: "B[ozzy] has long teased me for the story ab^t the *Broom Man,* as poor Bewley used to be called at Streatham—I have scrib[b]led it out" (Barrett).

4. CB started to correspond with Dr.

Johnson on 16 Feb. 1755; Johnson replied on 8 April 1755 (Chapman 1:68–69). The original of Johnson's letter is not extant, but the mention below of "*another* relic" suggests that CB did give Bewley the cover.

5. Dr. Johnson had moved from Gough Square to chambers in the Inner Temple Lane early in 1759 (Hill/Powell, 1:350 n.3). CB had first visited Johnson in the spring of 1758 during one of his periodic returns to London from King's Lynn (see Frag. 82).

6. According to Fanny's editor, Annie Raine Ellis, who does not give her source, CB "wrapped them in silver-paper, and enclosed them in a letter to . . . Lord Orford, in Norfolk, who gave these treasures to Mr. Bewley," who (says Fanny) "thinks it more precious than pearls" (*ED,* 1:176 and n.). CB did not confess his "theft" to Johnson till some twenty years later.

7. After the *Lives* came out in 1779, Dr. Johnson sent Bewley part of the set through the Burneys, addressed "For the Broom Gentleman" (*Mem.,* 2:180), who wrote to CB of "the delight I have received from *the lives* . . . procured through your means" (William Bewley to CB, 24 May 1780, Osborn). On 9 July 1781 Johnson sent him subsequent volumes (Chapman, 2:431).

8. Bewley died during his visit to London, on 5 Sept. 1783. Dr. Johnson had moved to 8 Bolt Court, his last residence, in 1776 (Hill/Powell, 2:427).

> 9. This house, where great Newton
>   once deign'd to reside,
>   Who of England, and all Human
>   Nature the pride,
>   Sparks of light, like Prometheus,
>   from Heav'n purloin'd,
>   Which in bright emanations flash'd
>   full on mankind.
>
> (*Mem.,* 1:289)

CB moved into Newton's house in St. Martin's Street in 1774.

10. John Montagu (1718–92), 4th Earl of Sandwich, First Lord of the Admiralty 1763–65, was something of a rake. On his return from a tour of the Middle East in 1741, he brought with him two Circassian girls, and the murder of his mistress Martha Ray was one of the great scandals of 1779. He was well known as a patron of the opera. After Lord Sandwich's admission to the Admiralty Board in 1745, Walpole wrote to Sir Horace Mann that he "put on such a first-rate tie wig . . . that nothing without the lungs of a boatswain can ever hope to penetrate the thickness of the curls . . . when he was but a Patriot, his wig was not of half its present gravity" (YW, 18:561; Walpole's editors point out that "this wig had a plaited tail, tied at the top with a large ribbon bow, and at the bottom with a smaller one. In Zoffany's portrait, Lord Sandwich's wig is tied with a large bow"). It is not clear on what occasion CB may have noticed his bewigged lordship. Later, in 1771, he met Lord Sandwich at Houghton and corresponded with him about his son James, who joined Captain Cook in his last voyage around the world, and in 1784 about organizing the Commemoration of Handel.

FRAGMENT 86   London, 1760–61

In 1760, finding his health considerably amended, he returned to London; where, from the zeal of his former friends, and the performance of his eldest daughter . . . he was instantly offered more scholars than he could undertake.[1] The late Duke of York,[2] to whom he had the honour of being introduced by the late Earl of Eglinton,[3] was so captivated by some of the most wild and *New scholars in 1761, & attachm[ts][4]* difficult lessons of Scarlatti, which he had heard his little daughter play, that his Royal Highness desired him to put parts to them in the way of Concertos, in which form he threw the principal movements not already turned to that account by Mr. Avison.[5] These were frequently performed to his Royal Highness and his friends by the late Mr. Pinto, at the head of a select band.[6]

The year after his return to London, besides his printed book of *Harpsichord Lessons*,[7] he composed several Concertos to display the abilities of his nephew and scholar, Mr. Charles Burney.[8]

1. CB specifies in a fragment in Berg that his increase in popularity was the result of "the powers of my little girl," Esther (see Frag. 84, n. 8).

2. Edward Augustus (1739–67), Duke of York 1760, George III's brother. Scholes (1948, 2:329) cites another version of his en-thusiasm for Esther's performance of Scarlatti.

3. Alexander Montgomerie (1723–69), 9th Earl of Eglinton, Lord of the Bedchamber 1760–66, who "loved wit more than wine, and men of genius more than syco-phants" (Hill/Powell, 2:66). He was "ex-

tremely fond of music" (Lonsdale 1965, pp. 54–55).

4. On his return to London, CB had among his scholars Jane Dutton (who later married Thomas William Coke) and her three sisters, who "went through my hands" "at Mrs Sheele's boarding-school" (CB to Fanny Burney, 2 Oct. 1789, Beinecke); and among his private pupils, Elizabeth Milbanke, later Lady Melbourne (CB to Charles Burney, 10 June [1805], Osborn), Lady Anne Lyon (CB to Frances Crewe, 31 Oct. 1802, Berg), Elizabeth and Catherine Cary (Frag. 88, nn. 6, 9), and Lady Mary Bertie (Frag. 95, n. 6).

5. Charles Avison (1709–70), native of Newcastle-upon-Tyne, where he settled after a visit to Italy with Geminiani, founded a small orchestra comparable to the German court orchestras, and composed for it some fifty concertos. CB here no doubt refers to his arrangements of Scarlatti, *I Concerto in seven parts done from the lessons of Sig^r Domenico Scarlatti by Charles Avison*, 1743; and *Twelve concerto's in seven parts for four violins, one alto viola, a violoncello, & a thorough bass, done from two books of lessons for the harpsichord composed by Sig. Domenico Scarlatti, with additional slow movements from manuscript solo pieces . . . by C. Avison*, 1744 (*RISM*, 7:S.1194).

6. Thomas Pinto (1714–83), violinist and conductor, born in England of Italian parents, replaced Giardini at Drury Lane in 1757.

See Appendix B.5 for CB's comments and anecdotes.

7. In March 1761 the following notice appeared in the *Public Advertiser*: "NEW MU-SIC Speedily will be published Price 10s. 6d. Six Sonatas or Lessons for Harpsichord composed by CHARLES BURNEY. Printed for the Author at his House in Poland Street." It was announced as "this day is published" on 27 April and several times thereafter (Scholes 1948, 1:101; *RISM*, 7:S.1194). These sonatas were criticized by the anonymous author of *ABC Dario Musico* (Bath, 1780): "His lessons hav[e] nothing remarkable, but frequent repetition of one note, which *trick* we think rather ill-adapted to the harpsichord" (p. 13); and more recently by Newman (p. 698) for skipping about "naively from one favorite Scarlatti keyboard device to another, especially hand crossing, hand exchanges and repeated notes."

8. "To perform at Drury Lane Theatre, where he played the Harp^d," CB adds in a Berg fragment. The fourteen-year-old Charles Rousseau Burney (Bridge: Frags. 87–88, n. 2) was to become a noted violinist as well as harpsichordist. The concertos referred to here are CB's *Six Concertos in Seven Parts for Four Violins, a Tenor, a Violoncello, and Thorough Bass for the Organ or Harpsichord*, opera quinta, which feature a *violino primo principale* part (*RISM*, 1:B.5053).

FRAGMENT 87

I heard nothing of her L^p[1] till I was grown up and settl[e]d in business in London previous to going into Norfolk. I had the honour to attend L^y Tankerville, now, during summer in the country, at   . The Earl was much afflicted with the gout, and seldom appeared, even at dinner. Her L^p began to learn accomp^t on the Harp^d but still practiced the G[erman] Flute, and was a good performer. On my quitting London to go to Lynn, I lost sight of her till after my return to London. During the 7 years war L^y T. went into Germany, & attached herself [to] the Princess Amalia,[2] sister to the King of Prussia, under whom she accepted of the place of dame d'atour to this amiable and accomplished Princess, of whom Voltaire was in love, according to the following Verses.

[Vers à la Princesse Amélie
    de Prusse

De plus d'une divinité
    J'adore en vous l'image;
Vénus avait moins de beauté;
    Minerve était moins sage.
L'Amour, timide et retenu,
    Suit sans cesse vos traces;
Vous faite aimer la vertu,
    Et respecter les Grâces.][3]

1. Lady Tankerville, née Alicia Astley (see Frag. 18). She "resumed her lessons with her early master, obligingly submitting her time to his convenience, be it what it might, rather than change her first favourite instructor" (*Mem.*, 1:135).

2. Anna Amalie (1723–87), favorite sister of Frederick II, was an amateur musician, tutored by Kirnberger, pupil of J. S. Bach. In 1762 she retired to Quedlinburg as abbess.

3. "I adore in you / The image of more than one goddess; / Venus was less beautiful, / Minerva less wise. / Love, bashful and discreet, / Forever follows your footsteps; / Because of you we love virtue / And respect the Graces." Voltaire knew her in 1743, when she was twenty; his flattering verses were published in 1761. The editors have supplied the verses, not in CB's text, from Voltaire, 32:424.

BRIDGE: FRAGMENTS 87–88

*Wife's bad state of
Health —ordered [to]
Bath & Bristol.
whither I go to her at
breaking up.*[1]

*Our fright in the
Forest opposite the
Pump room*

1. Of Mrs. Sheeles's school in Queen Square. The date is very probably June 1761, as the school reopened in mid-July (Frag. 104). Esther, who suffered from consumption and was expecting another child (Charlotte, b. 3 Nov. 1761), had evidently left London earlier.

2. They paid a visit to CB's brother Richard, who had left London c. 1755 for Worcester, where "he succeeded an elderly gentleman of the name of Weaver" and "removed to a very pretty house, about a mile out of Town, called Barborne Lodge." According to Worcester Mem. (p. 10), "Mr. & Mrs. Charles Burney paid a short visit to Barborne previous to their change of residence, from Lynn Regis to London," shortly after the birth of Edward Francesco Burney (late Sept. 1760). But it seems more likely that the visit

mentioned occurred a year later, in 1761, on the Burneys' return from Bath to London.

Richard had two musically talented sons. The first, Charles Rousseau (b. 1747), at the age of six showed "an extraordinary ear for music . . . for which he had talents very uncommon at that age." CB taught him by correspondence from King's Lynn "at the distance of 200 miles" (Worcester Mem.; CB to Katherine Raper, 12 Apr. 1776, Berg). Charles Rousseau later became a well-known harpsichordist. CB's eldest daughter Esther was then twelve. She and Charles Rousseau probably became acquainted during one of these visits; they were married in 1770. Richard's second son, Richard Gustavus (b. 1751), later a music teacher and dancing-master, became a favorite friend of the young Fanny.

FRAGMENT 88   London, 1762–63

Prosperity in the capital, & family
described

My eldest son had been entered on board a Man of War, the Princess Amelia, [commanded by] Capt. Montagu[1] in Octr 1760, where there was a regular school for younkers to pursue their naval studies and go on wth their education.[2] When he returned from this Voyage I placed him in an academy[3] to proceed in mathematics.

One of the first new families to wch I was recommended as a master after settling again in London, was that of the Honble Col. afterwards General Carey, brother to Lord Falkland,[4] and if I remember right, it was by means of Lady Milbank[5] that I had the honour of being known to this noble family, from wch I rec^d many acts of kindness. In relating to the Honble Col., whose daughters were my scholars,[6] the state of my family, and he found I had a son destined for the Sea, he s^d he thought he c^d get him a birth on board a Frigate commanded by Sir Thos Adams,[7] Bar^t who having been left an orphan, with no inheritance but his title, he (the Col.) had in a manner adopted him, had him educated for the Sea, & by the interest of his patron, seconded by his own merit & good conduct had got well through all the stages of examination, and finally was made post[8] & appointed to a Frigate. Col. Carey and his Lady had two daughters, but no son. Lady Amerst, still living, was married to the renowned General, afterwards Lord Amerst,[9] who was twice her age, in preference to many other more eligible officers, both in youth, person, and fortune. Miss Carey was rather beautiful, her complexion fine, and person good; but Mrs Carey, one of the most amiable, worthy, and most sweet characters I ever knew, used to say, that her eldest daughter's passion was somewhat romantic: she had fallen in love with a hero, not a man.

The Col. had a great turn for dry humour; and when I presented my son to him as to his patron, he was sheepish and silent, and had not a word to say; for being just come from Sea & from School, he was wholly ignorant of what was said or done anywhere else. "Oh, oh!["] (says the Col.) "the only way to get acquainted wth a School boy, is to give him a kick in the A." And by this kind of familiarity he drew him out; talked to him in Sea language, asking him how many knots there were, & how many splices, wch seemed to tickle his fancy; but I was out of my depth, and did not understand the joke. Soon after this presentation, he quitted his Naval Academy & was Rec^d by Sir Thos Adams on board his ship the Boston, in 1762, and afterwards in the Niger, where he was rated, and perfectly well treated till Feby 1765[10]

1. Capt. John Montagu (1719–95), later Vice-Admiral (1776) and Admiral (1782), in 1744 had testified at the court-martial of Vice-Admiral Lestock and in 1757 superintended the execution of Admiral Byng.

2. James was then ten years old. "At this period there were two officially recognized ways by which the sons of gentlemen might enter the Navy; one was through the Naval Academy at Portsmouth; the other as a 'Captain's servant.' After a two years' service at sea, they were rated as midshipmen; but as boys were not admitted to the Academy until they were twelve years of age, that method of

entry was not available to young Burney. Once again his father's friends stood him in good stead, and he was sent to sea in the ship of Captain John Montague as 'Captain's servant.' The rating, however, did not imply any menial capacity, but simply that of dependence, and a 'Captain's servant' was in fact his apprentice, who went to sea to be brought up in the professional duties of a sea officer." James was discharged from service on the *Princess Amelia* on 22 June 1762, to join the following day Captain Montagu, who was appointed to command the *Magnanime,* from which young James was discharged at

CB's request on 18 Sept. 1762 (Manwaring, pp. 4–5). In his letter to CB dated 16 Sept. 1762, Montagu wrote: "My friend Burney is a very ingenious good Boy and I sincerely wish him well; & hope he will answer all your Expectations" (PML).

3. Probably the Naval Academy at Portsmouth.

4. Hon. George Cary or Carey (c. 1712–92), Army Colonel, later General (*GM,* 42: 390). He was the younger brother of Lucius Charles Cary (c. 1707–85), 7th Viscount Falkland (Frag. 29, n. 1).

5. Lady Elizabeth (d. 22 July 1767), daughter of John Hedworth, of Chester-le-Street, co. Durham, M.P.; in 1748 married Sir Ralph Milbanke (1721?–98), Baronet of Halnaby Hall, Yorks., M.P. for Scarborough 1754–61 and Richmond 1761–68. He was connected with Lord Holdernesse, through whom CB probably met Lady Milbanke, whose two daughters he taught (Frag. 86, n. 4).

6. For the elder daughter, Elizabeth, see n. 9, below. The younger, Catherine (d. 1783), on 15 Oct. 1774 married Sir John Russell, Baronet, of Chequers, Bucks. (*AR,* 17:182; 26:239).

7. Sir Thomas Adams, Baronet (d. 12 April 1770), was then captain of the thirty-two-gun *Boston,* which James entered as "Captain's steward" on 19 Sept. 1762, the day after his discharge from the *Magnanime* (PRO

ADM 33/630). See n. 10, below.

8. Appointed captain, commanding a ship of twenty guns or more (*Oxford English Dictionary*).

9. Sir Jeffry (or Jeffrey) Amherst (1717–97), general, who had distinguished himself in North America. Having taken Montreal in 1760, he was cr. Knight of the Bath and Governor General of British North America (1761). Sir Jeffry, who lost his first wife in 1765, on 26 Mar. 1767 married Elizabeth (c. 1742–1830), eldest daughter of the Hon. George Cary. He was created Baron Amherst of Holmesdale in 1776 and, in 1778, Baron Amherst of Montreal (his seat in Kent); in 1796, he was appointed Field Marshal.

10. See n. 7, above. The *Boston* was soon put out of commission, and on 24 June 1763 James was appointed "Captain's servant" on the *Niger* under Sir Thomas Adams, who had taken its command 1 April 1763 (PRO ADM 32/222, 33/630). Manwaring (pp. 4–5) says that James took his discharge from the *Niger* on 7 June 1765, a few days before his fifteenth birthday (see n. 2, above). CB ends the sentence by referring to the "end of 2ᵈ addendum," which is missing. Judging by the pagination of the manuscripts, CB intended this section on his children (Frags. 88–91) to go after Frags. 96–97. Frag. 88 has been placed here in the interest of continuity with Frag. 89.

FRAGMENT 89   London, 1762–63

[James was good] at calculation, even before he knew his alphabet, or the numerical figures. But when he cᵈ read and was in possession of a penny, he [had] to go to the Bookseller's for a pennyworth of Roderick Random.[1]

My 2ᵈ daughter, Fanny, afterwards the Authoress, and now Madᵉ d'Arblay, was wholly unnoticed in the nursery for any talent or quickness of parts. Indeed at 8 years old she did not know her letters; and her brother, the Tar, who had a natural genius for hoaxing, and fore-castle jokes, used to pretend to teach her to read, and gave her the book topsy turvy, wch she never found out.[2] Her mother & I, who had often observed that children wch were thought Prodigies in early reading, repeated words like parots without knowing their meaning, began now to be uneasy at her backwardness; when, all at once, she read as if by intuition, nor did any of the family ever know how the talent was acquired. I was, however, told afterwards, by her play-fellows that in her sports she had a great deal of fun & humour in her early days;[3] and that after having seen a play, in Mrs Garrick's box, she[4]

1. Smollett's *Adventures of Roderick Random* (1748) had gone through several editions.

2. CB recalled that James "as soon as he c^d read, was furnished by his maid with one of the Ordinary of Newgates Sessions paper[s], wch delighted him so much in the perusal that he cries out to Fanny, my 2^d daughter . . . Sister! Sister! here's a *very* pretty murder—" (CB to Louisa Harris, [post–15 Feb. 1809], Osborn).

3. Joyce Hemlow quotes one of Fanny's playmates: "*You* were so merry, so gay, so droll, & had such imagination in making plays, always something new, something of your own contrivance" (*HFB*, p. 14).

4. Mme d'Arblay continues, "would mimick the actors," and expands this in print (as "copied from a Memorandum-book of Dr. Burney's, written in the year 1808, at Bath"): "take the actors off, and compose speeches for their characters; for she could not read them. But in company, or before strangers, she was silent, backward, and timid, even to sheepishness: and from her shyness, had such profound gravity and composure of features, that those of my friends who came often to my house, and entered into the different humours of the children, never called Fanny by any other name, from the time she had reached her eleventh year, than The Old Lady." She had "an excellent heart, and a natural simplicity and probity about her that wanted no teaching. In her plays with her sisters, and some neighbour's children, this straightforward morality operated to an uncommon degree in one so young" (*Mem.*, 2:168, 170).

FRAGMENT 90   London, early 1760s

There lived next door to me at that time in Poland Stree[t] a hair Merchan[t], who furnished peruques to the Judges, and Gentlemen of the law. The merchants Children & mine used to play together in the little gardens behind the House—and unluckily, one day the door of the Wig Magazine being left open, they each of them put on one of these dignified ornaments of the head, & danced and jumped about in a thousand antics laughing till they scr[e]amed at their own ridiculous figures; unluckily, in their vagaries one of the flaxen wigs, said by the proprietor, to be worth ten guineas fell into a tub of water, lost all its Gorgon Buckle, and was said by the owner to be totally spoiled. He was extremely angry with the whole party, and chid very severely his own children, when my little daughter, the old lady, says, with great gravity & composure— "What signifies making such a work about an accident?—The Wig was a good Wig to be sure; but what's done can't be undone."[1] Whether these stoical sentiments appeased the enraged Peruquier, I know not; but the younkers were stript of their honours and mock dignity, & my little monkeys were obliged to retreat without beat of drum or colours flying.

1. The expression "the wig is wet" became a standing joke in the Burney family.

FRAGMENT 91   1759–60?

[There was] a little natural trait of benevolence in a female child of mine[1] at the play of Jane Shore; who, being in the front of a stage box at a country theatre, and hearing the wretched Jane in vain supplicating "a morsel to support her famished soul," and, crying out, "Give me but to eat!"[2] the child, not five years old, touched with her distress, says, "Ma'am, will you have my *ollange*?" which the audience applauded much more than the artificial complaints of the actress.[3]

1. Susan (b. 1755). The editors have placed this here as part of CB's account of his children. This version is from a letter to Hannah More (see textual notes). See also Hill, p. 201.

2. Nicholas Rowe, *Jane Shore,* Act. V, sc. ii.

3. Mrs. Thrale comments: "This story I told to my two little Girls Susan & Sophy well says Sophy! now that was a *good natured* Ideot, if She *was* an Ideot. They have both been at a Play, and as Mr Johnson says, know y^t it is not true as well as the performers" (*Thraliana,* 1:228). In his letter to Hannah More, CB continued, "I must add to my little anecdote, that the charitable disposition of this child grew up with her growth, and has never quitted her in maturity" (CB to Hannah More, [6] April 1799).

But finding that he was smoked, and that we laughed at him—he never called it a *sturry* again, but a *cont*[*r*]*ivance.*[1] Our 4th girl born in London after we had left Lynn,[2] was out at Nurse; but when she grew up she did not write books, or, indeed, read many; but was an inveterate painter.[3]

1762

Though this was a very prosperous year professionally, yet it was marked by the greatest domestic calamity that c[d] befal a fond & tender husband, in the death of the best Wife, friend, & companion, wth w[ch] a mortal c[d] be blessed! She had been declining for more than twelve months; but on the 19th Sept[r] she was seized with a most violent bilious complaint, w[ch] terminated, after extreme torture, in an inflamation in the bowels, of w[ch] she expired on the 27th so calm and easy that for a short time she imagined she was recovering, and sh[d] live.[4] I was constantly by her during these terrible moments. The Apothecary[5] had insinuated

1762 equally prosperous in business but rendered comfortless by the bad state of my poor Wife's health of whom I am bereaved on Mich[s] day!

1. Here CB is no doubt speaking of Charles, born 4 Dec. 1757 at King's Lynn. Garrick used to call the boy Cherry-Nose, "on account of his skin being rather of the brightest" (*ED,* 2:279n).

2. Charlotte Anne was born 4 Nov. 1761.

3. In another fragment CB writes with pride about his children: "The eldest son was a seaman and a circumnavigator with Cook and Fourneau—the 2[d] son [Charles was] admitted in the Charter house and became one of the best scholars in the kingdom. My eldest daught[r] the best performer on the Harp[d] & Piano forte in her day; my 2[d] daughter the best Novelist for variety of characters, correct language, & purity of morals, w[ch] we can boast, perhaps in the English language. The 3[d] [Susan] had the best taste in all the Arts, particularly in Music sung with a feeble but touching & impressive voice and in a style

more truly Italian perhaps than any of Sacchini's scholars—besides this talent I may venture to say that she c[d] boast of being the best wife, parent, & most amiable friend w[ch] her rank in life c[d] boast. But she alas! was early lost, and left her afflicted family and 3 Children for ever to deplore her Loss!" (Osborn).

4. For the exact date (29 Sept.), see CB to Dorothy Young, [Oct.? 1762] (Scholes 1948, 2:288–90; *Mem.,* 1:140–45), where he gives a detailed account of Esther's last illness and death.

5. Probably John Reeve, Poland Street (Mortimer, p. 66). Mme d'Arblay emended CB's manuscript to "physician" and says (*Mem.,* 1:138) that Esther was attended in her last illness by Dr. William Hunter (1718–83), M.D. She was probably attended by both.

Thanked me for my good humour & kindness from the beginning of our Union; and without seeming to know that death was ⟨s⟩o near began to rattle in the throat, & to be insensible to every thing around her. I took the children away[1] & hovered over her in agony of mind equal to what she had suffered in body, to her la[st] Sigh! I shut myself up inadmissible & invisible [to] all but relations, without a thought on anything else till after the funeral, and then for a fortnight did nothing but meditate on my misery. I wrote elegyac Verses on her

Affliction described, & condoleances[2]

Virtues & Perfection.[3] Tried to translate 2 or 3 of Petrarca's most touching Sonnets on the death of Laura[4]—but was at length obliged to plunge into business, ⌈& attend at a school⌉. It was painful to me to see any one who knew & admired her as all my acquaintance did. But having my mind occupied by ⌈business⌉ was a useful dissipation of my sorrow; as it forced me to a temporary inattention to myself and the irreparable loss I had sustained ⌈While occupied on musical notes I was insensibly obliged to assume tranquility if not chear⌉

Domestic arrange-m^{ts} in consequence[5]

1. "Fanny, Susan, and Charley, had been sent, some days before, to the kind care of Mrs. Sheeles in Queen Square, to be out of the way; and little Charlotte was taken to the house of her nurse" (*Mem.*, 1:143). James was then at sea.

2. For an account of his affliction, see his letters to Dorothy Young, [Oct.? 1762] (Scholes, 2:288–90; *Mem.*, 1:140–45) and Elizabeth Allen, 1 Dec. 1762 (Berg).

3. Included by Mme d'Arblay in *Mem.*, 1:147–50.

4. CB later included translations of Petrarch's sonnets 124 and 135 in the second volume of *Hist. Mus.* (2:334–35; Mercer, 1:635). Sonnet 124 begins:

I saw on earth angelic virtues beam
And blaze with such celestial charms and grace
That since, no other excellence I trace,
But all appears a shade, a smoke, a dream.

5. Fanny, who was ten at the time, has left no clues about CB's arrangements beyond saying that "the idea of a governess, who, to him, unless his children were wholly confined to the nursery, must indispensably be a species of companion, was not, in his present desolate state of mind, even tolerable" (*Mem.*, 1:154). CB probably took the children to stay with his mother, who lived in York Street, Covent Garden (*ED*, 1:lxxx, n.), for Mortimer (p. 32) gives the following address: "Burney, Charles, Organist. Enquire at Grig's Coffee-house, York Street, Covent-Garden." His sisters Becky and Ann, "the best nurse in England," were no doubt also helpful (*ED*, 1:41; *HFB*, p. 12). In the summer of 1763, CB took his family to Battersea, while a "Welsh woman . . . took care of my house in Poland Street" (Frag. 96, n. 2).

FRAGMENT 94   London, 1762–63

In the midst of this Affliction, I was visited by M^r & Mrs Greville—M^r and Mrs Garrick, and others of my early friends, made previous to my going into Norfolk. ⌜These were Mr Sloper[1] and Mrs Cibber, with whom at breaking up time[2] in the summer vacation, I went to Westwood Hay near Newbury Berks, with my eldest daughter,[3] the little performer on the Harp^d where we passed our time very pleasantly.⌝[4]

1. William Sloper (1709–89) of West Woodhay, Berkshire, M.P. for Great Bedwyn 1747–56, Lord of Trade 1756–61, Deputy Paymaster of the forces at Gibraltar 1761–89. In 1728 he married Catherine (c. 1707–97), daughter of Major-General Robert Hunter. In the 1740s Sloper offered protection to Susannah Cibber, who had been exploited by her scoundrel husband Theophilus Cibber. Mrs. Cibber became his *amie* and had a daughter by him, Maria Susannah (for whom, see Frag. 106, n. 6; also Nash, pp. 108–12). CB had known Mrs. Cibber, Arne's sister, from his early days of apprenticeship under Arne (Frags. 31, 34) and probably met her again with the Slopers at Garrick's house.

2. Of the Sheeles school in June. A fragment in Berg provides the information that CB went to West Woodhay on "June 9th . . . and past 8 or 10 days there very pleasantly," and that "Miss Sloper" was present.

3. Esther (see Frag. 84, n. 8).

4. "It was an observation of my old friend Mrs Cibber, that in the separation of friends, after a visit, those who remained stationary were worse off than those who quitted them" (CB to Frances Crewe, 5 Aug. 1794, Osborn). In a letter to Mme d'Arblay, 18 Oct. 1794 (Berg), CB attributes the observation to Sloper. For CB's verses "For Fanny," composed at this time, see *ED,* 1:xlvi.

FRAGMENT 95   London, 1763

I renewed my acquaintance this year[1] wit[h] the Miss Macartneys,[2] Lord March,[3] Sir Charle[s] Sedley,[4] & Mrs Mackenzie,[5] who recommended me to the Duke & Duchess of Ancaster, as a master for Lady Mary Bertie,[6] & to several other scholars.

1763 Encrease of scholars

1. CB intended to insert this text at "p. 118—top" of the first volume of his memoirs. The year cannot be determined with certainty, but CB's index suggests 1763.

2. See Frag. 46.

3. William Douglas (1725–1810), 3rd Earl of March, succeeded 1778 as 4th Duke of Queensberry ("old Q."). He was known for his passion for betting. CB had probably met him through Fulke Greville (*ED,* 1:220).

4. Frag. 37, n. 6.

5. Frag. 74, n. 3.

6. Peregrine Bertie (1714–78), 3rd Duke of Ancaster and Kesteven, on 27 Nov. 1750 married as his second wife Mary (d. 1793), daughter of Thomas Panton, Mistress of the Robes to Queen Charlotte 1761–93. CB refers to their daughter, who died at a young age on 13 April 1767 (*AR*, 10:175).

FRAGMENT 96

An old Welsh woman, who looked after my town house during the absence of the family,[1] to whom I complained of being bitten by something when I last slept in town, wch I feared were buggs. She said nothing, wch made me fear the same w^d happen when I came again to Poland Street; but, contrary to my expectation I remained quiet, and slept undisturbed the whole night, and asked my Cambro-British House-keeper whether she had made use of any means to destroy the vermin wch had so annoyed me before: "Ay inteeet! (says she, with a sigh) I caave them a little waarm trink, I can assure you:" wch was pouring boiling water into the joints of the bedstead.[2]

1. It seems likely that this occurred in the summer of 1763 as one of CB's "domestic arrangements" after Esther's death (Frag. 93, n. 5).

2. Another version of the anecdote reads: "An honest little old Welsh-woman, who took care of my house in Poland Street, during the residence of myself and family at Battersea in summer, & to whom I complained after lying in Town one night, of my having been bit by bugs—the next time I remained a night in town, I told her in the morning that I hoped the bugs, if such had annoyed me before, had walked off—Ay, inteet! (she exclaimed)—I *caave* 'em a little waarm trink, I can assure you!" (Barrett, Egerton 3700B, p. 74). CB must have later told this story to Mrs. Thrale, who alludes to it in her letter to CB of ? Nov. 1780 (Osborn): her physician Dr. Jebb gave Fanny "a *little warm Trink: Ay inteet*!!!"

This story is followed by two more anecdotes about Welsh women: "Another old Woman, extremely deaf, who had a graceless son, with whom she had frequent disputes: on his going out of the room muttering— she says [']Hah! I don't know what you say, not I; but whatever you say you lie.' And in going out, when he slammed the door, she said, 'Why do you give yourself such trouble my head was not there.'" (In *Thraliana*, 1: 222, she became "a Clergyman's Widow at whose House he lived some time.") The second anecdote reads: "A cross old Welch woman—on being called a termagant, said—'I pless my God! I never wanted for a spiteful word at my need!'"

FRAGMENT 97   London, Summer 1763?

I c^d get to Battersea. And my brother Sculler[1] & I rowed his sisters & my children, to the great displeasure of the regular Watermen, who hoaxed, ragged & abused us in the most eloquent language of their element. I sometimes had a set too with them, when there were no females with us, and "out-Heroded Herod," till all their amunition of tropes and figures were expended.[2]

1. Neither CB's friend nor his friend's sisters have been identified.

2. "It is well known that there was formerly a rude custom for those who were sailing upon the Thames, to accost each other as they passed, in the most abusive language they could invent, generally, however, with as much satirical humour as they were capable of producing. Addison gives a specimen of this ribaldry, in Number 383 of 'The Spectator,' when Sir Roger de Coverley and he are going to Spring-garden. Johnson was once eminently successful in this species of contest; a fellow having attacked him with some coarse raillery, Johnson answered him thus, 'Sir, your wife, *under pretence of keeping a bawdy-house,* is a receiver of stolen goods'" (Hill/Powell, 4:26). For a comment on Johnson's retort, see *Times Literary Supplement,* 21 July 1961, p. 449.

FRAGMENT 98   London, Summer 1763

Garrick all this summer had been preparing to go abroad in Autumn, and meditating how best the business of the Theatre might be carried on during his absence. Colman,[1] who was joined to his brother George[2] & Mr Lacy, his brother Patentee, had prepared Philaster from Beaumont and Fletcher; & Powel, a new actor,[3] & his new farce of "The Deuce is in him," for the opening of the Theatre in 1764. Mr Garrick had himself prepared Midsummer Nights dream[4]

In the Autumn of this year, I past a week with the worthy Mr Vincent of Serjeant's Inn, King's Stationer,[5] whose daughters were the two first scholars I undertook in the city, after my return to London from Norfolk; a more worthy and friendly family I never knew in the whole course of my practice.

1. George Colman (1732–94), dramatist and friend of Bonnell Thornton, had become acquainted with Garrick in 1759. His adaptation of *Philaster* was eventually produced at Drury Lane on 8 Oct. 1763, and his two-act comedy *The Deuce is in Him* (based on Jean Marmontel), on 4 Nov.

2. George Garrick (1723–79), Garrick's

younger brother, in April 1747 had become co-patentee, with Garrick and James Lacy, of Drury Lane.

3. William Powell (1735–69), coached by Garrick, was to make a triumphant debut as Philaster in Colman's adaptation.

4. He asked CB to provide some of the musical settings, and CB noted: "My first excursion to Hampstead in consequence of this agreem^t was Sunday 6th March, and became more and more pleasant as the spring advanced" (Berg). "Hampstead" is evidently a slip for "Hampton." Garrick planned the musical adaptation of *A Midsummer Night's Dream* for the following season. It was to be staged after his departure for Europe, with Colman supervising the production during his absence. "I live in hopes of seeing it a favorite entertainment of next winter," Colman wrote to Garrick on 18 June 1763 (Lonsdale 1965, p. 57).

Later, on 21 March 1806, CB added as a footnote to this fragment: "I never knew till this moment, on looking into Mr Erskine Baker's edition of his Biographia Dramatica of 1782 for the precise time when it was performed, that this Cookery was not Mr Gar-

rick's He always spoke of it to me, with the anxious affection of a parent. But as I was less intimate wth Mr Colman than with the adorer & restorer of Shakespeare, he suffered me to suppose the *alterations* & *additions* to be his own, in order to interest me the more in its Fate. Mr Baker is in general so accurate and satisfactory in his information that I have not the least doubt of the foundation of his statements." In the 1812 edition of *Biographia Dramatica* [4:43], Colman corrects this, stating that "the original adaptation had definitely been by Garrick and that he, Colman, had only attended rehearsals and had been little more than a 'godfather' on the occasion." See Lonsdale 1965, p. 58.

5. Probably Robert Vincent, of Serjeant's Inn, who died 16 Feb. 1764 (*London Magazine,* 1764, p. 162). He and his two daughters, Miss and Miss S. Vincent, are listed among the subscribers to *Hist. Mus.* In 1763 he appears to have been succeeded by Edward Vincent (fl. 1745–90), stationer at Salisbury Court, No. 17 (1768–69), stationer to the Board of Ordnance 1790; he also figures among CB's subscribers. See Maxted, p. 233; and Nichols, 4:255.

FRAGMENT 99   London, 1763–64

I must now turn back a little to the time when I left Lynn Regis, to reestablish myself in London.

My friend Mr Stephen Allen, the Corn Merchant, soon after my final departure from Norfolk, by too great labour & anxiety in his mercantile pursuits, became consumptive & died ab^t a year after my poor first wife.[1] Mrs Allen his widow, one of our most partial Lynn friends, & I, frequently corresponded by letters & by reciprocal visits, wch she made to the capital in winter, & I to Lynn in the Summer. About the year 1764, a copy of verses wch I inclosed in one of my letters,[2] discovered my regard to be something more than mere friend^p and I laboured under an interdict more than a 12 Month, neither seeing nor being allowed to write to her. Previous to this interdict, I became very seriously impassioned; but after this rebuff I had very little hopes that our acquaintance w^d ever be renewed.[3]

1. Stephen Allen died on 11 April 1763.

2. Perhaps his verses entitled "The Witch" (Poet. Nbk, pp. 53–55), in which he describes Mrs. Allen's "magic spells":

> Then her voice, when she speaks or she
>   sings
> (For witches love music, you know)
> Each nerve & each fibre unstrings
> Such heart-piercing sounds from it
>   flow. . . .
>
> Her image by night & by day

> Still haunts me, both sleeping &
>   waking,
> Steals my peace & spirits away
> And my heart keeps incessantly aching.

3. "It will appear that the first *unsuccessful* overture was made more than twelve months prior to [Mrs. Allen's] establishment in Russell Street" (Mrs. Allen's son, the Rev. Stephen Allen, to C. P. Burney, 21 Nov. 1832, Osborn; he cites a letter that he owned, now missing, from CB to Dorothy Young).

FRAGMENT 100   London, November 1763

as well as artists, that the spirit of comparison sh^d not sour the one nor mortify the other; but that the whole praise or the blame, of a performer or production sh^d as much as possible appertain to one & the same individual—But in spite of all these fine reflexions, when in Dec^r [1] the performance of this drama was announced to the public with its new Music, scarce any body w^d come to hear it, and those who did come, could hardly be kept awake by the utmost efforts of the performers.[2] It was an old tale, wch had been so often told in different plays and farces taken from Shakespeare's original Sketch: such as the Fairies, Pyramus & Thisbe, Bottom the Weaver, & Queen Mab,[3] that no curiosity was excited by the present title. Messrs Colman & Geo. Garrick not seeing the cause of this indifference, and imagining that by compression it w^d become more elastic, withdrawing it after one representation, though heard through very quietly, cut down what they had imagined a *first rate* ship to a frigate or Farce,[4] wch turned out a bad Sailor, retaining only the comic songs, w^ch, however, shared the same neglect, and were withdrawn after one performance, to the great mortification of the actors and humiliation of the three musical composers[5] who had done their best, & severally expected to establish an interest in the Theatre and in the favour of the public.

So that we unfortunate champions being thus levelled by a general calamity, may be supposed to part better friends than we met.

1. CB made a slip here: Garrick's production of *A Midsummer Night's Dream* took place 23 Nov. 1763.

2. William Hopkins, the prompter, comments in his diary: "This Piece of Shakespeare's was greatly cut and altered,—the fifth Act entirely left out,—and many Airs introduced,—got up with a vast Trouble to all concerned, but particularly to Mr. Colman, who attended every Rehearsal, and had Alterations innumerable to make.—Upon the whole, I believe, never was a Piece so murdered as this was by the Singing-speakers, in which Mrs. Vincent and Mr. W. Palmer were beyond Description bad; and had it not been for the Children's excellent Performance (particularly Miss Wright, who ran away with all the Applause and very deservedly) the Audience would not have suffered them to have gone half thro' it.—The sleeping particularly displeased.—The next Day it was reported, the Performers sung the Audience to Sleep, and then went to Sleep themselves" (MacMillan, p. 100; *St. James's Chronicle*, 24 Nov. 1763).

3. *The Fairies*, set to music by Handel's assistant John Christopher Smith, had been produced by Garrick on 3 Feb. 1755 at Drury Lane; the mock-opera *Pyramus and Thisbe*, set by Lampe, on 13 April 1745 at Covent Garden; for *Queen Mab,* see Frag. 59. *Bottom the Weaver* may refer to *Pyramus and Thisbe, Lyon, Moonshine, and Wall,* a "Comic Masque, compos'd in the high Style of Italy"; words and music by Richard Leveridge (1670–1758). It was first produced 11 April 1716 at Lincoln's Inn Fields.

4. Colman and Garrick's brother converted the musical into *A Fairy Tale,* staged three days later on 26 Nov. 1763, in which only four of CB's fourteen songs were re-

tained (see n. 5, below). This version was somewhat more successful than CB would like to admit; it ran, off and on, until 1777 (Odell, 1:376).

5. John Christopher Smith (see n. 3, above), young Michael Arne, and CB himself. According to "A Table of the Songs, with the Names of the several Composers" prefaced to Thomson's 1763 edition of *A Fairy Tale* (BL, shelf-mark 642.e.19 [14]), this musical version contained thirty-three vocal numbers, twelve by Smith (all from *The Fairies*), three by Michael Arne, two by Jonathan Battishill (1738–1801), one by Theodore Aylward (c. 1730–1801), and the remaining fourteen by CB. No trace of CB's music has so far come to light, though it must have been in existence in 1816 when Sir Henry Bishop made use of it for his adaptation for Covent Garden. Alfred Loewenberg, in his informative article "Midsummer Night's Dream Music in 1763" (*Theatre Notebook* 1 [1945–47]: 23–26), on which this note is based, gives a list of the first lines:

1. Against myself, why all this art (Helena)
2. Most noble Duke, to us be kind (Quince, Starveling, Bottom, Snout)
3. Away, away, I will not stay (Oberon and Titania)
4. Our softer sex can't fight for love (Helena)
5. If, oh, if no flame return (Helena)
6. The ousel-cock so black of hue (Bottom)
7. These looks, these tears, these tender sighs (Demetrius)
8. I'll range all around till I found out my love (Hermia)
9. How can these sighs and tears seem scorn to you (Lysander)
10. Let him come, let him come (Lysander)

11. With various griefs my mind is torn
    (Helena and Hermia)
12. Up and down, up and down (Oberon)

13. Sweetest creature, pride of nature (Titan-
    ia)
14. Be as thou wast to be (Oberon)

FRAGMENT 101   London, January 1764

1764

In the midst of my professional prosperity as a teacher of Music, the first month of this year was rendered memorable by an event of considerable importance in my affairs.

Jany 28th, my liberal friend, Mr Honeywood,[1] died suddenly in his carriage, just as he had entered it from St James's Coffee house. He was an honourable man, with some singularities, wch had nothing vicious or immoral in them. He was rich enough to have lived splendidly without trade or commerc[e]; but established a banking house in Lombard Street wch was long in high credit, till by the great fire in Cornhill[2] he was burnt out. He then, after the streets wch had ⟨burned longest⟩ were rebuilt, removed to Cornhill, and took into partnership Mr Richard Fuller his principal Clark,[3] who succeeded to the Firm on the decease of Mr Honeywood, and the house is still in the possession of Mr Fullers descendants. Mr Honeywood stood a contested Election for Middlesex against Cook in wch he was defeated.[4] He was set up on the Dissenting interest, and always voted in Parliament on that side. He was many years Member for Steyning in Sussex. When he died it was found that he had no lineal descendants, but bequeathed his possessions wch were very considerable in Land as well as Money, to be divided among such persons of the name of Honeywood as c^d be found; and advertisements appeared for a long time after his decease in the public papers, informing such synonimous persons as could be found where and of whom to apply for their share of his property. Mr H. was a gentleman of good parts, and seemed to understand the Funds and Finances of this country very well; but he was cold and formal. He had read but little, except party pamphlets; had no taste for belles lettres, or Science, but that of the Alley;[5] as he had not early in life formed a taste for literature it was too late to acquire one. There is no plunging into the higher classes of learning without precognition. He had no ear for Music; yet thought that the study of its elements w^d divert him, and help to fill up his time; w^ch, from having no pursuit, hung heavy on his hands. The man that has no means of amusing himself but by walking or riding about, sh^d never detach himself from society; where without talking yourself, you may be amused by others: Nothing is more pleasing to loquacity than a silent & respectful hearer. With respect to Music, the mind, as well as finger, was too stiff and inflexible to assist him in the undertaking; and I believe he never was able to play the 100^dth Psalm, Lady Coventry's Minuet,[6] or to distinguish concord from discord before his departure from this world.

We agreed very well, but did not amuse each other much. His principal topic was confined to the politics of the day, concerning wch I was too indifferent, and, indeed, too prudent, to dispute; And though I was unable to make a musician of him, or to teach his ears to vibrate sufficiently true to musical tones to catch his attention; yet it was supposed by his Partner, Clarks, & domestics, that I sh^d rival them all in his favour, & be certainly well remembered in his Will. But in dictating his Testament, no such name as mine seems to have occurred to him, nor indeed of any of his Clarks or domestics, who were much better intitled to his remembrance.[7]

1. Frazer Honywood (d. 27 Jan. 1764) of Malling, Kent, M.P. for Steyning 1759–64, had married Jane Atkyns on 5 May 1736. He was a wealthy banker who speculated in government loans (Namier/Brooke, 2:635).

2. See Frag. 54, n. 6.

3. Richard Fuller (c. 1713–82), succeeded Honywood as head of the banking firm and as M.P. for Steyning, later M.P. for Stockbridge 1768–74 (Namier/Brooke, 2:477).

4. In 1750 he had been urged by Sir Hugh Smithson, M.P. for Middlesex, to stand for the county but lost to George Cooke (c. 1705–68). Earlier, in 1747, he had been an unsuccessful candidate in the Shaftesbury by-election (Namier/Brooke, 2:635).

5. Change Alley, scene of speculation in South Sea and other stocks.

6. Two copies of "Lady Coventrys Minuet" are in the British Library (shelf-marks: G.311 [70]; H.1994.a[43]). The score has no words to it, so that one cannot say with cer-

tainty whether the Lady Coventry of the title was Mary Gunning (1732–60), one of the prettiest and vainest girls in London, who in 1752 married George William Coventry, 6th Earl of Coventry. In January 1768, CB was teaching her two daughters Mary and Anne ("2 L^y Coventrys," Baldwin Diary frag., Berg): on 28 June 1777, Mary Alicia married Sir Andrew Bayntun Rolt, Baronet (c. 1740–1816), who divorced her 24 June 1783; on 24 Oct. 1778 Anne Margaret married the Hon. Edward Foley (1747–1803), M.P., who divorced her 21 May 1787 (Namier/Brooke, 2: 445, 69).

7. Honywood "gave me *£100* a year for dining with him at Hampstead of a Sunday; by whose sudden death I was supposed by his partner and connections, to have lost much more than the *£100* a year" (CB to Lady Crewe, 18 April 1806, BL, Add. MSS 37916, f. 16; Scholes 1948, 2:307).

FRAGMENT 102   5 February 1764

In April I rec^d the following letter from my friend Mr Garrick, dated Naples
Feb^ry 5th 1764[1]

Dear Sir

I have defer'd keeping my promise to you so long that I might be able to give
you some slight account (for you must expect no better from me) of the present
State of Musick in Italy[2]—

We have been here six Weeks and had not Mrs Garrick been lame for ye last
fortnight with a sort of Rheumatism, (as ye Doctors call it) wch has something
damp'd our Spirits, we should have no complaint to make of Naples—I mean
of the Climate, Situation, and Curiosities in and about the City, but for the
People themselves, they are literally and figuratively a Race of Thieves—we are
obliged to keep our hands in our Pockets at Noon day! and the best Merchant
has no shame, nor loses any Credit here to be caught cheating his Customers—
I am greatly delighted with their Characters, They are quite different from any I
ever yet saw. They are all pantomimers from the Prince to ye Beggar, & are
Harlequins, Scaramouches & Pantaloons according to their Vivacity Gravity or
Age—Should I represent a Neapolitan upon our Stage (and I have got their
tricks to a hair) it would be thought a most absurd unnatural Character—So
much for these worthless people, and now for a little Musick—to speak of it in
general here, I think the taste of it very bad—it is all execution without
Simplicity or Pathos—I have heard the famous Gabrielli,[3] who has indeed
astonishing powers, great Com-pass of voice, & great flexibility, but she is
always ye same, & tho you are highly transported at first with her, yet wanting
that nice feeling of ye passions, (without which every thing in ye dramatic way
will cease to Entertain), she cannot give that variety, & that peculiar Pleasure
which alone can support the tediousness of an Opera—in short the Musick
vocal & instrumental has lost its Nature, and it is all dancing ye slack rope, and
tumbling thro' ye hoop.—

Yesterday we attended the Ceremony of making a Nun She was ye Daughter
of a Duke, & ye whole was conducted with great Splendor and Magnificence—
the Church was ornamented from top to bottom, & there were two large bands
of Musick of all kinds—There was great Solemnity & I was much affected, &,
to crown ye Whole the first part was sung by ye famous *Caffarelli*, who tho Old
has pleas'd me more than all ye Sĩgers I have yet heard[4]—He *touch'd* Me, & it
was ye first time I had been touch'd since I came to Italy. The Theatre here is a

Most Magnificent one;[5] but ill conducted & the *Gabrielli,* who is ye only Performer of Consequence is so whimsical, that she scarc[ely] Endeavours to Sing once in three times—I have lately heard an Excellent Hautboy, & *Fabio* the Violin,[6] but they are not worth coming to Italy for—indeed *You* will get little by such a Journey[7] & I protest to you that I have felt more at y^e *first Air* of *Rousseau,*[8] than at all ye Operas I heard at Turin, Genoa, Leghorn, Rome, & Naples. I can say no More—what ye Carnivals will produce at Rome & the Theatres at *Bologna* & *Venice* I will tell you hereafter—pray let me have a letter from you directly, and a long one—& let me know what ye Winter has produced among You.[9]—I shall stay here about 3 Weeks longer, & then return to Rome, where I propose to stay a Month—now if you write directly, I shall receive it before I get to Venice; My direction is, a Monsieur Monsr Garrick, chez Monsr Barazzi, Banquier a Rome.[10] Take care to send it to ye right place; & (as I said before) to write immediately.—How goes *Phil* on?[11]

If you have any commands about Musick pray let me know them—I wish I knew more of it, to pick up something good for You, but I fear at present good Musick is ye Needle in a bottle of Hay—Should you write to *Venice,* instead of *Rome,* (for you may be idle like myself)—direct to me chez Monsieur Udney, Consul de sa Majesté Britannique, à Venise[12]—tell my Brother of this, tho he knows it by this time. My Wife sends her best Compl^ts, & I am most sincerely

Yours D: Garrick

I rec^d another letter from my frie[n]d, written at Naples on X^mas day, in wch he says, so mild is this climate, that we are now sitting with the windows open, eating Green Peas.[13]

1. The manuscript in Berg shows that CB intended to include this letter in his memoirs. It is printed here in full because previously only two fragments of it were known. One appeared in *Hist. Mus.* (4:420; Mercer, 2:819) and the other in Hill (p. 25); both are reprinted in Garrick *Letters* (1:404–5). Garrick's original letter, the text of which is reproduced here, is in Comyn. It is addressed: "A Monsieur / Monsieur Burney / Maître de Musique / at his house / in Poland Street / near Broad Street / London / Inghilterra."

2. Evidently by the end of the summer of 1763, when the Garricks set out for Europe,

CB was already contemplating the book that he published in 1771 as *The Present State of Music in France and Italy.*

3. Caterina Gabrielli (1730–96), soprano known as La Cochettina, came to Naples in 1764 after her success in northern Italy, where she sang in several operas by Traetta. CB gives an account of her at the time of her appearance in London in 1775–76 (*Hist. Mus.,* 4:502–4; Mercer, 2:881–82).

4. Gaetano Maiorano Caffarelli (1710–83), castrato, had sung in Naples since 1741 and returned to settle there after the Lisbon earthquake of 1755. He now sang only occa-

sionally. CB quotes this passage from Garrick's letter (*Hist. Mus.*, 4:420; Mercer, 2:
818–19), adding: "In 1770, I heard Caffarelli,
myself, sing at Naples. He was then sixty-
seven [in fact, sixty]; yet though his voice
was thin, it was easy to imagine, from what
he was still able to do, that his voice and
talents had been of the very first class." See
also *Tours*, 1:279, 281–82.

5. The Teatro di San Carlo, built in 1737,
was one of the largest and most impressive in
Europe, with a seating capacity of up to 1,500
spectators.

6. Ermagora Fabio, leader of the San
Carlo orchestra, with whom CB was to dine
on 7 Nov. 1770 in Naples: "He was so obliging and so humble as to bring with him his
violin. . . . In Italy, the leader of the first opera
in the world carries the instrument of his
fame and fortune about him, with as much
pride as a soldier does his sword or musquet;
while, in England, the indignities he would
receive from the populace would soon im-
press his mind with shame for himself and
fear for his instrument" (*Tours*, 1:283–84;
Poole, p. 197; "Fabio" in Rees).

7. Garrick was mistaken, but his remark

shows that CB had such a journey in mind as
early as 1763.

8. *Le Devin du village* was first produced
in Paris in 1752; Garrick was influential in
having CB's version of it produced in London in 1766. See Frag. 109.

9. He had learned before Christmas
about the failure of his and Colman's adaptation of *A Midsummer Night's Dream* (Garrick
Letters, 1:397). His letters to his brother
George and to Colman show his keen interest in what was going on in London during
his absence.

10. The name of the banker Francesco
Barazzi appears in Garrick's postal address at
Rome in several other letters at this time.

11. Garrick had left his favorite little spaniel with the Burneys in Poland Street before
he set out for Europe. See Bridge: Frags.
107–8, n. 3.

12. George Udny (1727–1800), British
consul at Venice c. 1761–76.

13. This letter to CB is missing. On 24
Dec. 1763 Garrick had written a long letter to
Colman, which ends: "My best wishes to M^r
Burney I shall write soon to him" (Garrick
Letters, 1:398).

FRAGMENT 103   London, June 1764

I was now meditating a journey on the Continent myself as far as Paris. I
wished to give my children as good an education as I c^d afford, to enable them to
shift for themselves as I had done, they being too numerous for me ever to be
able to leave them independant fortunes. And I found that learning French, for
females ⌐in servitude⌐ was absolutely necessary; but that having masters to teach
them at home, or to place them in a good boarding-school was equally tedious,
expensive and ineffectual.[1] I therefore, at the breaking up of Mrs Sheeles's school
June 6th for the Easter holidays set out with my eldest and third daughter[2] for
France, in order to abridge the time necessary in England for learning a little bad
French, by dipping them over head and ears in it, where being boarded in a

house where nothing else was spoken, they must drink or drown; and they being young and the Organs of speech ductile, they w^d acquire a better pronunciation & idiom in a few weeks, than at home in as many years, where it is book French wch children learn & English translated.

1. According to Fanny, CB discarded as well "the idea of a governess" (*Mem.*, 1:154). Later he advised Rosette to "practice *speaking French,* however well you may read it. You can neither enjoy conversation nor Theatres—I am sure that was my case during my first journey to France" (CB to Rosette Burney, 29 July 1806, Burney-Cumming).

2. Esther and Susan. Fanny was left at home—perhaps, says Joyce Hemlow, because "her 'tender veneration' for her Roman Catholic grandmother might easily turn to the Roman Catholic Church if she were in favourable surroundings" (*HFB*, p. 15). CB wrote her two letters from Paris, dated 13 and 18–[20] June 1764 (Berg; extracts in *ED*, 1: xlvii–l).

FRAGMENT 104

were of great use to me in all my purchases & transactions; but the most friendly and useful assistance wth respect to placing my children, was Lady Clifford, Sister of the then Duchess of Norfolk;[1] a Lady who on acc^t of her religion had lived many years in a private manner, in the capital of France.— She was rather in years; but chearful, full of anecdote, and able to give me the life and character of every person of consequence at the court of Versailles, as well as in the city. I met at her Ladyship's one morning the Duchesse de Mirepoix, consort of the Duke de Mirepoix, who had resided in England many years as Ambassador from the Court of France.[2] I was interrogated by the two Ladies, what news I brought from England; when I said I was a little ashamed of my countrymen, at present, they were very riotous, and great Mobs of Mr Wilkes's[3] fr^d[s] had frequently assembled together to the terror of the peaceable inhabitants:—"Ah! (says the Duchess) de English are de foinest people in de Vorld! I have see 50,tousand men assemble togeder, without break a Vindow— and in any oder country, day voud have occasion'd a Revolution."

Lady Clifford gave me my choice of two methods of having my children well placed & educated. One was at a Convent at Blois, where the best French was spoken,[4] and where the board, clothing, and Masters w^d cost no more than £20 a year for each, as they all wore a cheap black Uniform: no finery or distinction was allowed to excite envy or vanity in the rest, and the masters were poor priests whose worldly passions were subdued, & they c^d subsist upon a very small income. But the pensioners, or boarders must be all Catholics, and submit to the discipline & religious ceremonies of the House.

The other proposition was the placing my children in the hands, and under the care of some prudent & worthy female who w^d suffer them, if protestants, to attend the English Ambassador's chapel,[5] and allowed [them] to have such masters as I sh^d direct paying in proportion to their attendance & abilities. This I preferred, though instead of £20 a year for each, it w^d cost me a hundred. For as it was my wish that my children sh^d be brought up in the religion of their Fathers, that is, the established religion of our country, I thought it best, whatever might be the expence, to avoid putting them in the way to be prejudiced in favour of any religion but our own, as it might distract their minds, &, if opposed, render them miserable for the rest of their lives.

The good Lady Clifford, though a firm Catholic herself, indulged me in my wishes, and discovered for me an intelligent, worthy and kind governess, who having lived with the old Lady Sandwich,[6] was used a little to English customs, and suffered my girls to have their English prayer books, and to go on a Sunday to our chapel, and hear the service & a sermon by the Ambassador's chaplain.[7] This worthy person's name was Mad^e Saintmard.[8] She was married to the Maitre d'Hotel of the duc de la Valiere,[9] whose Lib^y was so celebrated.

Here my children were well and kindly treated during their whole residence at Paris. A Sister of Sir Willoughby Aston[10] was *en pension* in the same house, but was unfortunately seized with an acute Fever, wch in a few days carried her off, to the great grief of my children, for whom they had conceived a great affection.

Having settled my children much to my Satisfaction, visited the theatres, Public buildings &c.[11] I hasten back to England to be there at the opening of the Queen-Square School. I set off post, the 8th of July, see in my way the Abbey of St Denis, and Chantilly; landed at Dover the 11th, in London the 12th & attended the School and private Scholars on the 13th.

Though it was the height of the summer, I had 12 or 14 private scholars on my hands besides the School.

1. Lady Clifford née Elizabeth Blount (d. 1778), widow of Hugh Clifford (1700–1732), 3rd Baron Clifford of Chudleigh, whom she had married in 1725. Her younger sister Mary (1702–73) in 1727 married Edward Howard (1686–1777), 8th Duke of Norfolk. They were daughters of Pope's friend Edward Blount, of Blagden, Devon.

2. Anne-Marguerite-Gabrielle de Beau-veau-Craon (1707–post-1774), "Dame du

Palais" to the Queen. She was widow first of the prince de Lixin, and now of Pierre-Louis de Levis (1702–58), maréchal de camp, marquis de Mirepoix, cr. 1751 duc de Mirepoix, whom she had married as his second wife in 1739. He was French ambassador in London 1751–56.

3. John Wilkes (1727–97), the radical politician whose arrest, in spite of his being an M.P., had created a great scandal in London the previous year. Around Christmas 1763 he slipped off to France and in Feb. 1764, during his absence, was expelled from the House against the clamor of his supporters. He was now in Paris, and like CB, concerned with the education of his daughter. Subsidized by the French government, he cultivated the philosophes Diderot and d'Holbach, as well as a courtesan named Corradini; he returned to London in 1768.

4. Blois was known for the purity of its French, and many Englishmen, including Addison, resided there to "get the language."

5. The English ambassador to France from Oct. 1763 to June 1765 was Horace Walpole's first cousin Francis Seymour Conway (1718–94), 2d Baron Conway, cr. Viscount Beauchamp and Earl of Hertford 1750, and later (1793) Marquess of Hertford.

6. Lady Elizabeth (d. 2 July 1757), daughter of John Wilmot, Earl of Rochester, inherited some of her father's vivacity and wit. In 1689 she married Edward Montagu, 3rd Earl of Sandwich (1670–1729), and after his death resided in the rue Vaugirard, Paris.

7. James Trail (1725–83), D.D. 1760, Lord Hertford's chaplain, later (1765) Bishop of Down and Connor (YW, 37:430 n.21; 38:279).

8. Anne Saintmard or St. Mart (fl. 1757–65). According to Fanny, she "was accustomed to the charge of *des jeunes Anglaises*" (*Mem.*, 1:156).

9. Louis-César de La Baume (1708–80), duc de La Vallière. His maître d'hôtel has not been identified.

10. Sir Willoughby Aston (1714–72) of Rishley, 5th Baronet, M.P. for Nottingham 1754–61, CB's neighbor in Poland Street (Frag. 85, n. 1). Fanny says that two of his daughters, Selina and Belinda, were staying with Mme St. Mart (*Mem.*, 1:156). His sister has not been identified, unless she is "the lady of the late lord Aston" who died 11 Aug. 1764 (*GM*, 34:398; *AR*, 7:124), but this is most unlikely.

11. For a further account of CB's stay in Paris, see his letters to Fanny of June 1764 (Frag. 103, n. 2).

FRAGMENT 105   Summer 1764?

It was in the course of this Summer that my old friend Mr Samuel Crisp,[1] with whom I became acquainted at Mr Greville's in Wiltshire during my apprenticeship with Arne in 1747 and of whom I had lost sight 16 or 17 years, found me out. Indeed he had written to me once or twice while I was at Lynn; but I had not leisure to keep up such a pleasant correspondence. He wrote to me from Surry, and pressed me to visit him, giving me his instructions where to find him near Kingston.[2] But in 1763, having been at Wilbury, in returning to London I travelled across the country in search of my friend, and after wandering ab^t the country half a day in a post-chaise, I found Mr Crisp to whom I was admitted as a visitor but to my astonishment, and great disappointment, I saw a Gentleman I had never seen before, of age, form, and feature, totally different from my friend. I apologised for breaking in upon him by a

Trying to find him in Surry go to a wrong Mr Sam. Crisp

mistake of my Postilion: it was a gentleman of the name of Crisp of whom I was in search. "Sir, my name is Crisp"—but Sir, it was Mr Samuel Crisp whom I sought—"Sir, my name is Samuel Crisp."³—is there any person except yourself, Sir, of that name in this neighbourhood? "yes Sir, there is, 3 or 4 miles off"—is there a turnpike road to his residence, Sir? for I am famous for losing myself. "No Sir, it is a cross road—& I fear your postilion will find no quarter for his horses." Then Sir I must give up the search—am I far off the London road Sir? ["]No Sir, not above a Mile from the great West road"—but is the way to this road easy to find, Sir? "There are 2 or 3 gates to open; but I'll send a servant with you Sir, who shall direct your driver & save him the trouble of alight^g in order to open the gates["]—it was now growing dark, and I was much afraid of a cross road in the dark; I therefore with joy and gratitude accepted of the obliging offer of this gentleman, and arrived in Poland Street by midnight, with whole bones. I wrote my friend Crisp an acc^t of my Quixoteism in seeking him with as much zeal & ill success as La Manca's K^t ever wandered after his Dulcinea. This, as soon as gout w^d permit, brought him to Town, where our meeting was so truly cordial and affectionate that it promised, and produced, a duration for the rest of our lives.

Soon after this meeting, I visited him at the small stragling Village of Chesington near Kingston in Surry; where, to save the trouble of housekeeping he lodged & boarded all the year round in the decayed Mansion at least two hundred years old of a broken down old family, with a respectable maiden

Find him at last at Chesington

gentlewoman⁴ somewhat in years, the Lady of the Mannor, who, a little to encrease the small patrimony left, boarded gentlemen of a certain age who had quitted the world, and who in this Chateau only met at meals, at Tea, and afterwards at a game of cards. Crisp was the only reader and polished man among them who c^d amuse and instruct others, and had all the weight & importance here of a *capo di casa*. The rest saw no amusement beyond a walk or a ride about the common or fields round the Hall, for so it was still called, and had venerable remains of its anc^t dignity: a spacious garden, now a wilderness, with old fruit trees, flowers, box walks, peas, beans, weeds and ⟨cabbage⟩ mixt to-

Descrip. of the Hall & Village

gether: a ruined summer-house, with a distant view of Epsom, and an extensive prospect; an orchard, dove house, and, in front, an Ivy clad small parish church,[5] in wch the ancestors of the L^y of the Mannor for many generations, were entom[b]ed to wch there was an avenue planted with chesnut trees from the Hall, where the vicar had never ceased to dine of a Sunday since its foundation. My friend was such a martyr to the gout, that he seldom c^d enjoy the idle and rural rides of the gentlemen of his Mess; or quit his retreat, though invited by some of the first people of elegance and fashion; such as Lord Coventry,[6] Mr Conyers of Copt hall,[7] Mr Greville, & Mr.   [8] whom he had known in Italy, & who had a high opinion of his taste, learning, and knowledge of the fine arts. I visited him 3 or 4 times in 1764, and when my girls came from France, our attachment, and his fondness for all my children became so strong, that I made Chesington my country house as long as my friend lived. I sent one of Zumpe's Piano fortes[9] to the old mansion, and every summer all the new Music he w^d like to hear, and books he w^d wish to read. Here, out of the reach of London loungers, I c^d study in greater tranquility than anywhere else. But my friend, whose mind was richly furnished, and who still wished to know what was passing in the great world, was curious ab^t every thing that had passed in my professional pursuits; my courtship, & marriage after liberation from all claims on my time by Mr Greville; my establishment of an interest in the city, by gaining an organist's place there, & superseding Stanley at the King's Arms Concert; the foundation of the Society of the Temple of Apollo, and under that name, producing the Music of a Pantomime entertainment, an English Burletta, and [the] Music of the Tragedy of Alfred; my 13 weeks fever and [the] weak state of my general health afterwards, wch obliged me to lis[ten] to a proposal from Lynn, in hopes that change of

1. See Frag. 43, n. 1. Crisp had formerly owned a house in Hampton, London, furnished with antiques collected in Italy, but in the 1750s, in fear of debt, he gave it up, sold his collections, and joined his friend Chrysostome or Christopher Hamilton (1698–1758/9) on "some pic-nic plan of sharing expenses" at Chessington Hall, Surrey, owned by Hamilton (*ED,* 1:lvi; *HFB,* pp. 16–18; *JL,* 1:144 n.4).

2. Chessington lies about five miles south of Kingston-upon-Thames.

3. This particular Samuel Crisp (1705–84), namesake of CB's close friend, was an eccentric known as "The Greenwich Travel-

ler": he paid the owners of the Greenwich stagecoach £27 each year for his "daily amusement of riding in the coach from London to Greenwich, and returning in it immediately." See *GM* 54 (Jan. 1784): 73; and Annie Raine Ellis's account of him in *ED,* 1:xxvii–xxix.

4. Sarah Hamilton (1705–97) took over Chessington Hall after the death of her brother Christopher (n. 1, above) in 1759 and began to take boarders. Crisp, "perhaps out of kindness, and even charity," helped her to maintain herself "by becoming her first boarder" (*ED,* 1:lvii). She appears quite often in Fanny's *Early Diary and Letters.*

5. The thirteenth-century church, St. Mary the Virgin. Chessington Hall no longer exists, but a drawing of it by Edward Francesco Burney is mentioned in *ED* (1:lvii).

6. George William (1722–1809), 6th Earl of Coventry, Lord of the Bedchamber to George II and George III 1752–70.

7. John Conyers (1717–75), of Copt Hall, Essex, Tory M.P. for Reading 1747–54, for Essex 1772–75. On 15 Dec. 1763 he had lost a by-election by a narrow margin (Namier/Brooke, 2:247).

8. Left blank in manuscript.

9. Johann Christoph Zumpé (fl. 1735–83), "a German, who had long worked under Shudi, constructed small piano-fortes of the shape and size of the virginal, of which the tone was very sweet, and the touch, with a little use, equal to any degree of rapidity. These, from their low price, and the convenience of their form, as well as power of expression, suddenly grew into such favour, that there was scarcely a house in the kingdom where a keyed-instrument had ever had admission, but was supplied with one of Zumpé's piano-fortes, for which there was nearly as great a call in France as in England. In short, he could not make them fast enough to gratify the craving of the public" ("Harpsichord" in Rees. See also Boalch, p. 193; *New Grove*, 20: 1715–16).

FRAGMENT 106   London, 1762–64

the best compositions of that kind, both serious and comic, of wch the words were so free from licence and *Ladies' Catch Book*[1] indelicacy, that no female w^d be afraid to purchase it, or to let it lie open upon her Harpsichord deck. I had not time to print this collection before Bremner Warren and others published collections of the same kind.[2]

In Novr this year I first went to a meeting of the R.S. in Crane Court,[3] as Umbra to my Landlord, Keane Fitzgerald.[4] And became a Member of the Society of Arts, then in the Strand.[5] Attend a Committee of mechanics, when unpict Locks were under consideration; but no one produced was thought worthy of the premium. I frequently dined & supped at Mrs Cibbers. (Miss Sloper[6] began to receive instructions of *Accomp^y Mrs Cibber* me in accompaniment & Lesson playing in Decr 1762). *& Miss Sloper to* On Sat^y 24 Novr this year (1764) I accomp^d Mrs Cibber *Manzoli's 1st perform-* and Miss Sloper to the Opera of Ezio, to hear Man- *ance* zoli,[7] who now appeared on our stage for the first time under the new regency of Gordon & Vincent.[8]

---

1. In his article "Catch" in Rees, CB mentions "the institution of the Catch-Club, in 1762. This society was first suggested by the then earl of Eglinton, lord March, the pres-

ent duke of Queensbury, and—Meynel, esq. who soon inlisted under their banners the lords Sandwich, Orford, Fortescue, &c. &c. This institution has given birth to many excellent glees, in purer harmony and more polished melody than those of former times could boast; but of catches and canons the stock has not been equally augmented." As the Catch Club was all male, the catches were often hilariously bawdy. This gave CB the idea of publishing a different sort of catchbook.

2. In 1763 Edmund Thomas Warren (d. 1799) began a famous collection of *Catches, Canons and Glees* that he continued editing until his death. It contained 692 pieces and was printed by a number of music publishers; one of these was Robert Bremner (1713?–89), a Scotsman who came to London in 1762 and set up shop in the Strand opposite Somerset House. Several of CB's catches appeared later in various songbooks, such as the two-volume *Ladies Collection of catches, glees, canzonets, madrigals &c selected from the works of the most eminent composers by J. Bland* (1787–96), which CB had in his library (*Cat. Mus.,* no. 177).

3. The Royal Society had bought in 1710 two houses in Crane Court, in which it held its meetings until 1780. The MS Subscription Book 1754–63 of the society has the following entry: "Mr. Charles Burney, Organist. Poland Street. Elected a member Jan. 4 1763. Proposed by Mr. Fitzgerald" (information kindly provided by D. G. C. Allan, Curator-Librarian of the Royal Society).

4. Keane FitzGerald (d. 29 June 1782), experimental scientist, F.R.S. 25 March 1756, best known for his improvement of the barometer. For drawings and explanations, see *Philosophical Transactions of the Royal Society* 52 (1761): 146–76; 60 (1770): 74–79. He owned a house in Poland Street as early as 1753 and appears in the rate books of 1761–70 as CB's next-door neighbor (*JL,* 3:260–61 n.3). Fan-

ny described him in 1776 as "a hard featured, tall, hard voiced and hard mannered Irish man: fond of music, but fonder of *discussing* than of *listening*" (*ED,* 2:144).

5. The Society for the Encouragement of Arts, Manufactures, and Commerce was founded in 1754 with the aim of promoting "ingenuity and industry by bestowing premiums." For its history, see Hudson/Luckhurst; for Johnson's role in it, see Clifford, pp. 226–30.

6. Maria Susannah, or "Molly" (1740–86), Mrs. Cibber's natural daughter by William Sloper. She was a plain, amiable girl whose complexion was scarred with smallpox. After her mother's death (1766) she married the Rev. James Burton (Nash, pp. 123–24, 155–56, 278–83, 319–21).

7. Giovanni Manzuoli (c. 1720–82), Florentine castrato, came to London from Madrid. CB gives the following account of his performance: "The expectations which the great reputation of this performer had excited were so great, that at the opening of the theatre in November, with the pasticcio of E Z I O, there was such a crowd assembled at all the avenues, that it was with very great difficulty I obtained a place, after waiting two hours at the door. Manzoli's voice was the most powerful and voluminous soprano that had been heard on our stage since the time of Farinelli; and his manner of singing was grand and full of taste and dignity. In this first opera he had three songs, composed by Pescetti, entirely in different styles: *Recagli quell' acciaro,* an animated *aria parlante*; *Caro mio bene addio,* an adagio in a grand style of cantabile; and *Mi dona mi rende,* of a graceful kind, all which he executed admirably. The lovers of Music in London were more unanimous in approving his voice and talents than those of any other singer within my memory. The applause was hearty, unequivocal, and free from all suspicion of artificial zeal; it was a universal thunder. His voice alone was com-

manding from native strength and sweetness; for it seems as if subsequent singers had possessed more art and feeling; and as to execution, he had none. However, he was a good actor, though unwieldy in figure, and not well made in person; neither was he young when he arrived in London; yet the sensations he excited seem to have been more irresistible and universal, than I have ever been witness to in any theatre" (*Hist. Mus.*, 4:485; Mercer, 2:868). In his article on "Manzoli" in Rees, CB adds: "This great singer remained in England but one season. . . . In 1770 we heard Manzoli sing at Florence in a convent at the last consecration of six nuns; he had quitted the stage, and his voice, though in a small chapel, seemed much less powerful than when he was in England; and it was then said by those who had heard him before, that, powerful as his voice appeared to all who heard him for the first time, it had been still better." See also *Tours,* 1:183.

8. In 1764 John Gordon (see Frag. 40, n. 17) joined Peter Crawford (d. 1793), treasurer of the King's Theatre 1764–65, and Thomas Vincent in the management of the King's Theatre. They "spent £26,000 altering the auditorium and repainting and relining the boxes but did nothing about the 'Old & Dirty' scenery and costumes" (Highfill, 6:275).

FRAGMENT 107   London, 1764–65

Mozart.[1]

See M[r] D. Barrington's acc[t] of him. Phil. Trans. Vol. 60. p. 54.[2] & MS. Journal. wth original Certificate of his Birth, & Letter from Baron Haslang to L[d] Barrington.[3] Relate what I saw & heard myself at his Lodgings on his first Arrival in England & at M[r] Franks's[4]—Extemporary & sight Playing, Composing a Treble to a given Base & a Base to a Treble, as well as both on a given subject, & finishing a Composition began by another. His fondness for Manzoli[5]—his imitations of the several styles of Singing of each of these Opera Singers, as well as of their Songs in an Extemporary opera to nonsense words— to which were [added] an overture of 3[6] Movem[ts] Recitative—Graziosa, Bravura & Pathetic Airs together with Several accomp[d] Recitatives, all full of Taste imagination, with good Harmony, Melody & Modulation. After w[ch] he played at Marbles, in the true Childish Way of one who knows Nothing.[7]

1. These are CB's notes for an account of Mozart, written in 1772, that he intended for vol. 4 of *Hist. Mus.* but did not print. The young prodigy, accompanied by his father and sister, arrived in London on 23 April 1764. "During his residence in London we had frequent opportunities of witnessing his extraordinary talents and profound knowledge in every branch of music at eight years old, when he was able to play at sight in all

clefs, to perform extempore, to modulate, and play fugues on subjects given in a way that there were very few masters then in London able to do" ("Mozart" in Rees). As CB mentions young Mozart's "fondness for Manzoli," who made his debut in London on 24 Nov. 1764 (Frag. 106, n. 7), he probably saw the child after this date.

2. Daines Barrington (1727–1800), naturalist, published in the 1770 volume of *Philosophical Transactions* an "Account of a Very Remarkable Young Musician. In a Letter to Mathew Maty, M.D. Sec. R.S." (Barrington, pp. 280–88).

3. Barrington (ibid.) quotes his brother William Wildman (1717–93), 2d Viscount Barrington, a leading member of the administration: "I here subjoin a copy of the translation from the register at Salzbourg, as it was procured by his excellency Count Haslang, envoy extraordinary and minister plenipotentiary of the electors of Bavaria and Palatine." The reference to "MS. Journal" is not clear.

4. For Naphtali Franks, see Frag. 45, n. 4. The Mozarts lodged at Mr. Williamson's, No. 15 Thrift Street (now Frith Street, Soho). In the spring of 1765, Leopold Mozart repeatedly placed in the newspapers invitations to the public to hear and test Wolfgang's abilities at his lodgings "every day from 12 to 3, admittance 5s. each person" (*Public Adver-*

tiser, 30 May 1765, quoted in Pohl, pp. 133–34).

5. Giovanni Manzuoli (Frag. 106, n. 7) became a friend of the Mozart family in London (Pohl, pp. 110–11).

6. Originally "two Movem^ts."

7. Twenty-five years later, describing the talents of the twelve-year-old Johann Nepomuk Hummel, CB wrote: "It is odd that 30 years after his Master Mozart had been recommended to me, & played upon my knee, on subjects I gave him, that this little man sh^d also claim and merit my kindness" (CB to Fanny Burney, [13] Dec. [1790], Yale Center).

The Mozart fragment ends: "He's engaged to compose a 2^d opera for Milan next Carnaval (Vienna intelligence Septr 1772.)": that is, *Lucio Silla,* first performed at the Teatro Regio Ducale in Milan on 26 Dec. 1772. The sentence has been omitted from the text, as it refers to events later than the period covered by this volume. CB here recalls information on Mozart he had just received from the English diplomat Louis De Visme in a letter dated 20 Sept. 1772 (Osborn). See C. B. Oldman, "Charles Burney and Louis De Visme," *Music Review* 27 (1966): 93–97. For a further account of Mozart, when CB met him on 30 Aug. 1770 at Milan, see *Tours,* 1:162n; and on Mozart's *scena* for Tenducci, CB to Daines Barrington, 21 Jan. 1780 (Barrington, p. 288).

BRIDGE: FRAGMENTS 107–108

My Son the Tar dines at Mrs Cibbers and diverts her wth his Sea language

*Arne's Guardian out
witted d——d*[1]

*1765 Garrick arrives
from Italy Apr 25 the
day of M[rs] Cibber's
last benefit*[2]

**Come to Poland
Street**

Phil & Titter[3]
*Charlotte's play-
fellows*

*Sick Monkey—
published*[4]

1. Arne's comic opera *The Guardian Out-witted* was staged at Covent Garden on Wednesday 12 Dec. 1764 but lasted only until 18 Dec. For its reception see P. C. Roscoe, pp. 237–45, who quotes several satirical verses on Arne that appeared in the newspapers, including a parody of Gray's *Elegy* that Fiske (p. 347) attributes to Arne himself.

2. Mrs. Cibber acted Andromache in *The Distrest Mother* at Drury Lane. On 25 April 1765 Garrick "arrived at his house in Southampton Street" (Oman, p. 256).

3. When Garrick set out for Europe in September 1764, he left his "favourite little dog, Phill" with the Burneys (Frag. 102, n. 11). "The fondness of Mr. Garrick for this little spaniel was so great, that one of his first visits on his return from the continent was to see, caress, and reclaim him. Phill was necessarily resigned, though with the most dismal reluctance, by his new friends: but if parting with the favoured little quadruped was a disaster, how was that annoyance overpaid, when, two or three days afterwards, Phill reappeared! and when the pleasure of his wel-

come to the young folks [Fanny and Charlotte] was increased by a message, that the little animal had seemed so moping, so unsettled, and so forlorn, that Mr. and Mrs. Garrick had not the heart to break his new engagements, and requested his entire acceptance and adoption in Poland-street" (*Mem.*, 1:168–69). Phill was succeeded by "a trembling Italian greyhound." "Do you remember Frisk," writes CB to Fanny, "the pretty little slim dog we had, as successor to Mr. Garrick's favourite pet, Phill? who always pestered Garrick to let him lick his hands and his fingers,—till Garrick, though provoked, could not, in the comic playfulness of his character, help caressing him again, even while exclaiming, when the animal fawned upon him: "What dost follow me for, eh—Slobberchaps? Tenderness without ideas!" (CB to Mme d'Arblay, [May 1806], *Mem.*, 3:369–70; Scholes 1948, 2:308; and 9 Oct. 1806, Berg). "Titter" was no doubt another family pet.

4. While in Paris, Garrick composed satirical verses upon himself entitled *The Sick*

Monkey. These he sent to Colman in April 1765 "to be publish'd at my return." The poem was published with an engraving by Gravelot on 2 May but "fell *still-born* from the Press" (Garrick *Letters,* 2:447–48). In 1806 CB was checking up on this entry with his son Charles, a collector of Garrickiana: "One paper, I see advertises *The Sick Monkey* for the

7th of May, and another the 4th. It does not signify wch it was, it must have been written on the road; but the plate cd hardly be engraved there, though 10 days wd have been sufficient to throw off 10,000 copies of the Sick Monkey, wch is only the size of a pamphlet" (CB to Charles Burney, 16 April 1806, Comyn).

FRAGMENT 108   London, Spring 1765

My acquaintance wth Mr & Mrs Garrick was now improved into friendship; & of a Saty evening when he did not act or Sunday morning, he used to carry me with him to Hampton,[1] and brought me back to town on Monday.

I never was more happy than in these visits: his wit, humour, and constant cheerfulness at home, and her good sense, taste and propriety through life, rendered Hampton to me during these tete a tete Visits, to the time of our great Roscius's decease, so, a terrestrial Paradise.[2] Mrs Garrick had every quality of judgmt[,] good taste, & steadiness of character wch he wanted.[3]

visited by Mr and Mrs Garrick—our friendp [becom]es warm & permanent [   ] partiality to me & [   ]

She was an excellent judge of the fine arts, attended all the last rehearsals of new & revived plays to judge of effects, dresses, scenery, & machinery. She literally seemed the other half of a perfect mortal, and by her intelligence and accomplishmts to complete the Androgyne.

1. In 1759 Garrick had bought a house at Hampton, on the Thames, with five spare bedrooms, where he received his friends. CB first visited him there on 6 March 1763 (Frag. 98, n. 4).

2. Garrick's villa "was built in yellow brick, of a pleasant colour, between lemon and sand. Robert Adam's 'uniform front' was dazzingly white, 'with an Arcade and a Portico.'" Close by was Shakespeare's Temple, a lawn of more than an acre "skillfully reconstructed by 'Capability' Brown" with green serpentine walks, an orangery, and an underground grotto arch. The house had a

landing stage on the Thames and "emerging from it on to the Temple Lawn was like stepping into fairyland" (Oman, pp. 184–91). For illustrations of it, see Oman, pls. 7, 8; Garrick *Letters,* 1:212–13.

3. Eva-Marie Veigel (1724–1822), Viennese *danseuse,* came to England in 1746 and started her career at Haymarket and Drury Lane as "Mademoiselle Violette." Garrick married her on 22 June 1749. She brought him an annual interest of £5,000, settled on her by the Earl and Countess of Burlington, and was responsible for many improvements to their Hampton villa (Oman, pp. 116–24).

M^r amd Mrs Garrick, in speaking of t[he] music wch they had heard abroad, seemed t[o] prefer that of Rousseau's *Devin du Village* wch they had heard at Paris, where its success had been unbounded, to all the Music they had heard in Italy.[1] Now Burney, says he, if you who know French as well as Music, w^d but help us to bring on the stage in England this piece, the Airs are so beautiful, that I am sure it w^d have great success. And so thinks the Earl of Hertford the Lord Chamberlain, who was at Paris during its first run.[2] I then told him, that before I left Lynn, in the year 1760

Wishes to bring
Le Devin du Village
on the stage
with my Transl^o

to return to London, from a printed copy of the Music, wch Mrs Greville had sent me from Paris, I had been diverting myself at leisure hours with translating it [i]nto English, *totidem syllabis,* and a[d]apting my version to the original melodies. He, and Mrs G. came to my house a [d]ay or two after, and obliged me to sing most of the Airs, & some of the Recitatives, & [s]aid it was the very thing they wanted. Well, says I, I am going to Paris very [so]on to fetch home my eldest daughter, [a]nd shall be back the beginning of July; and if you find out before my return 3 good singers, who are likewise good actors, I will talk with you, and try to polish the translation, as well as I can, without losing a single passage, or even a note, of the original music. "Agreed (he says), I'll think of nothing else." And though I was all hurry in preparing for my 2^d journey to Paris, we had two or three consultations how to get the CUNNING MAN well performed early in the next Season. The part of the *Fortune-teller,* we destined, on finding no better for Champness, a Cathedral singer,[3] but little acquainted with secular Music, and no actor. *Colin* was cast for Vernon, the successor of Lowe, with an inferior ten[or] voice, but with more knowledge of m[usic] and a much better actor.[4] Mrs Cibber w[ish]ed very much to undertake the part of Pho[ebe,]and rehearsed it frequently with me at my return from Paris;[5] but her voice, howe[ver] sweet & touching, was too much in d[e]cay, as well as her constitution, to ri[sk] her reputation & that of the piece upo[n] a state of health so precarious as hers was now become. The Sig^ra Cremonini, 2^d woman at the Opera,[6] who sung in a good taste, but whose voice was likewise in decay, and who would have pron[o]un[c]ed the words very ill, wished to have the part, & studied it; but though a good singer with little voice may give great pleasure in a room; yet power is so necessary to fill a great Theatre, that it is dangerous to give a principal part to a feeble Voice; as the trying to enforce it beyond its natural power, in order to be heard in the most remote parts of the house, endangers the intonation; for however good the ear, and perfectly in tune such an organ may be, *sotto voce,* it never fails being out of tune when forced. The part was at length given to young Mrs Arne, late Miss Wright, the brilliant performer in the Padlock, particularly in "Say, little foolish flutt'ring thing."[7]

1. See Frag. 102, n. 8.

2. Francis Seymour Conway (Frag. 104, n. 5) was appointed Lord Chamberlain 4 Dec. 1766 on his return from Paris. But he was not in France when *Le Devin du village* was first performed at Fontainebleau 18 and 24 Oct. 1752 and at the Paris Opera 1 March 1753.

3. Samuel Thomas Champness had sung the Conjurer in CB's *Alfred*. He devoted most of his long professional career to singing in oratorios at the London theatres and in various professional and charity concerts (see Frag. 60, n. 4).

4. Joseph Vernon had as a boy sung Puck in CB's *Queen Mab* (Frag. 59, n. 5). "When his voice broke into a tolerable tenor, he was engaged at Drury-lane theatre to supply the place of Lowe, who was degraded into a singer at Sadler's Wells and Cuper's Gardens. Vernon, with a voice much inferior to that of Lowe at his best, was a much better musician and actor, and had not only Lowe's parts assigned to him at Drury-lane, but succeeded him at Vaux-hall, where, and at the theatre, he continued to perform till the time of his death.—Vernon was not only the professional successor to Lowe, but heir to his imprudence and debauchery" ("Vernon" in Rees). For Thomas Lowe, see Frag. 22, n. 4.

5. According to Mary Nash (who refers to this fragment on pp. 312–13), the rehearsals took place at West Woodhay. On CB's "part

these hours were an act of love," as he was aware of the decaying state of her voice.

6. Clementina Cremonini (fl. 1763–66) had made her debut at the King's Theatre in the Haymarket on 19 Feb. 1743 (Highfill, 4: 37–38). According to CB, "her voice, though a young woman, was in decay, and failed on all occasions of the least difficulty; which, however, did not prevent her from attempting passages that not only required more voice, but more abilities than she could boast" (*Hist. Mus.,* 4:480; Mercer, 2:864).

7. Elizabeth Wright (c. 1751–69) sang the role of a fairy at the age of nine or ten in *Edgar and Emmeline* on 31 Jan. 1761 and in *Queen Mab* on 23 Oct. 1761. She had a girlish beauty and a delicate voice that endeared her to the public. On 5 Nov. 1766 she married Thomas Arne's son Michael; on 3 Oct. 1768 she was a great success as Leonora in Isaac Bickerstaffe's comic opera *The Padlock*. This was her last performance; she died at the age of eighteen. CB said that her husband "sung [her] to death" ("Wright, Miss" in Rees).

CB's adaptation of Rousseau's piece as *The Cunning Man* was eventually performed on 21 Nov. 1766. His libretto appeared in two editions, the second dated 29 Nov. (Lonsdale 1965, pp. 71–73; Scholes 1948, 1:107–17; 2: 345–46). The score, which contains the unpublished recitatives in manuscript (*Cat. Mus.,* no. 9), is now in the library of the University of Chicago.

FRAGMENT 110   Paris and Lyons, June–July 1765

> *I set out for Fr. a 2ᵈ*
> *time—with Bremner.*
> *His complaints*[1]

In my first visit to the capital of France, I had only had time to run about from place to place to see sights: but now, in mixing with & studying the Inhabitants I found them[2] not so miserable as in England we are made to believe. They labour hard in the morning, it is true; but have their amusements and parties of an evening to the boulevard, the Theatres,

> *Arrive at Paris, see its*
> *Churches and public*
> *places [—] remarks*
> *on the Bourgeois*

Ginguettes,[3] or the Fields. The good Lady Clifford and my country man Arthur & and his sweet temperd & obliging little wife,[4] were of great use to me. I carried the Children who now understood French to the Opera comique, and to Versailles, where they saw the King and Queen sup *au grand couvert*, & were noticed by their Majesties: for being discovered by their dress to be *Angloises* they

> *See the K. & Q. sup*
> *au grand souper*

were put forward and allowed to approach them, much nearer than the children even of the native nobility. The custom of the grand Chambellan calling out, *Le Roi Boi*[*t*] "the King drinks," must, it shᵈ seem, have arisen from the fear he shᵈ be assassinated, or have his throat cut while off his guard: wᶜʰ was probably the origin of *pledging* people in our own country, when they drank, in Saxon times.

Before I quitted France, I was determined to take a peep at the interior of the kingdom; and went as far as Lyons, to approach as near Italy as my time wᵈ allow, without crossing the Alps. I took two places for that city: and the company being very good, and a lady of Noblesse among the Passengers, who caressed and countenanced my little traveller in the most amiable and endearing manner, we passed our time perfectly to the satisfaction of

> *Set off wᵗʰ Hetty*
> *for Lyons—Journey*
> *thither—*

all parties. As for my daughter's French, the gentlemen frequently cried out: "*pardi, elle n'a point d'accent!*", meaning no foreign accent.

I cᵈ easily fill a Volume in describing the persons & things which occurred in this agreeable voyage; they are still so fresh in my memory, though more than 40 years have elapsed since it took place. But as I went over the same ground again in my journey to Italy in 1770,[5] I shall add little more to this narrative, except to give a list of my fellow travellers, and a detail of the hospitality with wᶜʰ my girl & I were treated in this fine city.

We had a Brigadier des Armées du Roi; a Viscomte d'Arambure;[6] a Major des gardes Françoises, a very literary gentleman, who had all the best Fr. poets by heart, and furnished me with a list of such as were best worth purchasing wch I had not already in my possession: A M. Rigaud, a rich Merchant of Lyon;[7] his Lady, a most amiable & charming character, who I found afterwards, was of noble birth; and her Woman w^ch, with my little daughter and myself, completed the interior of the Diligence. M. & Mad^e Rigaud were inhabitants of Lyons and did the honours of that city. The three military gentlemen were going to Italy.

There was always a Whist table, and a party for conversation. On our arrival at Lyons, we were all   *hospitality there* invited to a most elegant entertainment at the magnificent mansion of M. Rigaud; and conducted by him to all the celebrated manufactories & curiosities of the place. The *Fête Dieu,* one of the greatest festivals in the Roman calendar,[8] happening at this time, we were all invited to the fire-works & water-works at the confluence of the Rhone and the Soane; and so great was the hospitality & politeness of M. le President to my little girl as an *etrangere,* that he made her take the match and give the signal for beginning the exhibition. Mad^e Rigaud was so kind as to take her under her wing & protection, wch qua[   ]

Dress of the times,
M. Pirnon[9]

Journey back to
Paris[10]

Schobert[11]

[End of Volume 1][12]

1. CB must have left for France toward the end of May, for on 6 June he was already in Lyons. For Robert Bremner, the music publisher, see Frag. 106, n. 2. "Mr Bremner we see often," wrote Susan in her journal on 19 Apr. 1767 (owned by Joyce Hemlow).

2. Mme d'Arblay scored through the first lines of CB's text here and interlineated this paraphrase.

3. A sort of café or cabaret, where one

drinks and dances in the open air.

4. Perhaps John Arthur (c. 1708–72), comedian, contriver of machines for Rich's pantomimes, and friend of Garrick. His first wife, whose name is unknown, died on 6 Aug. 1768 at Bath after giving birth (Highfill 1:129–32; and Garrick *Letters,* 1:27 n.2; 2:513–14 n.1).

5. See *Tours,* 1:34–38.

6. A "Capitaine Arambure" who served

in India under Law, 1756–60, is listed in *Dictionnaire de biographie française,* 3:218, but this may be a different man.

7. Probably "M. Rigod de Terrebuste," with whom CB corresponded after his return to London (see De Grange Blanche to CB, 27 Aug. 1766, Osborn).

8. Corpus Christi is celebrated on the first Tuesday after Trinity Sunday; in 1765 it fell on 6 June.

9. "You must remember how often I told the Story of M. Pirnon the Marchand de Velour at Lyons—whose civilities & confidence to & in me, an utter Stranger, without ⟨suite or shew⟩ of any kind to impose on his credulity, will never be forgotten" (CB to Mme d'Arblay, 30 July 1806, Osborn).

10. CB took Esther back with him to London, while Susan remained in Paris. Later he told Mrs. Thrale that while he and Esther "went about and amused themselves," Susan was "often if not always left . . . at the Lodgings with the Maid; one Evening the Dr recommended it to his Family to keep a Jour-

nal of what passed while they were abroad— and what *can I* put in my Journal Papa says Susan—I can only tell how many Shifts go to the Wash every Week" (*Thraliana,* 1:219). Mrs. Thrale, who probably did not listen well, mentions CB's first wife as being in Paris, too, though she had died three years earlier.

11. In Paris, CB became enamored of the music of the fashionable Johann Schobert (c. 1735–67): "In 176[5] we were the first who brought his compositions to England, when they had a run of favour of more than twenty years. His style never pleased in Germany so much as in England and France" ("Schobert" in Rees). See also Frag. 43, n. 8.

12. The evidence suggests that the first volume of CB's memoirs continued for perhaps another twenty pages. It appears that a considerably detailed account of Garrick followed (see textual note to Frag. 40). Of the second volume, which covered the years 1766–70, nothing is known to be extant but the fragments that follow.

FRAGMENT 111   London, September 1765–January 1766

⌜At Michs this year [1765] my Lynn frd Mrs Allen brings her eldest daughter[1] to town & places her at [   ]⌝

1766

In Jany this year, an acquaintance wch I had made wth that most agreeable of men, Dr Warren[2] ⌜at Mrs ⟨Ca   ley's⟩ where he & I attended every day for many years, and where I attended Miss ⟨Barsanti⟩[3] was improved into intimacy and friendp by teaching his eldest daughter at home and where I generally dined once a week⌝ [

        ][4] his conversation was the most pleasant & the most enlightened, without pedantry or dogmatism I had ever known. ⌜Miss ⟨Warren⟩⌝[5]

1. Maria (1751–1820), then fourteen years old. The name of the finishing school for girls illegible under Mme d'Arblay's attempted obliterations.

2. Richard Warren (1731–97), royal physician. Having received a medical degree at Cambridge on 3 July 1762, he replaced his father-in-law as physician to George III at the age of thirty-one. On 3 March 1763 he was elected Fellow of the Royal College of Physicians. Later he became a member of The Club and attended Dr. Johnson and Boswell in their last illnesses.

3. If our reading of the name is correct, this is Jane or Jenny Barsanti (1755–95), the "ingenious daughter" of the violinist and composer Francesco Barsanti. She "had been bound apprentice" to CB, who says he "had undertaken to prepare her for a public singer," and that under his instruction she "had vanquished all the difficulties of the art in point of execution" ("Barsanti" in Rees). Miss Barsanti would have been at this time ten or eleven years old. For her performance at CB's doctoral ceremony at Oxford in 1769, see Frag. 115, n. 2; for CB's subsequent patronage of her, see Highfill, 1:359–60.

4. Two lines are illegible here.

5. In 1759 Dr. Warren married Elizabeth Shaw, by whom he had two daughters.

FRAGMENT 112

L[y] Emily Stanhope was soon after married to L[d] Barrimore.[1] In July the next year her L[P] wished to resume her Musical Studies, particularly in thorough base to accomp[y] her Lord, who performed a little on the Violoncello. But instead of harmonizing this pair, & keeping them in humour with each other, it was the source of eternal disputes ab[t] who was in & who was out; and referring their disputes to me, after acting the moderator during two months, I was so tired of the warfare, that I slunk off and discontinued my visits, pretending that I was under the necessity of going out of town.

In Feb[y] this year L[y] Mary Bertie was seized with an acute fever and died, to the great affliction of her family.[2]

I was very sorry to lose her as a scholar, for though she had very little application or love for Music, she was perfectly good humoured & amiable.

In May following, her sister L[y] Priscilla[3] began Music, who had still less application and disposition for it than poor L[y] Mary.

1. Lady Amelia Stanhope (1749–80), daughter of the 2d Earl of Harrington, on 16 April 1767 married Richard Barry (1745–73), 6th Earl of Barrymore. This fragment was intended by CB as an insert "for p. 11" of the second volume of his memoirs, and probably narrated CB's activities early in 1767.

2. She died on 13 April 1767 (see Frag. 95, n. 6).

3. Lady Priscilla Barbara Elizabeth Bertie (1761–1828) on 23 Feb. 1779 married Sir Peter Burrell (d. 1820), Baronet, 1st Lord Gwydir.

In May 1768 she was seven years old.

CB's text at this point jumps to "the summer of 1777," when "the Duke of Ancaster applied to me to recommend a good Musician to go with the family into Lincolnshire, & to play & sing to himself & the Duchess at Night." CB recommended Piozzi, who had recently arrived in London.

FRAGMENT 113   1767

Mar. 12th [1767] I went to Lovatin[i's][1] benefit with my beloved Mrs Allen. How delightful is participation of pleasure wth thos[e] we love! On the 21st we go again to the Opera and the monday following,[2] in spite of all m[y] professional hurry, giving at this time betwee[n] 50 & 60 lessons a week,[3] besides school scholars, I contrived to spend the evenin[g] in Great Russel Street at Mrs Allens, out of sight of her imperious mother,[4] and she began to be weaned from her fears, by affection and consta[nt] importunity; and I flattered myself I was gaining ground. The only person in our confidence at Lynn was our com[mon] friend Miss D. Young;[5] and in London, Mrs Greville, on my side, and Mrs Strange, afterwards Lady Strange, the friend of us both: a woman of the most powerful understanding, and of more wit than I have ever known united in one individual female.[6]

On the 3d of April Mrs Allen's winter Season in the capital was closed & she returned to Lynn, to my great discomfort. And I had by letter to counteract all her mother's usurpations over her natural rights and affections. I used to sit up whole nights pleading my cause in letters addressed to her in a feigned hand or under cover to D. Young; & she to me or under cover to our zealous friend under different names and at different places. Our correspondence had all the Air of mystery and intrigue; in that we seemed 2 young lovers under age trying to out-wit our parents and guardians. But if second marriages are defensible, no two persons had a better right to dispose of themselves than we had.[7] I had been a widower 5 years, Mrs Allen 3. She had three children, two daughters and a son,[8] all amply provided for, exclusive of her dowery and an allowance of £100 a year for the maintenance and education of each, till they were of age, when their fortunes were to be paid by the Trustees into their own hands.[9] With my professional diligence, and the patronage and esteem of so many great families, wch made me in fashion with the less, I was well able to support and educate my children, without encroaching on the income of my wife. And this was fortunate: as Mrs A. had been persuaded by her friend & countrym[an] Dr King,

Chaplain to our factory at Petersburg,[10] to lend to Mr Gomm, a gr[eat] English Merchant resident in Russia[11] supposed to be extremely rich, her whole dowry of £5000, for the sake of the high interest of eigh[t] per cent. And during my last Norfolk tour in the midst of my courtship while a guest at her house in Lynn,[12] news arrived of the bankruptcy of Mr Gomm. This however had no effect on my affection, as my heart was attached to the lady's person not her property.[13] It was my wish & hope that our children w^d not be in each other's way, & that the children of my former marriage w^d be loved and regarded by my new partner as her own, being myself perfectly disposed & resolved to treat Mrs Allen's children with the same care and tenderness as my own.

1. Giovanni Lovatini (1730–post 1782), "a burletta singer, with the sweetest tenor voice and style of singing ever heard on the stage," had been the chief attraction of the 1766–67 opera season. See Frag. 56, n. 4. On 25 Nov. 1766 his company staged *La Buona Figliuola,* "written by Goldoni and set by Piccini," based on Richardson's *Pamela.* Its success rendered the name of Piccini, "which had scarcely penetrated into this country before, dear to every lover of Music in the nation." However, its sequel, *La Buona Figliuola Maritata* (31 Jan. 1767), failed: "The Music was excellent, full of invention, fire and new effects," writes CB, "but so difficult" that the spectators "were glad, as well as the performers, to return to the *Buona Figliuola* for their own ease and relief from a too serious attention" ("Lovatini" in Rees; *Hist. Mus.,* 4:490, 492; Mercer, 2:872–73). On this benefit night Lovatini sang in "*Il Signor Dottore. A new comic Opera*" composed in 1758 by Domenico Fischietti (c. 1725–post-1810) to a libretto by Goldoni.

2. To see, on Saturday 21 March *La Buona Figliuola Maritata,* and on Monday 23 March *La Buona Figliuola.*

3. A fragment of CB's Baldwin diary for early 1768 (Berg) shows that he was giving thirty to fifty-five lessons a week: "Lessons given this year / Jan^y—121 / Feb^y—196 / Mar. 219 / Apr. 191 / May 180." As he charged 10s. a lesson, he was earning from £60 to over £100 a month during the London season.

4. Mary (c. 1706–76), daughter of John Maxey, had married Thomas Allen before 1725. Her daughter Elizabeth had in 1765 rented a house in Russell Street for the London opera season.

5. See Frag. 69, n. 6.

6. Isabella Lumisden (1719–1806) was an ardent Jacobite. When she was being courted by her future husband, Robert Strange (1721–92), the famous engraver and rival of Bartolozzi, she made it a condition that he would fight for Prince Charles. Strange drew a portrait of the prince and designed printed money to be used in his reign. After Culloden, Isabella hid Robert under her hoopskirt when soldiers were looking for him, while caroling a Jacobite song in their faces. He was later (1787) knighted for his distinguished work as engraver. For a sympathetic account of her life, see Nora K. Strange, *Jacobean Tapestry* (1947). Her spirited letters, printed in *Memoirs of Sir Robert Strange,* ed. James Dennistoun (1855), reveal her keen interest in poetry, philosophy, physico-theology, and the business affairs of her husband—which she managed during his absence on the continent, though her Jacobite sympathies often prejudiced his interests. CB probably taught her daughters Mary Bruce (1748–84), then nineteen, and Isabella Katherina (1759–1849),

then eight years old. See also *Mem.*, 1:205–7.

7. Fanny, then aged fifteen, later wrote that "the 2ᵈ [espousal] is more in the common routine of life" (Mme d'Arblay to the Rev. Stephen Allen, *JL*, 12:782). She made her account of CB's courtship of Mrs. Allen (*Mem.*, 1:189–98) short, commenting that "I have tried to represent it as interesting, & certainly have rendered it respectable in the various motives I have drawn together for obviating ill-natured strictures upon 2ᵈ alliances. And There I thought I had best to stop, not to provoke madrigals & epigrams" (*JL*, 12:782). Almost none of CB's correspondence with Elizabeth has survived. After her death in 1796 he "destroyed near 500 letters of my own writing to the dear soul . . . [which], I am certain, produced an equal number from her" (CB to Christian Latrobe, 14 Nov. 1796, Osborn). Only a few of his verses to her remain: "Ode on a Lady's Birthday" (20 Oct. 1767); "But like a culprit unforgiven . . . ," c. 1765 (Poet. Nbk). Fanny mentions "amongst his posthumous relics" a "sedulous, yet energetic, though prose translation of the Inferno" (*Mem.*, 1:150–51), which is preserved in fifteen folio pages in Osborn, as "drawn by C.B. for Mrs. St. Allen abᵗ the year 1765."

8. Maria (see Frag. 111, n. 1), now sixteen and Fanny's correspondent, married Martin Folkes Rishton in 1772; Stephen (1755–1847), now twelve, was ordained deacon of Norwich in 1778; the youngest, Elizabeth, married Samuel Meeke in 1777. CB was instructing one of the daughters, probably Maria: "The hour for his instructions to Miss Allen was fixed to be that of tea-time; to the end

that, when he was liberated from the daughter, he might be engaged with the mother" (*Mem.*, 1:190).

9. Stephen Allen's will (PRO PROB 11/887/211) was proved 19 May 1763. The trustees, who inherited £100 each, were George Hogg, Daniel Dirkins, and Maxey Allen.

10. John Glen King (1732–87), native of Southacre, Norfolk. After attending Caius College, Cambridge, he was ordained deacon (1754), Vicar of Little Berwick, Norfolk (1760–64), and subsequently appointed chaplain to the English factory at St. Petersburg; later, D.D. (1771 Oxford), F.R.S. and F.S.A. (Fellow of the Society of Antiquaries). For a list of his works, see *Dictionary of National Biography*.

11. William Gomm (d. 10 April 1792), merchant in St. Petersburg, whose son William was born there in 1754 (Venn, *Alumni Cantabrigienses*). About 1767 he suffered considerable pecuniary loss when the government "seized upon an extensive naval and commercial undertaking just as it was about to become profitable." Later, in 1779–83, he served as secretary to Sir James Harris, ambassador to the court of Catherine II. He died in Bath, where he had for his health (*GM*, 62:390).

12. CB stayed "a Month in Norfolk" in the summer of 1766. Mrs. Allen's house was the present vicarage (Scholes 1948, 1:138 n.2), which her daughter Maria describes in a letter to Fanny of 3 Sept. 1778 (*ED*, 1:12–13).

13. For the dispute concerning the amount of property Elizabeth Allen brought to CB when she married him, see Appendix A.

FRAGMENT 114   1767

King's band the D. of Devonshire [   ] whom I was presented by Ld Orford.[1]

I Take a journey to Bristol with my 2^d daughter Fanny, to solicit the interest of Mr Edm. Allen[2] with his Mother to consent to his sister Mrs Ste. Allen taking me in marriage. (Fanny's only journey of 3 days of wch she made the most when she became an authoress)[3]

In June during my holidays, set out on a Visit with 2 of my girls[4] to Mrs Allen at Lynn, with whom and our dear fr^d D. Young, I visit every place and thing that is curious in Norfolk, making love chemin faisant, and in my addresses as well as my journey was able to report progress. I stay near a Month in Norfolk, and Octr 2^d my dear M^rs A consented to say B and to become one flesh—she came to town privately—after wch ceremony at St James's Church[5] we retired to an old Farm house at Talworth Court,[6] and at the end of 3 days returned to town, as if nothing had happened. We kept our union as secret as possible for a time, inhabiting different houses;[7]

1. William Cavendish (1748–1811) had succeeded in 1764 as 5th Duke of Devonshire. In 1767, at nineteen, he was probably instrumental in procuring for CB the appointment as "Extra Musician" in the King's Band. David Hume also wrote in this connection to Lord Eglinton, asking him to obtain an unspecified post for CB. See Lonsdale 1965, pp. 74–75; Scholes 1948, 2:321; and *Mem.*, 1:186–87.

2. Edmund Allen (c. 1737–72), Elizabeth's brother, on 15 March 1762 had married Jane Wilson, by whom he had two sons, John Wilson (b. 1 Aug. 1763) and Thomas (b. 16 Dec. 1764; d. Jan. 1765).

3. Fanny was then fifteen, but evidently a shrewd observer. The third volume of *Evelina*, published eleven years later (1778), takes place in Bristol Hotwells and Clifton (*HFB*, pp. 23, 77).

4. Fanny and probably Susan.

5. The ceremony was performed by the Rev. Matthew Pugh (1739–1810), curate of St. James's, Westminster, "for nearly fifty years" (Venn, *Alumni Cantabrigienses*), who

became a friend of the Burney family. The witnesses were Isabella Strange, Samuel Crisp, and Richard Fuller, banker of Cornhill, London (*ED*, 1:2), who in 1768 bought the Rookery in King's Lynn. CB disliked public weddings. When he saw one the next year in King's Lynn, he "said he would not have gone thro' those people in such a manner for 5000 a year" (*ED*, 1:18).

6. "In a little hamlet, a mile or two from Chessington Hall," which "Mr. Crisp had engaged for them" (*Mem.*, 1:195).

7. Elizabeth now "came openly to town to inhabit, for a while, a house in Poland-street, a few doors from that of her husband; while alterations, paintings, and embellishments were progressively preparing the way for her better reception at his home." According to Mme d'Arblay, "the secret, as usual in matrimonial concealments, was faithfully preserved," until "the loss of a letter, through some carelessness of conveyance, revealed suddenly but irrevocably the state of the connexion," which was "at the time, [a] cruelly distressing" experience (*Mem.*, 1:195–96).

FRAGMENT 115   1769

My Academic exercise was performed at three [subsequent] annual choral meetings at Oxford;[1] in the first & second of wch the principal soprano part was performed by Miss Barsanti,[2] & the next by Miss Linley[3] ere her marriage with Mr Sheridan was published.

I did not for some time after the honour that was conferred on me at Oxford display my title on the plate of my door; when Mr Steel, author of "An Essay on the melody of Speech",[4] says, "Burney, why don't you tip us the Doctor?" When I replied in provincial dialect, "I wants dayecity, I'm ashayum'd"—"Poh, poh, (says he) you must *brazen* it."[5]

1. The score of the anthem "I will love Thee, O Lord my Strength," which CB composed for his doctorate at Oxford (22–23 June 1769), is preserved in Bodleian, Ms. Mus. Sch. Ex. C.15. The ceremony is discussed in detail in *ED*, 1:55–58; *Mem.*, 1:210–14. See also Scholes 1948, 1:140–47; 2:346–47; Lonsdale 1965, pp. 77–79; and CB to Esther and Fanny Burney, 22 June 1769 (Berg).

2. For Jane or Jenny Barsanti, see Frag. 111, n. 3; for her performance of CB's academic exercise, see sources cited in n. 1, above, and Highfill, 1:359–62. In his article "Barsanti" in Rees, CB says that "she totally lost her singing voice, on going to Oxford to perform at a choral meeting, by sickness in a stage coach."

3. Elizabeth Ann (1754–92), the beautiful daughter of Thomas Linley, was known as the nightingale of Bath. In 1772 she eloped with Richard Brinsley Sheridan, whom she married 13 April 1773. For CB's account of her talents, see Appendix B.6.

4. Joshua Steele (1700–1791), member of the Society of Arts in 1756, author of *An Essay towards Establishing the Melody and Measure of Speech* (1775); 2d ed. renamed *Prosodia Rationalis* (1779). For CB's comment on Steele's attempt to transcribe Garrick's speeches into quasi-musical notation, see Hill/Powell, 2:327n.

5. In 1777 CB told this anecdote to Mrs. Thrale, who recorded it in *Thraliana*, 1:137.

FRAGMENT 116   London, October 1769

In October of this year (1769) I published an essay towards the history of Comets,[1] previous to the re-appearance of the Comet whose return Halley had predicted;[2] & the Countess of Pembroke[3] being reported to have studied Astronomy, & accustomed to Telescopical observations, though I had not the honour of being known to her, I dedicated anonymously this essay to her

Ladyship, much celebrated for her love of the arts & sciences, & many other accomplishments. I am not certain that she ever knew by whom the Pamphlet was written.[4]

1. "The absence of Scholars in Summer with an increasing family, used to alarm & make me so melancholy, that it first stimulated me to write, & not spend all my summers in reading and travelling ab[t] my own country for mere amusem[t], without any other object. I was very early in my life very fond of Astronomy and when the Comet whose return was predicted by Halley, was expected, I wrote, a short history of all the remarkable Comets that had appeared particularly [on] those of wch the elements had been settled in his Synopsis of Comets" (CB to Johann Christian Hüttner, 15 Aug. 1807, Osborn). *An Essay towards a History of the Principal Comets that have appeared since the Year 1742* (Scholes 1948, 2:331) has a postscript dated 25 Oct. 1769. CB had shown the manuscript to Bewley (William Bewley to CB, 27 Sept. 1769, Osborn) and prefaced his account with a *Letter upon Comets Addressed to a Lady by the late M. de Maupertuis, written in the Year 1742*, which his first wife Esther had translated from the French. According to Mme d'Arblay, CB wrote the essay "wholly in moments stolen from repose, though re-

quiring researches and studies that frequently kept him to his pen till four o'clock in the morning, without exempting him from rising at his common hour of seven," which "terminated in an acute rheumatic fever, that confined him to his bed, or his chamber, during twenty days" (*Mem.*, 1:218).

2. The return of Halley's comet was first observed on 8 Aug. 1769 by Messier in Paris; it disappeared on 13 Sept. On 23 Oct. it "was again observed at the royal observatory at Greenwich . . . and may be seen for sometime every clear evening toward the S.W. though gradually diminishing in lustre" (*AR*, 12:126, 131–32, 143).

3. Lady Elizabeth Spencer (1737–1831), 2d daughter of the 2d Duke of Marlborough, in 1755 married Henry Herbert (1734–94), 10th Earl of Pembroke.

4. Mme d'Arblay, who printed this fragment, comments: "Forty-three years after the date of this publication, the Countess Dowager of Pembroke acquainted this memorialist, that she had never known by whom this Essay was dedicated, nor by whom it was written" (*Mem.*, 1:218).

FRAGMENT 117   London, 1769

Before I terminate the transactions & events of this year I must mention, that amongst my new scholars, I had the honour of being called on by the bewitching and accomplished M[rs] Ploydel,[1] whose beauty, talents, & love of admiration were very dangerous, and operated so powerfully on an eminent Music Master at Bath,[2] as to bring on a violent fit of insanity, even to a strait Waistcoat; a proof that his passion had not been appeased by kindness; nor do I believe that this charming creature ever went further than coquetery. Her husband[3] was not an

Adonis, and had ⟨been forced⟩ on her by her father in India[4] on account of his[5]
[   ] ⟨very⟩ captivating, & required some[6]

1. Elizabeth (fl. 1759–71), daughter of Governor Holwell (n. 4, below), in 1759 married Charles Stafford Pleydell (n. 3, below). In 1768 the Pleydells returned from India to England, where they stayed until May 1771. CB evidently met her early in 1769. On 21 May 1769 he took his daughters to a party "at Mrs Pleydell's," who also attended CB's doctoral ceremony in Oxford in June (CB to Esther and Fanny, 22 June 1769, Berg). He read to her the verses that Fanny had sent to him on the occasion. Fanny says that "besides being so very beautiful," Mrs. Pleydell "would win a heart of stone": "There is a something, *je ne sai quoi* in the really amiable or agreeable [woman] which does not need intimacy or time to create esteem and admiration . . . she has something in her manners which engages the heart as effectually, immediately, as many thousand people would be able to do in years" (*ED*, 1:50–51, 61, 65; *Mem.*, 1:203).

2. Not identified.

3. Charles Stafford Pleydell (d. 28 May 1779) arrived in Bengal in 1744 and served in the East India Company as writer (1744), factor (1749), and later (1774) as superintendent of police and member of the Board of Trade at Calcutta (Holzman, pp. 10, 40, 157; *HMC* 163:252 n.4).

4. John Zephaniah Holwell (1711–98), in 1760 temporary governor of India where he had gone in 1732. In 1756 he was among the fifty-six survivors of the Black Hole of Calcutta, which he described in *A Genuine Narrative* (1758). After his return to England in 1761 he devoted himself to literary pursuits.

Mrs. Pleydell was one of his two daughters.

5. CB probably continued, "having gotten her with child." The baptism of their son Charles Brian Pleydell took place on 6 Nov. 1758, almost four months before the wedding; see *Bengal Past and Present* 21 (July–Dec. 1920):159.

6. "This lady," writes Mme d'Arblay, "in taking leave of Mr. Burney, upon her return to India, presented to him a Chinese painting on ivory, which she had inherited from her father; and which he, Governor Holwell, estimated as a sort of treasure" (*Mem.*, 1:204). She then gives "the following . . . description of it, drawn up by Mr. Burney, from the account of Mrs. Pleydell," which may have continued this fragment:

"It is the representation of a music gallery over a triumphal arch, through which the great Mogul passed at Agra, or Delhi, before his fall. The procession consists of the Emperor, mounted on an elephant, and accompanied by his wives, concubines, and attendants; great officers of state, &c., all exquisitely painted. The heads of the females, Sir Joshua Reynolds and Sir Robert Strange, to whom this painting was shewn, thought sufficiently highly finished to be set in rings."

"It hangs over the fireplace in my Bed room," wrote CB in his will (Scholes 1948, 2:271). This *"very rare and curious* Indian *picture"* is listed in *Cat. Mus.* as item 1030, but was "not sold." Its present whereabouts is unknown. It may have been disposed of by James Sansom (1751–1822), a relation of the Sleepes (*JL* 9:122n).

Appendix A

How Much Money Did Mrs. Allen Bring to Burney When She Married Him?

According to Stephen Allen's will (PRO PROB 11/887/211), his wife Elizabeth received £5,000 and "£100 during her Widowhood" in "2 equal half yearly payments as long as unmarried." The two houses he owned in King's Lynn were bequeathed to his children; they were to inherit at the age of twenty-one (at the time of his death in 1763 Maria was twelve, Stephen eight, and Elizabeth two years old).

In the late 1790s Burney wrote to Dorothy Young: "It is a very great satisfaction to me that, dependant as I was upon a laborious profession for myself & family, I never had a thought of anything belonging to the sweet soul but her person & Mind. Her own £5000 Jointure was *almost all gone* by Gomm's bankruptcy in Russia many months before our marriage. I knew this: & that she would lose 100 a year whenever that marriage took place. Yet all this only inflamed me the more by giving me an opportunity of despising all considerations & interests but those of the heart. And, after her Children, to whom she was left guardian, had all dropt off before they were of Age, &, consequently allowance for their Board, clothing, education, &c. When, *if single, she would have had a bare subsistence for herself.* I never touched a penny from the wreck in Russia; from her loan of £900 to Jemmy Sympson; nor even of the rent of the house in Lynn: *all this she had for Pin Money!*" (*JL* 12:780).

That letter itself is missing. It was sent to Mme d'Arblay by Mrs. Allen's son, the Rev. Stephen Allen, and she quotes this passage in her answer to him of 18 March [1833].

The £900 that the second Mrs. Burney had lent to James Simpson was her dowry, which she had in addition to the £5,000 from her husband. It was repaid to Burney on 30 July 1796 (CB's diary for 1796, Berg).

The Rev. Stephen Allen read Mme d'Arblay's printed *Memoirs* in December 1832 and protested "as a *Son*" that his mother Elizabeth Allen brought more property to the marriage than Mme d'Arblay had given her credit for. He sent her (via Charles Parr Burney) two of Burney's letters to Dorothy Young written in the late 1790s, claiming they showed "that with respect to the property, at least £1000 was saved from the Russian bankruptcy, that £900 had been previously lent to our friend Mʳ Simpson, & that, as I heard from certain authority, no less than £600 were then in my mother's hands. In this case full *half* of the £5000 bequeathed by my Father's will, was passed into her second marriage, exclusive of a small estate which was entailed on the two youngest children, & of a rent of £60 during nine years of her eldest Son's minority. The whole ⟨could be⟩ not actuated at less than £4000. Without this explanation it might seem from the *narrative* that my Mother was destitute of any provision when she consented to a second marriage" (Stephen Allen to Charles Parr Burney, 21 Nov. 1832, Osborn).

Mme d'Arblay replied, referring to her father's letter to Dorothy Young: "He then goes on to state that he did not investigate, did not know her resources. And to this it may be owing that he names not the £600 which you [Stephen Allen] count into her possession on marriage. Thus it clearly appears that she brought *him* no fortune whatever, neither towards his property, nor his establishment; nor his housekeeping; but merely what she expended & enjoyed, wholly at her will, in personals" (*JL* 12:780–81).

In 1776, after the death of her mother, Elizabeth inherited her mother's house in King's Lynn and £300 (PRO PROB 11/1024/410). How much of her property was used to support the family "establishment" and "housekeeping" can hardly be determined.

Appendix B

Excerpts from Burney's Articles in Rees and Manuscript Sources

B.1. WORGAN'S REVERENCE FOR SCARLATTI

In his youth, [John Worgan][1] was impressed with a reverence for Domenico Scarlatti by old Roseingrave's account of his wonderful performance on the harpsichord, as well as by his lessons; and afterwards he became a great collector of his pieces, some of which he had been honoured with from Madrid by the author himself. . . . At length he got acquainted with Geminiani,[2] swore by no other divinity, and on consulting him on the subject of composition, he was told that he would never be acquainted with all the arcana of the science, without reading "El Porque della Musica," a book written in Spanish per Andres Lorente, en Alcala, 1672.[3] But where was this book to be had? Geminiani told him, and told him truly, that the tract was very scarce. He had, indeed, a copy of it himself; but he would not part with it under twenty guineas. Worgan, on fire to be in possession of this oracular author, immediately purchased the book at the price mentioned; not understanding a word of Spanish, he went to work in learning it as eagerly as Rowe the poet, when Lord Oxford had expressed a wish that he understood that language, which Rowe thought would qualify him for a good place under government. But after hard drudgery, when he hastened to acquaint the minister of state that he thought himself a tolerable master of the Spanish tongue, "I give you joy (says lord Oxford); you are now able to read Don Quixote in the original."[4]

He composed several oratorios, in which the choruses are learned and the accompaniments to his songs ingenious. The *cantilena* was original, it is true, but it was original awkwardness, and attempts at novelty without nature for his guide.

His organ-playing, though more in the style of Handel than any other school, is indeed learned and masterly, in a way quite his own.

1. For John Worgan, see Frag. 36, n. 2; also Newton.

2. See Frag. 21, n. 3.

3. *El Porque de la musica, en que se contiene los quatro artes de ella, canto llana, canto de organo, contrapunto, y composicion* (Alcalá de Henares, 1672), by the Spanish organist and theorist, Andrés Lorente (1624–1703). "This is truly a very ancient treatise, which defines and explains the whole art of music, as far as it was known at the time it was written" ("Lorente" in Rees). See also Hawkins, 2: 657b.

4. The anecdote derives from Pope, who told it to Joseph Spence in 1736 (Spence, no. 221). CB probably read it in Johnson's "Life of Rowe"; he first recounted it in his letter to Thomas Twining, 30 Aug. 1773 (BL, Add. MSS 39929, ff. 59–64).

B.2. RICHARD CHARKE

[Charke][5] was a dancing-master, an actor, a man of humour, and a performer on the violin, with a strong hand. He was leader of the band at Drury-lane theatre.[6] As a composer, he only distinguished himself by being supposed the first who produced that species of musical buffoonery called a "Medley Overture," wholly made up of shreds and patches of well-known vulgar tunes.[7] But we believe that this very easy Species of pleasantry was first suggested by Dr. Pepusch, in the overture to the Beggar's Opera, brought on the stage in 1728, and Charke's medley overture bears date 1735.[8] There is a slang horn-pipe under Charke's name,[9] which used to be a favourite among the tars. We believe him to have been a facetious fellow, gifted with a turn for b. g.[10] humour, of which, and of his tricks and stories, Dr. Arne, in moments of jocularity, used to give specimens.

He was married to Charlotte, the youngest daughter of Colley Cibber,[11] a female not without talents as an actress; but of such an eccentric and indecorous character, that the memoirs of her life, though written and softened by being her own biographer,[12] could never be read by persons of her own sex, not wholly abandoned. For many years of her life she never appeared on or off the stage in a female dress. Mademoiselle d'Eon's male habiliments during many years, were a real disguise and concealment; but Mrs. Charke's sex and person being well known, her dress was no disguise, but a publication of her impudence.[13]

As long as Charke was the leader of Drury-lane band, his concerto on the violin was the lure in the second music, two or three times a week; which many lovers of music used to go into the theatre to hear, who never staid till the curtain was drawn up, before which time their money was returned, if demanded. His debts obliged him to leave his cara sposa; and, retiring to Jamaica, he there, in a short time, and in the prime of life, ended his days.[14] Though this couple was allowed to possess talents of various kinds, there was nothing in which they manifested more ingenuity than in plaguing each other.[15]

5. Richard Charke (c. 1709–37) made his debut in London in 1729. For an account of his theatrical career, see Highfill, 3:165–67; Fiske, pp. 124–25; *New Grove*, 4:156–57.

6. In 1729, according to Hawkins (2: 892), he succeeded "as first violin in the band at Drury-lane one who was called Dicky Jones."

7. *Six Medley or Comic Ouvertures,* performed 1732–44, were published in 1763. Of these, Charke was responsible for No. 3, performed on 4 Dec. 1732 at Drury Lane (Fiske, p. 161; *New Grove*, 4:157).

8. The 1735 edition has not yet been traced. It is not among the books in CB's library.

9. Hawkins (2:892) also mentions "a hornpipe that bears his name."

10. Bear-garden: i.e., rude, vulgar.

11. Charlotte Charke (1713–60), sister of Susannah Cibber, married Richard Charke on 4 Feb. 1730 at St. Martin-in-the-Fields. For an account of her career, see Highfill, 3:167–78.

12. *A Narrative of the Life of Mrs. Charlotte Charke . . . Written by Herself* was published in 1755, first in eight weekly parts and then in two duodecimo editions (see L. R. N. Ashley's introduction to the 1969 reprint for

Scholars' Facsimiles).

13. Charlotte was an exhibitionist as a child of four, when she put on "an enormous bushy Tie-wig of my Father's" and "a monstrous Belt and large Silver-hilted Sword," and "in this Grotesque Pigmy State, walked up and down the Ditch bowing to all who came by me." One morning she leaped on an unbroken donkey, and "rode triumphantly into Town astride, with a numerous Retinue, whose Huzzas were drown'd by the dreadful Braying" of the donkey's "tender Dam." Her father, seeing her, exclaimed "looking out of Window, *Gad demme! An Ass upon an Ass!*" (Charke, pp. 17–22). Highfill reproduces "An Exact Representation of Mrs. Charke walking in the Ditch at four Years old" and lists a score of male roles in which she appeared on the stage, such as Pistol in *The Humours of Sir John Falstaff,* Macheath in *The Beggar's Opera,* etc. For the Chevalier d'Éon (1728–1810), the famous French transvestite, see A. Rieu, *D'Éon de Beaumont: His Life and Times* (1911).

14. In 1736, before he sailed for Jamaica, he borrowed £100 to pay his mistress, "Sister to the famous Mrs *Sally K——g,* one of the Ladies of the HIGHEST IRREPUTABLE REPUTATION at that Time, in or about *Covent Garden*" (Charke, pp. 76–77). He

died in Jamaica, probably in 1737.

15. Charlotte herself was more charitable: "We ought rather to have been sent to School than to Church, in Regard to any Qualifica-tions on either Side, towards rendering the Marriage-State comfortable to one another" (Charke, p. 52).

B.3. KIRCKMAN'S COURTSHIP AND BUSINESS SENSE

[Jacob] Kirckman[16] himself used to relate the singular manner in which he gained the widow,[17] which was not by a regular siege, but by storm. He told her one fine morning, at breakfast, that he was determined to be married that day before twelve o'clock. Mrs. Tabel, in great surprise, asked him to whom he was going to be married, and why so soon? The finisher told her, that he had not yet determined whom he should marry, and that, if she would have him, he would give her the preference. The lady wondered at this precipitancy, hesitated full half an hour; but he continuing to swear that the business must be done before twelve o'clock that day, at length she surrendered; and as this abridged court-ship preceded the marriage act, and the nuptials could be performed at the Fleet or May Fair, "without loss of time, or hindrance of business," the canonical hour was saved, and two fond hearts were in one united, in the most summary way possible, just one month after the decease of Tabel.[18]

Kirckman lived long enough to stock the whole kingdom with his instru-ments, and to amass great wealth. He had no children, but as many nephews hovering over him as a Roman pontiff.[19]

[Kirckman] doubled the profits of his instruments, by becoming a pawn-broker and a usurer; obliging young heirs with money as kindly, and with as much liberality, as a Hebrew. . . . About 50 years ago,[20] [the] vogue [for the guitar] was so great among all ranks of people, as nearly to break all the harpsichord and spinet makers, and indeed the harpsichord masters themselves. All the ladies disposed of their harpsichords at auctions for one-third of their price, or exchanged them for guitars; till old Kirkman, the harpsichord maker, after almost ruining himself with buying in his instruments, for better times, purchased likewise some cheap guitars and made a present of several to girls in milliners' shops, and to ballad singers, in the streets, whom he had taught to accompany themselves, with a few chords and triplets, which soon made the ladies ashamed of their frivolous and vulgar taste, and return to the harpsi-chord.

He did not live enough to see his excellent double harpsichords of sixty or seventy guineas price, sold at auctions for twelve or fourteen pounds, and the original purchasers turn them out of their houses as useless lumber.[21] But such are the vicissitudes of this world, that descendants will, perhaps, know as little about the pianoforte, as we do now know of the lute or lyre.

16. For Jacob Kirkman or Kirckman (from German Kirchmann), see Frag. 41. After his arrival in London, according to CB, he worked for the harpsichord maker Hermann Tabel (d. 1738) "as his foreman and finisher till the time of his death" ("Kirckman" in Rees).

17. Susanna née Virgoe (d. pre–Oct. 1740) was Tabel's second wife (Boalch, p. 175).

18. Late in 1738. In his will dated 28 July 1738, Tabel nominated Kirckman one of his trustees and bequeathed him £5 for mourning (Boalch, p. 175). He also "left several fine Harpsichords to be disposed of by Mr. Kirckmann, his late Foreman, which are the finest he ever made, [and] are to be seen at the said Mr. Kirckmann's, the corner of Pulteney Court in Cambridge Street, over against Silver Street, near Golden Square"

(*Daily Gazetteer,* 8 May 1739).

19. Kirckman and his nephews subscribed for three copies of *Hist. Mus.,* no doubt because CB recommended the Kirckman harpsichords to some of his wealthy pupils.

20. In the 1750s, although Boalch (p. 84) suggests "about 1770."

21. According to Boalch (p. 85), "Kirkman harpsichords maintained their value very well in the second hand market, as is shown from the following prices paid at Christie's during the last decade of the eighteenth century: for single manual harpsichords—18 guineas (16 Apr. 1792), £19.8s. 6d. (25 Feb. 1792); for 2 manual instruments—£21 (16 May 1791), £50 (16 Apr. 1792), £36.15s. (25 Feb. 1793)." Perhaps CB had in mind the prices in the early 1800s when he wrote the article.

B.4. RANELAGH

RANELAGH, *Rotunda* and *Gardens,* built and opened for musical performances and public amusements in 1742. The building was erected in the spacious garden belonging to the residence, at Chelsea, of lord Ranelagh, one of the ministers of Charles II., when paymaster of the army.

It was planned by the late Mr. Lacey, afterwards joint-patentee of Drury-lane theatre with the great actor Garrick.[22]

At the first opening of this stupendous building, several experiments were made in placing the orchestra, in filling it, and in the time of performance, before it was settled as an evening promenade. The orchestra was at first placed in the middle of the rotunda. The performance was in a morning; and oratorio chorusses chiefly furnished the bill of fare. Sir John Barnard[23] complaining to the magistrates, that the young merchants and city apprentices were frequently seduced from their counting-houses and shops by these morning amusements, they were prohibited, and the doors opened at six o'clock in the evening. The performance, however, did not begin till eight o'clock, but was ended at ten.

It was intended to rival Vauxhall, and was little injured by bad weather; as the company, at such times, had a safe and pleasant retreat into the rotunda, and as few went thither but in carriages.

Its success as an evening's amusement remained undiminished more than 40 years. It was ruined by the late hours to which it was gradually brought by fine folks, who, at length, never came thither till past ten o'clock, when the musical performances were over, and sober people used to return home before eleven o'clock to their supper, which enabled them and their servants to go to bed, and rise, at their accustomed time.

But, at length, persons of rank and fashion made a debauch of this innocent amusement, and went to it and departed from it as late as at a masquerade. This precluded all that had any thing to do themselves, or any employment for their servants in the morning, and so much refined the company, that at midnight there had been seldom sufficient lamps, the terms of admission being only 3*s.*, for which, besides a good concert by the best performers in London, the company was furnished with excellent rolls, butter, and tea. In the year 1803 it was shut up, and only used occasionally for a masquerade, a festival, or an exhibition of fire-works. But since the period just-mentioned, the building has been pulled down, and the materials sold piecemeal, as was the case at Cannons, the splendid mansion of the duke of Chandois, (or *Pallazzo,* as it would have been called in Italy,) and the ground is now (1809) of no other utility than occasionally to drill and exercise the Chelsea volunteers.

22. James Lacy (1698–1774), Irish businessman, who had long served as Rich's assistant, became manager of Drury Lane after the riots of Nov. 1744 (Frag. 29, n. 1), when two bankers, Green and Amber, purchased the theatre and turned the management over to him (Nash, p. 198). Lacy "had been an actor in Barthol. Fair—afterwards, had a Booth of his own. He was an active experienced Man—& taken in as assistant Manager by the Trustees over Fleetwood's property in the Patent—afterwards the Projectors of Ranelagh, built first for a morning amusm[t] with the Orchestra in the middle of the room. . . . From a salary as assistant Manager, Lacy was invested with a share in the rec[ts] of D.L. and at last borrowed money to purchase the Patent, and was sole manager till Garrick quitting Covent Garden, purchased 1/2 the property of Lacy, and be[c]ame joint Manager—Introducing himself to the Town as such, by Johnson's admirable prologue, w[ch]

was called for every night for a 12 Month" (CB to Charles Burney, 19 April [1806], Comyn).

23. Sir John Barnard (1685–1764), merchant, Alderman of Dowgate Ward 1728–58, knighted 28 Sept. 1732, Sheriff of London 1735, Lord Mayor 1737. His pamphlet *A Present for an Apprentice* (1740) was very influential at the time.

B.5. THOMAS PINTO

[Pinto[24] was] an excellent performer on the violin, born in England of Italian parents. He was a miraculous player on his instrument when a boy; and long before manhood came on, was employed as the leader of large bands in concerts. He was, however, when Giardini arrived in England,[25] very idle, and inclined more to the fine gentleman than the musical student; kept a horse; was always in boots of a morning, with a switch in his hand instead of a fiddle-stick. But after hearing Giardini, who was superior to all other performers on his instrument with which he was acquainted, he began to think it necessary to practise, which he did for some time with great diligence. With a powerful hand, and marvellous quick eye, he was in general so careless a player, that he performed the most difficult music that could be set before him, better the first time he saw it, than ever after. He was then obliged to look at the notes with some care and attention; but, afterwards trusting to his memory, he frequently committed mistakes, and missed the expression of passages, which, if he had thought worth looking at, he would have executed with certainty. After leading at the opera, whenever Giardini laid down the truncheon, he was engaged as first violin at Drury-lane theatre, where he led during many years.[26] He married for his first wife Sybilla, a German under-singer at the opera,[27] and sometimes employed in burlettas at Drury-lane. After her decease, he married the celebrated Miss Brent,[28] and, quitting England, settled in Ireland, where he died in December 1782, aged 53 years.

His accuracy in playing at sight was so extraordinary, that he even astonished Bach and Abel by the extent of this faculty; and to embarrass him, if possible, they composed jointly a concerto for the violin, with solo parts as difficult as they could invent;[29] and, carrying it to Vauxhall as soon as transcribed in separate parts, told him that they had just finished a concerto, of which, as it was somewhat out of the common way, they wished to hear the effects, if he would venture to try it at sight. "Let me see it," says Pinto; and after a slight glance at the solo parts, and picking his teeth in his usual way, he said if they pleased he would try it as his concerto for the night. And the eminent composers who wished to make this experiment, declared that they did not believe any of the greatest performers in Europe on the violin, would have played it better with a month's practice.

Pinto, who in playing an adagio seemed to have so much feeling and expression, was a Stoic at heart, equally indifferent to pain and pleasure. While he led the band at Drury-lane, during the most affecting scene of Garrick's capital tragic parts, he used to fall asleep in the orchestra full in his view, which, after our *genuine* Roscius had with indignation seen, he never rested till his place in the orchestra was supplied with a leader on whose feelings he had more power. Indeed, we remember a more ridiculous mortification happening to our ever-to-be-lamented friend, Garrick, from a centinel at one of the stage doors, equally destitute of human feelings with Pinto, yawning aloud during the deepest distress of king Lear, which so completely turned "what should be great, to farce," that the vulgar part of the audience, being cocknies, burst into a loud *horse-laugh*; which so disconcerted and enraged the good old king, that he complained to the captain of the guard, and begged that so impenetrable a centinel might never be placed again on the stage to make the audience laugh, whilst he was doing every thing in his power to make them cry.[30]

Pinto died with the same indifference about worldly concerns as he had lived, and left his unfortunate widow, the once much famed Miss Brent, so literally a beggar, that she returned to England to solicit charity from the Musical Fund;[31] which, alas! she did in vain: for by his having during several years neglected to pay his subscription, all her claims were annihilated in an establishment which she and her husband had often by their gratuitous performance contributed, at its annual benefits, to support, previous to its being enriched, and rendered a royal institution by the commemoration of Handel.

24. See Frag. 86, n. 6.

25. In 1750; see Frag. 58.

26. In 1757 he replaced Giardini at the King's Theatre (*New Grove*).

27. Sibylla Gronomann, daughter of a German pastor, was known as "Signora Sibylla" (Highfill). Pinto married her c. 1745; she died before 1766.

28. Charlotte Brent (1735–1802), Arne's "most promising pupil," whose impeccable bravura singing made up for other defects, including halitosis (Nash, pp. 304–5n). She married Pinto in Nov. 1766. "Her history," writes CB, "if detailed, might furnish a useful lesson to female favourites of the public, possessed of greater vocal powers than human prudence" ("Brent" in Rees).

29. The concerto has not been identified.

30. CB gives a shorter version of this anecdote in his article "Cantare" in Rees, where

he introduces it by stating that "Garrick used to say, that applause was an aliment without which he could not live on the stage; and inattention to the part he was representing, he never forgave."

31. The Fund for the Support of Decayed Musicians and Their Families, established by Handel in 1738. For CB's accounts of this benevolent institution, see *Commem.*, pt. 2, pp. 129–39; and "Fund" in Rees.

B.6. MISS LINLEY (MRS. SHERIDAN)

This captivating performer[32] had acquired great reputation at Bath before she was heard in London, where she had likewise occasionally sung before she was engaged at the oratorios under the Direction of Mess[rs] Smith & Stanley 1772.[33] Her Musical renown tho' great and well-deserved did not excite more Curiosity in the Public Ear, than her History, & the Lawsuit concerning a Contract of Marriage, did in the Public Eye.[34] Both were insatiable; for the beauty of her Person with her modest, amiable, & interesting Deportment, rendered the Gazers as eager to renew their pleasure, as her melifluous voice, & correct and Natural Manner of singing did the Hearers. Never was a Theatre more Crowded, or an audience more generally delighted. There were not a sufficient Number of performances in the season to gratify mere Curiosity, much less to satiate the admirers of her Person & Performance by frequent Exhibition. No Performer c[d] excite attention but herself—nor was any Composition listened to in w[ch] she had no concern.[35]

The *present Times* want no reasons to be given for this universal Admiration; Posterity *may*. And as I have found in the Course of my Enquiries a great Number of old Books on the subject of Music w[ch] Chance has rescued from Oblivion unworthily, upon a supposition that equal blindness in the blundering God or Goddess Chance may poke into the Trunk of some Musical Newsmonger of future Times[, on t]his leaf of my Book I shall try to explain & discriminate the Vocal Abilities of M[rs] S.

That her voice, without the assistance of her beautiful Person; or her Person, without the sweetness of her voice, w[d] have been equally ravishing is impossible to believe. However great beauty alone will not support a Singer at the opera, and great musical Merit without Personal Charms has frequently done great Execution. However where united, both are rendered more irresistible. The Voice of M[rs] S. was as likely to make lasting Friends as any one w[ch] perhaps has been bestowed by Nature on a Young Female; not from its great Extension, or from its Force, but from a native Sweetness & true Intonation. Its original Quality was good, in point of *Tone*, & steady, in *Tune*. By being Educated from her Infancy by her Father, a Master of great experience & established Reputation for knowledge in his Profession,[36] Music was become a Language wch she read with as much facility as her Mother Tongue. And she had so long studied the Oratorios of Handel & so frequently sung the best songs in them that she seemed to execute them with more propriety of Expression than any one had ever done before. They were the sounds wch she first lisped in her infancy. There was something so pure, chaste & judicious in her manner of Executing them, that joined to her articulate & correct pronunciation of the Words, seraphic Looks,[37] and truely natural & Pathetic Expression, it was impossible for the most enthusiastic admirers of more modern music & Italian refinem^ts in singing not to be pleased. Indeed the most reasonable and distinguished Italians themselves confessed, that if Chance had made her a Native of Italy her powers of pleasing even in that Country w^d have exceeded those of any singer that ever existed. & at the same time allowed, in Justice to her Instructor, that they were much more surprised at what she *had,* than what she *wanted* on the side of refinem^t Taste & Expression. Her shake was perfect, her execution neat & articulate, & her Portamento unvitiated. She sometimes infringed a Rule wch Italian singers endeavour to preserve, of never taking breath ere the middle of a Close, or at least before she came to her shake; but this was perhaps occasioned by the extreme length, & difficulty of their Execution. Her closes had great variety, & were generally ingenious & fanciful, & as to the too great duration of These supposed extemporaneous flights, it is a vice as much to be complained of in Italy as in any part of the World.

32. See Frag. 115, n. 3.

33. John Christopher Smith (Frag. 57, n. 5), Handel's amanuensis, carried on the oratorios after Handel's death in conjunction with Stanley (Frag. 54, n. 7).

34. Samuel Foote's comedy *The Maid of Bath* (1771) exposed her rakish elderly suitors Mr. Long and Capt. Thomas Mathews. Her elopement with Richard Brinsley Sheridan to France in 1772, Sheridan's two duels with Mathews, and the marriage on 13 April 1773 were reported in the *Bath Chronicle.* See Black, pp. 23–112.

35. Young Fanny Burney, who went to "hear this Syren" in an oratorio "under Mr. Stanley's direction" during Lent 1773, wrote: "The applause and admiration she has met with, can only be compared to what is given Mr. Garrick. The whole town seems distracted about her . . . and the best and most critical judges, pronounce her to be infinitely superior to *all* other English singers" (*ED,* 1:208–10).

36. For Thomas Linley, whom CB had met at Bath when Linley was a boy, see Frag. 45, n. 6.

37. She sat for Sir Joshua Reynolds's *St. Cecilia,* and for the Virgin in his *Nativity.* CB (in Rees) calls her "sancta Caecilia rediviva."

B.7. GIOVANNI GALLINI

[Gallini][38] came into this country early in life, after having obtained considerable distinction as a dancer at Paris.[39] He seems to have come hither on speculation, without any previous engagement. He first appeared on our Opera stage in 1759, during the performance and management of the Colomba Mattei;[40] where his style of dancing pleased so much, that in a pas seul he was frequently encored, which we never remember to have happened to any other dancer. . . .

It was soon after his professional celebrity at the Opera house that he married lady Elizabeth Bertie, sister of the late earl of Abingdon, whose father, in 1727, married at Florence the daughter of sir John Collins, knight,[41] of a family originally English; but which had long resided in Italy. Signor Collino, brother to the then countess of Abingdon, was the last performer on the lute in this country. The earl, his brother-in-law, died in 1760, and his countess in 1763. The late lord Abingdon, celebrated at Geneva by Voltaire,[42] we believe, was not in England at the time of his sister lady Betty's marriage with Gallini; who, admitted at first as a dancing-master, by his vivacity, talents, knowledge of the Italian language, and manners, so insinuated himself into the favour of this noble family, as soon to be admitted as *amico della casa,* and afterwards to a closer alliance.

Many ridiculous stories were in circulation at the time, of Signor Gallini's expectations of the honours which would accrue to him by his marriage into a noble family; which he imagined would confer on him the title of my lord. But he was soon convinced of his mistake, and content with an inferior title: for when the marriage became a subject of conversation, we happened to hear in the gang-way of the Opera pit the following conversation. One of two ladies, going into the front boxes, says to the other, "It is reported that one of the dancers is married to a lady of quality;" when Gallini, who happened to be in the passage near the lady who spoke, says, "Lustrissima, son io."—"And who are you?" demanded the lady; "Eudenza, mi chiamo Signor Gallini Esquoire."[43]

This match, as is usual with such disproportioned alliances, was not the source of permanent felicity. They lived asunder many years. Lady Elizabeth died in the course of the year 1788.[44]

38. Giovanni Andrea Gallini (1728–1805), Florentine dancing-master, choreographer, author of *A Treatise on the Art of Dancing* (1762), and later impresario. See Highfill, 5: 444–49, which supersedes the article in the *Dictionary of National Biography.*

39. Antoine de Léris, in the *Dictionnaire portatif des théâtres* (1754), places him in the

company of L'Académie Royale de Musique as late as July 1754 (Highfill, p. 444).

40. The first mention of him, according to *London Stage,* is on 17 Dec. 1757, when he joined Miss Hilliard "'in a pantomime Ballet call'd *The Judgement of Paris*' . . . When Signora Mattei gave over the opera management to Giardini and Signora Mingotti in 1763–4, Gallini went back to Covent Garden" (Highfill, 5:445). CB's article lists half a dozen of Gallini's performances between 1759 and 1763, not mentioned in Highfill, which he found "in a collection of the *libretti*."

Colomba Mattei (fl. 1754–65), operatic singer and manager, had made her debut at the King's Theatre on 9 Nov. 1754. CB calls her "a spirited and intelligent actress, who soon after became a great favourite." In 1757 she took over the management of the opera until 11 June 1763, when she left England (*Hist. Mus.,* 4:464–79; Mercer, 2:853–67; *London Stage* pt. 4, vols. 1 and 2, passim).

41. Lady Elizabeth (c. 1724–1804), sister of Willoughby Bertie, 4th Earl of Abingdon (1740–99). Their father, Willoughby Bertie (1692–1760), 3rd Earl of Abingdon, in August 1727 had married Anna Maria Collins (d. 1763). "Sir John Collins" had been known to English travelers as the "owner of the best Inn in Florence" (Ross, p. 137). Gallini's marriage must have taken place before 12 April

1764, the date when Horace Walpole (YW, 38:367–68) mentions "Lady Betty Gallini" in connection with the scandal caused by the marriage of Lord Ilchester's daughter, Lady Susan, to "O'Brien the actor," and comments: "The shopkeepers of [the] next age will be mighty well born." By 13 Oct. 1766, when she gave birth to twin sons, she had assumed the name Gallini.

42. The 4th Earl, brother of Lady Elizabeth Bertie (n. 41, above). Voltaire praises "Milord Abington" in *La Guerre civile de Genève* (1768) for having given "cent livres sterling" to a starving Genevoise (Voltaire, 9:538–39n).

43. "It was after this period," writes CB of the early 1780s, "in going to Italy to engage performers," that the Pope "made him 'Cavaliere del speron d'Oro,' Knight of the golden spur, the only order which his holiness has to bestow. But lord Kenyon, when his title was introduced in court on a trial [1784], refused to acknowledge it, and treated the assumption with indignation and contempt. Sir John, however, continued to retain it, and was abetted by the public, in spite of the lord chief justice" ("Gallini" in Rees).

44. An error on CB's part: she died 18 Aug. 1804 "in Great Quebec-street, aged 80" (*AR,* 46:497). For Gallini's later career, see the end of CB's article in Rees; and Highfill.

B.8. FELICE DE GIARDINI

If Giardini[45] has been surpassed by a few in taste, expression, and execution, his tone and graceful manner of playing are still unrivalled, nor does any one, of all the admirable and great performers on the violin, surpass all others so much at present, as Giardini did, when at his best, all the violinists in Europe.

That a man with such talents and intellects as art and nature scarcely ever allowed to the same individual, who might have realized 40 or 50,000*l.,* should, by extravagance, caprice, and a total want of benevolence and rectitude of heart, die a beggar, unfriended and unpitied, is scarcely credible![46] It is painful to probe the private character of such a man; yet it should not be concealed. Truth and morality require it to be recorded. The kings of Egypt used to be tried after their decease.

And if young musicians of great talents, who are prone to deviate from propriety of conduct, should chance to read this article, it may serve as a beacon, and remind them of the possibility of surviving favour and talents, however great, and terminating their existence in misery and mortification.

A respectable professor,[47] who, from Giardini's first arrival in England, was constantly attached to him, and a sincere admirer of his talents, his wit, and even the ingenuity of his spleen and spite; before he quitted this country in 1784, delineated his character in the following manner, a copy of which came lately to our hands, accidentally.

Sketch of the private character of a great musician.—"There exists a man who would rather gain half a crown by superior subtilty and cunning, than a guinea by usual and fair means; who is of so difficult a commerce, that the utmost circumspection, attention, and complaisance, can only prevent an open rupture, but never put him off his guard, or warm his heart with the faintest glow of friendship; so capricious and splenetic, that he has had disagreements and quarrels with all the first personages, as well as professors of the same art, in the nation, with whom he has had any intercourse; yet such are his talents, and entertaining qualities, that, in a short time, all else is forgotten, and those whom he had offended, are as ready to court his acquaintance as ever; though his rank in his profession and great abilities should set him above the envy and petulance of indigent inferiority; yet the success of any one of his acquaintance is as torturing and intolerable to his mind, as the gout or stone could be to his body. He can bear no musician who does not solely depend on his favour, whom he can lift up and put down with a *coup de baguette,* bring into light, or extinguish, at pleasure. He seems, himself, to despise all favour from superiors or even equals, yet he is constantly at war with favourites of every kind, public and private. His disposition is so truly diabolical, that, preferring the evil principle of the Manicheans to the good of the Christians, if it is a matter of indifference to his interest, whether he shall serve or injure an individual, he would always chuse the latter. He has constantly trifled with fortune as well as favour, and having, in the course of his life, acquired great sums, is indigent, and though so much courted, has not one friend.

I[48] was three times engaged with him in business; but was so much the dupe of his Temper & inadmissible Demands, that against reason & conviction, I consented to deliver in proposals of his framing to those with whom we were in treaty wch were so offensive & impracticable as to overset the whole business. By the 1st I lost setting the Ode and conducting the band for the D. of Grafton's Installation at Cambridge as well as a Doctor's Degree in that university;[49] by the 2^d was lost and annihilated the Plan for a Conservatorio at the Foundling Hospital; wch had been unanimously voted, & established in all its branches, wth a salary for each [i.e., Burney and Giardini] of £200 per An:[50] And 3dly by abetting his insolence & tyrannical Governm^t at the Pantheon I not only lost the weight I had acquired with the Proprietors, but their Friendship, & a Sal^y of £100 p^r Ann. wch had been voted me for carrying on their foreign Correspondence for 3 years, & wch w^d have been readily renewed had I chosen to relinquish him & his Principles.[51] With the best intellects and clearest Ideas for business, his temper renders it so impossible for any enterprise to thrive under his direction, that the most favourable & propitious beginnings, constantly end in Enmity & Misfortune. Though so far from being qualified to write a book, if he is able he is never willing to read me in any Language; yet he has never forgiven me for doing even what he despises.

He is as inveterate and powerful an enemy to the opera, oratorio, pantheon, and public and private concerts, when they are not under his direction, as an ex-minister usually is to the government; and yet, notwithstanding the attractions of his performances, abilities as a composer, and experience as a manager, so much are his tricks and tyranny held in abhorrence by patentees and proprietors, that they would shut their shops, rather than open them by his assistance. His interest is now as totally annihilated in the nation, as that of the Stuart family, who, whatever convulsions or revolutions were to happen in the state, would never be called into power.

45. For CB's account of Giardini's arrival in England, see Frag. 58. This bitter assessment of Giardini's character was written later, when CB reflected on what his close association with this temperamental genius had cost him. The account, except for the penultimate paragraph (see n. 48, below) is taken from CB's article "Giardini" in Rees. See also Lonsdale 1979.

46. Giardini died in Moscow on 8 June 1796.

47. The professor (as Lonsdale 1979 points out) was CB himself. Giardini did leave England in 1784 but later returned (see n. 51, below); he left permanently between 1792 and 1794 (Highfill, 6:166).

48. This paragraph was too personal to be published: see textual note.

49. The installation took place in July 1769. Gray was supposed to furnish the ode and CB the music. According to Mme d'Arblay (*Mem.,* 1:211–12), CB

engaged, as leader of the orchestra, the celebrated Giardini, who was the acknowledged first violinist of Europe.

But, in the midst of these preliminary measures, he was called upon, by an agent of the Duke, to draw up an estimate of the expense.

This he did, and delivered, with the cheerfullest confidence that his selection fully deserved its appointed retribution, and was elegantly appropriate to the dignity of its purpose.

Such, however, was not the opinion of the advisers of the Duke; and Mr. Burney had the astonished chagrin of a note to inform him, that the estimate was so extravagant that it must be reduced to at least one half.

Cruelly disappointed, and, indeed, offended, the charge of every performer being merely what was customary for professors of eminence, Mr. Burney was wholly overset. His own musical fame might be endangered, if his composition should be sung and played by such a band as would accept of terms so disadvantageous; and his sense of his reputation, whether professional or moral, always took place of his interest. He could not, therefore hesitate to resist so humiliating a proposition; and he wrote, almost on the instant, a cold, though respectful resignation of the office of composer of the Installation Ode.

CB's manuscript passage suggests that it was Giardini's extravagant "Proposals" that were responsible for this fiasco. See also Lonsdale 1965, pp. 77–78; Scholes 1948, 1:140–42.

50. For CB's abortive plans between 1770 and 1774 to establish in London a "Public Music-School" on the model of Italian conservatorios, see *Mem.*, 1:233–44; Scholes 1948, 1:261–63; Lonsdale 1965, pp. 149–53; Kassler; and CB to Felice de Giardini, 21 June 1772 (Osborn). Giardini was then Governor of the Foundling Hospital, "in charge of such musical activities as already took place there." CB here puts the blame for the fiasco on Giardini, though in Aug. 1774 he was disposed to blame "a small Junto, a Cabal . . . collected together from 2 or 3 neighbouring streets" (Lonsdale 1965, p. 153).

51. On 17 June 1789 the Pantheon burned down, and a year later a patent was issued to convert it into an opera theatre. CB early in 1790 "purchased a share, wch cost me £700," and was on the board of trustees, with "a place of *100* Guineas a year as foreign secretary to engage singers from Italy and Germany" (CB to Charles Burney, 21 July 1790, Osborn; CB to Lady Crewe, 18 April 1806, BL, Add. MSS 37916, f. 16; Scholes 1948, 2:308). In 1788 Giardini was in Madrid (Felice de Giardini to CB, 25 Aug. 1788, Osborn), and it seems likely that CB, in his new capacity, had imprudently engaged him for the opening of the new theatre, for in 1789 Giardini was back in England. For the complicated disputes during the rebuilding of the new Pantheon, see R. B. O'Reilly, *An Authentic Narrative of the Principal Circumstances relating to the Opera-House in the Haymarket: from the origins to the present period* (1791). CB lost his £700 when the new house burned down on 14 Jan. 1792, but the present text suggests that Giardini was responsible for his loss of the 100 guineas "as foreign secretary," before the fire.

Textual Notes

With the exception of Fragment 85, which is taken from the Yale Boswell Papers, and Fragment 102, for which the Garrick original in the Comyn Collection provides the text, all manuscript sources for the fragments are found in the British Library, the Osborn Collection, and the Berg Collection. (The Berg fragments are preserved in a "Collection of miscellaneous holographs, with MS. notes and deletions in Fanny Burney d'Arblay's hand, including various fragments from volumes of diaries and books of memoranda, etc., *c.* 104 pieces in 11 folders," call number m.b. There is little order within these folders, but they are numbered: further reference will therefore be to folder number only.) From the following notebooks, only those fragment-sheets dealing with the years before 1770 have been used for the present edition.

Nbk 1805 (Osborn; BL; Berg), 15.6 x 24.5 cm., mutilated and partially destroyed, provides text for approximately two-thirds of the fragments (see the editors' introduction). Frags. 115–17 (Osborn) are presumably from vol. 2 of this 1805 redaction.

Nbk pre-1805 (Berg Folder 5). The 3 surviving sheets, 11.6 x 18.4 cm., furnish full, partial, or variant text for Frags. 37 and 44–46.

Interesting sundries (see List B, Item 8b, in editor's introduction) designates what may

be remnants of a notebook or notebooks of an early draft of the memoirs. Two scraps are in BL, Add. MSS 48345 (ff. 1 and 17), one in Berg (Folder 7), and another in Osborn, all approximately 10 cm. wide and of varying lengths because torn. They furnish full, partial, or variant text for Frags. 13, 16, 18, 63, 65, 70–71, 87, 89, 93, 108, and 114.

Addenda (Berg Folder 4; Osborn) derive from 6 of the surviving sheets of a notebook 11.6 x 10.0 x 18.3 cm. that contains passages intended for insertion into Nbk 1805; they furnish text for Frags. 12, 29, 34, 95, 109, and 112–13.

Johnsoniana & Bons Mots (BL, Barrett Collection, Egerton 3700B), surviving sheets of an 11.5 to 11.8 x 18.5 cm. notebook (evidently part of vol. 3 of the 1782 version of the memoirs), furnish text or variant text for Frags. 8, 40, 72–73, and 96.

Autobiographical sketch (BL, Add. MSS 48345, f. 22), 19.6 x 30.7 cm. This holograph account of CB's life to 1760 was written c. 1804 and furnishes full or partial text for Frags. 9, 32, and 84.

Two *Musical Nbks* (Osborn, shelf-marks c.97 and c.100) furnish text for Frags. 31, 62, 107, App. B.6, and part of App. B.8. Notebook c.97 (15.8 x 19.8 cm.) carries the title "Manuscript / Notes &c.— / Dr. Charles Burney / Mus. Doct." Sec. 1 is paginated 1–166; sec. 2, 1–110; sec. 2 begins at the end of the volume and is upside down with respect to sec. 1. Notebook c.100 (16.2 x 20.3 cm.) carries the title "German Music (2)" and consists of 133 pp.

Continuation of Memoranda N° V (Berg Folder 3), 9.9 x 16 cm. furnishes text for Frag. 90.

Fourteen fragments derive from previously published material. Mme d'Arblay's *Memoirs* furnish text for Frags. 41, 68, and part of 84; sources for the other eleven are indicated in the textual notes to Frags. 10, 15, 35, 48, 57–58, 67, 82–83, 86, and 91.

Of Burney's own revisions, only the most significant are listed (variants are cited by manuscript page and line numbers). His frequent insertions have been silently incorporated into the text and the words he crossed out, if they do not significantly alter the meaning, ignored. The text has been cleared of Mme d'Arblay's editorial interventions, and they have not been recorded. Irregularities in shape resulted in the occurrence of more or less meaningless bits of text at the top or bottom of some fragments; these have been removed from the body of the text but are recorded in the relevant textual notes below.

Burney's Index. BL, Add. MSS 48345, ff. 18ʳ–19ʳ

Fragment 1. Nbk 1805, pp. 1–4 (Osborn), 15.5 x 24.5 cm.; scored and heavily edited, with obliterations. Docketed by CB: "Transᵈ Decʳ 26. 1805 / Commenced."

p. 1	line 2	Appointments] Virtues
	line 11	these advantages were] it was
p. 2	line 7	first] highest
	line 19	respective] several
p. 3	line 18	wᶜʰ he delivered] wᶜʰ he did not fail to deliver

Fragment 2. Nbk 1805 (Osborn), 7.6 to 6.0 x 12.3 cm.; scored and edited. On verso Fragment 3.

Fragment 3. Nbk 1805 (Osborn); scored and edited. On recto Fragment 2.

Fragment 4. Nbk 1805 (Osborn), 7.9 to 5.9 x 12.1 to 11.5 cm.; scored and edited. On recto Fragment 5.

Fragment 5. Nbk 1805 (Osborn); scored and edited. On verso Fragment 4.

Fragment 6. Nbk 1805 (Osborn); 8.1 to 6.5 x 11.9 to 11.5 cm.; scored and edited. On verso Fragment 7.

Fragment 7. Nbk 1805 (Osborn); scored and edited. On recto Fragment 6.

line 11   [from Condover] added by Mme d'Arblay

Fragment 8. Johnsoniana & Bons Mots, p. 70 (BL, Barrett, Eg. 3700B); unedited.

Fragment 9. Autobiographical sketch (BL, Add. MSS 48345, f. 22ʳ); unedited. Recto also furnishes text for Fragment 32. On verso Fragment 84.

Fragment 10. Commem., pt. 1, p. 26.

Fragment 11. Nbk 1805, bottom half-sheet (BL, Add. MSS 48345, f. 4ʳ), 15.6 x 11.7 to 12.5 cm.; scored and edited. On verso Fragment 21.

Fragment 12. Addenda, pp. 3–4: insert "a" (Berg Folder 4); unedited.

line 6   soldier! When] soldier, &

Fragment 13. Interesting sundries (BL, Add. MSS 48345, f. 1ᵛ). On recto Fragment 16.
Fragment ends: "The aerial Castles I now built,"

Fragment 14. Nbk 1805, bottom half-sheet (BL, Add. MSS 48345, f. 2ᵛ), 15.6 x 11.7 to 12.5 cm.; lightly scored. On recto Fragment 17 and partial variant text of Fragment 18.

Fragment 15. Hist. Mus., 3:102n, 561; Mercer, 2:88 n., 445.

Fragment 16. Interesting sundries (BL, Add. MSS 48345, f. 1ʳ), top and bottom cut away. On verso Fragment 13.

line 12   Instructions] encouragemᵗˢ (*crossed out*)

line 13   &] me (*both crossed out*)

Fragment ends: ⟨Possession⟩ & of which I ⟨long⟩

Fragment 17. Nbk 1805, bottom half-sheet (BL, Add. MSS 48345, f. 2ʳ); lightly scored. Recto includes Fragment 18. On verso Fragment 14.

Fragment 18. Interesting sundries, p. 57 (Berg Folder 7), 10.2 x 22.5 to 22.0 cm., bottom cut away. Verso, docketed by CB "1776," is lightly edited, and furnishes text for Fragments 18 and 87, continuous in MS. Recto, heavily obliterated, furnishes text for Fragments 108 and 111.

Last two sentences are from Nbk 1805 (BL, Add. MSS 48345, f. 2ʳ), which provides a more accurate account than Berg: "In 1739 she married Lᵈ Ossulston, the son of the earl of Tankerville; I remember seeing them come out of Sᵗ Julian Church after the Wedᵍ."

Fragment 19. Nbk 1805, bottom half-sheet (BL, Add. MSS 48345 f. 3ʳ), 15.6 x 11.7 x 12.5 cm.; heavily scored and edited. On verso Fragment 20.

line 9   in the summer or autumn] abᵗ the beginning

Fragment 20. Nbk 1805, bottom half-sheet (BL, Add. MSS 48345, f. 3ᵛ); heavily scored and edited. On recto Fragment 19. Photographic reproduction in Lonsdale 1965, facing p. 448 (pl. 5).

Fragment begins: ⟨the 2ᵈ⟩ principal.

line 1   1743] 1742

line 15   being in form superior] being in \ form, style and execution / superior

Fragment 21. Nbk 1805, bottom half-sheet (BL, Add. MSS 48345, f. 4ᵛ), 15.5 x 11.5 to 13 cm.; scored and edited. On recto Fragment 11.

Date: August] the Autumn

Fragment begins: new exertions.

Fragment 22. Nbk 1805, bottom half-sheet (BL, Add. MSS 48345, f. 5ʳ), 15.5 x 11.5 to 12. 5 cm.; heavily edited. On verso Fragment 23. Fragment begins: in his times.

line 23   cᵈ] can

Fragment 23. Nbk 1805, bottom half-sheet (BL, Add. MSS 48345, f. 5ᵛ); scored and edited. On recto Fragment 22.

Fragment 24. Nbk 1805, bottom half-sheet (BL, Add. MSS 48345, f. 6ʳ), 15.5 x 11.5 to 13 cm.; lightly edited. On verso Fragment 25.

Fragment 25. Nbk 1805, bottom half-sheet (BL, Add. MSS 48345, f. 6ᵛ); lightly scored. On recto Fragment 24.

Fragment 26. Nbk 1805, bottom half-sheet (BL, Add. MSS 48345, f. 7ʳ), 15.5 x 11.5 to 12.7 cm.; lightly scored and edited. On verso Fragment 27.

Fragment begins: and spend the day with him [   ] wᵈ give me permission

Fragment 27. Nbk 1805, bottom half-sheet (BL, Add. MSS 48345, f. 7ᵛ); lightly edited. On recto Fragment 26.

Fragment 28. Nbk 1805, bottom half-sheet (BL, Add. MSS 48345, f. 8ʳ), 15.5 x 11.5 to 13 cm.; lightly scored. On verso Fragment 30.

Fragment 29. Addenda, pp. 8–9; insert "e" for "Vol. I. top of p. 39" (Berg Folder 4); un-edited.

p. 9   lines 3–4   was too manifest] made the contrast too strong

Fragment ends: In April he had a benefit (*crossed out*)

Fragment 30. Nbk 1805, bottom half-sheet

(BL, Add. MSS 48345, f. 8ᵛ); scored and edited. On recto Fragment 28.

Fragment 31. Musical Nbk c.97, sec. 2, pp. 85–86 (Osborn); unedited. These pages also furnish text for Fragment 62. Nbk 1805, bottom of p. 155 (Berg Folder 9) contains the beginning of another version: "It may seem strange & ungrateful in me, perhaps, not to have spoken with more respect and regard of my Master Arne, than I have hitherto done, but I had too much reason to complain of his selfishness." In MS this directly follows Fragment 40.

p. 86   line 7   examining how] an examination of

line 8   wᶜʰ] &

Fragment 32. Autobiographical sketch (BL, Add. MSS 48345, f. 22ʳ); unedited. Recto also furnishes text for Fragment 9. On verso Fragment 84. "Page to Queen Caroline . . . festivity" is from Nbk 1805, bottom half-sheet (BL, Add. MSS 48345, f. 9ʳ); lightly scored. On verso Fragment 33.

Fragment 33. Nbk 1805, bottom half-sheet (BL, Add. MSS 48345, f. 9ᵛ), 15.5 x 11.5 to 12.5 cm.; heavily scored. Verso also furnishes text for Fragment 34. On recto Fragment 32. Fragment begins: ⟨on her⟩ vocal ⟨studies⟩

Fragment 34. Addenda, pp. 9–10, insert "e" for "Vol. I. top of p. 39" (Berg Folder 4); unedited. In MS follows Fragment 29. Furnishes text up to "12ᵗʰ of April 1746"; remainder from Nbk 1805, bottom half-sheet (BL, Add. MSS 48345, f. 9ᵛ), heavily scored, which also furnishes text for Fragment 33. On recto Fragment 32.

In Addenda, p. 10, second part is insert "f"; it reads: "On the 12ᵗʰ of April 1746, Mʳˢ Cibber acted at Drury Lane for Mʳ Arne's benefit Monimia in the Orphan. As soon as this play was advertised &c Vol. I. p. 40—to French House. p. 41."

Fragment 35. Hist. Mus., 4:637n.; 636n.; Mercer 2:988n.; 987n.

Fragment 36. Nbk 1805, bottom half-sheet (Berg Folder 6), 15.6 x 13.6 to 13.0 cm.; unedited. In MS followed by the indication "—in Hanover Square. p. 57," succeeded by the last sentence of Fragment 47. On verso Fragment 40.

Fragment 37. Nbk pre-1805, pp. 21–22 (Berg Folder 5).
poliçoneries] espiegleries

Fragment 38. Nbk 1805, bottom half-sheet (Osborn), 15.7 x 12.5 to 11.6 cm.; scored. On verso Fragment 39.

Fragment 39. Nbk 1805, bottom half-sheet (Osborn); scored. On recto Fragment 38.

Fragment 40. Nbk 1805, bottom of p. [153] (Berg Folder 6); scored and edited. Furnishes text for "I, of course . . . of doing, he." Remainder on pp. 154–55 (Berg Folder 9), scored and edited, followed by variant text of first sentence of Fragment 31. The pagination suggests that in the 1805 redaction this followed CB's return from France in July 1765 (Fragment 110) and described his renewed acquaintance with Garrick, with flashbacks to his early experiences with Garrick and Drury Lane. We have placed the passage here because its events occurred in the mid-1740s. An unedited version of the section "Mʳˢ Clive . . . sent it back" in Johnsoniana & Bons Mots, p. 7 (BL, Barrett, Eg. 3700B, f. 4ʳ), has no significant variants.
Fragment begins: as usual."
p. 154   line 10   whispers] says

Fragment 41. Mem., 1:26–33.

Fragment 42. Nbk 1805, p. 56 (Berg Folder 9); scored and edited. In MS the text follows Fragment 46, which occupies recto (p. 55), part of verso, and is followed by first part of Fragment 47.

Fragment 43. Nbk 1805, bottom of p. [52] (Berg Folder 9), 15.7 x 12.4 to 11.3 cm.; scored and edited. On recto partial variant text of Fragment 45. "Mr Arne play . . . my studies" is on top half of p. [53]—erroneously paginated "52" (Berg Folder 6); lightly scored and edited. On verso Fragment 44.

Fragment begins: Greville took ⟨lessons⟩ [   ] long asunder

Fragment 44. Nbk 1805, top of p. 54 (Berg Folder 6), 15.7 x 13.1 to 12 cm., furnishes text up to "in the evening"; edited. On recto Fragment 43. Followed in MS by "Mr. Crisp had," but only two lines of this 1805 version are extant. The full text is from Nbk pre-1805, p. 31 (Berg Folder 5); scored and lightly edited. Pp. 31–32 continue with alternate text of Fragment 46, as far as "beauty she possessed."

Fragment 45. Nbk pre-1805, pp. 27–28 (Berg Folder 5). Nbk 1805, bottom of p. 51 (Berg Folder 9), furnishes text "I can remember . . . transferring"; lightly scored and edited. On verso Fragment 43.

Fragment 46. Nbk 1805, pp. 55–56 (Berg Folder 9), furnishes text down to "personal appearance"; scored and edited. In MS, preceded by last two lines of Nbk 1805 version of Fragment 44, and followed by Fragment 42 and part of Fragment 47. Another version of the text, to "beauty she possessed," is in Nbk pre-1805, pp. 31–32 (Berg Folder 5). "I had been . . . romantic" is in Nbk 1805, top half of p. 57 (BL, Add. MSS 48345, f. 10^r), 15.5 x 12 to 13 cm.; lightly scored and edited. This half-sheet begins with the continuation of Fragment 47. On verso Fragment 49.

Fragment 47. Nbk 1805, p. 56 (Berg Folder 9) and top of p. 57 (BL, Add. MSS 48345, f. 10^r). Last sentence from Nbk 1805, bottom half-sheet (Berg Folder 6), where it follows Fragment 36 and is preceded by "—in Hanover Square. p. 57," which probably refers to "M^r

Greville marries Miss Macartney" in CB's Index (Fragment 46, n. 13).

Fragment 48. Hill/Powell, 1:197 n.5, 538.

Fragment 49. Nbk 1805, top half of p. 58 (BL, Add. MSS 48345, f. 10^v); scored and edited. On recto Fragments 46, 47.

Fragment ends: the most ami-

Fragment 50. Nbk 1805, top half of p. 59 (BL, Add. MSS 48345, f. 11^r), 15.5 x 13 cm.; scored and edited. On verso Fragment 51.

Last sentence revised by CB to read "then went abroad with his L^y & family," but original reading has been retained.

Fragment 51. Nbk 1805, top half of p. 60 (BL, Add. MSS 48345, f. 11^v); scored and edited. On recto Fragment 50.

Fragment 52. Nbk 1805, top half of p. 61 (BL, Add. MSS 48345, f. 12^r), 15.5 x 13 cm.; lightly scored and edited. On verso Fragment 53.

Fragment 53. Nbk 1805, top half of p. 62 (BL, Add. MSS 48345, f. 12^v); unedited. On recto Fragment 52.

Fragment 54. Nbk 1805, top half of p. 63 (BL, Add. MSS 48345, f. 13^r), 15.5 x 13 to 13.5 cm.; heavily scored and edited. On verso Fragment 55.

Fragment 55. Nbk 1805, top half of p. 64 (BL, Add. MSS 48345, f. 13^v); heavily scored and edited. On recto Fragment 54.

Fragment 56. Nbk 1805, top half of pp. 65–66 (BL, Add. MSS 48345, f. 14^r–v), 15.5 x 13 to 13.5 cm.; scored and heavily edited. Last sentence ("going . . . cause") on verso, folllowed by Fragment 59.

Fragment 57. Commem., pt. 1, pp. 34–36.

Fragment 58. Hist. Mus., 4:522; Mercer, 2:896; "Giardini" in Rees. Musical Nbk c.97, pp. 41, 57, contains preliminary draft of material in *Hist. Mus.* with slight variants, supplemented later by his severe criticism of Giardini's character; much but not all of later part published in "Giardini" in Rees (see Appendix B).

Fragment 59. Nbk 1805, top half of p. 66 (BL, Add. MSS 48345, f. 14ᵛ); scored and edited. On recto and part of verso Fragment 56.

Fragment 60. Nbk 1805, top half of p. 68 (BL, Add. MSS 48345, f. 15ᵛ), 15.5 x 12. 5 to 13.5 cm.; scored and edited. On recto Fragment 61.

Fragment 61. Nbk 1805, top half of p. 67 (BL, Add. MSS 48345, f. 15ʳ); scored and lightly edited. On verso Fragment 60.

Fragment 62. Musical Nbk c.97, sec. 2, pp. 85–86 (Osborn). In MS, precedes Fragment 31 on p. 85, and follows it on p. 86.

p. 85   line 2   qualified him wᵗʰ] called him
                         by
         line 4   Attorney] Lawyer

Fragment 63. Interesting sundries (BL, Add. MSS 48345, f. 17ʳ), 9.7 x 10.1 to 10.9 cm. Provides text for first sentence ("Having . . . health") and for Fragment 65. On verso Fragment 71 and alternate version of Fragment 70. Remainder in Nbk 1805, top half of p. 69 (BL, Add. MSS 48345, f. 16ʳ), 15.5 x 13.5 cm.; scored and heavily edited. On verso Fragment 64.

Fragment ends: ⟨as before⟩ Sutton's & B

Fragment 64. Nbk 1805, top half of p. 70 (BL, Add. MSS 48345, f. 16ᵛ); scored and edited. On recto second part of Fragment 63.

Fragment 65. Interesting sundries (BL, Add. MSS 48345, f. 17ʳ), which also provides text for first part of Fragment 63. On verso Fragment 71 and alternate version of Fragment 70.

Fragment 66. Nbk 1805, bottom half-sheet (Berg Folder 6), 15.6 x 12.4 to 12.0 cm.; scored and edited. On recto Fragment 72.

Fragment 67. Tours, 1:148–49.

Fragment 68. Mem., 1:107–9.

Fragment 69. Conflation of two fragments. Interesting sundries (Osborn), 9.8 to 9.0 x 16.3 cm., recto furnishes unedited text. On verso, heavily obliterated, text for Fragment 94. For text "though no card-player . . . Mʳˢ Allen," variants incorporated from Nbk 1805, top half of p. 83 (Osborn), 15.7 x 12.5 to 12.1 cm.; scored and edited. On verso Fragment 70.

Fragment 70. Nbk 1805, top of p. 84 (Osborn); lightly edited. On recto Fragment 69. Interesting sundries (BL, Add. MSS 48345, f. 17ᵛ) provides another version, also unedited text for Fragment 71. On recto Fragments 63, 65. Earlier text in BL differs considerably from 1805 redaction in Osborn but provides no significant new information.

Fragment 71. Interesting sundries (BL, Add. MSS 48345, f. 17ᵛ); unedited. Also provides variant text for Fragment 70. On recto Fragments 63, 65.

Fragment 72. Johnsoniana & Bons Mots, pp. 71–73 (BL, Barrett, Eg. 3700B, ff. 8ʳ–9ʳ). Partial variant text on verso of Fragment 66 (bottom half-sheet, Berg Folder 6); lightly scored; variants, but no new information.

p. 71   line 1   so innocent a shot in his
                         younger days] so bad
p. 72   line 21   is] was

Fragment 73. Johnsoniana & Bons Mots, p. 73 (BL, Barrett, Eg. 3700B); unedited.

Fragment 74. Nbk 1805, bottom half-sheet (Berg Folder 6), 15.6 x 12.4 to 11.9 cm.; scored and edited. On verso Fragment 75.

Fragment begins: [arri]val at Lynn, ⟨this⟩

Fragment 75. Nbk 1805, bottom half-sheet (Berg Folder 6); lightly scored and edited. On recto Fragment 74.

Fragment 76. Nbk 1805, bottom half-sheet

(Berg Folder 6), 15.6 x 12.4 to 11.9 cm.; scored and edited. On verso Fragment 77.

Fragment 77. Nbk 1805, bottom half-sheet (Berg Folder 6); scored and edited. On recto Fragment 76.

Fragment 78. Nbk 1805, bottom half-sheet (Berg Folder 6), 15.6 x 14.2 to 12.7 cm.; lightly scored and edited. On verso Fragment 79.

Fragment 79. Nbk 1805, bottom half-sheet (Berg Folder 6); scored and edited. On recto Fragment 78.

line 8   This Gentleman] My friend who
line 10   ⟨&⟩ Soon became so intimately] but we got so well

Fragment 80. Nbk 1805, bottom half-sheet (Berg Folder 6), 15.6 x 14.6 to 12.5 cm.; scored and edited. On verso Fragment 81.
Fragment begins: [ac]cording to

Fragment 81. Nbk 1805, bottom half-sheet (Berg Folder 6); scored and edited. On recto Fragment 80.

Fragment 82. Hill/Powell, 1:328–30.

Fragment 83. Boswell's *Life of Johnson,* 3rd ed. (1799), 1:378n.

Fragment 84. First part provided by *Mem.,* 1: 101–2; text from "Yet though he" taken from autobiographical sketch (BL, Add. MSS 48345, f. 22ᵛ); unedited. On recto Fragments 9, 32.

Fragment 85. Yale Boswell Papers, *Life,* Papers Apart, M 145, pp. 816–17, 18.5 x 11.2 cm. A portion of the sheet, 14 x 11.2 cm., was folded over and left blank. Docketed by Boswell: "The following curious Anecdote I insert in Dʳ Burney's own words." The MS text, which Boswell edited lightly, differs slightly from that in Hill/Powell, 4:134.

p. 816   line 5   from the Ramblers & plan of his Dictionary] while the Ramblers were publishing

line 6   by the Dictʸ itself or any other work] by subsequent works
line 10   he happening to] it happened that
line 12   appartment] room
p. 817   line 4   wᵗʰ] by
line 9   scission *appears above the word* segment—*neither is scored through*
soon after] some years after

Fragment 86. *European Magazine* 7 (March 1785): 163–64. Interesting sundries (Osborn), 9.8 to 9.0 x 16.3 cm. (entirely obliterated) has variant text of final sentence.

Fragment 87. Interesting sundries, p. 57 (Berg Folder 7). In MS, immediately follows Fragment 18. On recto Fragments 108, 111.

Fragment 88. Nbk 1805, pp. 121–22 (Berg Folder 9); heavily scored and edited. Recto also furnishes text for Fragment 96, verso for Fragment 99. Interesting sundries (Osborn), 10 x 11.7 to 11.2 cm. (entirely obliterated) has partial variant, followed by variant text of Fragment 89.

Fragment 89. Nbk 1805, top of p. 113 (Berg Folder 6), 15.7 to 15.1 x 12.7 to 12.2 cm. On verso Fragment 92. Interesting sundries (Osborn) has variant text of "My 2ᵈ daughter ... topsy turvy."

Fragment 90. Continuation of Memoranda Nᵒ V, pp. [2–3] (Berg Folder 3), 9.9 x 16 cm.; unedited. Cf. *Mem.,* 2:170–71.

Fragment 91. Burney to Hannah More, [6] April 1799, in William Roberts, *Memoirs of Hannah More,* 1834, 3:69–74.

Fragment 92. Nbk 1805, top of p. 114 (Berg Folder 6); scored and edited. On recto Fragment 89.
Fragment ends: [mor]tification was

Fragment 93. Interesting sundries (Osborn), top half of p. 21, 10 x 11.7 to 11.2 cm.; edited with obliterations. On recto, heavily obliterated, are earlier versions of Fragments 88, 89.

Fragment 94. Interesting sundries (Osborn), 9.8 to 9.0 x 16.3 cm.; heavily obliterated. On recto first part of Fragment 69. Partial variant directly precedes second part of Fragment 98.

Fragment 95. Addenda, p. 4 (Berg Folder 4), insert "b." for "p. 118—top"; unedited.

Fragment 96. Nbk 1805, bottom of p. [120] (Berg Folder 6), 15.7 x 12.3 to 11.5 cm., unedited; and top of p. 121 (Berg Folder 9), heavily scored. Text in Folder 6 preceded by Fragment 97; on recto variant of Fragment 94 and partial text of Fragment 98. Text in Folder 9 continued on recto and verso with Fragment 88; on verso also Fragment 99. Variant text in Johnsoniana & Bons Mots, p. 74 (BL, Barrett, Eg. 3700B). See Fragment 96, n. 2.

Fragment 97. Nbk 1805, bottom of p. [120]; unedited. See textual note, Fragment 96.

Fragment 98. Nbk 1805, bottom of p. [119]; scored. See textual note, Fragment 96. The second part directly precedes in MS.

lines 9–10   Garrick had all this summer been preparing to go abroad in Autumn] Garrick was now preparing to go abroad in the spring of next year

Fragment 99. Nbk 1805, p. 122 (Berg Folder 9); scored and edited. On recto part of Fragment 96, with Fragment 88 continuing on recto and verso. In MS, Fragment 99 follows Fragment 88.

At bottom of page Mme d'Arblay added, as though CB were writing: "I lost, also, at this time, the charming society of the admirable Garrick & his amiable Wife. They went on a long tour to France and Italy. But they left to me, & my Children, a pleasing Charge, in

their favourite little Spaniel, Phil. of whom we were all very fond." ("Phil." turns up again in an index entry for missing p. 141 of Nbk 1805; see Bridge: Fragments 107–8, n. 3.)

Fragment 100. Nbk 1805, pp. 125–26 (Berg Folder 9); vertical scoring. Verso continues in MS with Fragment 101.

p. 127   line 21   learning] literature

Fragment 101. Nbk 1805, pp. 126–28 (Berg Folder 9); scored and edited. P. 128 ends with variant text of Fragment 103.

Fragment 102. Comyn, letter transcribed in Nbk 1805, pp. 129–32 (Berg Folder 9); lightly edited. P. 132 continues with Fragment 103.

Fragment 103. Nbk 1805, p. 132 (Berg Folder 9); scored and edited, with an obliteration. Burney began the topic on p. 128 (see textual note, Fragment 101) but evidently decided to transcribe the Garrick letter (Fragment 102) first. Pp. 133–34 are missing; last line ("it is book French . . . translated") taken from Burney's deleted version, p. 128.

Fragment 104. Nbk 1805, pp. 135–36 (Berg Folder 9); scored and edited. P. 136 continues with beginning of Fragment 105.

Fragment 105. Nbk 1805, pp. 136–38 (Berg Folder 9); and top of p. 139, 15.7 x 14.0 to 11.6 cm. (Berg Folder 6), with Fragment 106 on verso; scored and edited. Text continuous in MS; fragment containing text of Fragments 43 and 44 pasted to pp. 137–38.

Fragment ends: [sha]⟨tt⟩ered nerves, and at the distance [   ] to the capital. He obliged [   ] of life in Norfolk, &

Fragment 106. Nbk 1805, p. 140 (Berg Folder 6); heavily scored and edited. On recto Fragment 105.

receive instructions] take lessons

Fragment ends: Th[   ] his fame was great

Fragment 107. Musical Nbk c.100, p. 10 (Osborn); unedited. P. 11 contains account of Mozart's "Scene for Tenducci," composed in Paris in 1778.
line 15　3] two

Fragment 108. Interesting sundries, p. [56] (Berg Folder 7). On verso Fragments 18, 87.

Fragment 109. Addenda, pp. 4–7 (Berg Folder 4), insert "c" for p. "140"; unedited.
how to get] how best to get

Fragment 110. Nbk 1805, pp. 143–44 (Berg Folder 9); heavily scored and edited. Punctuation apparently added by Mme d'Arblay has been removed.
character] woman

Fragment 111. Interesting sundries, p. [56]; heavily obliterated. See textual note, Fragment 108.

Fragment 112. Addenda, pp. 13–14 (Berg Folder 4), insert "(2) for p. 11 [Vol. II]"; unedited.

Fragment 113. Addenda, pp. 10–13 (pp. 10 and 13 in Berg Folder 4; pp. 11 and 12 in Osborn); Berg sheets unedited, Osborn sheet lightly edited.

Fragment 114. Interesting sundries (Osborn), bottom of sheet, 10 x 10.9 to 10.0 cm.; lightly scored and edited. Text on verso provided in Fragment 92, n. 3.
line 5　taking me in marriage] marrying

Fragments 115–17. Text furnished by a fragment (Osborn), 15.4 to 14.8 x 12.5 to 10.6 cm. from vol. 2 of the memoirs; lightly scored and edited. Recto provides text for Fragments 115 (second paragraph) and 117; verso for Fragments 115 (first paragraph) and 116.

App. B.1. "Worgan" in Rees.

App. B.2. "Charke" in Rees.

App. B.3. "Kirckman" and "Guitarra" in Rees.

App. B.4. "Ranelagh" in Rees.

App. B.5. "Pinto" in Rees.

App. B.6. Musical Nbk c.97, sec. 2, pp. 73–75 (Osborn).

p. 73	line 12	eager] greedy
p. 74	line 1	rescued from Oblivion] preserved
p. 75	line 15	refinem^r] Delicacy
	line 23	generally] very
	line 24	too great duration] length

App. B.7. "Gallini" in Rees.

App. B.8. "Giardini" in Rees; next to last paragraph from Musical Nbk c.97, sec. 2, pp. 41, 57 (Osborn); p. 39 also contains draft of part of the article.

p. 41	line 1	three times] twice
p. 57	line 5	intellects] head
	line 6	for any enterprise to] that any business sh^d
	line 7	constantly end] finish
	line 8	qualified] able

Index